SURVIVING JUSTICE
AMERICA'S WRONGFULLY CONVICTED AND EXONERATED

VOICE OF WITNESS
SAN FRANCISCO

SURVIVING JUSTICE

AMERICA'S WRONGFULLY CONVICTED AND EXONERATED

EDITED BY

LOLA VOLLEN AND DAVE EGGERS

MANAGING EDITOR

COLIN DABKOWSKI

PRODUCTION MANAGER

CHRISTOPHER YING

GENERAL EDITORS

NORIA JABLONSKI • AMY JOHNSON
MARC HERMAN • MICHAEL McCARRIN
STEVE SANDER • SARAH STEWART TAYLOR

Interviews and reporting completed by students at the
University of California, Berkeley Graduate School of Journalism

NEIL BERMAN	LEONIE SHERMAN
SARAH WIENER-BOONE	JONATHAN JONES
MICHAEL CHANDLER	KRISTA MAHR
ARWEN CURRY	JORI LEWIS
TRACI CURRY	ELLA McPHERSON
REBECCA GOLDMAN	KHUSHBU SHAH
NICOLE HILL	ANNA SUSSMAN

Additional reporting by:

DOMINIC LUXFORD • ALEX CARP • CANDACE CHEN
JAMES BARMANN • CHRISTOPHER YING • JORDAN BASS
EMILY TAGUCHI KLIGENSMITH

VOICE OF WITNESS

VOICE OF WITNESS

McSWEENEY'S BOOKS
SAN FRANCISCO

For more information about McSweeney's, visit www.mcsweeneys.net.

Copyright ©2005 McSweeney's

ISBN: 1-932416-23-4

PROCEEDS FROM THIS BOOK GO TO VOICE OF WITNESS,
A NONPROFIT ORGANIZATION

Printed in Canada.

EXPERT CONSULTATION AND ASSISTANCE

Edward Blake
Forensic scientist
Forensic Science Associates

Ernest Duff
Executive Director, Life
after Exoneration Program

Teena Farmon
Former warden, Central
California Women's Facility

Thomas L. Goldstein
Exoneree

Dr. Terry Kupers
Psychiatrist, Professor
The Wright Institute

Lawrence C. Marshall
Professor
Stanford Law School

Natasha Minsker
Death Penalty Policy Director,
American Civil Liberties
Union of Northern California

Barry C. Scheck
Co-founder
The Innocence Project

LEGAL CONSULTATION AND ASSISTANCE

Janice Brickley
Supervising Attorney
Golden Gate University
Innocence Project

Judi Caruso
Director, Juan Melendez Voices
United for Justice

Karen Daniel
Senior Staff Attorney
Northwestern Center on
Wrongful Convictions

Madeline DeLone
Executive Director
The Innocence Project

Jon Eldan
Legal Coordinator, Life After
Exoneration Program

Jill Gibson
Paralegal, Public Interest
Litigation Clinic

Brian Gray
Law Professor, University
of California, Hastings

Susan Gray
Attorney

Ray Hasu
Attorney, Morrison and
Foerster

Geoffrey Haynes and
Courtney Noble
Law Firm of Shartsis Friese,
LLP

Jill Kent
Staff Attorney, Northern
California Innocence Project
at Santa Clara University

Laurence O. Masson
Attorney, Lurence O. Masson
Law Offices

Sean D. O'Brien
President and Executive
Director, Public Interest
Litigation Clinic

John Pray
Associate Professor, University
of Wisconsin Law School

Kathleen Ridolfi
Director, Northern California
Innocence Project at Santa
Clara University

Susan Rutberg
Director, Golden Gate
University Innocence Project

William Sothern
Staff Attorney
Capital Appeals Project

Christina Swarns
Director, Criminal Justice
Project, NAACP Legal
Defense & Educational Fund

Jim Wagstaffe
Attorney and Partner,
Kerr and Wagstaffe

Rob Warden
Executive Director
Center on Wrongful
Convictions at Northwestern
University

Elizabeth Zitrin, J.D.

PHOTOGRAPHER: Courtney Jones; COPY EDITORS: Libby Stephens and Sarah Manguso; PROOFREADING: Aimée Macpherson, Otto Saumarez-Smith, Matt Werner, Noria Jablonski, Jim Fingal; DESIGN ASSISTANCE: Natalie Davis, George Slavik, Alvaro Villanueva, Brian McMullen; EDITORIAL CONSULTATION: Eli Horowitz, Andrew Leland

VOICE OF WITNESS

The Voice of Witness series allows those most affected by contemporary social injustice to speak for themselves. Using oral history as its foundation, Voice of Witness seeks to illustrate human rights crises through the voices of its victims, and in some cases, its participants. These books are designed for readers of all levels—from high school and college students to policymakers—interested in a reality-based understanding of ongoing injustices in the United States and around the world.

The editors would like to acknowledge the tremendous support of Orville Schell, Mark Danner, and the students, staff and faculty of the UC Berkeley Graduate School of Journalism. Most of all, the editors would like to thank all those exonerees who participated in this project, and their families. The time required of them was enormous. Their dedication to ensuring their stories were told, and told correctly, was deeply appreciated.

CONTENTS

FOREWORD

by SCOTT TUROW

Now and then when I'm asked to say what I think the law is for, meaning what use it actually is for humans, I answer that law is meant to make the little piece of existence that people can actually control more reasonable. The universe will continue to contain impulses to chaos and humanity will always be full of folly. But we dignify civilization with the hope that our communities will operate by standards that most of us regard as rational.

Which goes to explain why we are so peculiarly horrified by the notion of imprisoning the innocent, or even worse, condemning a guiltless person to death. Law cannot go any farther off the tracks. Our criminal justice system is supposed to err on the side of innocence, sifting the clearly guilty from those less-obviously culpable. In the same vein, the death penalty, whatever one thinks of it, is intended, even by its proponents, for the so-called "worst of the worst"—those cases where there is not the slightest ambiguity about the moral blameworthiness of the defendant. Imprisoning—or condemning—the innocent exposes a host of procedural defects in our criminal justice system: the manner in which confessions are obtained and the vulnerabilities that prompt some persons to confess falsely; the reliability of eyewitnesses; the way investigators sometimes predetermine who committed a crime; the occasional inadequacy of appointed counsel;

the overreaching zeal of some prosecutors; and, of course, the pervasive and distorting effects of race. But these mistakes are also a sobering reminder to everybody who makes his life in and around the law about the very limits of the enterprise. Justice must be our eternal aspiration, but we should greet skeptically those who ever claim it's been fully achieved. Even if we were to do much, much better, we would still tragically miss the mark on occasion.

The accounts in this book are not works of lofty philosophy or jurisprudence. They are humble first-person tales told in everyday terms, of how injustice happened, one blunder at a time. They are moving stories of living out that most Kafkaesque of nightmares—being imprisoned for something you did not do. There is a uniquely literary aspect to that cruel dilemma, because no one on earth knows better than the person wrongly imprisoned how unjust his situation is. Even devoted loved ones or dedicated lawyers can never have the same certainty as the defendant, who knows absolutely he or she has done nothing wrong. As such, these accounts are in the end eyewitness testimonies to the epitome of human isolation—wronged, separated from society and loved ones, and trapped in an existence defined by what you alone know without doubt to be a lie.

As bleak as that is, these are also redeeming stories. While it is impossible not to be overwhelmed by the injustices each of these people endured, their tales are also testimony to their resilience, and to the families and lawyers who often helped them escape the prison cell where they did not belong. Even the law managed to do better in the end. But each story is a reminder that freedom is not merely a matter of confinement, but also the chance to dwell with the truth.

INTRODUCTION

by DAVE EGGERS AND LOLA VOLLEN

At first glance, the group defied all stereotypes we might conjure of those who have served time behind bars, deservedly or not. The five men present were affable, good-humored, gentle even, dressed in sweaters and khakis and loafers. Beverly Monroe, the one woman in attendance, was the epitome of southern gentility— gracious, warm, and impeccably mannered. Among the six of them, they had served seventy years in prison for crimes they did not commit. In two instances, there had been no crime at all. That these people had served time for murder, for rape, for molestation, was almost incomprehensible.

In a living room in Berkeley, California, these six wrongfully convicted Americans sat, discussing their lives before, during, and after their incarcerations. They had been brought together under the auspices of the University of California, Berkeley Graduate School of Journalism, to begin telling the stories that comprise this book. On the coffee table before them lay the front section of that day's *San Francisco Chronicle*, across which roared the word GUILTY! The headline referred to Scott Peterson, the man convicted, the previous day, of murdering his pregnant wife. In the weeks leading up to that verdict, the residents of the Bay

Area had made clear, in countless television and newspaper man-on-the-street interviews, their desire to see Peterson sent to prison and, for a good portion of those who were sure of his guilt, executed. Now Peterson's guilt had been affirmed, and the public could rest assured that justice had been done. When the word GUILTY appears in four-inch-high letters across the daily newspaper, there can be no doubt about its veracity and finality.

John Stoll would disagree. In 1982, he was convicted of molesting dozens of children in Bakersfield, California; the case implicated a group of other adults, was wildly lurid in its details, and extremely public. The newspapers there and nationally reported that children had told stories of ritual abuse at Stoll's house; that they had been photographed in sexual poses, given sleeping pills, and molested repeatedly. By the time both local and national media had broadcast the children's stories, it is difficult to imagine any citizen of the Bakersfield community believing that a man accused by so many children—including his own son—of molestation, was in fact innocent. The carefully conducted work of the community's law enforcement officers, social workers, prosecutors, jurors, and media would never, the public assumed, collectively convict the wrong person—much less convict a man of a crime when there was no crime. But indeed they did convict an innocent man. John Stoll served nineteen years and was released in 2004, when his accusers, children now grown, recanted their testimony; they had all been coerced or confused into fabricating their stories.

Stoll was forty-two when he entered prison. He is now sixty-one. Male life expectancy in the United States is seventy-five. The American system of justice stole almost one third of his life, and now Stoll struggles to reconcile his body, which is that of an older man, and his mind, which often forgets that he's no longer forty. Stoll, like many exonerees, has to a certain extent set aside, or even blocked out, the time he served in prison. He wants his life to begin again where he left off, but he's now coming to grips with the fact that his body can't do the things it could before he was imprisoned. Even gardening is difficult. "My body is telling me, 'What are you doing?' I'm thinking I'm forty."

Next to Stoll sat Beverly Monroe, who was convicted of the murder of her lover, who in fact took his own life. Monroe, sixty-seven, is graceful and soft-spoken, with teardrop eyes that she directs with palpable warmth into the face of anyone she's addressing. With a degree in organic chemistry and three grown children—one a lawyer who helped overturn her conviction—Monroe is difficult to picture as an inmate. Monroe was the victim of an overzealous investigator, who, after the coroner declared the death of her lover a suicide, was convinced Monroe was the killer. There was no evidence to corroborate this theory, and yet she was convicted. He fabricated a confession, and told Monroe, "I can make you out to be the black widow spider of all time." After serving seven years for the murder, her conviction was overturned in 2002, by a U.S. federal district court. In his ruling, Judge Richard Williams labeled Monroe's case a "monument to prosecutorial indiscretions and mishandling," and called the state police's interviews of Monroe "deceitful and manipulative."

Monroe, and the rest of the exonerees represented in this book, demonstrate that wrongful conviction can and does happen to people from any background, from any socioeconomic group. A grandmother can be convicted of a murder when there is no evidence against her. A father can be convicted of molestation, based on nothing but the coached testimony of five-year-olds. In many cases, the victims of wrongful conviction are literally plucked off the street, and their lives are thereafter altered irreversibly. In the case of John Stoll, he was taken in the middle of the night. He was woken in the early hours, dragged to the police station in his pajamas, and did not see his home again for nineteen years.

That afternoon in Berkeley, champagne was opened for Peter Rose. He had been released from prison only a week before, and the rest of the exonerees knew exactly how he was feeling. They toasted him—"To freedom!" they said—and Rose tried to muster the appropriate words, but couldn't. He was still overcome, over-

3

whelmed.

One day in 1994, while walking in town with his young son on his shoulders, Rose was stopped, handcuffed, and arrested for the rape of a thirteen-year-old girl. Rose served ten years for the crime, and was exonerated when DNA evidence proved his innocence. Rose, tall, trim and clean-cut, sat in a leather chair, joined the discussion when addressed directly, and otherwise sat quietly, shaking his head at it all. Rose, though affable and quick to laugh, was still adjusting to life outside. "When I went to San Francisco last night," he said, "it's just so much traffic and so much things going so fast that my eyes was trying to pick up everything at the same time and it actually made me dizzy." John Stoll nodded in recognition. Rose continued, "I got nauseated from it. I got dizzy, because I couldn't focus on what I was doing. I'm trying to look everywhere at the same time. My eyeballs were just going, 'Whoop!'"

As the afternoon wore on, John Stoll—boisterous, loud, quick with a joke—led most discussions, and had a story to illustrate any subject matter, from prosecutorial misconduct to prison violence. Ulysses Charles was animated, exasperated, sitting on the edge of his seat, while Monroe was reserved, speaking only when the room had quieted down enough to hear her reed-thin voice. When the discussion turned to how the men had managed to survive in prison, Beverly Monroe was aghast. During her years incarcerated, she hadn't seen anything like the violence described by Rose, Ulysses Charles, and even Stoll, whose own actions were startling—but by all accounts necessary to survival at San Quentin. When Stoll described walking across the prison yard to confront a potential enemy, Monroe took in a quick breath and held a hand to her mouth.

The seven graduate students present had volunteered for this class for many reasons, chief among them their astonishment that wrongful imprisonment—perhaps the most galling human rights abuse possible in the United States—was still possible. Before this gathering, the students had read about these exonerees, had researched each of their cases, but to meet them was something else entirely. To know that these exonerees were not only sane and well-adjusted, but also willing to discuss their experiences at length, if only to reduce the likelihood that it would happen to someone else, was at once bewildering and profoundly inspiring.

But meeting these highly intelligent people begs the question: How could this happen? How can Americans, including those with no prior record, be convicted of crimes with which they had no involvement? In many cases, the first and gravest mistake the wrongfully convicted made was in trusting too much. Because they were innocent, they cooperated with investigators, not suspecting that the investigators were targeting them. Many of the victims waived their Miranda rights and agreed to hours or even days of interrogations, all in an effort to solve the crime. They trusted the police to act with integrity. They took investigators at their word. Even after they were charged, they reasoned their predicament would get straightened out in a fair trial. They trusted that the system worked.

Many Americans rightfully have a general sort of faith in the soundness of their system of justice. Not so those inside the system. Peter Neufeld worked as a criminal defense lawyer for fifteen years before he and Barry Scheck started the Innocence Project in New York City. "Those of us toiling in the trenches," he says, "the defense attorneys, prosecutors, and judge—assume we get it right 99.9 percent of the time. But I've learned that's not the case at all. The system is much more vulnerable to error."

The findings of a 1996 study, conducted by C. Ronald Huff of Ohio State University, confirms this. For the report, Huff and his researchers surveyed 188 judges, prosecuting attorneys, sheriffs, public defenders and police chiefs in Ohio, and forty-one state attorneys general. The survey asked respondents—of whom, it should be noted, only 9 percent were public defenders—what percentage of U.S. convictions they estimated were in error. Over

70 percent of respondents estimated an error rate of anywhere from .1 percent to 1 percent. Huff thus estimated that if a conservative average of .5 percent of convictions were in error, that would indicate that for the year 1990, of the 1,993,880 convictions for index crimes—murder, non-negligent manslaughter, forcible rape, aggravated assault, robbery, burglary, larceny-theft, motor vehicle theft and arson—there were 9,969 wrongful convictions. A more recent study, by Ohio State University's Criminal Justice Research Center, concluded that police and courts are right 99.5 percent of the time. In 2005, there are currently 2.2 million men and women in United States prisons. If even .5 percent of them have been wrongfully convicted, this indicates that approximately 11,000 innocent people are currently behind bars in America.

The advent of DNA identification technology, first used to exonerate in 1989, has suggested that, at least for many serious crimes such as rape, the error rate has been significantly higher. In 2002, the FBI compared the DNA from 18,000 suspected rapists to the DNA from their alleged victims' rape kits. In 5,000 of these cases, about 30 percent, the suspect did not match the perpetrator's DNA profile. Thus, almost one third of suspects were spared trial and therefore the risk of wrongful conviction. And, although some might have been acquitted even in the absence of DNA evidence, the eyewitness testimony that is usually at the core of the prosecution's case has been shown to be among the most persuasive evidence when presented to juries. DNA evidence was not used widely until the mid-1990s; the possibility therefore exists that one third of rape convictions before that time might have been in error.

Error in eyewitness identification is one in a handful of frequent causes of wrongful convictions. Many such cases involve the testimony of "snitches"—paid or otherwise compensated witnesses, often prisoners seeking to reduce their own sentences. Ineffective defense counsel, dubious science, prosecutorial misconduct, and forced confessions are the other factors commonly seen in wrongful conviction cases. Add to these factors the more passive, or systemic elements: poorly paid, overworked, and sometimes incompetent public defenders; juries picked for their willingness to convict; the indifference of the community and the media to the plight of indigent defendants, particularly non-white defendants. It's a system assured of making mistakes.

Those who manage to prove their innocence are of an extraordinary breed. Displaced from all that is familiar—home, family, identity, freedom—the wrongfully convicted person sets about proving his innocence in the most adverse of conditions. They and those who have faith in them—their families, friends, attorneys and innocence advocates—must be relentless, sometimes over the course of decades, in their quest to prove their innocence. The amount of time, determination, money, and faith that is required to reverse a wrongful conviction is so daunting that only the most stalwart and unwavering can hope to achieve it.

Some simply can't muster or maintain the strength; their anger is too great. Like most exonerees, Joseph Amrine, convicted of murder, first couldn't believe it was happening: "I didn't think there was gonna be a trial," he says. Once in prison, and knowing that his situation was all too real, he had to come to grips with his conviction, and work toward his release. But first he had to find a place for his outrage. "I couldn't just sit here and be thinking about my case… and then thinking about these guards harassing me, and then think about this lawyer that I don't like, and then the jury, and all these different problems that I got, different things that are just bothering me… I had to learn how to put stuff in different areas. It's like, if I got my problems with family over here, and right now I'm dealing with the problem with my lawyer or my case, well then, my situation with my family don't even come into play. It's locked in a box. And these are all in little boxes. Now, if all them boxes was to open up at one time, I'd probably lose my mind."

Of the exonerees represented in this book, almost half considered suicide at one time or another. After being convicted of murder, Juan Melendez could not bear the double burden of his imprisonment and the knowledge that society as a whole was not listening to his pleas to be heard. "This is what the demons used to tell me all the time," he says. "Why you got to satisfy them? Why let them kill you when you can do it yourself? You supposed to be a real Puerto Rican man, a real macho man. Don't satisfy them. Do it yourself. You say you didn't do the crime, you think they gonna believe you? They gonna kill you anyway. Don't satisfy them. Satisfy yourself. Do it yourself."

Even if they can stay sane and focused, exonerees must first educate themselves about their own cases. As James Newsome, exonerated after twenty-two years in prison, puts it, "The problem is, the wrongfully convicted person has the hardest time proving his innocence, because he doesn't know anything about his own case." Proving innocence from inside prison is a backwater proposition, where there is little connection to the outside world, where the state has control over everything—the mail one sends out, the visitors received. And prison is now meant for suffering. The days when American prisons were interested in rehabilitation, in releasing prisoners back into society as improved, reformed individuals, are long gone.

While all defendants are entitled to an attorney to represent them at trial, only those sentenced to death are automatically provided an appellate attorney. This fact drives some to extraordinary measures. Joseph Amrine, knowing that his case would receive more attention and legal assistance if he were given the death penalty, campaigned for it. "I tried my best to get the death penalty," he says. "I'd seen a lot of other guys there who had life and fifty years without parole—they didn't have no lawyers or nothing. So I'm thinking, rather than spend the rest of my life in prison, I'm gonna take my chances getting the death penalty for a murder I didn't commit. If nothing else, I'll have a lawyer throughout my appeal." In lieu of state-sponsored legal assistance, the wrongfully convicted try to cobble together their savings and those of their families, or represent themselves *pro se*. Many become experts in the law, and slog through the mired appellate process. All the while, they struggle with varied obstacles, from the storage of legal documents in their cells to the long, debilitating waits between motions, appeals, and decisions. Bright moments and developments in their cases come from the unlikeliest places. One man, convicted of multiple rapes, learned of the possibility of proving innocence with DNA on *Oprah*. Twenty-two years into his sentence, DNA results freed him.

When the wrongfully convicted are released, they might be initially exultant, but they enter a world very different than that which they left. They usually have no marketable skills, they've received little to no vocational training in prison, and in most cases, the exonerees are released with nothing — no compensation, no apology, no ability to fend for themselves. In 2005, only nineteen states had laws providing compensation for the wrongfully convicted. Only a few exonerees have been successful in suing the counties where they were convicted.

More often, the exonerees become dependent on relatives, and some are simply too damaged to function successfully. Michael Evans and Paul Terry were convicted, at age seventeen, of the rape and murder of a young girl on the South Side of Chicago. They spent twenty-seven years in prison, before their release due to DNA evidence and the assistance of the Center on Wrongful Convictions at Northwestern University. Michael Evans is a talkative and optimistic man, now middle-aged, struggling to move forward after being incarcerated for more than half his life and the entirety of his adult life. Paul Terry, though, was left a shell of his former self. He has no aspirations for the future and is content to hold a set of keys to his sister's house, where he lives.

The inevitable questions addressed to exonerees—"Are you angry? Are you bitter?"—are difficult for them to answer. Often asked on the very day they are released, the day the fortunes of the wrongfully convicted turn, they are joyful, optimistic, ready to begin their lives again. But this period of grace is often short-lived, as the realities of their post-prison quandary become clear. What seems to irk exonerees is that few seem to care about what happened to them, much less how it continues to happen to others. Apologies from states, courts, and officials involved in their conviction are a rarity, and there is no review process, whereby a police department, prosecutor's office, or court would reflect on its errors. Christopher Ochoa was convicted of a rape and murder and served twelve years for a crime that he didn't commit. "Nobody, nobody," he says, "has come out in public and said, 'We screwed up.' Not the DA, not the cop, not anybody. Nobody's even apologized to me."

Exonerees want something meaningful to grow from their horrific experience. But without recognizing and trying to correct the causes of wrongful convictions, without accountability for mistakes made at all levels, the decades these men and women spent in prison can seem to have been for nothing at all.

America has long played the role of watchdog for human rights abuses abroad—China, Iraq, Palestine, Kosovo, South Africa, Argentina—in each instance condemning the perpetrators and insisting on change, sometimes tied to sanctions and public censure. We are not accustomed to bearing witness to victims of systemic injustice at home; the lens is always pointed outward.

And yet wrongful conviction is a shocking and preventable injustice that affects countless numbers of Americans. This book gives voice to thirteen exonerated Americans. Their stories are told in plain language, and the issues raised by their narratives are elaborated upon in sidebars. We have attempted in this book to present stories that highlight different aspects of wrongful conviction—witness misidentification, forced confession, the preservation of biological evidence, prosecutorial misconduct, and so on. Selected on that basis, it should be noted, the racial composition of the book's exonerees does not precisely match that of the wrongfully convicted at large; the incidence of wrongful conviction is considerably higher among African-Americans than any other minority.

Those unfamiliar with the phenomena of wrongful conviction very often assume that the wrongfully convicted person had something to do with the crime. One of the students in the UC Berkeley graduate class, when asked about her preconceptions about exonerees, said that she imagined that most were "African-American, poor, involved in some criminal activity," and that "they were known by the cops, and saddled with some crime that they couldn't solve otherwise." Even the wife of exoneree Kevin Green, many years after his exoneration, still believes that "the police don't just pick you off the street."

But in the narratives of *Surviving Justice*, it becomes clear that wrongful conviction can and does happen to virtually anyone. Until stories like these are widely known and from them lessons learned, it will continue to happen to anyone.

Christopher Ochoa

MY LIFE IS A BROKEN PUZZLE

NAME: Christopher Ochoa · **BORN:** 1966 · **HOMETOWN:** El Paso, Texas

CONVICTED OF: Murder and sexual assault · **SENTENCE:** Life

SERVED: 12 years · **RELEASED:** 2001

A GUN TO YOUR HEAD

Let's say you sit at a bus stop, and an hour earlier somebody just robbed a bank and left a big bag of money there. A bad guy. It's under the bench at the bus stop. Somebody else found it—it's gone.

He goes back to get his money. He says, "Where's my money?" What is he talking about? You don't know.

He's got a gun, and he puts it to your head, but what you don't know is that this gun has no bullets.

"Tell me where the money is or you're dead."

You tell him, "No, no, no, no. I don't know."

You're just like shaking, because you don't know. If you knew, you would tell him, because you don't want to die. "I don't know. I don't know," you're thinking, "I don't want to die; I got to think of something."

"Where is it at? Where is it at?"

And then you're like, "Okay, somebody took it from here. I saw somebody running away from here. He went that way." Knowing darn well you didn't ever see anything.

Then the guy pulls away his gun and for some reason you see that it doesn't have any bullets, and you feel like such an idiot. But you didn't know. And that's how I felt. [They were] saying I was going to die.

In late 1998, during a two-day interrogation, Christopher Ochoa was persuaded by police to confess to a rape and murder he did not commit. Threatened with a death sentence, Ochoa also implicated his co-worker Richard Danziger in the crime.

IF THERE'S ANYBODY YOU CAN TRUST, IT'S A COP

I grew up in El Paso, Texas. From what I remember, I was always a good kid. One time, when I was a kid, a cop scared us. A mean neighbor, she said that we cussed her out and she called the cops. We're like ten years old at that time. The cop came into our house illegally. He had no probable cause; he just went in and scares the living daylights out of us. "You know I can take you to jail for this?" he said.

And then I called my uncle, and my uncle got on the cop: "What the hell are you doing scaring little kids? Isn't your job to try to be friends with them?" And the cop really didn't know what to say. That was the only run-in that I had. I trusted them. You're a kid, the cops give you candy.

I was a patrol boy in high school. They gave me a coupon, a

14

little certificate: "We're here to protect you, just call us." If there's anybody you can trust, it's a cop. And I did, and there it happens.

When I went to high school, I was playing sports, I was studying. For some reason I became a C-student, and then I went back to being an honor student. I was the assistant editor of a literary magazine. I took some law class; we did a mock trial. I was the prosecutor and I won the case. And it felt good. Maybe I could do this law thing. Either a lawyer or a major-league baseball player. That's really what I wanted to do. But things happened.

MY FUTURE WAS BRIGHT

When I graduated high school, I didn't go to college right away, 'cause we had a teacher that said that sometimes when you go to college right after high school, you don't do as well as you would normally. So she advised, "You can go to college, or you can take a year off or two." And I did.

I was optimistic. My future was bright. Really bright. I was a typical twenty-, twenty-one-year-old, having fun, going to rock concerts. Drinking. Working. Primarily working. I used to go to Dallas for big rock festivals—Aerosmith, Van Halen, Boston, all these older bands. I worked at an amusement park during the summer. I was a ride operator at the amusement park, and then I moved on to Pizza Hut in El Paso. After a couple of years in El Paso, I went to Austin, where I worked at different jobs until I settled at Pizza Hut.

I had worked [at Pizza Hut] with Richard Danziger. We were both cooks, and he left, he quit. And then he came back maybe a couple months later. He came back looking for a job. I was an assistant manager at Pizza Hut by then, and he was a good worker. He really worked hard so I gave him a job.

I saw him living at the YMCA. I think he told me he had

been convicted of something or other, or he was on probation, and so I said, "You can stay with us until you get on your feet. You just have to pay rent." I was living with another roommate, Roger Lewis, before I even met Danziger. I was living with him for a while, then my brother came to Austin.

I had a manager, a boss. I think she and Richard started seeing each other, and he would spend most of the time at her house. So it was like I had a roommate, but I didn't. I was not that tight with Richard. The media portrays us to be really tight, which we weren't. He was a cool person. He was a little bit, I don't know, he was really open, I think, whereas I was not. But other than that, he was just a cool guy. He wanted to be a psychologist. So maybe that was why he was so interested in behavior and stuff.

But I didn't go out with him and have dinner with him, no. I went out with my roommate, Roger, or my brother, Ralph. And I had other friends that I would hang out with. I guess they were more down to earth, more normal. So it's not like we had this relationship. I just know he was a hard worker and he was a really nice guy. It's kind of impossible for me to sit here and tell you how he really was.

I got the bug to go back to school, so I went to look into the Austin Community College. I was going to go in the spring of '89. That was my plan.

SUSPICIOUS CHARACTERS

On the morning of October 24, 1988, Nancy DePriest, a twenty-year-old Pizza Hut manager and mother, was raped and murdered at the Reinli Street Pizza Hut in Austin (a different Pizza Hut than the one where Ochoa worked). After the attacker sexually assaulted the victim, he handcuffed her to the restroom counter and shot her in the back of the head with a .22 caliber pistol. Before leaving, he flooded the restaurant in order to destroy any physical evidence he might have left behind.

October of '88, there was a murder in another Pizza Hut—a robbery, a rape, and a murder. A young woman was opening the store. I had seen her at managers meetings, but I didn't know her personally. The murder was one of those with virtually no leads, and they closed the restaurant for a couple of weeks. Everybody was shocked. All the Pizza Hut employees in the city were shocked about what happened to that young woman.

A couple weeks later they reopened the restaurant. My roommate Danziger was taking me home from somewhere. He wanted to stop by the Pizza Hut where the murder occurred. And I really didn't. He was curious about the scene, and I found that kind of weird. He was driving, so I had no choice. He drove up to Pizza Hut. I was in the car, and we were outside in the parking lot and I didn't want to go in. We were arguing and arguing, and I said, "Fine, let's just go in."

We go in. He ordered a beer. The whole time I was nervous. I've always been the kind of person that wants to follow the rules. In high school, I went to the principal's office once. Once. Never went again. Well, there was a Pizza Hut policy you couldn't drink beer at any other restaurant, so we're drinking beer there. He's only eighteen, I'm twenty-one.

And then he wants to look at the scene of the crime. I go, "I don't understand." So he makes a toast, and I toast, but you know, I didn't feel comfortable. I wanted to leave. We left shortly after, but as we were walking out, my roommate stopped to talk to a security guard, and asked him a lot of questions about the crime scene. I don't know what he asked him—I was at the car when he was asking questions.

And we drove off. Apparently, the police officers—the detectives that were investigating this crime—had talked to the Pizza Hut employees. They said, "Whoever did it might come back. And if they come back, if you see anybody suspicious, call us." So that looked suspicious, toasting, and you put it all together, we looked like suspicious characters.

A couple days later, on Friday morning, I was working and two detectives asked for me, and they said they wanted to ask me questions about a burglary. And they asked me if I wanted to go down to the station and answer them, and I said yes. They said I could drive my car or I could go with them; if I went with them they'd bring me back or whatever. Of course, they never brought me back.

THIS IS WHERE THE NEEDLE'S GONNA GO IN IF YOU DON'T COOPERATE

So I go with them. I was naive. I didn't know nothing about the system. I figured they were asking every employee at the Pizza Huts around the city. They take me into some kind of cubicle, what I know now is an interrogation room. What I later found out is that I was already a suspect in the murder. It was never about a burglary. They lied.

It was a Hispanic [detective] that walked in. When he walked in, he slammed his fist on the table. He starts asking me about why I was inquiring about the murder, rape, and all that kind of stuff. And then he's telling me that if I know something, I should just tell him. Typical interrogation, but he's yelling this whole time. He's not being so nice.

He spoke to me in Spanish initially, but I was speaking to him in English, so he laid off Spanish. He was trying to get this Chicano bond thing, and like, you're a cop—how can you ever get that? When it comes to detectives, they want to get their man.

They don't care.

He taps his finger on my arm at one point. "This is where the needle's gonna go in if you don't cooperate." He's telling me, "You know, if you know something about it, you can still get charged with capital murder and get the death penalty, 'cause you know something about it." And I told him, "I don't know what you're talking about. If I knew something, I would tell you. I would help you, but I don't know."

So he kept yelling at me, saying, "If you don't cooperate, I'm just gonna throw the book at you. They're gonna send you to death row; you're gonna get executed." This is going on for hours. At one point a female detective walks in. I was getting tired, and I asked her, "Can I have an attorney?" And she got really upset. She said, "No, you can't have one till you're officially charged."

At some point they give me a polygraph test. I failed. I failed all three polygraph tests. Even the ones where I said I didn't pull the trigger, I failed. I mean, there's nothing that I passed.

"If you don't cooperate, this is where you're gonna live the rest of your life, in this cell. Take a good look at it, 'cause that's gonna be your home. You're not gonna be able to hug your mom or your family anymore; you're gonna die in the death chamber. You'll live there until you die."

I don't know what's going on. Everything's spinning.

"Your partner on the other side is gonna testify. He's about to talk. I don't want him to get the deal. The Hispanic always gets the shaft, and the white guy always gets the deal."

I tell him, "I don't know what you're talking about."

He shows me pictures of the autopsy.

"Don't you feel sorry for her?"

"Yeah, I do, but what do you want me to do? I can't help you."

This is going on for hours. He said, "I'm just getting tired of this BS. I'm gonna book you. You're young, you're fresh for the

CALLED INTO QUESTION
Deceptive police interrogation tactics result in false confessions

In 1936, the U.S. Supreme Court outlawed the use of physical force during police interrogations. Since then, interrogators have focused primarily on psychological tactics, including intentional deceptions, role-playing exercises and a variety of other subtle mind games. Psychological tactics can be as coercive as physical tactics and can induce false confessions, a factor that shows up in at least 15 percent of wrongful convictions.

According to social psychologist Richard A. Leo, psychological pressure can cause a suspect to "temporarily doubt the reliability of his memory, to believe that he probably did, or logically must have, committed the crime under question, and to confess to it despite having no memory or knowledge of... the offense." As a result of a role-playing exercise, Gary Gauger was briefly convinced that he had killed his parents. This hypothetical exercise, in which Gauger was asked to describe how he would have murdered his parents, was then used against him at trial.

In Palo Alto, California, police falsely claimed to have a videotape of Jorge Hernandez entering a ninety-year-old woman's apartment just before she was beaten and raped. Hernandez then falsely confessed and was later exonerated by DNA. It remains legal for police to lie and employ trickery during interrogations.

Most psychological interrogation tactics used today by U.S. and Canadian police forces trace back to *Criminal Interrogation and Confessions*, a seminal police training manual co-authored by Northwestern University Professor Fred Inbau and former police officer John Reid, first published in 1962. In detailing the appropriate steps to an effective interrogation, the book, often called *The Reid Manual*, outlines psychological tricks to play on the suspect, and specifies when deception is appropriate. Its value as a method of extracting reliable information has been called into question by numerous false confession cases.

In Alberta, Canada, after interrogation tactics from the Reid model induced false confessions from three young men accused of raping and murdering a fourteen-year-old girl, a judge described the Reid technique as a "huge psychological brainwashing exercise."

Concerns about deceptive and coercive police interrogations have prompted some municipalities to begin videotaping interrogations—not just confessions, as many do. The Reid model, however, remains the standard method for interrogating suspects.

continued on page 22

prison. You've never been in prison, they're gonna have you."
I took that to mean rape.

That was when I gave him the first statement.

I JUST WENT ALONG WITH THEM

The Hispanic cop, Hector Polanco, was writing a statement. He wanted me to say my codefendant [Danziger] was the one that did it, and he came and told me about it, that he did it, all this kind of stuff, and I just went along with what the detective was saying. Signed the statement.

Then I wanted to go home. He says, "You can't go home. We want you to stay at a hotel for your own protection." Then he asked me for some lab samples. Some semen and hair and all that. I gave him the semen and the hair. I wanted to. While at the hotel, now I'm getting really worried. I'm scared, really scared. I call my roommate Roger. "I think I need an attorney."

I was there [at the hotel] for the weekend. Come Monday, the detectives walked in and they picked me up. And they said, "Okay, now we know you're guilty, 'cause you wanted to call for an attorney, and only guilty people call for attorneys." So now, I don't know what's going on. They take me to another interrogation room. Now they got a tape recorder on. "We think you had something to do with it, we think you were the lookout. If you don't cooperate again, the death penalty's there, it hasn't gone away, we're gonna execute you."

So I just say, "Okay, yeah, I was the lookout." I just want to go home. All this time they're saying, "Oh, well, you'll get twenty years." By this time, I know I'm sunk. I'm scared. I didn't know what they could do. You just don't know what can happen. So that confession, alleged confession, was pretty easy, but then all of a sudden they wanted more. They wanted me to be in there,

"THE NINE STEPS TO EFFECTIVE INTERROGATION"

An excerpt from Criminal Interrogation and Confessions, Third Edition, *pgs. 82-83*

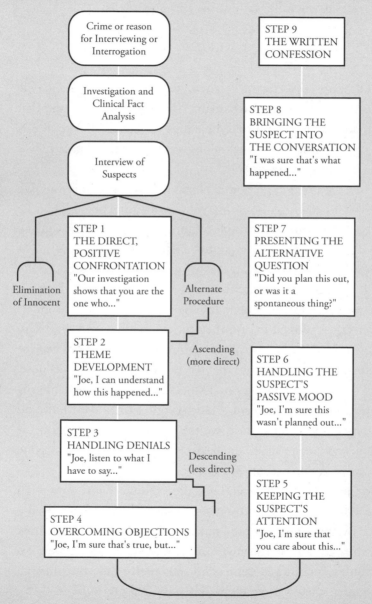

Crime or reason
for Interviewing or
Interrogation

STEP 9
THE WRITTEN
CONFESSION

Investigation and
Clinical Fact
Analysis

STEP 8
BRINGING THE
SUSPECT INTO
THE CONVERSATION
"I was sure that's what
happened..."

Interview of
Suspects

STEP 1
THE DIRECT,
POSITIVE
CONFRONTATION
"Our investigation
shows that you are the
one who..."

Elimination
of Innocent

Alternate
Procedure

STEP 7
PRESENTING THE
ALTERNATIVE
QUESTION
"Did you plan this out,
or was it a
spontaneous thing?"

STEP 2
THEME
DEVELOPMENT
"Joe, I can understand
how this happened..."

Ascending
(more direct)

STEP 6
HANDLING THE
SUSPECT'S
PASSIVE MOOD
"Joe, I'm sure this
wasn't planned out..."

STEP 3
HANDLING DENIALS
"Joe, listen to what I
have to say..."

Descending
(less direct)

STEP 5
KEEPING THE
SUSPECT'S
ATTENTION
"Joe, I'm sure that
you care about this..."

STEP 4
OVERCOMING OBJECTIONS
"Joe, I'm sure that's true, but..."

See Appendix A for further excerpts from the Reid manual

sodomizing her and raping her, and I was like, "No."

But again, the death penalty's there, so I'm like, "Whatever, okay." By this time I just want to get it over with. This is a long time. I've been there a while. They tell me, "We think you were there," and all this stuff, so I say yeah—I just went along with them. I don't know why, I was just scared.

They start tape-recording it, but the problem was that any time I came to a detail in the restaurant, it was wrong, and then they would get mad. They would say, "Well, was this item there?" I would say, "Yeah…" "Then what color was it?" They had me guessing for the right color. They would start the tape and then would have to stop it 'cause I got the detail wrong. So they would start it, stop it, till they got the details. It took a long time.

At one point the sergeant got up and threw the chair he was sitting in, at my head. He missed, but he threw it with such force, and I was really scared 'cause those guys were really big.

THERE'S A DETAILED CONFESSION, YOU GOTTA BE GUILTY

The interrogation lasted two full days, during which the police repeatedly threatened Ochoa with the death penalty. His requests for a lawyer were denied. By 10:00 P.M. on the second day, Ochoa had signed two separate statements, each typed by one of the officers. In the first, he claimed to be the sole murderer of DePriest. In the second, he claimed that while he had participated in her rape and murder, Richard Danziger had pulled the trigger. Ochoa later retracted this accusation in a third statement, made on March 7, 1989, in which he implicated Danziger in the rape and the robbery, but asserted that he himself was the shooter.

I sign the confession, I get arrested. I went to the magistrate. She was really upset that I didn't have a lawyer on a capital murder case. So she took me to chambers. She yelled at people, said, "I want this guy to have a lawyer. Immediately."

The lawyer they sent me was just out of law school. Young. I didn't know it, but that's bad news on a capital murder. I tell him exactly what happened, and he said, "Okay, fine." He leaves, and then the cops tell him, "No, he's got a confession." And he says, "Okay, you've gotta be guilty." So I told him, "No, I'm not, I'm innocent."

So they get another attorney—a lead attorney, an older attorney. I tell him the same thing. And he got mad. He wanted me to plead guilty. I said, "No. Isn't it your job to prove me innocent?" He says his job was to save my life, which I guess it was, but he didn't even try to investigate. "There's a detailed confession, you gotta be guilty." He didn't even believe in my innocence. I guess the DA, everybody wanted me to plead guilty, to testify against Danziger. I didn't want to do that 'cause I was not guilty. So I told him no.

But the problem was, they were calling my mom every day. "He's guilty, he's guilty. You got to get him to plead guilty and to testify. If not, your son is gonna die on death row." So you can imagine what my mom is going through. And she would keep on calling me, telling me, "You got to save your life." No, I don't want to. I don't want to testify. I don't want to plead guilty. I don't want to admit to it.

But eventually, she had to go to the hospital—had she gone later she would've had a heart attack. People didn't want to tell me. Nobody wanted to tell me till my grandma let it out on the phone when I called from the jail. She told me what had happened with my mom and I got really sad, and it was the hardest choice I ever had to make. I called whoever I had to call: "I'll plead guilty to this."

And I go talk to them, and they want me to plead guilty, but Danziger has to be convicted. They really wanted him.

I testified against Danziger. I'm coached before I go into the courtroom and told what to say.

Ochoa pleaded guilty to murder and sexual assault on May 5, 1989. His sentencing was suspended until after Danziger's trial in late January 1990. At Danziger's trial, Ochoa testified that he had shot DePriest, but that he and Danziger had planned the crime together, and that they both had raped her. Although Danziger's girlfriend testified on his behalf that she was with him at the time of the murder, she also wavered under the prosecution's threats to bring charges against her, and her statements were ultimately not enough to convince the jury. Danziger's defense, furthermore, could provide no explanation for Ochoa's testimony. Danziger was found guilty of aggravated sexual assault and sentenced to life in prison. Soon after, on March 6, 1990, Ochoa also was sentenced to life in prison.

LOSING ALL SENSE OF DIRECTION

It's like you don't have a choice. Life sentence, death penalty. Life sentence in prison—you're going to die a slow death at an old age—or you're going to die in the death chamber. It was no choice. You're twenty-two years old. What do you do?

And if people notice, every confession, every time there's a wrongful convicted guy, most people were in their mid- to early twenties. The cops are trained. They're going after people that want to live. They know your weakness, and your enemy knows your weakness. That's what he's going to look for.

Danziger's girlfriend, they brought her in. She was saying, "No, he was with me." They interrogate and say, "You know what? We think that you were there. You and Ochoa and Danziger were there—you held her down while she was being sodomized. So what's going to happen: we're going to send you to jail. They're going to take your kids away." A mother's kids. What does she do? She caves in. That's her weakness.

THE LONELIEST FEELING IN THE WORLD

They send me to prison. The first night, they put me in the cell, and then they close the door. They close the door, and it was the loneliest feeling in the world. I was all alone.

So many things you see in prison. I don't know. I started seeing body bags roll down the hallway. I saw a guy stabbed. A riot broke out in the kitchen where I working. And you just start smelling the pepper spray, and you put a towel on you and it just makes it worse. Tear gas is different. You can put a wet towel on your nose and it's okay. But pepper spray, it just makes it worse.

I had to go through riots. I had to go through lockdown. They would lock the prison down because people were killing each other. And it was pretty bad when they locked down the prison. When we were locked down in the summer it was hot, humid. I remember I sometimes had to put the fan on the toilet so that the fresh air that was bouncing off the water would hit the fan. Or throw water on the floor. You would lay in it.

It smelled bad, it felt even worse. Tennessee County, Texas. Three days without a shower, three days in the same cell. Fortunately I always had plenty to read. That's all you do, read and listen to the radio. They didn't allow TVs in the rooms in Texas. They do in other prisons, but we didn't have them.

The bars were navy blue. The color would supposedly make you more mellow, instead of the higher, brighter, sharper colors, that make you vicious or whatever. And we wore white all the time. That's why you will never see me in a pure white shirt.

CHRISTMAS EVE

I'd been there almost ten years. I'm thirty years old, I'm looking back on my life. I'm a failure. I have no family, I have no kids, I have no education, no car, no house. I used to get the newspaper from back home. I used to see these people I went to high school with. They had kids, beautiful homes, beautiful wives, and all this stuff, and I had nothing, and I didn't know what I did to deserve it.

Christmas Eve, I was really depressed. No cards came for me. People can tell when you're going to kill yourself in prison—they know. They saw me really sad, and they said, "You'll get a card." Mail call came. I didn't get anything.

I went up to my cell, I took a razor and I busted it open and I got the razor blade itself and I put it on my arm, and I was going to kill myself on Christmas Eve. I was in so much pain that I didn't want to live anymore. It hurt too much to live. So I just wanted an end.

But somehow, before I did the deed, my morals, everything came flashing back—my family, my religious upbringing. I didn't have the right to take anybody's life, not even my own. It really took all I had not to do it. I dropped the razor. I flushed it down the toilet.

I went to sleep, woke up the next morning. I was still in pain. I mean emotional pain, not physical. I started going to church, not because I wanted God to save me or give me release or whatever—no. I needed peace.

I found peace. I would go to school, I would work out, weight-lift, do all this stuff. I would read everything: Bible, love novels, horror novels, everything under the sun. I pursued my college education, got two associate's degrees.

FAVORITE GRANDSON

When I was a little kid, I would go to my grandfather's house, and if I had a hole in my pants or my shirt, he would take the hole and just rip it all to shreds, and I would have no clothes. And I thought that was funny. I would laugh, and my mom would get mad. He would do it to my little brother and my brother would cry; I was laughing. My grandfather was my best friend. I found out later that I was his favorite grandson.

Ochoa (center) and his parents Dorna and Samuel at the Wynne Prison Unit in Huntsville, Texas (1999)

When I was in prison, he would write me. He would send me money every month. Fifteen dollars to put on my books. It wasn't much, but it was something.

One day, my parents said he was getting sick, he was about to die. The doctor gave him I don't know how many months, or a year. I would tell him, "You can't die, you can't croak." He would say, "I'm not going to kick the bucket, I have to wait for you to get out."

At some point, I just stopped writing. I was like twenty-four. You take people for granted at that age sometimes. He would get mad. Why didn't I write? And I don't know what possessed me, one day I wrote him a letter. A long letter. I thanked him for everything he did, specific instances where he helped me. A heartfelt letter.

My mom said that he died at three in the morning, and my letter got to his house at like seven. And it totally devastated me, that my letter didn't get to him on time. Because I wanted to say that. I mean, I guess something inside of me felt that he was

going to die, and I didn't get to say goodbye to him.

But he would always tell us not to cry—never cry for him when he died. He says, "Always cry for people when they're alive, because that's when they want to hear it the most. I'm dead, what the hell are you going to cry for me then?" He even told my family, "The first person you see crying over my grave, you push them in the coffin with me—push them in the hole with me."

So I didn't cry.

I HAVEN'T STOPPED BELIEVING IN MYSELF

In 1990, convicted rapist Achim Josef Marino learned from his cellmate that two other men had pleaded guilty to murdering DePriest. Marino had a religious conversion as a result of his participation in a twelve-step program, and in 1996, seeking atonement, he wrote letters to the Austin Police Department and the Austin American-Statesman, *in which he confessed that he was the sole perpetrator of the crime against DePriest. The letters described the crime in detail and informed police of the location of the pistol with which he had shot DePriest, as well as handcuffs he had used to bind her, and a bank bag he had stolen. These items were recovered shortly after the crime, but investigators, unsure as to whether the gun was the real murder weapon, took no further action.*

In 1997, Marino again wrote letters, this time to Governor George W. Bush, to the police department, and to the district attorney's office. In response, a homicide detective and a Texas ranger were sent to interview Ochoa.

In '98, two cops came to see me, a Texas ranger and an Austin police officer. They asked me if they could interview me. They said, "There's this guy that's saying that he did this crime with you guys."

I didn't know then, at all, what was going on. I didn't know that this guy, who actually did it, had already wrote them a letter, had wrote Governor Bush a letter, had wrote DAs that we hadn't done the crime, that he had done it. He did a Christian conversion. But I guess they were trying to link us together. Well, I didn't know this guy; he didn't know us.

During that interview I ask one of the detectives, "Hey, what if I call Barry Scheck? What if I get in contact with him?" I had kept up with all the DNA exonerations that Barry Scheck had done. I remember the cop had mentioned DNA initially, and that's the only thing that stuck to my mind when I was first arrested.

He says, "I wouldn't do that if I were you. You're gonna make it worse for yourself." I didn't respond to that. I just looked at him like, wait a minute, they know damn well that if I'm guilty I'm not going to do that. So this guy's got to be hiding something. I was very afraid that if I gave him any clue whatsoever, or say that I'm going to contact an attorney, they would destroy evidence that might be used to help me.

Distrustful of the officers, Ochoa repeated what he had said at Danziger's trial—that he and Danziger had raped and murdered DePriest. The officers suspected he was lying to protect Marino. For the next two years, the police searched for a link between Ochoa and Marino. In the meantime, Ochoa began to pursue information about DNA testing.

So I went and I talked to this [prisoner] from El Paso that was going home, a pretty good friend of mine. I told him to type Barry Scheck's name in the search engine. And finally somebody from the Innocence Project emails him back: "Your friend might have a case, because he has DNA." And he sent me the add-

resses of the schools with innocence projects.

So for some reason I circle Wisconsin. That's the one I'm going to write. Wrote them an eight-page letter and I sent it off and I said, "That's all I can do, God. That's the best I can do." Told them the whole story from the beginning to the time that I wrote them. Just the legal stuff. And I told them, "You know what, I've given up on the system, I've given up on everyone, I don't trust anybody. I've given up on the world, I don't have faith in the system, but I haven't stopped believing in myself."

That was enough for them to take the case. They called me up a couple of months later, and I was really happy.

In 1999 the lawyers and students of the Wisconsin Innocence Project began their search for evidence that would help prove Ochoa's innocence. In the spring of 2000, John Pray, law professor and co-founder of the project, sent a letter to the police department requesting that DNA evidence be preserved. The DNA laboratory at the Texas Department of Public Safety had saved the evidence, and the police department immediately agreed to testing. At the request of the district attorney's office, the tests were performed in the summer and fall of 2000. The results matched Marino and conclusively excluded Ochoa and Danziger.

Eventually, in 2000, the cops came to see me again. This time they were friendlier. They gave me another polygraph. I flunked it again. And that's when I told them, "I don't care what your polygraph says, I'm innocent. I don't care what that crap says." So September, October, I don't know when it was, I got the test that exonerated me. The DNA test. They said it matched Marino, and I said, "Who the hell is Marino?" And my attorney said, "You don't know?"

I said, "No. What are you talking about?" So then he started

AN EXCERPT FROM ACHIM JOSEF MARINO'S 1998 CONFESSION LETTER TO TEXAS GOVERNOR GEORGE W. BUSH

Re: Murder Confession

Governor's Office
Received Feb. 25 1998

Dear Governor Bush Sir,

My name is Achim Josef Marino, #573514 and I'am currently confined in the McConnell Unit of the T.D.C.J-I.D. [Texas Department of Criminal Justice Institutional Division] serving three life sentences plus three ten-year sentences for crimes committed at Austin, Texas in both 1988 and 1990. While in Austin in 1988, I also robbed, raped and shot a 20 year old women at the Pizza Hut at Reinli Lane. This was in late October of 1988, after purchasing the murder weapon via the Austin American Statesmans classified section. The womens name was Nancy Lena Dupriest, and I have not been convicted for this crime. Approximately a month after this crime, I was arrested in El Paso, Texas, where the murder weapon was confiscated by the El Paso police department, however, the federal government ultimately convicted me for it. At the time of my arrest, I had to keys as well as two currency bags from the Pizza Hut with the name of Pizza Huts bank on the bag, in my possession and which remained in my personal property in the county jail for approximately 14 months. My friend, ▮▮▮▮▮▮▮▮▮▮▮▮▮▮▮▮▮▮ ▮▮▮▮▮▮▮▮▮▮, picked up my personal property after I was transferred to T.D.C.J-I.D for parole violation. She later took these items to my parents home where they remain to this day. Included with this confession to you is a B.A.T.F. report in conection with the confiscated murde weapon, and the purchase of it in Austin, Texas, shortly before the murder. In 1990, after I was re-paroled by T.D.C.J.-I.D., I was once again arrested in Austin, Texas for robbery on approximately 5/30/90 While in the county jail, I was told by my cell mate, ▮▮▮▮▮▮▮▮▮▮▮▮▮▮, that two men named Dansiger and Ochoa had been convicted for that crime. I told ▮▮▮▮▮▮▮ at that time that they had gotten the wrong people, that I knew the guy who had done it. He then told me that Dansiger and Ochoa had plead guilty to the murder. Governor Bush Sir, I do not know these men nor why they plead guilty to a crime they never committed. I can only assume that they must have been facing a capitol with a poor chance of aquittal, but I tell you this sir, I did this awful crime and I was alone...

telling me Marino is this guy, the actual perpetrator. In a way I was grateful, but in a way I was really angry, 'cause Marino is the one that cost me a lot of years. He took somebody's life. He's caused so much hurt. I don't know him. I don't want to know him.

They tell me I'll have to wait for two months. They'll try to get me out before Thanksgiving, before Christmas. Finally, January 16, they took me to court and they released me.

When I was released it was celebratory. Every talk show host that I've talked to, they said they admired me, or whatever—because, I guess, I didn't come out angry. I think people like that. I think the media like that I was forgiving and not this angry convict. I went on *The O'Reilly Factor*. He was angry at what happened. He said, "Why aren't you angry? I would be really angry." I guess he was trying to draw me in to a confrontation.

I said, "No, I'm not bitter." And he said, "Thank you very much, Mr. Ochoa." I didn't last but ten minutes on his show.

THIS IS WHERE I BELONG

I know that my uncle believed in me. My mom says she didn't have her doubts, but she had her doubts. My uncle never did. When I got out, my uncle and his partner had a room ready for me. He had an extra room in his house. So they fixed it up. They had a bed and a TV for me, and they had my Dallas Cowboys helmet-phone—a phone that's a helmet. I would stay with my mom, but I decided that being at my uncle's there was more freedom. You should be able to do whatever you want to do. You don't want people telling you... That's part of getting out.

I had a good relationship with [my relatives]. I was really socially awkward. I couldn't look anybody in the eyes; I still don't. When I would go out and I would not be very talkative, they would try to draw me out. Everybody I've seen that just gets out, they're not ready to talk when they get out. So [my uncle] would take me out dancing to the clubs. He would, like, make the sacrifice.

My uncle, when I got out, he taught me how to dress. He took me to get my prescription glasses. I paid for half, he paid for the other half. I remember picking out my glasses, and I'm looking at the 1980s style, those teardrops. And him and his partner come up and go, "No, no, no! The teardrops are gone. We'll get you some nice, in-fashion little ones."

For a month or two I did nothing. I traveled around the country. I started working in about May, April—worked at a concrete company. And then I started school, went to finish my bachelor's degree. I was a business major. Accounting came naturally to me. When I started taking business classes I really took to them well.

And then I took a business law class and I thought, "This is where I belong." I decided to go to law school, and I decided to apply to Wisconsin, and then eventually I got my settlement.

Barry Scheck, Johnnie Cochran, and all them, their law firm sued the city. Well, I did, I sued the city of Austin and the police department. Eventually we settled. We settled for $[5.3] million.

Barry Scheck was the first famous person I ever met. Somebody told me that most lawyers can walk into an airport and not get recognized, but Barry Scheck and Johnnie Cochran go to an airport and they get recognized. They're like rock stars of the law. Barry Scheck is a hero to people in prison. But I met him and he was really, really humble. I expected somebody that was full of himself, but he was so warm, so genuine. He said, "You're going to be in front of the media. Here's some tips for talking to the media." And he told me how politicians speak to media, how you pick three points and stay on them. And when I talk to the press I always remember what he told me, and I carry that through law school.

BRAND-NEW START

Ochoa was admitted to the University of Wisconsin Law School in 2003, where he became a student of John Pray and Keith Findley, the professors who had worked to free him. He joined the Wisconsin Innocence Project in 2004.

The [acceptance] letter came, and I realized I was going to law school. I couldn't believe it. A couple of years before, I was at the bottom of the barrel, here now I was going to one of the top law schools in the country. It all seemed surreal. I felt it was like a brand-new start for me. I felt, I finally felt, like there was something that was my own, my very own. It felt like finally my life, it's beginning again, which it actually has.

I was so excited when Wisconsin said yes. When I was in East Texas, in prison, you can tell you're looked down on you're Hispanic, you're black. They won't say anything, but you can feel it. And here, walking in Madison, the first time I walked to State Street, it was like they didn't even, you know, they didn't stare, it was nothing different to them. My biggest thing is that I want to be part of society. I want to be normal, whatever normal is. I just want to walk through a mall, or walk through a street, not be treated different because I was in prison.

I did my first year here, and now I'm doing my second year. I do pretty well when I set my mind to it here in school, when I really study. When I read for class, and I go prepared, I really understand it.

But I can't sleep. I wake up in sweats. You know, when you take the law school finals, because those things are like four hours long—I have to get eight hours of sleep. Well I can't... I haven't got eight hours of sleep in forever. When my finals roll around, I have to go to bed at six o'clock at night in order to get the rest.

Because I wake up lots of times. That really is affecting my law school work.

My social skills, they were lacking. I'm a thirty-eight-year-old working with twenty-year-olds. I didn't fit in. And I'm still shy by nature. People think I'm this conceited guy, but it's not that. People didn't mean to on purpose, but it happens—I say something and it gets dismissed. I would make a suggestion, and they would act like, "What do you know? You've been in prison." A couple months later they would see that I was right.

I HAD NO EMOTION IN MY HEART

It's hard for me to be close to people. My family doesn't understand at all. It's kind of hard to trust people. And then, in the prison, you learn not to trust people. You're taught very early on, don't trust anyone. No one. If you want to survive prison you have to not trust anyone. You're a kid; you're learning these things. You're twenty-two years old.

One thing you do learn is, you have to shut off your emotions. You have to have no emotions, 'cause other prisoners, when they see weakness they attack, physically and mentally. So I had no emotion in my heart. Just because you don't have emotions doesn't mean you're not a cool person, doesn't mean you're a mean guy, you're just a jerk. You still treat people with respect, you still help them, but you don't show anything.

And that was very difficult for me. I didn't want anybody to see me, and now I don't let anybody see me break down. I have dreams, I have nightmares. I don't tell anybody. I don't tell my mom, I don't tell anybody. They don't see what I go through.

I've dated before. It was the sex part that I had a difficult problem with. When I care about a woman, I have problems performing sexually, because prison, you really couldn't look at

women. If you look at them wrong, the female guards, you were
beat up pretty good. Sex is so very prohibited. Of course, people
still do it—naturally, you're human—but they suppress it as
much as they can. The masturbating and stuff, they don't want
people to do that. You know, prison just did a lot of things to me.

I think my problem was that I don't want to be controlled.
I don't want to be told what to do, and when I am dating somebody and she tries to tell me what to do, it's not going to happen,
because I've just been told what to do all my life.

THAT'S ALL THE MONEY DID—PUT ME
WHERE I WAS SUPPOSED TO BE

I met this wonderful woman. Her name's Robin. I'm kind of
happy that now I know, okay, there's nothing wrong with me.
Robin shows me how to manage my money. I'm an electronics
freak. I used to buy remote control cars, which we always wanted when we were kids, me and my brother. Remote control
cars—it seemed like a good idea. Now, Robin would just kill me.
There's a robot I bought at Sharper Image, sale rack. It dances
and stuff. A hundred dollars. She said, "Why did you get that?
You don't use it." I was going to go buy this $300 robot one time,
a big one, I mean he actually serves drinks and stuff. He has a
camera, so you send him in to spy on people. But she won't let
me. I mean, I could, 'cause it's my money. She would say, "It's
your money," but she shows me how to control myself.

My family was pretty poor. When I was growing up, I didn't
have much—and I sure as heck didn't have it in prison. I didn't
have a TV, I had a little radio, worth eight bucks—that's all
I had. And now I come out here and they give me money. It's not
so much that I go nuts. Every guy that's middle class, thirty-eight
years old, with a wife and kids, they have the ability to go buy a

Ochoa (center) with Barry Scheck (bottom row, second from right) and the Wisconsin Innocence Project lawyers who helped to free him (2004)

plasma [TV]. That's all the money did—put me where I was supposed to be.

THAT GUY STILL TOOK HER LIFE

Sometimes I do interviews, and I have to remind myself that it's Chris Ochoa, it's Richard Danziger, it's Jeanette Popp [the victim's mother], but we can't forget the victim, Nancy DePriest, the woman that died.

I felt horrible. Everybody did. That guy still took her life, and I won't sit here and tell you everybody's not guilty and you shouldn't be punished when you hurt people—physically hurt people. I don't believe in physically hurting people at all. I'm just as mad as anybody else.

I feel bad for her mom, her family. Especially her mom, Jeanette Popp. That's not the only tragedy she's gone through. She doesn't talk to me much anymore, but Jeanette's somebody that's really, really special.

What happened is that she saw it on *Good Morning America* that I was probably going to be exonerated. She was rather upset. She calls the district attorney: "What is going on? I mean, these guys are guilty, what are you trying to do?" They weren't very truthful. So she calls my attorney. I'm scared, because once the victim puts up a fight, the exoneration is going to be longer.

So my attorney, John Pray, tells her everything from the get-go—what happened, honestly. And Jeanette was so grateful that finally someone was telling her what was going on, and she felt so bad that she asked John if she could write me. I get the letter in prison. She says how sorry she is, kind of saying that it was her fault. I wrote her back, and we start writing each other. I asked her if she could be at my exoneration. I really wanted her to be there. So she went to Austin. I felt so bad for her. She was crying because, you know, she saw my mom. My mom got her son back, but Jeanette didn't get her daughter back.

She was the biggest advocate. She was a very, very big part of why I was released so quick and why society accepted me so quick. She talked to the press, she talked to the DA—that was very instrumental, believe me, when a victim stands up and says, "I want him out." We went to do TV shows together. I would speak, she would speak from her perspective, and it was a really nice one-two punch.

Now, I don't know where she's at, mentally or emotionally, but during the time I think it helped her. It's helped me a lot. But I didn't take her daughter's life, so I don't know how much it's helped me, in that way. It's like I don't need closure. The guy [who] needs closure is Marino.

I need closure from the police officer. My whole deal is not between me and Jeanette or Nancy. My deal is between me and the police department. I have an issue with [Officer] Polanco.

That's the guy I need to talk to.

YOU KNEW I WAS INNOCENT. YOU KNEW.

They were going to make [Polanco] go to the [civil] trial. They were going to subpoena him. I said no, I don't want him there. "Do you want to talk to him?" No, I don't want to talk to him.

I didn't know how I would have reacted. I'm not saying I would have been mad. I'm not saying I would have done anything bad. Maybe I would break down. I didn't want to cry, because I was taught not to cry in prison. Not in front of people. Sometimes now I do want to confront him.

I would ask him, "Why? Why did you do this?"

"Well, I really thought you were guilty," he would say.

"No, don't lie to me. You destroyed evidence. You knew I was innocent. You knew. You were a cop for fourteen years or however long; you were one of the most experienced homicide detectives, and you knew, you knew. Why was it so important for you to wrap this up? There was an MO [modus operandi] on the guy that did it. He had already done stuff like this—why don't you use standard procedures? Why don't you go to the FBI? They would have given you an MO. You didn't follow procedure."

And the second question I would ask is, "How in the hell can you live with yourself? Are you happy that my life is destroyed, and I have to pick it up? 'Cause you're not doing anything to pick it up for me. My grandfather—are you happy that all you left me was a grave?"

You know, sometimes I feel like I'm a little kid, that I'm a little kid that had this gigantic puzzle, and then he came and kicked it, and I'm here left with this puzzle, all by myself, trying to put the pieces back together.

I mean, I know I have money, and I have school, and I have

friends and support. But I'm alone. In the end, when I'm in my room, and when I have nobody, like right now, I'm left alone trying to pick up these pieces, and nobody's helping me. You know, I never thought about it that way, but I'm thinking about it now. My life is a broken puzzle. People say I'm young. Come on, I'm thirty-eight. I don't have much time to put my life back. And it's frustrating, because sometimes the pieces that I need are not there, and I'm trying to fit pieces that don't fit. And there are times that it works well, I get a little piece. That's what I would ask him. Why did you kick my puzzle? Why did you destroy it?

You sit there and you fight me when I sue you. Why don't you just admit you messed up and you violated every right that I had under the Constitution? People have helped me pick up the puzzle, it hasn't been you. It's been the courts; it's even been the DA, Barry, the Innocence Project, even Congress, even President Bush.

When I started my relationship—I don't want to bring in our sex life, but I couldn't perform. And I got so mad at Polanco because this is what you've done to me. I was crying in bed. I said, "Why did he do this to me, why?" I can't even function. Finally I got through it, but I had to fix that—to put those pieces of that part of the puzzle together.

People tell me, "You can go to the therapist." The therapist, in the end, is not going to help me. I have to help myself. I can talk to the therapist; he can guide me, but in the end, I'm in the room alone.

TAKING RESPONSIBILITY

In 1991, Richard Danziger was knocked down and repeatedly kicked in the head by an inmate who had mistaken him for someone else. Danziger suffered severe brain damage from the attack, leaving him in need of lifelong care. He was released in 2001.

HARD TO RELATE

Exonerees often struggle with romantic relationships after release

Contrary to popular belief, not all inmates are sexually ravenous when released; actually, after years of suppressing sexual urges, many exonerees experience substantially decreased sexual drives—one of a host of challenges exonerees face upon re-entering the dating world.

The average exoneree has spent more than twelve years in prison. During that time, dating customs and trends can change dramatically.

Christopher Ochoa with his girlfriend Robin Dalton

After his release, Peter Rose was approached by a young woman at a local bar. "She told me I was handsome and asked me what my name was," he says. "Women didn't do that ten years ago. I'm not really sure what a man is supposed to do these days."

Exonerees who entered prison as teenagers often have difficulties even with very basic aspects of relationships, having missed a crucial maturational stage in their youth. After his release, Donnell Johnson began to date a fellow undergraduate at Mississippi Valley State. "I was still discovering myself when I met her," he says. "I was twenty-one, but after spending my teenage years in prison, I didn't really know about real simple stuff that most people take for granted, like how to even talk to a woman."

Trust can be particularly challenging for exonerees. Many, unable or unwilling to express their rage and despair, engage in avoidance or distancing behaviors. After so many years of restriction, many become annoyed if a partner tells them what to do.

Basic romantic expression can be difficult for exonerees. "When I came home it was difficult for me to relate to a woman," says exoneree Michael Austin, "because I'd been around men for so long. It was difficult for me to be somewhat gentle."

And for exonerees accused of rape, physical intimacy brings additional anxieties. "When I first got out," says Ken Wyniemko, "and even to some extent to this day, I am real paranoid. If a woman walks up to me that I don't know, I keep my distance, because in the back of my mind, I'm worried that she's going to accuse me of molesting her."

I asked for forgiveness, through the media, through the press. And then later on I asked [Danziger's] sister Barbara Oakley personally, and she was really nice. She said, "You know what, Chris, you just do me a favor and go be a lawyer. The biggest help you can do is believe people when they tell you they didn't do it, believe in them, even when nobody else does. Don't let something happen to somebody else like happened to you and Richard."

Everybody started blaming me, everybody. "Chris Ochoa did it. It wasn't the DA, it wasn't the cop, it wasn't Danziger, it was him." They never wanted to take responsibility for their actions. And I did. I have. You know how much responsibility I've taken in my life? I did somebody else's time. I blamed myself when I got out. I took responsibility for what I did wrong.

I don't think I need to ask forgiveness from the victim or victim's family at all, 'cause I didn't do the crime. [Danziger,] yeah. Him and his family. Because the one thing I am guilty of is being a coward. I was a coward. I should have just faced up to it.

He got beat up. He got hit in the head. He was very hurt. He needs care for the rest of his life. It's mental stuff—they say he might not live too long. And it's sad, and some part of me feels really bad about it, but there's nothing I can do. I did as much as I could. I'm taking some responsibility. We presented our cases at the same time. I settled for $[5.3] million, he settled for nine. Then all of a sudden I get sued by Danziger for a million dollars. I settled with him—I gave him $500,000 out of my settlement.

I don't know what's going through his mind. I wish I could write him. His sister gave me his email, but I'm worried. I guess I'm afraid that he'll reject me. I just want to know that it's okay. I hope that one day it's okay. But who knows? That's out of my control.

As soon as I came out, I took 5 percent or 2 percent responsibility for being a coward. Nobody, nobody has come out in

THE POLITICS OF APOLOGY
Exonerees endeavor to have their innocence fully acknowledged

When Calvin C. Johnson Jr. was freed after serving sixteen years for rapes he didn't commit, he received a handshake from the prosecutor who had convicted him. But even while shaking Johnson's hand, the attorney remained convinced that Johnson's arrest and conviction were warranted.

Calvin Johnson Jr. with his lawyer Peter Neufeld (1999)

Prosecutors and investigators tend to be loath to offer apologies to the wrongfully convicted, in part because they can be sued for their roles in wrongful convictions, and in part because an apology can be construed as an admission of guilt.

Prosecutors sometimes maintain that an exoneree is guilty, concocting strained theories to justify their positions. In the case of Michael Evans and Paul Terry, two seventeen-year-old Chicagoans wrongfully convicted of rape and murder in 1976, prosecutors clung to what has become known as the "unindicted co-ejaculator" theory. Though they had been excluded as the source of semen recovered from the victim, prosecutors maintained that Evans and Terry committed the crime, along with an unidentified man who deposited the semen. The supposed third man was never identified, and Evans and Terry were released in 2003 after serving twenty-seven years in prison.

Victims, too, often have difficulty believing a wrongful conviction has occurred. Victims who misidentified a suspect can find it particularly difficult to accept that their memory of the crime was simply wrong. Those who do admit their error often suffer guilt as a consequence.

Jennifer Thompson, a rape victim who misidentified Ronald Cotton and helped send him to jail for eleven years, was grief-stricken when she discovered she had identified the wrong man. A few weeks after Cotton was exonerated, Thompson apologized to him in person.

"If I spent every day for the rest of my life telling you how sorry I am, it wouldn't come close to what I feel," Thompson told him, according to *The Toronto Star.*

Cotton responded, "I'm not mad at you. I've never been mad at you. I just want you to have a good life."

public and said, "We screwed up." Not the DA, not the cop, not anybody. Nobody's even apologized to me, saying, "I'm sorry." Like really saying the words, "I'm sorry."

I sit and read cases where the court says, "No reasonable person would ever confess to something like this." But was I a reasonable person at that time? You can't use that standard. There's no rational thinking when you're doing this kind of stuff. A lot of people use that standard: a reasonable person would never have pled guilty. You're reasonable when you're in a normal environment.

Everybody that drives is taught that when you hit an ice patch or you go into a skid, you turn your wheel into the skid to correct the car. What do people do when they get into a skid? They go the opposite way. Why? Because they're panicked. You lose all sense of direction.

I was very tired. I think that people don't know that interrogations, when people are asking you questions in an interrogatory manner, it drains you, your energy. I was tired. I wanted to go home. I don't know if I had eaten. They wear you down, they don't let you go till they wear you down.

I just wanted to go home. I was living my life one day, and all of a sudden I'm here in this room, and they're saying that I killed somebody and I'm probably going to go to the electric chair. I'm so tired of telling them no, and then the good cop [says,] "If you tell us, you can go home." I'm so mentally drained, I want to go home and sleep. I don't want to do this anymore. I want to go home and sleep. "Oh, you can't go until you say something."

And then at this point you're just defeated. I mean, you don't have anything else. You just say, "Well, whatever—just let me go home." You say whatever it takes, whatever they want to hear.

ONE MILE AT A TIME

I came out of prison with no scratches, nothing.

Sometimes I'll get in my truck and I'm driving alone, and it's such a smooth ride and stuff. It overwhelms me. I'm just like, "Thank you, God, for everything, for all this I have." I mean, this is a nice house I'm in. I got a forty-two-inch plasma, and people would kill for one of these things.

I'm in law school, and I have met some beautiful people—friends, and Robin. And I've always wanted someone to love me, someone that I could laugh with, and somebody to have intelligent conversations with. She'll give me the good and the bad. There's times when she'll just look at me and I'm like, "I'm falling in love with you."

I just want to be a normal part of society, contribute to society like everybody else does, in a good way. I want people to know that everybody's human whether they're in prison or not—they still live and breathe and they still go to the bathroom like all of us do; they still put their pants up the same way. I think I've learned both sides of the street now.

I plan for the future, but I live my life one day at a time. Kind of like when I'm driving to Chicago: I want to get to Chicago. I have a map, but I know to take it one mile at a time because I may have to catch a detour. But then, I get back on the road.

Juan Melendez

MY MAMA DIDN'T
RAISE NO KILLERS

NAME: Juan Roberto Melendez · **BORN:** 1951 · **HOMETOWN:** Maunabo,
Puerto Rico · **CONVICTED OF:** Murder and armed robbery · **SENTENCE:** Death
SERVED: 17 years · **RELEASED:** 2002

I DID NOT COMMIT THIS CRIME

*Juan Melendez was born in Brooklyn in 1951, but fled to Puerto
Rico when he was eight years old to escape an abusive stepfather. At
seventeen, he moved to Delaware, where he got a job harvesting vegetables, picking fruit, and pruning trees. After several years, several
barroom brawls, and frequent run-ins with the police, he quit his job
and hustled on the streets. In 1975 he was arrested in Florida and
sentenced to ten years for an armed robbery. After an early release
from prison in 1982, he returned to the life of a migrant farmer.*

I had to leave Florida early that year, 1984, in February. The cit-
rus fruit was hit with a frost and all the grapefruit and the
oranges, they just fell down and all we had to do was pick them

up. We was done with the job in no time.

Then I was without a job, so I decided to migrate to Pennsylvania, where I knew there was a farmer that would give me a job pruning and trimming apple and peach trees, getting them ready for the next harvest.

In 1984 [on Tuesday, May 15], while we was under an apple tree eating lunch, here comes a whole bunch of FBI agents in their cars. They pull out guns and we got scared. They told us to hit the ground and we did. Then they call my name and I was afraid to get up because of the guns that was pointed at me. So I raise my arm. Then they told me to get up and walk towards them. I did. Then they told me to lift the sleeve of the shirt on my left arm; they want to see a tattoo. I show it to them. And then they told me to open my mouth and I did. They want to see if I had a missing tooth and I did.

And then they told me I was the man they was looking for. They said that I was wanted for unlawful flight to avoid prosecution. They had warrants for my arrest in the state of Florida for first-degree murder and armed robbery. And then they read me my rights, slapped the handcuffs on me, and threw me in the car.

On September 13, 1983, Delbert Baker was found dead at his Auburndale, Florida cosmetology school. His throat had been slashed, he had been shot in the head and chest, and his gold jewelry was missing. On May 15, 1984, the FBI arrested Melendez for the crime.

They took me to a federal prison. The next day they took me in front of the magistrate, a federal judge. And he was talking about extradition and I did not know what extradition was. I did not know the language, did not know nothing about law. So they brought an interpreter to explain to me what extradition means.

"You either waive it or fight it. They going to take you back anyways," he told me in Spanish.

These are the things running in my mind: I did not commit this crime, I am not a killer, my mama didn't raise no killers.

So I say, "I will waive it. As soon as they see my ugly face in Florida they will let me go." How wrong I was.

So they extradite me from Pennsylvania all the way to Florida. Two weeks later I arrive and they take me in front of a judge and he read me the charges.

"You are arrested, indicted for first-degree murder and armed robbery. And the state of Florida is seeking the death penalty," he said to me.

I'M NOT O.J. SIMPSON, I DON'T HAVE MONEY TO HIRE NO LAWYER

Two weeks after that the court appointed a lawyer to me, a public defender. I'm not O.J. Simpson, I don't have money to hire no lawyer, so the court appointed this lawyer to me. He came and he talk to me. I can't understand what he saying because I don't know the process, I don't know the language. But he was patting me on the back all the time, every time he see me.

"Don't worry about it," he tells me.

He also says that I going home. I understood that, that going home stuff. I did not commit this crime. I should go home.

Then we going to trial. The trial: Monday we start picking the jury. Tuesday we still picking the jury. Tuesday evening after we pick eleven whites and one African American person. They read instructions to the jury how to conduct themselves in a capital murder case where they seeking the death penalty. No Hispanic in the jury and I'm Hispanic.

Wednesday, this is the same week, that's when the evidence come in.

PROSECUTORIAL MISCONDUCT
Misrepresentations by prosecutors factor into wrongful convictions

The case that sent Juan Melendez to death row for murder contained no physical evidence of his part in the crime, only the testimony of witnesses who placed him there. These same witnesses, during investigation, gave the state prosecutor different information than they provided at trial. One witness, a police investigator, based his court testimony on his police report, which was written months after the murder occurred. Another witness had given varying accounts of his involvement in the crime, admitting to the murder himself more than once. Although this information was recorded in the prosecutor's notes, none of it was made available to Melendez's attorney.

Prosecutors have a constitutional duty to disclose any evidence that would be favorable to the defense, even if the defense has not requested this information. All too often this fails to occur. In fact, a study of the first seventy wrongful convictions overturned by DNA evidence found that prosecutorial misconduct, in some form or another, played a role in thirty-four of the wrongful convictions—nearly 50 percent of the cases.

The American Bar Association charges the prosecutor with a duty "to seek justice, not merely to convict." In doing so, a prosecutor must represent a variety of constituencies. According to the Vanderbilt Law Review, "The prosecutor is simultaneously responsible for the community's protection, victims' desire for vengeance, defendants' entitlement to a fair opportunity for vindication, and the state's need for a criminal justice system that is efficient and seems fair."

A prosecutor has two very different responsibilities: investigation and conviction. Before a suspect is formally charged, prosecutors collect and evaluate evidence, investigate suspects, and explore hypotheses about the crime until they believe they know where the guilt lies. After bringing formal charges, many prosecutors rely on this belief in the defendant's guilt.

"I don't think prosecutors ever try to convict the innocent," says law professor Rory Little. "They may be mistaken about who's guilty, and they may get tunnel vision."

All too often, rather than reevaluate their original conclusions, prosecutors may instead bury conflicting evidence. Sometimes, even after new, incontrovertible evidence comes to light, prosecutors continue to cling to their initial conclusions.

This is what they had against me: They had a police informant, what they call on the streets a snitch. He claim that I confess the crime to him. He also implicates another man in the crime, an African American person, John Berrien, a black man that I know. He gets arrested. He gets interrogated. He incriminates himself in the crime, he get charged with the crime, first-degree murder, armed robbery, and they threaten him with the electric chair. It's time to make a deal. Prosecutors love to make deals. So he strikes a deal with the state to testify against me.

He gets the charges dropped from first-degree murder and armed robbery to accessory after the fact. He gets two years probation with two years he already got.

I was convicted on the word of David Luna Falcon, an ex-con who had charges of home invasion pending when he testified against me, charges that were later dropped. I did not know David Falcon but he knew about me because I knew his brother and father.

The father had a house in the country outside of Polk County, Florida, and he wanted me to take care of the animals and to paint the house while he was in Puerto Rico. Things didn't work out well. He got kind of angry because some of the animals died, and some other things like that. It was not my fault; he just didn't want to pay me. So I left.

Because of a dispute concerning some odd jobs he had done for Falcon's brother and uncle in Puerto Rico, Melendez parted on bad terms with the Falcon family. David Falcon retaliated by telling investigators that he had heard Melendez confess to killing Baker. Later, several witnesses for the defense said Falcon admitted that he received $5,000 from the police department for his testimony. Furthermore, Falcon was never prosecuted for an incident in which a married couple claimed he had invaded their home by impersonating *a police officer, then threatened them and fired bullets into their car. When the couple contacted the police, the detective they spoke with— who was already working with Falcon on Melendez's case—told them he could not protect them against further attacks unless they dropped charges against Falcon, which they did.*

Two questionable witnesses. No physical evidence against me, just two questionable witnesses with a record from one end of the country to the other. Two questionable witnesses that make deals with the state to get leniency for their own crimes they commit.

This is what I had in my favor on the defense side: I had an alibi witness, I had four witnesses that corroborate the alibi's testimony. Other witnesses saying that the police informant witness, the snitch, had a grudge against me.

But I had a problem. Every witness that I had was an African American person, a black man, a black woman. And when a black man and a black woman testify for the state, all of a sudden they got good credibility, they even dress them up all fancy, I seen that with my two eyes. But when a black man and a black woman testify for the defense, all of a sudden their credibility is gone.

There was no physical evidence implicating Melendez in the murder. The prosecution based its case primarily on the testimony of two key witnesses, John Berrien and David Luna Falcon. On September 20, 1984, a jury found Melendez guilty of murder and armed robbery. The next day, he was sentenced to death and sent to Florida State Prison (now Union Correctional Institution) in Raiford, Florida.

Thursday, the same week, they found me guilty. Friday, the same week, they sentence me to death. And the judge complained that it was taking too long.

It takes two [phases] for a death penalty case. You have the verdict, the guilt and innocence trial, and then you have the other [phase], based on the sentencing, to decide if a man deserves the death penalty or deserves life in prison. That came in on the Friday, around ten o'clock. The vote was nine to three, nine for death and three for life.

The truth is, in a courtroom, nobody knows English, only the lawyers and the judges and the prosecutor, because they got a different language. I was real naive, I didn't know how to read, I didn't know how to write, I didn't know how to speak English well. I did not understand no legal terms, I did not understand none of that stuff.

Everything that they show in the trial indicated that I did not commit the crime. But they did not believe me because all my witnesses on my side was African American people.

I told them, "I will be back because I'm an innocent man. In the name of Jesus, I will be back."

When they sentenced me to death, I became an angry man. I hated the prosecutor. I hated the jurors. I hated the judge. And I hated that one that pat me on the back, my defense attorney, because I feel he betrayed me.

I'd rather be in a prison population than on death row. You all by yourself in there.

WE FIGHT TO THE END

When I was extradited to Florida after my arrest, I went to the county jail in Polk County, Florida. They say it was the worst county jail in the state, because you can't get to phone, no air, the ventilation is bad, the food is bad. When they put you in the county jail they put you in the bullpen. In the bullpen you play cards, you see a lot of fights, you see people get hurt, people get raped, all that stuff. Most of the people that get raped and get messed up in there, it's because they act scared when they go in and they make mistakes, borrow money.

I used to fight, I used to box, I was always a fighter. I never be looking for trouble, but I know how to defend myself.

I was scared. I was real scared to die for that crime I did not commit. They took me to death row November the second. I'll never forget that day. The place was horrifying. It was dark. It was cold. They always kept me with shackles, handcuffs, chains, every time they move me. I thought we Puerto Ricans was real macho mens but I found out different. I was scared, real scared to die for that crime I did not commit.

When I went in there I made it 230 men condemned to death. Today, it's 360. Every one of them have their own cell. It's what you call super-max, super maximum security. You got to be by yourself.

The things is running in my mind when I got there is: They executing people in here every week. How long is gonna be for them to come and get me?

This is the things running in my mind: I know how to box, and I know all these exercise where you can keep your muscles flexible, you can swing with your hands if you're gonna fight. I'm thinking if they come over here, I just gonna fight them to the end. I'm not walking to that chair.

I decided to take the sheets on my bunk, cut 'em in pieces, and make little ropes with it. Then I take them little ropes and I tie the bar doors. When they push the button in the control room, the door ain't moving nowhere. So I'm thinking by the time they cut these ropes to come inside and get me, I got a good warm-up, and I can fight these people to the end. I ain't goin' to that chair, I ain't walkin' down there.

Here I am doing push-ups, around count time, with the doors already tied up. I'm sweating good. I'm starting to get muscles coming out of my eyeballs. Because I'm trying to intimidate these people, I'm trying to scare these people. But all the time I'm the one intimidated. I'm the one scared.

So here comes the guard. And he sees the door tied up. And he gets angry at me. And he start cursing. "Why you got the damned doors tied up?" and I don't know too much English, but I know how to curse. So I remind him of his mother, father, all the way down.

The rest of the condemned mens, they get involved in the argument, and to my surprise it was against me! They tell me that I am wrong. So now I get angry with them.

I say, "You mean to tell me that they killin' people in here every week and we ain't doin' nothing about it? We supposed to take this place and burn it down. We supposed to fight these people. We Puerto Ricans, we don't go out like that, we fight to the end!"

WHY THEY GOT TO GIVE YOU AN EDUCATION WHEN THEY GONNA KILL YOU?

They still told me that I was a fool. They told me that when I get up in the morning, all I do is curse and cry and nag about my innocence. They told me I did not know how to read, I did not know how to write, I did not know how to speak English. And then the other prisoners told me the most beautiful thing I could hear at that time. They told me they would teach me how to read, how to write, how to speak English.

When I learned how to read, how to write, how to speak English, I was able to communicate better with my lawyers. I was able to communicate better with the pen pals that wrote me, that showed me kindness and love.

It's a group in there learning, but we teaching each others.

Nobody in there is teaching us. There's no education programs. Why they got to give you an education program when they gonna kill you?

I was in there with people that ate people. I was in there with the worst of the worst. The ones that the United States wants to see dead. The ones that the prosecutors call monsters—they taught me how to read, how to write, how to speak English. If they would not have taught me how to read and write and how to speak English I would never have survived that place.

On death row, it's more secure because you more segregated, you more in solitary. But when it boil down to it, it's more suffering because you alone, you all by yourself, it's hell. You got to deal more with loneliness than if you was in the prison population walking around.

Also, people on death row probably change better than people in the prison population. Because people on death row, when they change, they change for something divine, they know they not going nowhere. They know they gonna kill them. So they want to get closer to God. In order to get closer to God you got to have a great change of heart. So a lot of them become real religious, they become real good people, people that teach others how to read and how to write, how to respect, stuff like that. When they execute them, they're not the same person that committed the crime, ^ they committed the crime.

You got time to think. You all by yourself in there. You got time to think, and think positive. Don't think negative. You in a negative situation and you try to transform that to a positive situation. And that's all I did. I feel a change. I learn how to forgive, how to have compassion. I learn how to love people, how to appreciate all God's creations.

Three things you have on death row: You got the future, which is death. You got the present, which is hell. And you got the past, which is the only thing that you can grab to have some comfort. You got to remember the old days, the good times that you have. You tell the good times you had to the guy next door to you. And he tells you the good times he had. That way you kill the day.

SECURITY GO BEFORE LIFE

The conditions at Florida State Prison are terrible. The place was infested with rats and roaches. The worst part was when they bring the food in. Breakfast is the worst one. They put the food in a cart on a tray, and they slam that tray through a flap they got in the cell door. At breakfast time they put the tray in there through that flap. They don't wake you up. If you stay five seconds in that bunk, you out of luck. The roaches already beat you to it; they waiting for the breakfast, too.

And it get cold in northern Florida. They supply you with a thin blanket. I cover myself from the foot all the way to the head because I don't want to see nothing. But the rats, they also get cold, and they want to get warm so they climb into that blanket. You can feel that rat, running from my foot all the way to my chest. I was waiting for it to get to my face. I don't want to look at him. If I look at him then I not going to be able to sleep. So I wait. And when I feel that rat in my face, I grabbed the blanket with my wrists real tight and I shake that blanket hard as I can. boom! I can hear that rat hit the floor. It's a big one.

A friend of mine, Frank Smith, he was wrongfully convicted of killing an [eight]-year-old black girl. He's also black. He got cancer, and so when the DNA evidence showed up, he was begging for them to check the DNA in the case. And then he died. He died a horrible death. And you know cancer, you lose your bowels, you defecate in there, urinate in there, everything. And

AT THE BREAKING POINT

Standards in U.S. prisons are often breached

*Prisoners sleep on the floor in the Marion County
Lockup in Indianapolis, Indiana (2001)*

Though regulations vary by state, every state requires its prisons to uphold certain minimum standards concerning food, lighting, health, bedding, plumbing, general cleanliness, and personal hygiene.

Even so, reports have repeatedly revealed discrepancies between standards outlined in state regulations and inmates' actual living conditions. Common transgressions include vermin infestations, bed shortages, lack of hygienic privacy, and rooms filled beyond their intended occupancies.

These discrepancies are largely the result of the explosive growth of the U.S. prison population. With the average cost per inmate at roughly $25,000 per year, state resources are often insufficient. As a result, in 1993, forty states were under court orders to address overcrowding issues.

Poor prison conditions can lead to years of torment. Paralyzed in his right leg, Clark McMillan was undergoing physical therapy and pain management when he was arrested and convicted for rape and robbery. Prison authorities confiscated his leg brace; denied him any medication beyond Tylenol; subjected him to harsh sleeping conditions, unregulated temperature changes, hard physical labor, and solitary confinement; and left him vulnerable to physical attacks from other inmates. After twenty-two years McMillan was exonerated by DNA in 2002.

after he died his lawyers still had the DNA evidence tested. After he was dead they found out that he was not the man that committed the crime.

The problem with the medical conditions on death row is this: Security go before life. If a condemned man have a heart attack in the cell, they not gonna rush that man out of there and take him to the clinic, to aid him. They got to put the handcuffs on him. They got to put the shackles on him. They got to put the chains on him. And all this take time. Then they got to make sure that it's an emergency call. It takes about forty-five minutes to an hour before they get that man out of that goddamned cell. By then, he's dead.

Melendez at Florida State Prison (1998)

One day we all went to the yard. All the ones that taught me how to read and write and speak English, we all went to the yard. But this particular one, this African American person, this brother, that's what I call him, he was there, too. They all taught me, but this one, he was pushy. He always trying to get the best out of me, like, "You need to learn this, you need to learn that." And I love him dearly for that.

The brothers, the African Americans, they love to play basketball. So he went out there to play basketball. Some of them play basketball, some of them play volleyball, some of them lift weights. I lift weights; I can burn steam and go back to the cell and rest a little bit better.

This particular friend of mine, he's playing basketball. And suddenly he falls to the ground, to the concrete—'cause that's all they got in there, steel and concrete. I stop lifting weights and I go and shake him out to see what's wrong with my friend. I notice that white foam was coming out of his nose and mouth, so I assumed immediately that it got to be a stroke, a heart attack.

I tell the guards in the gate, "You have a man down that need some medical assistance."

They take their time with the walkie-talkie, they call the clinic. And here come the so-called nurse, this big ol' white man, with a great belly. They let him inside the gate and they told us to put our backs to the fence. They bring the guns out and they point 'em at us, because they think as soon as they let this so-called nurse in the yard one of us going to snatch him.

So we got our backs to the fence with the guns pointed at us. Now they gonna let the so-called nurse in the yard. And here he comes, but he ain't got no medical bag with him. But he had something. He had about a half a pound of chewing tobacco in his mouth. You can see the black stuff that's running down the side. Every once in a while he spits.

He looks at my friend on the ground.

We tell him from a distance, "He's not breathing!"

And he spits. And he say, "I need to go back to the clinic and get an oxygen tank."

He take his time and walk real slow back to the clinic to get this oxygen tank. Then he comes back, walking real slow, and comes back inside the yard. Bends down and put that oxygen tank in my friend's mouth and then gets up.

We tell him from a distance, "Man, he still not breathing, he need air."

Then he spits. And he say, "I got to walk back to the clinic to get another oxygen tank, this one is broken."

And I say, "You don't have to do that. You can do CPR, mouth-to-mouth."

Telling one of them to do mouth-to-mouth to a brother on the ground, you wastin' your time. This big ol' nurse, he looks up, then he looks down, then he spits. And then he made a statement using these two [curse] words, the M and the N, and, "I not gonna put my mouth in there."

I tell him, "You don't have to, I do it. You just do the counting." And he agreed. I'm so glad that he agreed, because I want to save my friend's life, I want him to live. So I rush down there, I take my T-shirt off, I wipe that white foam my friend had on his mouth and nose and the so-called nurse start counting.

One-two-three, and I blow air.

One-two-three, and I blow air again.

One-two-three, and I blow air and my friend open his eyes.

When my friend open his eyes, I saw a sign of hope, he's gonna live. But all the sudden my friend's eyes, they roll back and he made a frown with his face and mouth that I still see right now, because it never left me. Then he breathe real hard and air came out. I believe that was his soul that left him because he die right there in my arms.

So now I get angry. And I wanna do something to this so-called nurse that let my friend die in the yard like a dog. And when I swing at him, the rest of the condemned mens came in there and they grab me, and they put me in a corner and they tell me, "Puerto Rican Johnny, don't get in any more trouble than you already are in. We got other ways to handle this."

I still go to confinement for ninety days for disrespecting a member of the staff. But I learn a lesson. I learn that I have to trust something more powerful than the system.

I COULD NOT FIGHT THE SYSTEM ON MY OWN

The truth is that the condemned men that don't turn to something spiritual either go crazy or commit suicide. Some of them become Muslims, and they praise Allah, and they teach others how to read, how to write and how to speak English. Some of them become Buddhists. I don't know what they praise, but they

PRISONERS FIRST, HUMANS SECOND

Health care in the nation's prisons leaves inmates suffering

Ten months before DNA would prove him definitively innocent, Frank Lee Smith died shackled to a hospital gurney.

"Essentially he was naked, and… in excruciating pain," says Jeff Walsh, a defense investigator for Smith. "He was just dehydrating, starving. The truth of the matter is that they just didn't care about him."

From 1990 to 1999, health care costs for the Federal Bureau of Prisons rose an average of 8.6 percent per year, with state prisons seeing similar increases. In response, prisons have cut staff, reduced pay, and have often left inmates' medical concerns unaddressed.

Though the Eighth Amendment requires jails and prisons to provide health care for inmates, courts have ruled that only "deliberate indifference to a serious medical need" qualifies as a violation of a prisoner's constitutional rights.

Frank Lee Smith

In federal prisons, regulations require a medical professional to be available twenty-four hours a day. Additionally, once a week, a "sick call" is to be conducted, and when medical problems arise that cannot be handled by the on-site doctor or other resources available at the prison, the medical staff must refer the inmate to a hospital.

Qualifications for prison health care practitioners vary widely from state to state. In Florida, one investigation found 30 percent of prison doctors had blemishes on their records ranging from "medical malpractice" to "defrauding federal insurers." In May 2005, California's prison health care system was wrested from state control and placed under federal control after disturbing discoveries of medical malpractice.

In an effort to cut costs, states are increasingly hiring private companies to handle their health care, an industry now worth roughly $2 billion. Prison Health Services, one such private health care company, is responsible for providing medical care to 10 percent of the more than two million inmates in the United States. It was also the focus of an extensive series by *The New York Times* in 2005. The *Times* reported that investigators found "medical staffs trimmed to the bone, doctors underqualified or out of reach, nurses doing tasks beyond their training, prescription drugs withheld, patient records unread and employee misconduct unpunished."

teach others how to love, how to have compassion, how to forgive. Some of them turn to Christianity. That's what I did. I had
to go back to my roots.

I could not fight the system on my own. So I had to rely on
something spiritual. All them in there, if they want to make a
positive change, they have to rely on something spiritual.

I remember we had a chaplain that never come inside the
death row facility. And we ask him why he don't come inside the
death row facility at [Florida State Prison]. He sent a message
that we already going to hell, he don't need to come over there.

I don't pick no sides. My faith is this: You do good deeds, you
make good choices, you respect. You love. You have compassion.
You forgive. You believe in God, in something that's more supreme than you are.

YOU KNOW EXACTLY THE TIME
THEY'RE KILLING HIM, BECAUSE THE LIGHTS
GO OFF AND ON

The hardest thing for me was when they kill somebody. This guy,
he's beside you, you share your deepest thoughts with him, and
then they snatch him out of there and it takes about thirty or
sixty days before they execute him. You praying all the time they
gonna give him a stay of execution, or some appeals gonna happen. You know exactly the time they killin' him because the lights
go off and on, because they got to generate the electricity to put
the electricity in the chair.

You can hear the sound *rrrrrrrrr, rrrrrrrrr* as the electricity
runs through the chair and kills your friend. Then the lights go
off, and you know exactly the time they taking his life. And you
cannot do nothing about it. When I stop and think about it, the
truth is I'm scared of electricity anyway.

When that happened, nobody talks. Everybody be quiet. And the new ones that come in that don't know what's going on, when they start talking, nobody pay attention to them. Nobody want to talk about that. Can't stop it. It's gone, it's gone. It's not something that people want to talk about.

THEY GONNA KILL YOU ANYWAY...
DO IT YOURSELF

After ten years I was tired of it. I wanted out of there. And the only way out is to commit suicide.

I saw plenty of my friends commit suicide. You can tell when one of them is gonna commit suicide. He stop talking, stop eating, stop going to the yard. Stop being social, stop caring for himself, stop going to the bathroom and taking a shower, stop combing his hair. He looks real weird, you know sooner or later he gonna kill himself. You can tell. You can smell it coming.

I never see my friends kill themselves, because I cannot see through the walls. But I see when they wheel the body out. Something in the back of my head says, "You not gonna look at your friend for the last time?" I grab a mirror. I stretch my arms through the bars, and I look when they wheel the body out. This is what I see: I see a purple-blue face that do not look like my friend. I also get to see something else that always in my mind. I get to see the noose in his neck because they never take the damned noose out. The truth is, the guards don't do nothing. All they do is watch. And give you a hard time when they can.

I will tell you how they kill themselves. They got what they call a runner who's doin' time in population. He's an inmate, he's not condemned to death. He does work in the death row facilities. This runner is the one that supply us with food, with the toothpaste, the toothbrush, the soap, the toilet paper, the broom and the mop so you can clean the floor yourself.

This runner also supply you with the tool that you can kill yourself with. He knows it. All you have to do is give him four stamps so he can write to his pen pal, or give him a packet of loose tobacco, and he will swing that tool in your cell. He will watch the guards. When they not looking, he will swing that tool in your cell.

The tool is real simple. It's a plastic garbage bag, the one that you see around in the garbage can, the strong ones. You take that plastic garbage bag and you twist it all up and you make a rope with it. You put a noose in it. You put the noose on your neck. You tie the other part on the bars. You throw yourself down. And you dead, but you free.

This is what the demons used to tell me all the time: "Why you got to satisfy them? Why let them kill you when you can do it yourself? You supposed to be a real Puerto Rican man, a real macho man. Don't satisfy them. Do it yourself. You say you didn't do the crime, you think they gonna believe you? They gonna kill you anyway. Don't satisfy them. Satisfy yourself. Do it yourself."

So now I wanna take this trip. I want out of there. I'm tired of it. So I tell the runner to give me that bag and I give him four stamps. He gives it to me, and I twist it all up. I make a rope with it. I put a noose in it. Then I look at what I just made and I look at the bunk. And I say to myself, I better lay down and think about this a little bit more.

So I take that rope and I throw it under the bunk so the guards when they walk by they don't see it, and I lay down. When I lay down I fall in a deep sleep and I start dreaming. I start dreaming that I'm a little kid again doin' the things I used to do when I was a kid, things that make me laugh, the things that make me happy.

PUSHED TO THE BRINK
Suicides in prison call policies and conditions into question

Suicide is the number one cause of death in jails and the third most common cause in prisons.

Past lawsuits and outside investigations have revealed numerous inadequacies in preventing prison suicides. This includes cases where "patients' charts were missing, alerts about despondent inmates were lost or unheeded, and neither medical nor correction officers were properly trained in preventing suicide," according to a February 2005 article in *The New York Times*.

Nicholas Yarris

Instead of receiving one-on-one therapy with mental health professionals, suicidal inmates are often written up as having "disciplinary problems." They may be kept in solitary confinement until they renounce any suicidal intentions. With two-thirds of all suicides occurring in solitary confinement, it is a particularly poor strategy for treating despondent prisoners.

For the wrongfully convicted, incarceration can have an especially devastating effect. "The sense that harsh punishment is being imposed unfairly makes it much more difficult to tolerate," says psychiatrist Terry Kupers. "The kind of hopelessness that can lead to suicide is intensified by the knowledge that even though one is innocent, nobody cares about the unfairness of the punishment."

Nicholas Yarris, a man wrongfully convicted in 1982 of kidnapping, rape, and murder, attempted suicide while in solitary confinement. "Because of my suicide attempt," Yarris says, "I was stripped of all clothing and given one wool army blanket and a plastic mattress. Period. For three days I tried to fend off the cold of January in a cell that had broken windows. I was naked in a wet blanket, and of course, the guards saw nothing."

When suicides do occur, they are often met with muted reactions from the general public. "There is little outrage when a prisoner dies," writes Jim Oliphant, editor of the newspaper *Legal Times*. "Their deaths pass largely unnoticed, reported in the back pages of local newspapers, when chronicled at all."

Like I told you before, I grew up in Puerto Rico. On the east side of my house I have a wonderful mountain. If I go up six minutes to the south I find myself on the most beautiful beach in the world. In this dream, here I am swimming in the Caribbean Sea, doin' the most wonderful things I used to do as a kid, the things that make me happy, the things that make me laugh. The water's warm. The sky is blue. The sun is bright. The palm trees look so good; it's a beautiful day. And I'm having fun on that beach in the Caribbean Sea. And then I see something that I never seen before. I see four dolphins coming my way. They start flipping and jumping, like dolphins do. I'm having a ball in there, I'm so happy.

And then I look to the shore and I see an old lady, she's waving and she's smiling, she seems so happy. I know why she's happy. She's happy because I'm happy. That's my dear mother.

Then I wake up. When I wake up, the bunk smell like a beach. I go under that bunk and I get that rope and walk straight to the toilet. I look at the rope and I look in the toilet. I say to myself, "I don't wanna die." And I flush that rope in the toilet.

THEY WAS KILLING PEOPLE IN
FLORIDA LEFT AND RIGHT

I believe my mama suffered more than I did. I got all the letters. Still got 'em, but this particular one, I keep it with me all the time because if I'm down or if I need a little energy I can grab that letter and read it and it picks me up.

The letter go like this: she say, "Son, I just build an altar, and in that altar I put a statue of the Virgin of the Guadalupe. I cut roses and put them in it. I pray five or six rosaries a day, seeking for a miracle. And the miracle will come. I know you innocent and God know you innocent. But you got to put your trust in

God. You got to put your faith in God. Be good. Keep thinking that you gonna make it. And you will."

Well, sometimes when you get an appeal and you lose your appeal, all your hope is gone. So you do like a little kid. When a little kid is trying to learn to walk, he falls, and when he falls he cries and he's mad, but then he gets up and he try to walk again. That's what I did.

I'm probably the luckiest man in the world. I should have been dead, 'cause they was killing people in Florida left and right. In fact, they never signed my death warrant, which is real strange 'cause I seen a lot of people in there that came after me—they signed their death warrants and killed them. That's when I was worrying about it, when they was killing the ones that came after me.

One day I remember my lawyer came to see me,. She had tears in her eyes and she tells me that she no longer can handle my case. I say, "Why? I don't need no new lawyers in the stage where my case is now, you know my case better than anybody."

And she say, "You know why. I lost five clients." And you know what I mean when she say she lost five clients: she means five clients got executed.

She say, "You know all of them, they're your friends, I cannot do it no more. But I'm gonna talk to the agency and get the agency to assign the best three lawyers they got. And the best investigator."

I finally got the dream team.

Here comes my new lawyer that's been assigned to me. He say, "Melendez, you done lost too many appeals."

The truth is, when you lose appeals, you getting closer and closer to death. You become what they call a great candidate for the governor to sign your death warrant. And I'm already in that stage.

He say, "We're gonna try one more time, but if you lose this one, you'll be lucky if you live three years."

I say, "If I lose this one I be lucky if I live a year and a half. You know who the governor of Florida is? His name is Jeb Bush, he be glad to sign [the death warrant]."

He said, "I'm gonna try one more time. I'm gonna send an investigator to go and see your trial defense attorney"—the one that used to pat me on the back—"to see if he have any files of your case left. To see if we missed something."

In the summer of 2000, Rosa Greenbaum, an investigator who had just been assigned to Melendez's case, contacted Cody Smith—the defense investigator from the original trial—and asked him for his notes and files. Smith, now living in Pennsylvania, told her that any files he had would be in storage in Florida. Smith and Greenbaum went to Florida to look for these files; they found nothing.

While in Florida, however, Smith had lunch with Roger Alcott, Melendez's defense attorney from his initial trial.

So here the first miracle occur. My trial attorney, the one that used to pat me on the back, he becomes a judge. He's a judge now and I'm so glad that he became a judge. Because by him becoming a judge it created what we call in the legal world a conflict of interest. And I was able to move my case out of that racist county, out of that county where the good-old-boy network operate. Out of that county where the crime occur. Out of that county where they fabricate the case against me.

My case moved from Polk County, Bartow, Florida to Hillsborough County, Tampa, Florida. And it fell in the hands of a courageous woman, a woman who wants to do the right thing, a female judge by the name of Honorable Barbara Fleischer. I can sincerely say she saved my life.

Because Melendez's lawyers were arguing that Alcott had provided ineffective counsel, all of the judges in the county—who had become Alcott's colleagues as a result of his recent appointment—recused themselves from presiding over the case, forcing it out of Bartow. Another unexpected consequence of Alcott's new position manifested itself while he and Smith were at lunch: Alcott mentioned that when he was cleaning out his old office, he had, by coincidence, noticed some boxes with the name Melendez written on them.

As they were going through the boxes, Alcott came across a transcript of a taped interview with Vernon James—a man who all of Melendez's attorneys had repeatedly contended was the murderer of Delbert Baker. In the interview, which occurred one month prior to the trial, James admitted to having been at the scene of the murder. Furthermore, he stated that Melendez was not there.

Although Alcott had himself argued that James was the real perpetrator of the crime, the interview had not been presented to the jury as evidence. And while the prosecution also had a copy of the transcript, somehow none of Melendez's subsequent attorneys knew of its existence. A series of discoveries followed. Numerous documents were found, including notes, reports, and letters, which supported Melendez's innocence, but which the prosecution had failed to disclose. At the same time, a series of fortuitous events led investigators to new witnesses, whose testimonies corroborated the contents of the documents, all supporting Melendez's claims of innocence.

When my investigator goes to get some files from my trial attorney—who became a judge—he tells her, "I'm a judge now! I'm in a new office. But in the old office where I used to do defense work I think there's a box in there with the name Melendez in it. You can go in there, you can get it, and you can have it."

She left his new office and went to the old office, where he used to do defense work. She went to that shelf and grabbed that box. Guess what! The confession of the real killer was in [the box] and my trial attorney had it a month before my trial. This open up a can of worms now. The case is in the hands of a courageous woman, a woman who wants to do the right thing. The truth is that all the problems I had with my case was that judges was looking at my case bit by bit, but Honorable Barbara Fleischer, she wanted the entire pie, she wanted to look at the whole thing.

She immediately made a court order to the prosecutor's office and demand that he send any files of my case if he had any, with a court order. And he did.

Guess what! He also had the confession of the real killer one month before trial. And he had documents that corroborated that tape confession, documents that he never turned in to the trial defense lawyer at the time of the trial, creating what they call in the legal world withholding exculpatory evidence, prosecutorial misconduct.

Among the documents withheld from the defense was a handwritten report suggesting that the detective on the case had—in exchange for Falcon's testimony—coerced the married couple into dropping charges against Falcon, telling them, "If I lock up Falcon, he'll just bond out and he may come back [and] get you."

So [Judge Fleischer] had all this ammunition. With all this ammunition she wrote an opinion. In that opinion she chastised the way the prosecutor handled the case. She chastised the investigator for the way they handled the case. And she chastised that one that pat me on the back.

The way I look at it, it's all about indictments. The confession came after the indictment. In order for a prosecutor to get a first-degree murder indictment and seek the death penalty, he got to go through a grand jury. The indictment is done behind closed doors. The defense is not there. The only evidence in there is the ones they got against you. You not there to defend yourself.

So he goes and tells the reporters, "I got the man that committed this crime, I'm gonna get a grand jury indictment." After he got that indictment against me, he was not going to turn it around, not for this Puerto Rican anyways. He done told reporters, "I got the right man, this is the man that going to trial, this is the man that killed Delbert Baker." See, when he got that tape in his hands, I'm on my way to trial already, he's not going to turn back. He already in the newspaper saying, "Hey, Melendez the one that committed the crime." How he gonna look?

So Barbara Fleischer ordered a new trial. She told [the prosecutor] that the case was terrible, that everything indicates that you have an innocent man on death row. The prosecutor decided not to appeal the judge's opinion, not to process the case. That's why I'm here right now, thank God.

THEY DIDN'T STOP CLAPPING
UNTIL I LEFT THAT PLACE

I never know the time I was going to be released. It caught me totally by surprise. Here comes a guard right in front of my cell and tells me I got a call-out. A call-out mean that you goin' outside, to court, to take care of legal business. Since I got a new trial I was thinking that the prosecutor is appealing the judge's decision and is still going to try to kill me, is going to still try and keep me on death row for some more years.

You never in front of an officer without the handcuffs. They snap the handcuffs on you from the inside. This is what they do: You give 'em all your clothes and you put 'em through a flap in the door, and they search those clothes. Then they do what they call a corporeal search. Believe me, it's very humiliating; they want to see everything. So when he get through with that he throw the clothes back to you through the flap of the door. When you get done putting them back on, you turn around and through the flap in the door he slap the handcuffs on you. And then he opens the door.

But he ain't through with you yet. He got to put shackles on your legs, chains in your waist and then he got to change the handcuffs to the front. Then he change it to the front and they got a black box, they put the handcuffs inside that box and they twist your arms and you can hardly even move your fingers. You walk like a penguin. All the way down.

So now I'm going downstairs. I got to go and take a van and go where they take this photo. It's in the same building, it's in the same prison, they just don't want to parade a so-called killer in the prison population.

The reason they take the photo is 'cause they want to know how you look when you leave that place, in case anything happen down the road.

So here comes a whole bunch of guards toward me and I got paranoid. I don't trust these people. Every guard that came toward me had a white shirt. When you see a guard with a white shirt it means that he's a colonel, a superintendent, a guy with higher rank. Even the chief of the prison, the warden, was coming toward me. I got real paranoid. I stop and I didn't want to move nowhere. They order me to move.

And here come the superintendent of the prison, the biggest man in the prison. He gets behind me and pat me on the back and tell me to move. He remind me of my trial attorney, the one that used to pat me on the back. I say to myself, I'm doomed, they gonna kill me.

Then this officer he say to me, in Spanish, he say "Melendez, don't start no trouble, man. Move. You going to the information room, and I believe you gonna have good news."

I'm still skeptical, paranoid, but I decided to move. They take me to this office, and they sit me in a chair. There's a desk in front of me and behind the desk is a lady working on computers. She asks me for my Social Security number. In my mind, I say what the hell she want to know about my Social Security number for? But I know it by heart and I give it to her. Then she ask some more weird questions: "Where you gonna live at? What type of work you got? What you like to do? Who's living with you?"

I must have given her a weird look because she got up and put both hands on the desk that was in front of me and look straight in my eyes. She say, "You do not understand what's going on in here, do you?"

I say, "Lady, I don't have the slightest idea. I live cross the street and I been in there for almost eighteen years. I'm on death row. They don't have no jobs in death row."

Then she say, "We fixing your papers to release you today."

I don't know if you watch cartoons. You see this cartoon hit another with a sledgehammer over the head, and you see this big knot come straight out, and you see stars going around him, and he's in a state of shock. But he's smiling. That's how I was. In a state of shock, but smiling. And I'm still smiling today.

All of the sudden, the guards, they start acting different. They start offering me soda pops and sandwiches. I told them, "I don't want no soda pop, I don't want no sandwiches, I want to get back to my cell, pack up, and get the hell out of here."

Then they start calling me something they never call me before, they start calling me "Mr. Melendez." And I like that.

By the time I get upstairs, everybody knew that I was gonna be released. I pack my personal stuff and the pictures of my aunts, my grandchildren, and my nieces. And all the letters. I take all the cosmetics and stuff and I give them to my friends because I know I can buy them in the streets.

Then I hear steps in the hallway. All of the sudden my cell door pops right open. I got scared again. 'Cause I don't trust these people. Three guards and the captain of the prison come inside my cell. I got super-scared. But I turn around so they can slap the handcuffs on me.

When one of the guards was ready to put the handcuffs on me, the captain of the prison told him "No! You don't put the handcuffs on Mr. Melendez today. Mr. Melendez walks out of here without handcuffs. Mr. Melendez is going home. Mr. Melendez is a free man." And I liked that, too.

So now I'm gonna say goodbye to my friend in the next-to-last cell. I want to say goodbye to him but I cannot speak. I'm happy... I got a smile on my face and tears that's running down, but part of me that's still sad. Because I got to leave them behind, and I know their destiny. If we don't get this death penalty abolished they gonna kill them all.

He was crying but he was able to tell me, "Don't forget about us. Don't get in no trouble out there. Take care of yourself." And the last thing he told me was "Take care of your mama." They all know my mama.

Now I got to walk this hallway, and there's about all of them telling me the same thing. Then I get to that door that gonna lead me out of that wing. Before they open that door, I hear one clap, then I hear the second clap, and I hear a third clap. I heard a whole bunch of claps. The entire death row facility was clapping their hands. They was clapping so loud that the guards got mad at them and told them to be quiet. But they didn't stop clapping until I left that place.

I DON'T WANT TO TALK ABOUT BAD THINGS, AND EVERYTHING INSIDE THERE IS BAD

When I get out of prison some of the press was there. I never had talked to reporters before, first time in my life, and to me it just came natural. When they asked me how I feel, I told 'em I feel happy that I'm going home. Then they ask me where I want to go, what I want to see, and I told 'em the truth. I told 'em what I had in my heart: I wanted to see the mountains, the stars, the moon, I wanted to climb a tree, I wanted to hold a little baby in my arms, and I wanted to talk to some beautiful womens.

The reporters wanted to know the treatment I had inside, and I cut it short. I said I don't want to talk about bad things, and everything inside there is bad. I want to say good things. I want to say how happy I am to be out. I want to go and see these things, the moon, the stars, that's all. It was a good day for me, I didn't want to mess it up with thinking bad things, talking bad about the prosecutor, talking bad about the guards, I didn't want to get into that.

I cut them short. I told them the simple things, that I want to go back to Puerto Rico and be with my mama. I told them they could not pay me for what they did to me in there. The only way they could pay me is give me my time back, and that's impossible. They could give me a billion dollars, and that don't pay for what they did to me.

That first night, staying in my lawyer's house, I couldn't sleep. I was thinking about lots of things. I was thinking about going home, I'm gonna go home and see my mama. I was in a dream. I was in a state of shock like in a dream. I just laid down with my eyes closed and I just think. Think how lucky I am and all that stuff.

I DIDN'T KNOW WHAT RESPECT WAS
UNTIL I GOT OUT OF DEATH ROW

I got out January the third and I got back to Puerto Rico January the eleventh.

It was just a little after 9/11, so there was a big thing about airplanes, taking airplanes was real restricted. In fact, the airplane I was on, there was not too many people in it; 9/11 was coming to my mind, it was messing with me. It's kind of scary in the plane.

When we get in the island, they call my name. They say, "Melendez. Juan Roberto Melendez, we want you to come out last. Stay where you are and come out last."

That freaked me out, I'm thinking what the hell's going on here now? It's been only eight days exactly since I been out. So when everybody heard, they're all looking at me. I don't know what's goin' on, just then everybody's going out. Then here come the men to get me.

They say, "Come on, Mr. Melendez."

There was about five mens in the group and they all look like law enforcement officers to me. They were security officers from the airport. One of them say, "You from my hometown."

I looked at him, and then he say, "And you are a hero."

That's what he tell me. He say, "You all over the news."

And I say, "Damn!"

They get me out of the plane and they put me in a golf cart. That's the same golf cart they put the governor and all them politicians in there. Ha ha ha! They put me in a golf cart, that was a good feeling, you know what I mean? I'm just riding and riding and riding, and then they put me in the conference room where the governor speaks and all the big shots go.

I get in this room and I got all my family in there, and friends from my hometown that I grew up with. There's a caravan outside from my hometown with a school bus. There was all kinds of reporters from all of the channels. They stop every program they had to put me in there. That was amazing to me. I didn't know what respect was until I go out of death row. That's the truth!

In comes my mama and she just grabs me and hugs me and we cry. I say, "Mama, Mama!"

And in come a dude that I don't even know, he's my uncle and I don't even remember him. He grab me and look at me, when he say his name that's when I remember. Uncle Rob? I never did like him too much! But I grab him, I was happy to see him then.

After that my brother came, he grabbed me, and all my aunts and all that. It was a hell of a feeling. Every time I feel bad about something I just remember that day and forget about everything else.

A Puerto Rican newspaper announces Melendez's return to his hometown (2002)

When I left Puerto Rico it was a whole bunch of sugar cane fields. And where the sugar cane fields was, now they got beautiful houses and highways and stuff. Lots of cars. When I left the island it was lots of horses!

They put me in a school bus with all my friends. The school bus like a convoy, so the school bus is the head. I'm in the front. With the school bus I got a good view of everything, better than a car. The school bus is full of friends of mine that I grow up with and people I know, friends of my mama. My aunts are in there and we all going to my hometown Maunabo.

In the road, there was so many people, they even make a poem out of it. I'm not lying—they even made a poem out of it!

I got the book with the poem in it. Every time we go through the towns there's people standing out and saying "Hi."

Before we get to my hometown we going down a hill and I can see the beach where I dreamed. I have to stand up and go where the door is so I can get a better view. I say, "Look at this. That's what saved me, that's one of the things that saved me."

When we get to the town they took me straight to the mayor's office. He was in the bus, too, the mayor of the town. They took me inside and they had food and everything for me. I didn't want to eat. I wasn't hungry, and I knew they had something for me in my house, that's what I wanted. I just taste a little bit; they understand.

Melendez sits on a panel at the second World Congress Against the Death Penalty in Montreal, Canada (2004)

I leave the mayor's place, the government building in that town, and they're taking pictures. I go to the plaza and people are playing dominoes so I go in and I sit down. And this old man that know me, he say, "Come on, you know how to play."

We start playing and we win. And then we got up and went to my house.

My house was full of people, in and out, reporters and people from everywhere. There was people bringing me food from all over: "There you go, I know you ain't eaten this one in a long time." They put it all in pots. Oh, I had food for about a month! All that food that I ain't eaten in all them years and they know it.

There was teachers coming in there with food, they taught me at school when I was young. I was thinking that they never forgot me. The strange thing is, I never forgot them either.

THE PROBLEM WITH THE DEATH PENALTY IS THIS: PEOPLE DON'T HAVE ALL THE DETAILS

Every time I have an opportunity to speak about the death penalty I will do it. I think the problem with the death penalty is this: People don't have all the details. And it's our duty to educate them. I think that's what I should do.

The persons that can educate the best is people that been through it, people that been incarcerated like myself. Not everyone can do it, and you cannot expect all of them to do it because they did some damage. I suffer what any person suffer that's been in a war. Post-traumatic stress—whatever the name they wanna give it. I got nightmares. And I find ways, believe it or not, to enjoy that part. It's all about not letting things get to you.

Sometimes I just like to be by myself. I think and I pray and I go all by myself because all these is things I got to do by myself. Everybody got problems, everybody got things they got to talk to themselves about. I just got more than anybody, probably. Because I left people in there behind.

It's painful. Every time I got to tell my story I go right back in there again, which I don't want to do. But I know it's necessary. It's not easy to live with this. It's about learning how to live with it. And that's what I do, I learn how to live with it. It's negative, but I try to convert it to something positive. The only way to convert it to something positive is to abolish the death penalty. Since I see there's a problem, I address the problem. It's painful but I thank God that I am able to do it.

Gary Gauger

I STEPPED INTO A DREAM

NAME: Gary Gauger · **BORN:** 1952 · **HOMETOWN:** Richmond, Illinois

CONVICTED OF: Murder · **SENTENCE:** Death, reduced to life in prison

SERVED: 3 years · **RELEASED:** 1996

MOM TOOK US TO FIRST GRADE
IN A SIDECAR HARLEY

We grew up on the farm. It was all farm and dairy country when we grew up. It was a pretty normal childhood, I suppose. We were always kind of plugged in and involved in the farming, planting potatoes. My grandparents grew sweet corn and we would sell it by the side of the road. It seems like I was only six years old when they had me out pushing hay.

Grandpa bought the farm in 1923. They started with dairy farming like everybody else. He was only sixteen when he was in charge of his own team of horses. Grandpa was great with animals. Until he retired in 1960, he always worked with a team of horses. I don't think I ever saw him driving a tractor. Grandpa was the guy that got me interested in farming. He was a great farmer.

Dad was a mechanic. He started out repairing bicycles for the neighbors and stuff at an early age. Around here, a lot of the farm boys, once they got old enough to drive, had the old Harley-Davidsons and the old Indians. Dad got into motorcycle repair, and then he got into selling used bikes. He helped my grandfather on the farm, but when Grandpa sold the cows in 1960, my dad became a full-time motorcycle dealer.

On the first day of first grade, my mom took us to school in a sidecar Harley. She was a little lady, five foot three. She'd kick over this big Harley and put us kids in the sidecar, take us to school. Even when I was a first-grader, I thought, "Yeah, this is cool." I never thought of myself as different. I blended in pretty well with all the different groups. I had good enough grades. I fit in with the brown-nosers. I fit in with the farming kids and the greasers. I liked mechanics, so I blended in with all the groups really.

The Vietnam War really shaped my emerging adulthood. The hippie thing started in the mid-'60s. When the Beatles went from mod to hip, I just went "Wow! This is going to change the world," and I just embraced it and everything that went with it: the drugs and the alcohol and the partying and the traveling and the self-imposed poverty and all that goofy stuff. I thought that was really cool. The only thing I didn't embrace was free love. I had a steady girlfriend and married her right out of high school, so I missed the whole free love thing. But it's probably just as well. I went to college for a year and we got married after that.

We had our third baby in Austin, [Texas]. But by this time our marriage was falling apart. We got married way too young. Neither one of us had a clue what we were gonna do in life. My wife thought she wanted to be a back-to-lander hippie, and I did too. She liked the romantic part of it, but not the dirt and the poverty and the hard work. She became more and more conservative and kind of liked the yuppie lifestyle her friends were leading, and I just kind of rebelled against it. Plus I was an alcoholic, which didn't help things at all. It's a hard life to be a drunk. It just disappoints everybody. A lot of people in AA feel that you're born an alcoholic. I tend to agree with that. The first word I could spell was sauce. I just took to it like a duck takes to water.

I moved back home in 1989. I was getting tired of Austin. I wanted to get back into farming. I'd tried a lot of jobs. I'd been a tax examiner for the IRS. I'd had my own business. I'd worked with landscapers. I tried bricklaying, but I never liked any of these things. The only thing I ever wanted to do was be a farmer, so I came back up here and moved in with my folks and started helping my dad repairing motorcycles and got started with my vegetable business.

I liked it. Dad was busy with his motorcycles, but he would help me out with the farming and I worked on the bikes. I put some buildings up on the farm and built myself a greenhouse. I was working all the time. I liked it. We'd pretty much have dinner together every night. I might read the newspaper, watch a little TV with them, go to bed. Other than that, we pretty much did what we did.

My drinking pattern was getting a lot better. I was growing up. I was still a binger—I would drink for a week or so and sober up for a month, take care of business, and get everything done. Even when I was drinking, I would still be working. I got two DUIs in a row and I said that's it, so I quit driving, and then I quit drinking two years after that.

My parents were killed in 1993, thirty-two days after I quit drinking.

IT SEEMED TOO QUIET

On April 8, 1993, Gauger's parents, Morris and Ruth, were murdered, their throats cut to the spine. A day after the murders, Gauger discovered his father's body and called the police, who found his mother's body inside a trailer on the family's property.

After investigators scoured the crime scene, police arrested Gauger and took him in for questioning.

It was a rainy morning. I slept late. There was no sense to getting an early start, because my plans were to take stuff out of the greenhouse and into the hotbeds, which is virtually impossible in the driving rain. I finally got up at nine o'clock. Basically, I did the same thing I do every morning: I make myself a sandwich, make it over to the greenhouse and go to work.

I noticed the house seemed quiet. It wasn't really unusual. By this time my dad would be out working in the garage and my mom, if she wasn't in the house, would either be out helping my dad find something in the garage, or running errands in town. It seemed too quiet.

You know, they were just gone. I looked around for a note or something to see if they'd gone somewhere, but I didn't find one. They had been planning a trip to look at an old tractor, so I just assumed their friend had come by that morning and said, "Well hey, let's go to Sugar Grove and look at this tractor."

So I went to work, came home that night. When I did get back, I was a little surprised no one was home, because usually we had supper together. I checked the garage door at six when I walked back to the shop.

I figured rather than just stay at home worrying, I grabbed a bite to eat and went back over to the greenhouse to finish up some work I was doing. I came home just after ten. Then I went and looked up in the barn and in my mom's car, because I was worried about my folks at this point.

They'd always be home by dark or a little after dark. I didn't know what to do. There was nobody I could think to call. I couldn't call the police. They wouldn't investigate missing people until twenty-four hours had elapsed. My brother was in Whitewater [Wisconsin]. My sister was in Colorado. So there was really nobody else to call. So I just stayed by the phone until midnight and then went to bed. I was hoping somebody would call.

I went to bed, got up the next morning, looked around right away. They hadn't come home. Then I was really worried, just trying to think what to do next. Around 10:45, a customer of my dad's, Ed Zender, and his girlfriend, Tracey, came walking up the driveway. I was just relieved to have somebody to talk to. Ed said he needed a part. We didn't go into the shop right away, but Ed specified that he really needed one part to keep going on this project, so he kind of talked me into it.

So we went in the shop to look for this one part. He needed an English camshaft nut, so I looked in the box of English bolts. We didn't find it in the one box, so we went to the back to the BMW parts room, which is poorly lit. In the doorway between those two rooms, that's where we found my father's body.

He was just kind of laying in a semi-fetal position. There was a pool of blood around his head. It looked to me like my dad had had a heart attack, or stroke, or fallen and hit his head. He was seventy-three. He had very bad circulation. I mean, he had some major circulatory problems and he just absolutely refused to see a doctor.

It was a shock. It was like I stepped into a dream. I stepped over his body, felt his pulse, and his body was cold. He had no pulse, so I realized he was dead. Nothing made any sense. My father is dead. My mother is missing. Ed was a couple steps

behind me. Then Tracey came up behind us, and she started crying. We were just stunned. I didn't even really know who to call,
so I walked back to the house and called 911. I talked to the
operator and said I'd found my father's body, and my mother
was missing.

They called the paramedics. They were there really fast. In
five, six minutes, the ambulance got there. I was surprised. They
called the police right away. At this point, Ed and I are looking all
around the immediate buildings to try and see if we could find
my mother, or any signs of what had happened to my mother.

When the police came, I told them my mother's missing, my
father's dead. I tried to help them. One officer went through the
house with me. He told me foul play was suspected but he didn't
elaborate. I talked to a coroner, I talked to another officer,
I talked to a detective. I tried to give them everything I could give
them to help with an investigation because there wasn't much.
I mean, I had supper with them, I woke up the next morning,
went to work, and then the next morning, I found my dad dead.

At one point they had quit questioning me. The sun was
coming out, so I realized I needed to open my cold frames over
at the farm. When the sun's shining in the spring, you can cook
your plants in about twenty minutes, twenty to thirty minutes.
This was my whole tomato and pepper crop. So I came over,
opened up the cold frames. It's a time-honored tradition. I mean,
if there's a death in the family, you still milk the cows. The cows
have to be milked. You still take care of business.

I was only there about twenty minutes, and then I went back
in case I could be of any help. I came back to the house and
nobody wanted to talk to me, so I went in the kitchen and made
myself a cup of coffee. I was just hanging out by the driveway
over by the house in case anybody wanted to ask me any more
questions. By this time, the driveway, which is about 400, 450

feet long, was car-to-car from the house to the road. There were a lot of people. Lot of cars, three squad cars, and about four or five uniformed officers.

A policeman asked if I knew where there was a key to the rug trailer and I told him where some keys were kept. None of those fit, so I told him to just take a hammer and pop open the lock, because it was a little suitcase lock. It wasn't much of a lock. They opened it. I was maybe fifty feet away. I could see when one officer went in and then he came out and said something and three, four other officers just rushed into the rug trailer. Then one of them came out, pointed at me, and said, "Don't let him go." At that point, I was surrounded by three uniformed officers, frisked, taken over to the squad car, and locked in the squad car. It was 1:30 p.m.

I realized they must have found my mother's body. By the way they acted, the way everybody was acting, it was pretty obvious. They put an officer in the front seat to guard me, and I asked if they had found my mother's body and he said yeah. That was a shock. It was just all shock at this point.

It felt like I was dreaming. Everything looked real, felt real. It just lacked all depth. There was no emotions. I wasn't acting like a character in a made-for-TV movie, which is not how real people act. There's no telling how anyone's going to act. I was just going through the motions.

I sat in the car over three hours. I was under guard the whole time. I didn't see anybody I recognized. At this point, they'd found my mother, they'd found my father, so there wasn't a lot of commotion anymore.

IF I KILLED MY PARENTS,
I WANT TO KNOW ABOUT IT

During an all-night interrogation, police posed hypothetical questions to Gauger. His answers were later presented as a confession. Gauger says that he made these hypothetical statements after investigators suggested the possibility that he committed the murders during an alcoholic blackout. At the request of Gauger's lawyer, the names of the detectives have been changed.

Two of the detectives, Carol Dunne and Ken Trager, showed up. They did a preliminary investigation of the scene, and then they took me to [the police station] for the interrogation. They were taking me in for questioning, is what they told me. That would be about four in the afternoon. I was numb. My parents had been murdered. I was trying to help.

I had never been in the police building before. We go into the basement and upstairs and into an interrogation room. I'm not told I'm under arrest, but I'm read my Miranda rights, and I said something flip. I said, "Qué?" I used to say flip things when I was uneasy—just to try to change the tone of the conversation a little. There had just been a big case in McHenry County about a guy who was Hispanic, who didn't speak English, and they only read him his Miranda rights in English, so they got in all kinds of trouble for doing that, so there I am, thinking I'm just there for questioning. So just to say something a little off the wall, I said, "Qué?" They didn't like that.

The room wasn't that big. The interrogation table would've sat maybe eight to ten people. It was a sturdy table, sturdy enough for a three-hundred-pound policeman to lean on it. The chairs were comfortable enough, with padded seats and wooden arms. It wasn't like folding chairs or anything like that.

The questioning began. And I told 'em everything about my parents that I could. I told 'em about my habits, my parents' habits, what had been going on at the farm. It was just normal questioning. I was trying to tell them what I was doing the last few days before my parents were killed.

This went on for an hour, hour and a half. Agent Trager was doing most of the questioning and he became more like he couldn't believe it. He had a real problem with the fact that when we found my father's body, we went through a back parts room and up into the other parts room rather than walking into the garage and going straight over to the first parts room. That way, we would have found my father's body a few minutes sooner. I kept trying to explain to him, it was because we went to the mechanics first to look for this part and once you're back there, it's quicker to cut through the back room. He kept asking me to repeat that, repeat that, repeat that. It just made absolutely no sense at all.

I kept going over my memory of what I'd been doing the last two to three days. By eight o'clock, I'd run out of things to say. I was getting tired of it. I didn't really want to go home because there was nothing to go home to. I assumed the place probably still had police looking around for evidence and stuff. There wasn't much to go home to, but there wasn't any reason to stay. I just asked if I could leave. And he said, "Nope, you can't go."

So we just kept questioning. I ran out of things to say about my folks and the last couple days, so their questioning got a little broader about what I'd been doing my whole life—going to school, going to Texas, my family, just stuff that didn't seem to have much bearing. But I'm trying to help. I'm as cooperative as I possibly could be. I told them everything. I told them what I could remember from when I was eighteen months old to present. How I'd never been abused, how I wished I could have been closer to my father when I was growing up, everything I'd done the last ten years in Texas, events that led to my divorce, organic farming, my children—I mean, everything. This went on until about ten o'clock, and I said, "Man, can I go home?" and he said, "No, we can't stop now. We can't stop. We've gone too far." So again they told me I couldn't go.

I asked if they'd let me go if I took a polygraph test. I'd heard they were unreliable, but I was looking for reasons to get out of there. This thing had gone far enough. So they arranged right away for a polygraph examiner. The closest one was in Rockford, which is about twenty miles from Woodstock [where Gauger was being questioned]. They decided to take a break and ordered out for sandwiches. Things got a little calmer.

We talked about the polygraph test a little bit. I told them I heard they're unreliable. By this point, I probably had about seven or eight cups of coffee at the police station and probably three or four cups at home, so I was wired. I was really caffeinated. I haven't had anything to eat all day, except coffee. My blood sugar was plummeting.

"Oh no, no," Trager said. "These things are real reliable. If you pass it, we could probably let you go." So okay, it sounded like a good deal. The sandwiches came. I wasn't hungry; I took a few bites of one. I didn't feel like eating. I told them I'd probably throw up now because my stomach was upset. I was upset.

The polygraph examiner got there a little bit before midnight. I'm taken to another room, set down in a chair, strapped up. It's quite an elaborate system. There's eight different readings they take so they got a couple things around your waist, you got things on your wrist, things on your fingers, things on your hands. It's uncomfortable. And I told the examiner this and he says that's normal. I was afraid that if it's digging into your rib cage, it would give a false reading or something. I asked him, "If you start wincing is it gonna to give a false reading?" He said, no, that's normal.

It was just me and the polygraph examiner. The detectives were not in the room. The first thing he told me was that my parents had had their throats cut, which I didn't know. He said that my mom's throat had been cut so badly she'd almost had her head cut off. This made me very upset. I'd known they'd been killed, but this just makes it seem so much more real.

The test took about an hour. I answered all the questions truthfully and thoroughly, except they give you a control question that you're supposed to lie on. He said, "I'm gonna ask you where you live. Tell me some place other than where you live." So I did. And what they do then, they calibrate the machine for when you tell a lie. All the time, he's fiddling with the knobs and stuff. At one point during the test, I heard the needle going *clack clack clack* like it's way off the graph, but it was just some mundane routine question—it didn't have anything to do with anything, so I assumed he was calibrating the machine again.

Mostly, he was asking questions specifically about whether or not I killed my parents. "Did you cut their throats?" "Did you kill them?" I was being honest. I mostly just felt exhausted. It took about an hour, and I assumed I passed with flying colors—there was no reason not to. I didn't lie about anything. After the examination, the interrogation took a bizarre turn. Trager met me right outside the room and he asked, "Gary, if you were going to cut somebody's throat, how would you do it?" And I'd seen Rambo movies, you know, too much TV. We shouldn't even know about these things, we really shouldn't. It really messes up your subconscious. So I started to act like, "Well, if you had a knife..." I started to make the hand motion, and then I thought, wait a minute, this is too bizarre. So I just put my hands down.

Detective Trager took me back to the interrogation room. As

A USEFUL FICTION

The reliability of polygraph tests is widely contested

Polygraphs, also known as lie detector tests, do not actually measure whether a person is lying. Rather, they chart the physical changes usually associated with lying: sweaty palms, racing hearts, shaky breaths. Sensors are used to measure skin conductivity, blood pressure, and chest and abdomen girth.

The accuracy of polygraphs is hotly contested. While the American Polygraph Association claims accuracy rates of 80 to 98 percent, others disagree. "Polygraph accuracy is effectively negligible," says David Lykken, polygraph expert and professor emeritus of psychology at the University of Minnesota. "I would estimate that the result of a lie detector test has a fifty-fifty chance of being correct, and the best examiners are accurate only 60 percent of the time, maximum."

A typical polygraph machine

To settle the matter, the United States Department of Energy commissioned the National Research Council in 2002 to evaluate scientific evidence on the validity of polygraphs. The resulting report concluded there was "little basis for the expectation that a polygraph test could have extremely high accuracy."

The Supreme Court has not yet ruled definitively on the admissibility of polygraph evidence. But as of 2002, thirty-two states have judged polygraphs absolutely inadmissible and seventeen states and the District of Columbia have judged polygraphs admissible only upon the agreement of both defense and prosecution before the test takes place.

Polygraph examinations continue to play a large role in pretrial investigations because investigators believe polygraphs do often lead to the truth—not by detecting lies but by encouraging confessions. This is why investigators spend so much time in the pretest phase convincing examinees that the lie detector test is infallible and omniscient.

"If I were running a police department, I would be inclined to use the polygraph test," says Lykken. "It's a bloodless third degree, highly effective as a questioning device, and an interrogation tool for producing confessions."

we walked back, I said, "I passed, didn't I?" and Trager said I failed. I was stunned. I really felt I had passed. A third officer, Trent Howard, came in. He had stayed at the house longer and done a more thorough investigation. They asked me to sign a search consent form. I looked at it closely because I had maybe seven or eight grams of marijuana right under my worktable. I saw the search warrant was only for the farm, so I didn't have a problem with signing that.

By this time, I was exhausted. One guy said, "Did you hear what property values are going for in our area?" Things like that, but not a lot of questioning. I think he was implying that I would kill my parents to inherit the property so I could sell it. They were just throwing a few questions out. They were fishing.

This is when it got really bizarre. Dunne asked me, "What would you say if I told you we have a stack of evidence against you this tall?" indicating about eight to ten inches tall. I said, "I'd say you were crazy." She said, "Well, we do."

She kept going over about why did I go through the back two doorways. Trager was becoming more belligerent, more confrontational. Trager was more of a buffoon, a blusterous buffoon. They were playing good cop, bad cop. Dunne was always the sympathetic one and he was always the blustery one. At one point, I accused 'em of that—playing good cop, bad cop.

At one point they said that they found a bloody knife in my pants pocket. Another time they said they found bloody clothes in my bedroom. They said they found bloody sheets.

I asked them, I mean I told them, "This is impossible. I don't believe it." I asked them, "Can you lie?" They said, "No, we can't lie. If we lied, we would lose our jobs." I asked them, "How do you like your jobs?" They said, "We love our jobs." They seemed so believable. I couldn't understand why they would lie. I was still looking at these people to help me solve the murder of my parents. Nothing made any sense. I was exhausted. They wouldn't let me go home.

I asked at one point to let me lie down. I said, "Hey, I am exhausted. Can we start this up tomorrow morning? And Trager was getting more confrontational. "No! No, we can't! We've gone too far. We have to keep going." A couple times, between one and three in the morning, I asked to lie down. They wouldn't let me lie down, and I was just exhausted. They kept saying they had all this evidence. They said they had all the evidence they needed against me. They didn't need a confession. I asked, "When can I see the evidence?" They told me Monday. I don't know why they told me Monday. This was on Friday night.

They said something must have snapped. I couldn't keep this inside. I had to let it out. We all live on the edge. It could have happened to anyone. They said they had plenty of evidence, didn't need a confession. It was someone my parents knew and trusted. There was no robbery. They told me my mom's body had been covered with blankets and pillows like someone had cared.

I was still trying to cooperate. At some point I thought, "Man, maybe I oughta ask for a lawyer." But I'd done nothing wrong, and I knew they weren't going to be able to get a lawyer at one-thirty on a Friday night. I had this mental image of the real killers' trail just growing colder and colder, so I was still thinking that if I could just pin down my activities for the last three days, to the minute—so I could just account for everything I'd done over the last forty-eight hours—they'd finally believe me. So I pinned down, to the minute, how long everything took me. This took twenty minutes, trying to give them just a really accurate account of what I'd been doing, trying to convince them that I'm innocent.

They told me I'd failed the polygraph test. They said the machine wouldn't lie—some of the answers were so bad, they jumped the needle right off the graph. At one point, [the polygraph examiner] had two pictures of my parents' bodies, very graphic pictures. They weren't pictures at the crime scene so much as pictures to show the extent of my parents' injuries. My folks' throats were cut to their spine. It was horrible. He slapped these down on the table. It's like he's got a winning hand of cards and I'm gonna just blurt out and confess that I did the crime. He slapped them down and he said, "How could you do this? How could you kill your mother, the woman that gave birth to you?" And he was yelling at me now, very confrontational. I just winced and looked away. It was just horrible.

This is the way it went on. Dunne suggested maybe this happened in a blackout, that this often happened with family members, that you would black it out. They're telling me that I killed my parents, that they had the bloody knife, that they had the bloody clothes, the bloody sheets, a stack of evidence. The polygraph says I'm lying. They told me they couldn't lie, they'd lose their jobs. Finally, they suggested we go through a hypothetical and reenact the crime. Maybe I'd done it in a blackout. If we just went through, maybe it would jog my memory. I agreed to this. This is when the alarm bells really went off in my mind: Maybe I should get a lawyer. But I was trusting them. I was still trusting them at this point. I'm assuming that they must be telling the truth, which is very traumatic, thinking you killed your parents in a blackout. I'm still thinking, if I killed my parents, I want to know about it. I'm not going to try and hide it, so I didn't ask for a lawyer to try and stop the interrogation.

So they asked me to go through a hypothetical account of how I must have killed my parents. And I mean they're not asking me if I killed my parents, they're telling me that I did kill my parents and they wanted to know what happened, and if I would go through a hypothetical account with them, using facts they'd fed me about what I must have done, it might jog my memory.

There wasn't much memory here. I had no memory of my own, so it's very short. Basically, I said I would have gotten up in the morning, got dressed, because I remembered that. I had a dim memory of having a knife in my pocket, but I didn't have the knife in my pocket on Thursday morning, I had the knife in my pocket on Wednesday morning, because I'd worked late the night before and it was a little dark in the greenhouse, and I put it in my pocket, because I used it for transplanting too, and sometimes I lose stuff, and I needed it the next morning, so I woulda had it when I went to work Wednesday morning, the day before. When I got up Thursday morning there was no knife in my pants pocket, but I'm just taking former memories I had with things I'd done and lumping it all to try and fit their scenario to jog my memory.

I tried to imagine doing it. I said I would have gotten up, walked into the living room, and seen my mother outside the trailer folding clothes, because I had a memory of her two weeks earlier outside of the trailer folding clothes. Well, that particular morning, it was blowing and windy and there was no way she would have been outside folding clothes, but I'm trying to jog my memory with a hypothetical situation here. And then, the next thing I said, I would have gone in the trailer, come up behind her, grabbed her hair, and cut her throat, because you could see in the one photo that somebody had grabbed her hair and pulled it back. But I mean, that's all I could tell, because that's what the picture looked like. I said I would have grabbed her by her hair, cut her throat, and then I would have caught her and laid her down because I wouldn't want her to get hurt.

At this point, I just completely broke down and cried. This was the first time I cried since finding my father. The police had told me everything that had happened, but I couldn't understand where the image of me catching my mother and lowering her to the ground came from. Now this is the first emotion I'd felt since I'd found my father's body. I'm crying now and I'm thinking, "Oh my gosh, this is doing something here. This must be jogging a memory," and that's when I first thought maybe I had actually killed my parents. They'd said I did it, and there was all this evidence. I said I would have gone out to the garage, come up behind my father, grabbed his hair, cut his throat, and let him fall. They said, "What did you do with the weapon?" And I said, "I would have left it there," 'cause I had no memory of doing anything with a weapon.

Immediately upon saying it, I said, "But this is just hypothetical. I have no memory of this." But they've got me thinking now that I did it. And they're making no bones about this. I'm crying pretty much now. At this point I'm feeling some emotion. And whenever I look up and stop crying, either Trager or Dunne said, "You did it. We know you did it. There was no struggle. It was someone they trusted. We've got the clothes. We've got the bloody knife. We can see it in your eyes. You killed your parents. We know you did." I mean, this went on for about an hour and a half.

And I'm still looking at them to help solve this crime. I'm feeling really bad, and I'm thinking through this now. I'm believing that I actually had killed my parents in a blackout. I told Trager I was afraid. He was wearing his .45 pistol on his side. I told him I was afraid I'd grab that gun and kill myself. I told him, "Man, what are my brother and sister going to think?"

It calmed down a little and we start working on a motive. They have all this proof, and we're sitting around trying to decide what my motive could have been and we couldn't come up with one. I mean, I loved my parents. There was no motive.

Five o'clock in the morning, Howard comes in, and we're all exhausted. Howard had a paper bag and said, "We'll take your clothes now." He put the bag on the table. It was prison clothes: cotton slippers, black cotton pajamas, and a white short-sleeved cotton shirt. It said McHenry County Jail on the back. It was a prison outfit. So they made me strip naked in the interrogation room.

Howard said, "Gary, just tell us what happened the other morning when your parents were killed." And this flood of relief just went over me and I thought, "Oh my gosh, this was all just part of the investigation. They made this all up. I didn't kill my parents." So I started to tell him what I did. I said, "I slept late, I made a sandwich, I took the sandwich, I walked across the field to go to work," and about the time I said that he stood up and he just started hollering at me. "No, No! We don't want to hear that! We just want to hear about you killing your parents!" He was very belligerent, very accusational, and I just gave up. I gave up. I wasn't in my right mind. They wouldn't let me lie down. They wouldn't end the interrogation. They just kept going.

But immediately when I finished it I said, "But I'm not signing a confession, because I have absolutely no memory of this." I was very adamant about that. I'm not signing a confession. I thought I'd killed my parents at this point in a blackout, I really did think I had, but I told him, "I'm not going to sign a confession if I have no memory of it."

I asked Dunne for a hug. She was sympathetic. She was the only one who hadn't been browbeating me, basically. She was very believable. She was very good at what she did.

I realized that the door's open, and sometimes people are coming and going now and we're still talking about it. I'm still sitting in this room with some cops, and I'm thinking, "Man, some policeman who hasn't been privy to the whole conversation might take something I said as some kind of admission of guilt," and I want it to end, and finally I say, "Man, I guess I need an attorney, don't I?" And it was like, that's it, we're done. Now they're going to pay attention to the laws. They put their papers in their folders. They said we're done now, and they were gone.

It was the end of the interrogation. I'm taken down to the booking room. I'm booked for murder.

POLICE DO LIE

The next three days were probably the worst three days of my life. I was booked at ten in the morning. The booking sergeant asked if I had blackouts and I said, "Yeah, I had one two days ago," because they told me I did. The only blackouts I ever had were alcoholic blackouts after a heavy episode of drinking, but I'd been thirty-two days sober when this happened. Even when I had alcoholic blackouts, my pattern was I'd remember what bars I was at and I'd go back and make apologies because these were my friends. When I'd get drunk, I was a loud drunk. I'd just repeat myself. I didn't fight. I'd like to dance and sing. I'd just repeat myself and I'd get really loud. My language got a little vulgar. I'd know enough so I'd know where I went, retrace my steps, make apologies because I wanted to go back to these places, and I'd walk into these bars and people would say, "Gary, Gary, Gary..."

So I was booked, put in a cell. Dunne came in about an hour later. She wanted me to sign some kind of release. I thought it was a confession. I told her, "I'm not signing a confession." It was a release for my clothing or something stupid like that. At this point, I'm thinking I must have done it. I'm in observation in the holding tank. There's a booking desk. They're looking right into the holding cell. She asked if I was suicidal and I said yes. So they put me in observation. I felt suicidal.

It did not escape me that this was Easter weekend. This was all happening on Good Friday. I didn't eat for the next three days.

I felt horrible. At one point I took toilet paper, wadded it in little balls, and inhaled it into my trachea, and the police saw me. I kind of pulled the covers up over my head so they couldn't see me and inhaled this toilet paper. And I started to convulse. They came in and basically Heimliched me, and I also realized it would be very hard to kill yourself, doing that. This was the only thing around, and I felt so horrible. So they took away my toilet paper, so if I needed toilet paper, I had to ask for it. It's very humiliating being in jail. It's a very dehumanizing experience.

Sunday morning, my sister called and they came and put me on the phone, and I'm crying and she's crying. And I don't know what to say, and the police are telling her I confessed, that I killed my parents, and I'm thinking I did it. That was a horrible time. Very emotional. It was just very emotional, very bad. This was Easter Sunday.

Monday morning, my sister and her husband had flown back from Colorado. She got me a lawyer. Monday morning was the first time I talked to an attorney. I told my attorney the police had me believing I killed my parents. He explained to me that police do lie. He also explained to me that innocent people are convicted. That helped me feel a little better, and that's when I realized I hadn't killed my parents. That was Monday morning.

My sister came and visited on Tuesday. She still had a few questions for me. I answered those, and she realized I was telling the truth. So she didn't think I killed my parents, so that was good.

They put me in the observation room. I was trying to write my lawyer what happened and all I had was a stubby pencil and I'm starting in the middle of the paper and I'm going out and around and I got an arrow going over to the other side of the paper and I'm not writing in a normal pattern or fashion at all. It took me a week to concentrate enough to play simple games.

I couldn't play chess. I couldn't play cards.

They had brainwashed me so thoroughly that even as late as June, I'm still thinking that they're just telling me things just to keep me from killing myself and that maybe I still had done it, just from the brainwashing. By late May, early June, I was still having bad dreams, still confused, and still thinking possibly that my family might be hiding evidence from me that actually existed. But when I read the police discovery, and I realized the police were lying about the nature of the interrogation, I realized they're lying about this, and I'm totally innocent.

Once I realized I hadn't killed my parents, I was thinking this is just a big misunderstanding, and once everybody gets the facts straightened out, I really thought I'd be let out of jail any day. When I told my attorney what happened, I figured he'd talk to the prosecution, they'd talk to the police, they'd understand the nature of the interrogation, and within a couple weeks or a month, when they realized there was no evidence that tied me to the crime, that I'd be cut loose. It wasn't until the discovery started coming back in late June that I realized the police were lying about the nature of the interrogation. That's when I realized I was probably going to go to trial.

After Gauger was charged with double murder in April 1993, he was held in the McHenry County jail for more than six months, as preparations were made for his October trial. He was represented by two private attorneys.

It took six months to go to trial, which I thought was an eternity. It's actually very fast on a homicide case—I didn't know that at the time. I was very naive about how much trouble I was in and I think that really helped me, or I would have been a lot more depressed and despondent than I was. I was very naive. I always thought I'd get out, but I didn't know how much trouble I was in.

Trial was a terrible thing for me. All of these horrible things the prosecution is saying, all these lies the police are saying about you. These are supposed to be pillars of the community, but they're just lying their asses off. I'd stay up after the trial, just writing down all the things to be used for rebuttal the next day about things they said, questions to ask them, points to drive across. I'd give them to my lawyer when we'd meet before trial. He'd put them in his pocket. Never used any of them. He never prepared anything the night before.

He told a couple friends of mine that these trials are not won on the trial level, they're won on appeal. Here you have a trial where no motive is established, no confession is written down or signed, no physical evidence ties me to the crime, and yet he's not even trying to win the trial. He wants to win it on appeal, which takes about three years.

It lasted two weeks. The prosecution took all but the last two days. I testified for five and a half hours. Very detailed, very accurate. Mostly it was the prosecution and this was all non-witnesses—they had forensic experts, property experts. Other than the police's testimony, nothing else had bearing to the case.

The prosecution used the hypothetical account I'd given. The police's official version is that I was never under arrest, that I was chatting with them, sitting around chatting with them in street clothes, when actually I was wearing a prison uniform. They denied the whole nature of the interrogation from one o'clock onward. They testified that they were never heavy-handed, they never showed me the pictures, they never said they had evidence against me—they said none of this existed. Trager testified we were just chatting, that he was walking on eggshells, he just wanted to keep me talking when I suddenly became very still and issued a confession, which contained details only the killer would know.

The jury deliberated for less than three hours before convicting me. When they read the guilty verdict, I wanted to get up and shout, "Wait! You forgot to say *not!*" It was like they made a mistake. I thought it was a no-brainer and a slam-dunk, I'd be out. I was so convinced I'd be found not guilty. I never thought I'd be convicted on no evidence. No motive, no evidence, no signed confession.

People don't understand how false confessions can take place. After I was found guilty, my attorney asked the jury foreman, how could you convict a man when there was no physical evidence? And the jury foreman said, "We just couldn't understand why somebody would confess unless they did it." Well, I never actually even confessed, so that tells me that they couldn't even consider that the police could be lying.

MY SHIP-IN-A-BOTTLE DAYS

In October 1993, Gauger was convicted of two counts of murder. On January 11, 1994, he was sentenced to death. Gauger was held in McHenry County jail for another nine months as his case went through post-trial motions.

I was tried and convicted in October 1993. I was sentenced to die in January of 1994. Then we had post-trial motions, which lasted for a year.

I was writing anybody I could possibly think of. You know, there are law firms that do pro bono work. I was writing all the TV news shows, I was writing all the magazines, I was writing all the newspapers, laying out my case about what a miscarriage of justice I'd received. These were my ship-in-a-bottle days, and I'd spend all day writing one or two letters. I mean, these are not form letters. These are thought-out, one-page, handcrafted letters, each one targeted to that specific address trying to get help. I wrote at least fifty letters that way. The first batch of letters I sent out, I thought within two, three weeks, someone will get ahold of this, take it to a judge that's outside the county court system.

While Gauger was writing letters from jail, his friends and family at home were trying to get him another lawyer. That winter, after his death sentence, Gauger's sister and a group of his friends drove in a blinding snowstorm to Northwestern University to meet law professor Larry Marshall. They told him about Gauger's case. In August 1994, Marshall met with Gauger and decided to take his case.

The day before his final post-trial hearing, the judge reduced Gauger's death sentence to life without parole based on mitigating evidence about Gauger's background. After this hearing, Gauger was sent downstate to the Stateville Correctional Center in Joliet, Illinois.

I was sent first to Joliet, which is a clearinghouse for all prisoners before they're sent into the penal system. I was scared. I'd never seen anything like this. There was probably 150 to 200 people on our wing. It was dirty. It was loud. It was dangerous. The tension level was tremendous. You go to chow and there's signs on the wall that has a picture of a gun with a bullet coming out of it and the sign says "IF SHOTS ARE FIRED, SIT DOWN." The ceiling is full of bullet holes. The guards sit in steel towers in cages, armed with shotguns. That's where you go and eat.

There was a fight broke out and the whole place almost went up. One of the Latin Kings stole the big Kool-Aid barrel from one of the black gangs' dining tables and took it over to his table, and I seen him do it. This guy's a big Hispanic with probably a fifty-gallon jug of Kool-Aid and he's laughing about it, and it was just something to do because he was bored. And it almost started this huge gang riot.

It was the ugliest thing I had ever seen in my life, and I've seen car accidents and stuff. You have all these gang members up on the tables now. About two-thirds of the whole dining area rushed to the area because they were all associated with one gang or the other. I mean, this was going to be a tremendous rumble. Shots are being fired into the ceiling by the guards. I'm seeing these Gangster Disciples, I think it was, standing up on the table, flashing gang signs, saying "Forks down." "Forks down" means "Rumble's on, this is happening." Everybody was so bent on violence and destruction at this time. And then there, all of a sudden there, up on the table, is my cellmate. He was a mid-level Latin King gang member and he managed to calm everybody down.

I was off to the side. I didn't associate with the gangs. I was a neutron. At Stateville, 98 percent of the prisoners were hooked up in gangs. The rest of the guys were called neutrons, and they were on their own. There's a gang called the North Siders which is a loose collection of mostly white guys—it's only a prison gang, it does not exist outside the prisons, and it's made of skinheads and Aryan Nation and I had nothing in common with these guys. I was basically just on my own. You fend for your own as best you can.

While Gauger was in the Stateville Correctional Center in 1994, federal authorities were conducting a separate criminal investigation into a Wisconsin motorcycle gang known as the Outlaws. They taped a conversation between Outlaws members Randall E. Miller and James Schneider as they talked in detail about how they had planned and carried out the murders of Gauger's parents. The two gang members had heard rumors that the Gaugers kept large amounts of cash in the house. In recorded conversations, they talked about how they carried out the murder, but found only $15 on the Gaugers, which *they took and spent on breakfast later that morning. Prosecutors knew about these conversations as early as 1995, but failed to disclose this to Gauger's lawyers.*

Meanwhile, Gauger's case was gong through the appellate process with the help of Marshall. The U.S. Second District Court of Appeals heard Gauger's case in February 1996. A month later, the court unanimously reversed the conviction and remanded the case for a new trial on the grounds that Gauger's alleged confession should not have been admitted at trial and that he had been arrested without probable cause. Without the confession, McHenry County State Attorney Gary W. Pack did not have evidence to retry the case, so he appealed the ruling to the Illinois State Supreme Court. In August, with the appeal still pending, Gauger was released on a leg monitor. When the Illinois Supreme Court refused to overturn the appellate court decision in October 1996, Gauger was exonerated.

In 1997, eight months after Gauger's release, Miller and Schneider were charged with thirty-four federal counts of racketeering related to the murders of Ruth and Morris Gauger. Both were convicted of the racketeering charges in 1998 and 2000. Pack, the prosecutor who had fought Gauger's appeal so vigorously, officially charged the gang members with the Gaugers' murders in 2004. As of 2005, they were awaiting trial in McHenry County.

Released after three and a half years behind bars, Gauger moved back home. He now lives in a farmhouse with his second wife Sue, just a few hundred yards away from where his parents were killed.

I MUST HAVE BEEN KILLED, TOO

I'm an organic vegetable farmer now. We sell at four farmers' markets and a roadside stand. I'm able to produce clean, healthy food for individuals, which I think is a good thing to do. The vegetable season lasts from early February to mid-November and

Gauger with his wife Sue on their Richmond, Illinois, farm (2004)

I equate it to being an eight- or nine-month-long sprint. It's hard making a living farming.

The first four years especially after my release, my routine was basically to work. I couldn't sleep. I had real problems with sleep disturbances and not sleeping at all, so what I would do is just work really hard all day and be absolutely exhausted at night, so I could just go to bed, go to sleep, and just get up the next morning to do the same thing.

I really like the fact that we're staying on the family farm. It's been in the family for eighty years. My first attorney was really amazed when I told him I had no intentions of leaving. There's no way I'm going to let the police and the prosecution run me out of town like that. They're the ones that were wrong, not me. We've always been a very stubborn, dig-in-your-heels kind of a family.

Living on the farm, it's a daily reminder of my parents, but this is something that never goes out of your head anyways. The fact that I do a lot of interviews every year keeps it very fresh in my mind, too, so that's really irrelevant. I kind of like the fact that I've got my dad's old tractor collection, and we still use several of the tractors to farm the land. It just reminds me of when my grandfather was using some of this stuff. It's good. I'm glad I'm able to do that.

Since his release, Gauger has become a speaker and an activist. He has been featured in dozens of articles, documentary films, and the play The Exonerated. *He talks about his experiences at speaking engagements around the country.*

When I have public speaking gigs, I have panic attacks. I do the engagement, and then I come back and I have these weird psychological things and sometimes it affects me really strongly and

Gauger speaks about his wrongful conviction at a meeting of the Kentucky interim Health and Welfare Committee in Frankfort, Kentucky (October 1999)

sometimes it doesn't. I don't always know why or what. One time, I went in to Northwestern University and saw a film about a man who had been framed by the police and just spent the last thirty-five years in jail for a crime he didn't do. It was just so traumatic that the next day, it's like I had a stroke. I couldn't concentrate on simple tasks, I couldn't articulate simple thoughts. Sometimes it's a lot worse than others.

I'LL SPEAK OUT FOR THE REST OF MY LIFE

This last year, it's gotten a little better, but mostly it's because I've been avoiding speaking engagements. I've just been working on the farm. We went to Alaska four years ago. The Coalition Against the Death Penalty invited us up there, and I did a two-week tour where I was doing engagements sometimes three or four times a day, and I was hoping this would desensitize me to the whole process, but it didn't. What it did is it just totally exhausted me. When I wasn't speaking I'd just go to bed.

But every time I think about getting out of a speaking engagement, all I have to do is remember what it was like waking up one day behind bars to the sound of the guards coming with your breakfast, waking up from a sound sleep thinking, "Shit, I'm still here." And remembering what it feels like. And if I can prevent this from happening for one person, I'll speak out for the rest of my life.

I found one of the common denominators I had with a lot of these other guys that were convicted and put on death row and then exonerated is that we all felt we were fairly street-smart and yet we were really naive and ignorant about what goes on in the court rooms, the interrogation room, and the criminal justice system in general. So it's a campaign to just educate people and wisen them up to what's going on. Hopefully to stir some people to want to change things, and if not to change them, at least to say, "Hey, look out! Bridge out up ahead."

My case is an excellent example of why we need transparency in the police department and interrogation rooms. Bare minimum, you need video cameras in the interrogation rooms so that when the light switch goes on, the camera goes on. They have it in all the convenience stores. It's not an issue of cost. The departments that are honest and upright, they say this helps them in their convictions. In my case, if we had had a video camera in the interrogation room, not only would the case not have gone to trial, I never would have been charged—because the police would not have done what they did. The case has been instrumental in that it's being recommended now in Cook County that this take place in all police precincts and around the state.

In 2002, Gauger received an official pardon from Illinois Governor George Ryan.

I have very vivid memories of the injustice that I went through. Sometimes I'm out in the fields driving the tractor where nobody can hear me, and all of a sudden I'll get a memory and I'll just scream. And if I'm by myself sometimes, [the memories] will come out, and I'm by myself you know most of the time, so I get rather introverted. I spend a lot of time just going over my whole life and sometimes, you know, I'll remember what the police did, how they perjured themselves so much, just for promotions really, and I'll just, sometimes, I'll just curse. And you know, it's not healthy when I get into these veins. I realize that, so I try to get away from it.

I try to stuff all these memories, but I equate it to being like you're putting all your memories in your closet—your feelings, emotions, and memories in a closet. But you've got so much garbage you can't even close the door anymore. So when you start tripping over the stuff, you just throw it up into a pile and just lean your shoulder to the door and try to close it. I mean it's right there. The whole experience is always right there.

I've really retreated to the farm. I don't leave the farm unless I have to. I've got some kind of emotional problem. I mean, my sister, she's been one of my biggest supporters, and I'm scared even to talk to her and it makes absolutely no sense at all. It's been eleven years since my arrest, and I'm getting over it a little bit, but you know, the phone rings and I curse the phone. I won't answer it. I have really avoided any contact with people. It's my fault; I don't understand it. I went to a psychologist three times, but I wasn't getting much out of that, so I dropped that.

I've had maybe five emotional episodes since my parents were killed. You get this tightness in your throat and you start crying. The only emotion I was left with pretty much is frustration, you know, which was with me in prison all the time. Once in a while I'll get little glimpses. It's kind of like the movie *Pleasantville*

THE PSYCHOLOGICAL TOLL
OF WRONGFUL CONVICTION

Post-traumatic stress disorder disrupts the psyches of exonerees

A typical inmate is exposed to acts of prison brutality—including rape, stabbings, and killings—for years on end. Wrongfully convicted inmates must also attempt to come to terms with the fact that the justice system has failed them. Not surprisingly, an exoneree's years in prison can exact a severe psychological toll. Typical psychological disorders among exonerees include post-traumatic stress disorder, depression, and mental "institutionalization."

David Quindt

Following the Vietnam War, the term post-traumatic stress disorder (PTSD) was coined to describe the psychological toll of the war on returning veterans. The symptoms—including flashbacks, panic attacks, nightmares, paranoia, and detachment from society—were also common among victims of torture and other extremely traumatic events.

David Quindt, who served fourteen months for a robbery and murder he did not commit, often wakes drenched in sweat after nightmares of being handcuffed and taken to prison. Fear overwhelms him whenever he passes police officers on the street. One year after his release, when an officer who had investigated the crime that led to Quindt's conviction pulled into the Jiffy Lube where Quindt worked for an oil change, Quindt fled in panic. He never returned to that workplace.

Exonerees may suffer the classic symptoms associated with PTSD, such as avoidance, reexperiencing their trauma, and hypervigilance. This may be complicated by a concomitant depression and anxiety that relates to the massive loss of years of freedom. At least one study suggests depression may be even more common than PTSD. According to psychologist Craig Haney, exonerees' attempts to reconcile their incarceration with their innocence can lead to "suffering that is impossible to make sense of, suffering that becomes very difficult to build from or grow out of."

"All inmates, including exonerees, are at risk of becoming institutionalized," says Terry Kupers, a psychiatrist who has testified in more than twenty cases relating to the effects of prison conditions on prisoners. "They are so used to the institutional schedule where all their daily activities are regimented that when they leave, they are unable to think for themselves and interact spontaneously and naturally with the nonprison world."

where everything is black and white for me now, and it's not real anymore. Sometimes I think I must have been killed, too, and I'm just acting out a mental dream of what my life would be if I had survived. I don't feel like I'm alive.

I get glimpses once in a while of emotion. There was a conference at Northwestern in 1998 where for three days there were like thirty-five of us telling our stories and talking to reporters and everybody else, and when I came home I was just sitting on the couch and it was like the movie *Raiders of the Lost Ark*, when they opened up the ark and you see this light start coming out of the ark. It was like I could see this light and it was going right into my chest and a hole opened up and I could see this world of color and sound, and it was beautiful and it was just really beautiful, and then it just snapped shut again. And after that, once in a while I'll get a glimpse of emotion, but as soon as I get to feeling any emotion at all, I just start crying and it's like I'll never stop if I ever let it just come out. So I mean there is emotion in there somewhere, but it's really locked in there tight.

James Newsome

I AM THE EXPERT

NAME: James Newsome · BORN: 1955 · HOMETOWN: Chicago, Illinois

CONVICTED OF: Murder and armed robbery · SENTENCE: Life

SERVED: 15 years · RELEASED: 1994

GUIDING FORCES

I'm James Newsome from Chicago, Illinois. All my life I've lived there, with the exception of fifteen years, two months and four days, when I was an enforced transplant of the Illinois Department of Corrections for the murder and armed robbery of someone that I didn't know.

The first person I can think of in terms of influencing me in the best way she could was my mother. When you come up in a one-parent home and you don't have the constant vigilance of both parents, and your mother is off to work, you're living under a situation by which you have to fend for yourself. You do your own thing until your mom comes home tired at the end of the day.

Other guiding forces in my life were ordinary people in the community like the Black Panther Party. I can't say that they were necessarily influential, but they left a lasting impression on me with respect to their advocacy, their community awareness and their activism. But they were being portrayed as a negative element in our community by people who didn't understand them, who looked at them as being disruptive radicals. All these terms you heard in the '60s—the radical left, the Black Panthers, the Conspiracy Seven in Chicago—they were part of a group of people who were against the Vietnam War and many ideals held by "White America." These were things that people in the minority class were sick and tired of and wanted to commit themselves to changing. They were people who used their voice toward change from the status quo. They didn't want to be mastered over anymore. Those are the people who really gained my respect and gave me a better understanding of how I should stand.

I was going to Operation Bread Basket. That was an adjunct of SCLC, the Southern Christian Leadership Conference, which Martin Luther King was a part of. He had an offshoot called Operation Bread Basket that was run by Jesse Jackson. Every Saturday they met in my community at the Capitol Theater for the purposes of rallying the troops, addressing the community's agenda, whether it be the local urban community's agenda with respect to Chicago and the Midwest, or even the national agenda.

I'm a kid fourteen, fifteen years old. Just imagine me standing across the street from Operation Bread Basket, just looking at the activities. I'm a kid just sitting there, maybe on a cinderblock, just looking and trying to absorb all that's going on around me.

I'm coming out of the '60s where I'm in segregated schools, where we weren't allowed to branch out to other schools that had much better resources than ours. I want you to get this picture in your mind of a young boy—it's almost like a movie that gives you a retro look at your life. I'm looking at this activity, at the Capitol Theater across the street, trying to understand. It was giving me an opportunity to understand what my social consciousness should be and if I wanted to be a part of my community's progress and change.

I was always smart in school. They weren't giving A's out then, they were giving E's, F's and G's. E for excellence, G for good, F for failure. I was always an E, G student—mostly E's. But something happened to me. Something happened to Operation Bread Basket, where it all of a sudden changed its course. There was some discord between SCLC's headquarters in Atlanta and Operation Bread Basket. Because of that discord, Jesse Jackson was asked to step down from Operation Bread Basket. So he started his own group, People United to Save Humanity. From that point on he moved from the Capitol Theater to 50th and Drexel, where their present location is.

You have to remember I'm a young kid, I can't move with them because I don't have any money to travel over there. And then the only other influences I had around me were the negative ones because I was just hanging around on the street. Four or five of us used to be together on a daily basis and we were really close friends—kids I went to grammar school and high school with. We would just spend our days walking around the community, just experimenting and experiencing things that we shouldn't have been doing—marijuana on occasion, drinking on occasion.

My first encounter with being wrongfully accused of something came when I was fourteen years old, after Operation Bread Basket had died and Jesse Jackson had moved on. I was accused of burglarizing somebody's house that I didn't burglarize. I had to spend four months in a juvenile detention center called Audy

Homes. I immediately took to taking advantage of a bad situation, tried to make it positive by concentrating on academics.

Because of my academic interests, I went to an advanced program there and got involved with some people who were coming in on a daily basis from Malcolm X College. We were being taught by, believe it or not, Black Panthers, radical leftists, and those are the people who were influencing me to get on the academic track—do positive things, contribute to the community. They said the uplift of our community is going to be contingent upon you empowering yourself with the academic tools that are necessary to be able to take positions for us. We had to contest the establishment if we wanted to move up in the world.

I graduated from high school and did general labor jobs in Chicago. But after that, there came a period of time that I allowed myself to become stagnated, in the mid-'70s—not working, just moving around here and there. I wasn't doing what I should have been doing to make myself the kind of person that I was capable of making myself. That was the time I was arrested.

WELL, WE GOT THE FINGERPRINTS

On October 30, 1979, a white grocer named Mickey Cohen was shot and killed at his convenience store on the South Side of Chicago. The man who fired the shots had previously asked for Kool-Aid and had browsed around the store. After the shooting, the killer went through Cohen's pockets and took at least $100 from the cash register before leaving through the front door. Three regular customers witnessed the murder, and described the murderer as an African American man dressed in black. The three witnesses also noticed that the assailant touched various items with his bare hands. Police arrived, secured the scene, interviewed the witnesses and dusted for fingerprints.

Thirty-six hours after the crime occurred I was on the North Side of Chicago helping a friend move. We took a break from the move, and went to get something to eat and shoot a game of pool. On our way home to my friend's residence we were stopped by the Chicago police on an unrelated matter—guns pointed at us and everything. There was an armed robbery that happened on the North Side. Somebody, at least the police were saying this, wrote my brother's license plate down. I was using his car. We went to the police station and got that cleared up.

Chicago Police has a bulletin they circulate every single day about different criminal activity. So they had an illustration of the guy wanted for the robbery and murder [of Cohen].

They first focused on my friend and asked him what his address was. Now, we knew from our encounters with the police that you limit your conversation with the police because anything you say can and will be used against you—you know, the whole Miranda thing. So he gave them an address. His address was a North Side address, far away from where the crime occurred. Then they shifted to me. I had a South Side address which was in close proximity to where the murder occurred. Lo and behold, they started concentrating on me.

They took me from the police department to the South Side headquarters, Area 2. Area 2 is infamous for its brutality and torture. Police induce suspects to confess to crimes they didn't commit. As we were driving to Area 2, they tried to get information. They said, "Well, we got the fingerprints." The guy who robbed the store had handled some items and so there were fingerprints. They were trying to goad me into confessing. They said, "Oh, we have fingerprints."

The police did have a set of fingerprints from the items that witnesses said the assailant touched, but the fingerprint examiner assigned to

THE LIMITS OF MEMORY
Faulty identifications can lead to wrongful convictions

The leading cause of wrongful conviction is misidentification by an eyewitness. In a study of exoneration cases between 1989 and 2003, 64 percent involved misidentification by an eyewitness.

Sometimes this misidentification is intentional: the suspect is being framed. But this accounts for only about 20 percent of misidentification incidents. Much more commonly, an eyewitness simply makes a mistake. And it's a mistake with extremely serious consequences. Evidence suggests that eyewitness testimony is one of the critical determinants in jurors' decisions.

A variety of factors can affect an eyewitness's accuracy. A perpetrator's weapon can distract a witness; this so-called "weapon focus" can create a dramatic dip in the accuracy of recall. A witness's mental state during the crime may also affect accuracy. Drugs, alcohol, and mental illness can all contribute to memory distortion. In fact, memory distortion can even be caused by something as simple as poor weather conditions.

The stress felt during a crime can also erode recall accuracy. Research suggests that whenever the threat of violence is high, only 30 percent of victims make a correct identification in a live lineup (as opposed to 62 percent of a low-stress control group). In a photo lineup, the differences may be even more dramatic: in one study, only 32 percent of a high-stress group made the correct identification versus 88 percent of a low-stress group.

Additionally, the faculty of memory is itself highly malleable. Verbal suggestion can initiate false memories, and memories can become scrambled when a witness attempts to reconstruct an event.

Certain police procedures also contribute to misidentifications. Eyewitnesses are often shown a "six-pack" of mug shots—six photos grouped on a single page. But when confronted with a six-pack, witnesses have been shown to use a "relative judgment" strategy: picking the photo that most closely resembles their memory of the perpetrator. Often, witnesses are not even told that the perpetrator's face may not be among the photographs they are shown.

Another police procedure that can contribute to eyewitness inaccuracy is the "show up," in which police present the witness with only one suspect. Albert Johnson was thus "identified" by a rape victim from a moving police car. After spending a decade in prison, he was exonerated in 2003

continued on page 122

the case could not match them to James Newsome. At the time, the Chicago Police Department stored prints on paper cards.

At Area 2, a Chicago police station on the South Side known for extracting confessions by using physical abuse and torture, two witnesses looked through a mugshot book and picked photographs of someone else—not Newsome.

An officer thought Newsome resembled the composite sketch of the suspect. Newsome was then put into a live lineup and the eyewitnesses identified him as the man who shot Mickey Cohen. One of the eyewitnesses, Anthony Rounds—who became a key witness on Newsome's behalf in his 2001 civil trial—testified that when he was placed in front of the police lineup, he was told by officers to "Pick number three." Newsome was number three.

When I got back to the headquarters after the lineup, I was informed by the police, "You might as well confess to the crime." They drove me to an alley on the way to another police station to try to scare me. The officers said, "We know you committed the crime, you'd better admit to it." When we got to the station they officially informed me that I've been identified. I said, "You've got to be crazy, this is another trick." The state's attorney comes in and I didn't give any statement. I was taken back to the North Side, where they transported me to Cook County Jail, where I remained for almost a year and a half through trial and sentencing.

AN ALL-WHITE JURY FROM SUBURBIA

At my trial, when I started to understand how potential jury members could be struck from the jury pool, I knew that I could end up with an all-white jury. I understood what that meant for me. I grew up in an era when segregation was so prominent that

on the basis of DNA.

Race also figures prominently in cases of eyewitness misidentification. According to the U.S. Justice Department, less than 10 percent of rapes are of white women by black men. However, of the 120 rape exonerations studied by the Justice Department, 45 percent involved misidentification of black men by white women.

Jennifer Thompson, a white woman, misidentified Ronald Cotton in 1985. She had studied her African American attacker closely during the assault with the intention of identifying him later. With police, she produced a composite sketch which she said matched a photo of Cotton. She then picked Cotton out of a lineup. "I picked out Ronald because, subconsciously, he resembled the photo, which resembled the composite, which resembled the attacker," Thompson says.

As a result of her identification, Cotton received a lifetime sentence. After more than a year in jail, Cotton was retried when an appeals court ruled that evidence of another rape that occurred just after Thompson's should have been allowed in the first trial. In Cotton's second trial, Thompson was presented with the actual rapist, Bobby Poole, whom she did not recognize. She identified Cotton again and sent him back to prison to serve a life sentence.

Eleven years after Cotton's conviction, analysis of DNA evidence confirmed that Poole was the rapist. After Cotton was exonerated, he and Thompson reconciled and became friends. Thompson has since become an outspoken critic of the death penalty and the dangers of misidentification. To this day, when she closes her eyes, it is Cotton's face that Thompson sees as the rapist.

Ronald Cotton

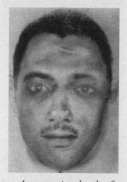

A composite sketch of Thompson's rapist

Thompson's rapist Bobby Poole

I understood about the misunderstandings that any culture can have for another. I understood that white people wouldn't grasp the significance of the concept "innocent until proven guilty." People believe that when you sit at the defense table, you're guilty.

I ended having an all-white jury from suburbia. They can definitely convince an all-white jury that a black man killed a white. All you gotta do is say it. That's the naiveté of maybe eight out of twelve jurors. "He wouldn't be sitting there if he wasn't guilty. They must have something against him."

The prosecutor did such a good job in my case that when he got through closing arguments, I said to myself, "I'm guilty." He did that good of a job. They can manipulate, they can manufacture evidence, they can fabricate it so well that you can almost believe that you're guilty yourself.

An innocent person always holds out hope that the system will work. That's the naiveté. You're brought up that way, looking at *Dragnet* and all these law enforcement programs on TV. You're induced to believe that the good guy always prevails. That's a bunch of bullshit. The good guy ends up last.

My lawyer was a private attorney by the name of William Wise. I didn't know anything about the law, so I'm thinking I'm getting good representation. Hindsight tells me that I wasn't. He didn't do any investigation whatsoever. If he had done any basic, rudimentary investigation, I wouldn't have been found guilty. There's no two ways about that.

The bottom line that I learned well from this situation is that you don't have to play dirty, but you can't be a passive person in these kinds of fights. You have to be aggressive, you have to fight hard, you have to play tit for tat. That's why some attorneys, like the Cochrans, they go to the edge; that's how they win. A lot of people don't know how well-resourced the district attorneys are. They have the citizen's money to work with.

RACE MATTERS

Whiter juries create racial bias in verdicts and sentencing

More than two-thirds of exonerees in the United States come from racial or ethnic minorities. Out of 328 exonerations between 1989 and 2003, 55 percent were black and 13 percent were Hispanic. Many of these exonerees were convicted by juries that were either all or mostly white. Whether conscious or unconscious, race can affect both an individual juror's perceptions and the selection of jurors itself.

Just as defense lawyers want a jury sympathetic to their client, prosecutors want one inclined to convict the defendant. Prosecutors are not allowed to reject jurors on the basis of race; a prosecutor must be able to provide a "race neutral" reason for any rejection to stand. But this offers only a weak protection against racism. In 1999, when Jessie Hoffman, an African American man, was tried for the murder of a white woman, all three prospective black jurors were summarily rejected. One woman was dismissed on the supposedly "race neutral" grounds that her body language was "inappropriate for someone who is a decisive individual."

Once the jury is actually selected, a juror's racial biases can be triggered by both the defendant's race and the victim's race. These biases seem to be strongest when the jury itself is racially uniform. In capital cases with a black defendant and a white victim, the presence of at least one black man alone on a mostly white jury appears to reduce the likelihood of a death penalty verdict anywhere from 36 percent to 70 percent.

Thus, for an innocent defendant of minority descent, simply being tried before an all-white jury can become a critical determinant of the outcome of his trial.

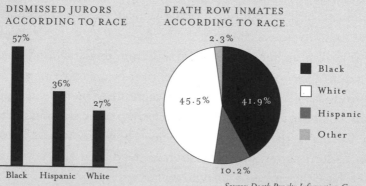

DISMISSED JURORS
ACCORDING TO RACE

57%

36%

27%

Black   Hispanic   White

DEATH ROW INMATES
ACCORDING TO RACE

2.3%

45.5%   41.9%

10.2%

■ Black
□ White
■ Hispanic
■ Other

Source: Death Penalty Information Center

I was out-resourced. My attorney was an asshole. He was trying to save overhead. He didn't want to spend any money. My
family was poor. My family gave him $15,000. What we paid
him was a lot of money for us. My uncle got a second mortgage
on his building because I was facing capital murder.

I was sentenced to life, which is the flip side of the death sentence. Death row people get a little more attention, a little more
scrutiny, but I didn't want to take that chance. It's a big gamble.
Through the grace of God, I didn't get it. I was sentenced to die
in prison.

*In September 1980, Newsome was convicted of murder and armed
robbery. His conviction was based on the testimony of three eyewitnesses who had previously identified people other than Newsome as
Cohen's murderer.*

GOD GOT MY ATTENTION

I was an ordinary kid growing up. Well, I can't say I was ordinary,
coming out of a one-parent home. At the age of ten my mother
and father separated, but I had a life. It wasn't a terrible one, but
it wasn't hunky-dory either.

I could've been anything I wanted to be. I could have been
mayor of the city of Chicago. I really believe that. There are so
many opportunities for people who have the support systems
around them that cultivates them, that finance them, that allow
them to understand what's available and what they can seize
upon if they applied their abilities and their talents in the right
way. And I just didn't have a lot of that. It's not that my mother
didn't want me to have those things, but because her tireless
effort to support three kids made it difficult for her to fund any
of the things that could've been available for me.

That anger was there from the very beginning—when I was convicted, when I was arrested. But I was able to temper the anger, and use it again in a way so it didn't allow me to become eaten up inside. Some people sit in jail or in prison for years and years and maintain their innocence, and do nothing about it. And they get angry with the system, they get angry with their families, they get angry with other forces that have nothing to do with them being there. People have to take responsibility for their own actions.

I can say to this very day that I made a contribution to my own wrongful incarceration. If I had an education, if I had the intellectual prowess, it would've never happened to me because I would've known how to deal with that situation in a way that would have prevented the Chicago Police Department from fabricating the case against me. When you work from the disadvantage of being intellectually powerless, being academically powerless, people do what they will with you.

You know what, my incarceration wasn't by mistake. God doesn't make mistakes. God doesn't have puppets. He gives us the will to choose. I made some bad choices. I wasn't involved in the killing, but I was in the wrong place at the wrong time and God got my attention. I was a Christian and baptized, but I wasn't perfect. God got my attention.

I ATE BOOKS

The shock of my being incarcerated—I'd already overcome that in the county jail. I was doing the best I could to get access to the law library in the county jail, but I couldn't. It was a dormant time—soap operas and just sitting around chewing the fat and deteriorating intellectually, academically, because you don't have a lot of material to read. You're just sitting around all day, not really doing anything to challenge yourself. And physically, you don't get enough exercise. You become weakened all over.

I overcame the shock. I knew I had to do something within myself to correct this injustice. I took a hard look at myself. What did I need to do to prepare myself, to get the kind of audience I needed and deserved? I had to prepare myself academically to be able to talk and write well. I did that once I got to prison. In prison I went back to school.

I immediately started working on myself just for my general education. I hadn't finished high school, and I did that. Immediately after that I did a college program; I got my bachelor's degree in legal education administration from Northeastern Illinois University. I worked in an accelerated program in prison where I completed my college work in less time than I would have on the street. And after that I did a master's degree in political injustice studies from Governors State University, and I completed that when I got out of prison.

I read anything I could get my hands on. I ate books. My study was anywhere I could open a book. My headquarters, where I spent the majority of my time in prison, was the prison library, where I was a jailhouse lawyer. In between the job responsibilities I had in the prison library—where I helped other prisoners with their legal concerns like writing and filing pleadings—I would squeeze in my academic studies. I intertwined both of those programs, working in the prison library thirteen or fourteen hours a day, along with my independent studies.

Because of my zeal to improve myself academically, people who came to tour the prison and the prison library would learn about me. I would be the spokesperson for the library, giving them an overview of the operations. People liked my spiel, and they would, out of curiosity, ask about me. I was different than everybody else. I wasn't trying to make myself different, I just *was*

IN-HOUSE LEGAL EXPERTISE
Jailhouse lawyers exchange legal services for protection

A jailhouse lawyer is an incarcerated person who provides legal services to others. Sometimes called a 'writ lawyer' due to the number of petitions they write for the writ of habeas corpus, jailhouse lawyers are usually, but not always, self-taught. Typically, jailhouse lawyers trade their services for small sums of cash or items such as cigarettes and postal stamps.

Gloria Killian

In the United States, every prison is required by law to provide legal materials for those inmates seeking redress through the courts. However, an inmate's right to provide legal assistance to others wasn't recognized until a landmark U.S. Supreme Court ruling in 1969.

In *Johnson v. Avery*, the Supreme Court ruled that the right of an inmate to assist another with litigation is inherent in the First Amendment. Johnson, a prisoner in Tennessee, was disciplined for helping other prisoners prepare writs. The Supreme Court asserted that "unless and until the State provides some reasonable alternative to assist inmates… it may not validly enforce a regulation… barring inmates from furnishing such assistance to others." Thus the rights of the jailhouse lawyer were legally recognized.

It is a position of importance within prison society, often held by the wrongfully convicted whose only source of reliable legal help may come from themselves. Jailhouse lawyers, often also the prison librarians, assist other inmates not only in cases of exonerations and prison-related abuse, but also in private issues of a civil nature.

Gloria Killian, a California woman wrongfully convicted for a robbery and murder in 1981, served as a jailhouse lawyer throughout her sixteen years in prison. Fellow inmates have compared her to Johnnie Cochran. In the case of Brenda Arris, a battered woman who killed her husband, Killian wrote thousands of letters and was instrumental in Arris's eventual grant of clemency and release.

"People treated me differently," said Killian, who was two years into law school when she was incarcerated. "They'd know if they got in trouble, I could help them… When I came back to the yard, there was this whole new level of respect for me."

different. They would look at me as someone who stood out, someone who didn't belong here. "What is he doing imprisoned?"

I guess it made me feel good. But I never wanted to be separated from the other guys in prison, in terms of wanting myself to stand out. Of course I did, though, because I was an intellectual and a lot of the other guys weren't. You gotta remember the setting we were in: prison. You have murderers, thieves, kidnappers who probably haven't cracked a book since the second or third grade. They were raised up in some bad conditions and lived under some very threatening circumstances, so academics was not one of the things they were ever considering to be a part of their life.

Newsome and his mother at the Stateville Correctional Center in the late 1980s

With a life sentence I'm disempowered from being able to effectively challenge the authorities who had put me in prison for something I didn't do. I didn't have the intellectual equipment. That intellectual equipment is not necessarily the books, but the information that allows me the confidence and gives me the strength to be able to articulate my position better than any other lawyer can ever do.

Once I started strengthening myself academically with my liberal arts education, I knew how to put an effective written package together to make a statement about my wrongful incarceration. I knew that I was going to have to fend for myself. After your direct appeals, you're on your own, so I knew that if I didn't know how to read or write well, if I didn't know how to speak well, I wasn't gonna be able to communicate to those who I wanted to enlist to help me.

Lawyers probably hear from thousands of guys every day who say, "I'm wronged." How does James Newsome make himself different from the other guys who make that same statement? I made myself different by making my story more intriguing. I'd practice my case all the time, in front of the mirror, in my cell, walking back and forth in my cell by myself. I was going to be my best representative.

I had to use the lawyer, because I knew I wasn't gonna be respected no matter how articulate, how knowledgeable I had become. No matter how seasoned I could have appeared, I was gonna be approached as a litigant. I don't want to say that everything has to have some hidden agenda, but with respect to the profession that a lot of people hold so dear, the profession of law, they would say, "Who is this smartass son of a gun who would think he can tell me what *sua sponte* means or *mens rea*,"—all the Latin terms and the nuances about the law, and all the procedural tricks, understanding procedural standards better than them. As somebody who's been sent to prison, who's never had a formal legal education, just being able to have an intelligent legal exchange with judges and lawyers makes them irate.

But I did have a legal education. Mine was in that prison law library where lawyers were coming down every week training us, giving us seminars. Sometimes we would have six-month seminars with lawyers who had an interest in educating us and training us, giving us an understanding about criminal, civil, and constitutional procedures.

My audience was much more critical than any audience you can get in any old class where the professor is standing you up and embarrassing you in front of the whole class, asking you Socratic questions. I've been grilled worse than that by some of the hardest critics, by some of the toughest intellects imaginable. Those are the guys I knew in prison. Everybody in prison is not

dumb. People think everybody in prison is stupid or intellectually inferior. I know some giants in prison, some intellectual
powerhouses in prison. They eat books, they know everything.
Cicero, John Locke, Thomas Aquinas—just name them and they
can tell you everything from head to toe about these people.

ARE YOU SITTING DOWN?

*Before digital technology became widely available, fingerprints col-
lected at crime scenes were typically compared only with those of
known suspects. In the mid-1980s, law enforcement agencies began
employing electronic systems, such as the Automated Fingerprint
Identification System, which allowed fingerprints to be compared
with thousands of potential matches. As this technology became
available in Chicago, Newsome actively campaigned to have unidentified fingerprints from Cohen's murder checked against the
Chicago Police Department database.*

*Police ran the prints through their database in 1989. The prints
matched a man named Dennis Emerson, who was already serving a
life sentence for murder. Police did not reveal this information until
1994, when Newsome's lawyers obtained a court order requiring the
Chicago Police Department to run the fingerprints again.*

It was my intellectual empowerment that got me out. That's not
a brag, that's a fact. As I became stronger intellectually from a
legal standpoint, I became unrelenting in the positions I took in
terms of missing or implausible evidence like the fingerprints.
The fingerprints were what exonerated me.

Automated Fingerprint Identification Systems (AFIS) came
into Chicago in 1986-87. There were six thousand prints in the
Chicago Police Department, and in order to have them fully
loaded into the computer system, it was going to take some time.

SCHOOL'S OUT

The once-thriving prison education system has been gutted

In 1993, the Federal Bureau of Prisons (FBOP) and all forty-three state departments of corrections granted associate's degrees. Fifteen states conferred bachelor's degrees, nine states and the FBOP conferred master's degrees, and pre-release prisoners in Indiana, Maryland, Massachusetts, and the FBOP could even earn Ph.D.s.

Inmates attend class in the South Dakota Women's Prison

Many of these higher-education programs flourished in part due to funding from Pell Grants, instituted in 1972 to help low-income individuals, incarcerated or not, pay for tertiary education.

There are many known benefits of correctional education, including improved disciplinary records, diminished parole revocation rates, and higher employment rates after release. But the most significant benefit is the strong correlation between schooling in prison and reductions in re-incarceration, or recidivism. Indeed, many of the studies conducted on this phenomenon find that recidivism rates are cut by more than half when a prisoner commits to a program of education.

However, in the early 1990s, politicians began denouncing what they called "country club" prisons. And thus, the Violent Crime and Law Enforcement Act was passed in September 1994. "No basic grant," the act states, "shall be awarded under this subpart to any individual who is incarcerated in any federal or state penal institution." The clause essentially eliminated bachelor's and master's degree programs for prisoners.

By 1995, 342 of the 350 prison college programs in the United States prison system had been eliminated, including those in the Illinois prisons where James Newsome earned his two degrees in legal education administration and political injustice studies. The average exoneree emerges after twelve or more years of incarceration with the equivalent of an eleventh-grade education and ill-equipped to compete in the employment marketplace.

I solicited the man who was in charge of AFIS at the Chicago Police Department with a letter. He was initially willing to run the fingerprints because he was excited about this new technology and, of course, also because there was the possibility that there was an innocent man in prison. But, once it was discovered that he was doing this, the state's attorney told him to stop. The state's attorney didn't want to go further with the AFIS investigation because it would impugn the integrity of that office.

Years later, those fingerprints were finally loaded in. The fingerprint examiner did it on his own as a courtesy to Chris Scott, a law student who worked at Chicago–Kent College of Law.

Chris Scott subscribed to my theory, about me being innocent, but also about being able to use AFIS to get me exonerated. She believed that could happen. She was able to convince the Chicago Police Department to run those fingerprints, and lo and behold we were able to get a hit.

My attorney called me right away. I was in Cook County Jail. I was back there to have a hearing on my post-conviction petition. My attorney called to the jail and he asked the guards to tell me to call him. I figured it was one of these routine bad news things.

He said, "Are you sitting down?"

I said, "What do you want, Richard?"

He said, "Are you sitting down?"

I said, "No, I'm standing up talking to you on the phone."

He said, "We found the guy."

I said, "What guy did you find?"

He said, "We found the guy who committed the crime."

I said, "You did? What?"

It got really quiet.

And I said, "Are you sure?"

He said, "I'm positive."

This is at five minutes to five. Then the five o'clock news comes on and my picture pops up on the news. It was the lead story. Before you know it, my attorney was down at the jail. The story had blown up. They didn't know what to do. They were trying to figure something out in terms of tailoring the right kind of petition or writ they needed to get me out of there. Richard came down and asked me because I'd been a jailhouse lawyer. He said, "What do we do?" I said, "Richard, I think it's a habeas corpus. But we need to go in front of the chief judge because it's just too big."

On December 6, 1994—fifteen years, two months, and four days after Newsome was arrested—Thomas Fitzgerald, a Cook County circuit judge, ordered Newsome released from jail and restricted him to home-monitoring while prosecutors decided if they wanted to retry him.

At the court, media was everywhere: NBC, *Good Morning America*. They got into a fist-fight. The courtroom was packed. The story was in every newspaper in Chicago. The judge was under a lot of scrutiny to do the right thing.

A state's attorney was trying to contest my release. He said, "We would like time to investigate this, can you give us thirty days?"

The judge said, "Yes, but I'm not giving you thirty days with Mr. Newsome in jail."

The judge said, "I'm gonna let you go home, but I want you to be on home-monitoring for thirty days."

I said, "Your honor, I'd like to be able to go to church."

He said, "James, I'm letting you out of jail. Don't be asking for nothing."

I WROTE *YOU*, I WROTE *YOU*, I WROTE *YOU*

The sheriff took me out. I wasn't excited at all. I was angry. It came, but it came too late. It came at a time when they had taken a lot of my life. Almost all of my twenties, every year of my thirties—how do you give that back to me?

It wasn't like I was having a birthday party. One thing about being in prison and being a wrongfully incarcerated person—and understanding that things can be taken away from you so quickly—is that you take one step at a time and you don't believe it until it actually happens. And because of the way I was put in, because of the mistrust I had for the system, anything could have happened. That's not to say I'm paranoid. I have trust for things, people and systems and bureaucracies, things like that. I'm the kind of person who believes that the benefit of the doubt should be given to a person. I'm just really more grounded, more humble in my approach. I don't jump up and down about things. This life is a short one. Prison has given me a perspective I probably wouldn't have gained anywhere else. I like to have fun, I like to smile and laugh, I like to joke around. My not getting overly jubilant about my release was because of how bad I was treated with respect to them not letting me out the first day, the first year, the second year. The evidence never changed. The facts were always there.

I took the long route home because I hadn't seen the trees in a long time. When I got to my mother's block, they had the whole block blocked off. There were like a hundred newspeople on my mother's porch and in between was my mother. She grabbed me. I went into the living room downstairs and I went to the dining room area and I went to the head of the table with the news media, cameras clicking. I said to them, "You know what, it's a shame." I pointed all over the living room. I said,

"I wrote *you*, I wrote *you*, I wrote *you*. Fifteen years you didn't respond, didn't give me the time of day. You all don't even deserve an interview." Every time I gave an interview, I always admonished them. I said, "Don't dismiss people so easily. Give people the benefit of the doubt."

I became a vegetarian in prison. I've been a vegetarian for like twenty-four years now. One thing about prison is you want to stay as healthy as possible because you don't get good medical care. So you don't want to ingest a whole lot of garbage. I told my mother, "I want spaghetti and cornbread." It tasted all right.

After Newsome spent thirty-days on home-monitoring, the prosecutor decided not to retry the case, and Newsome was officially released from custody on January 5, 1995. On July 14, 1995, Illinois Governor Jim Edgar granted Newsome a full pardon.

I WAS FRACTURED

People always ask me, "Were you angry? Are you still bitter?" I can be angry, but not bitter. I have defined bitterness as a consuming hostility that can stagnate you. Anger can be a fuel that ignites you. Anger allows you to catapult. Anger allows you to springboard into action. Anger can allow you to turn a negative into a positive. Anger can allow you to say, "Listen, I'll retaliate by doing what's right." Anger can make you a success. But one thing it won't do, for me at least, is allow me to go back where I was before. It can serve as a positive emotional energy that will move me in the direction that I need to go in, all because of the fifteen years that I lost, that I will never be able to recapture. And because of that I am able to see a little further, I'm able to enjoy a little more because I allowed my anger to become a positive force in my life.

You know, it's kind of strange when you're incarcerated and you come out. What made me most happy? The ability to choose whatever I wanted to do, whenever I wanted to do it. Eat whatever I wanted to. Walk wherever I wanted to. Drive. Just having the choice to enjoy some of the basic freedoms.

I lived with my mother for five months after I got out of prison. My family was totally supportive. They did everything they could to try to make me whole. I was fractured.

One thing about being incarcerated is that if you're gone for a long period of time, you'll never be completely the same again. It becomes even more difficult for someone who's been jerked around the way I was.

I was not lonely when I got out. Hell no. I was smothered. There's some people who come out and don't have any family. They've been locked up twenty years and their families died off and splintered and they don't have nobody to help them, to help to restore them. We need to have a process or system by which these guys can go to a program or project so that when they are restored to the free community they're able to address some of their immediate concerns—the clothing, the housing issues, the medical issues, the therapeutic issues, even relationship issues. These guys have been without mates or spouses or whatever, for a period of time. Guys need to be reoriented on how to cultivate that kind of relationship.

What a person needs is some independence. He needs some resources, but he needs to be able to fend for himself.

NOTHING'S BEEN EASY

The easiest part? Nothing's been easy. There's nothing that can prepare you for transition of getting out of prison. You just want out. The preparation for me personally was understanding that if

I wanted to be gainfully employed, if I wanted to make a life for myself, I had to concentrate on education and academics, and that's what allowed me to make myself a little more attractive than most who come out. I didn't have to work cooking fried chicken or something like that. And that's not to denigrate people who have to do that, but I knew when I was in prison that this was a period of preparation for me. Not just for me getting out, but just for getting myself confident in terms of who I was and who I wanted to be.

Did I feel different after I got out of prison? Yes, I felt different. I felt more confident, much more assured. I felt more directed. I was no longer directionless. I knew where I wanted to go, I knew where I was going, and I knew that if I allowed myself to be embraced by the right people, that there were so many opportunities out there waiting for me. All I had to do was pick and choose as I pleased.

I just want to be happy. I just want to be happy. I just want to be happy. I want to be a contributor. What do I want my legacy to be? I think it's important that we add something to this life. So somebody can build on what is left.

DISPOSABLE PEOPLE

Does law enforcement frighten me? No, they should be frightened of me. I'm empowered now. Police have an exaggerated sense of who they are. They have this authority that they believe allows them to do whatever they want to. They become almost despotic.

The people coming out of prison who have been wrongly incarcerated—it's because law enforcement committed some malfeasance. They exceeded their authority. That includes the prosecutors, the Chicago Police Department, or the various law enforcement authorities throughout the United States.

The police will never investigate themselves. We have to understand how police come to do what they do. It's an indoctrination that has been in place for eons that permits them to believe that what they're doing is right.

I don't want to sound like some kind of extremist when I say this, but the prison-industrial complex is about a continuation of what has been going on for years and years, for decades, for centuries or more. It's about enslaving people.

Prisons are places where some people—I'm clear evidence of this—where some people shouldn't be. If the right thing was done, the i's were dotted and the t's crossed, I shouldn't have been there. The police didn't care. I was disposable, I was expendable. They didn't care—African American, they didn't care. They don't care about the Paul Terrys, the Michael Evans, the Anthony Porters, the James Newsomes, the Ford Heights Four. They don't care about them, you know why? Because all of them are of African American descent. It's sad.

It's important for us to understand the phenomenon from that perspective. If we just look at wrongful incarcerations as being just some guys that somebody made a mistake about, that's wrong.

FOOD AND RAIMENT

Illinois law allows for compensation of up to $140,350 for wrongful imprisonment of more than fourteen years. In 1997, two years after Newsome was released from prison, he received all $140,350 from a compensation claim with the state of Illinois.

Though state officials are generally immune from civil action, in October 2001, a federal jury found that two of the five Chicago homicide detectives involved in Newsome's case framed him by coach-

ing the eyewitness.

Attorney Philip Beck, who was on President Bush's legal team in the battle for Florida's electoral votes, represented Newsome.

In 2003, Newsome received a multimillion dollar award from the same federal jury. The verdict came after less than two hours of deliberation following Newsome's testimony concerning how he survived fifteen years in state prison. Newsome was awarded $1 million for each year he was wrongfully incarcerated. To date, this is the largest award based on a wrongful conviction. The vast majority of exonerees receive no financial compensation following their release.

Let me put it bluntly: Money doesn't change me. I'm only a temporary custodian of all that I have. I learned something in church today, and First Timothy, Chapter Six, Verse Seven. This was so poignant, it hits the nail right on the head. It says, "For we brought nothing into this world and it is certain that we can carry nothing out. And having food and raiment, let us therefore be content." In other words, this money ain't changed me. It doesn't belong to me. I'm a temporary custodian of what God allowed me to have for the moment that I'm here. I'm satisfied with being able to have food on my table and a roof over my head. All the other stuff is a plus.

Money is supposed to immediately change you. What it has done is made other people uncomfortable. People believe that you should be able to do a little bit more for them. It becomes obligatory for you to do more for them. The check that the city of Chicago awarded me, and the state of Illinois gave me—you know what it said on my check? "James Newsome." I didn't see anybody else's name on the check.

Some people are interacting with me because of the money. They've never had any money, and all of a sudden they become financial experts. "Well, you should do this, you should do that.

Newsome talks to a class in Chicago shortly after his release (1994)

Can you loan me this, can you loan me that?" No. They don't
have any money; now what they want to do is manage me out
of mine.

I'm very protective of this money. I've extended myself to my
family and my friends. I bonded a guy out for $20,000. But one
of my friends expected me to give him $300,000. Those are the
challenges. You know Biggie Smalls? He did a rap record that
said, "More money, more problems." He was absolutely right.

I should have taken this money and run away, gone to live
somewhere like Aruba or Hawaii. Before I got the money, I did-
n't even have this many bills. Now I have State Farm, I have
umbrella protection, I have car protection, I have condo protection. I have a house on the South Side me and my sister bought.
I have some beautiful things, but you won't see me looking like
one of those rap stars on TV with gold hanging around their
necks, and a gold tooth, and five or six rings on my fingers.
I don't need that.

After I got out of prison, women were writing to me from

their prison cells from all over saying, "Do you have a girlfriend? I'm available." I'm like, "I'm sure you are. You're in prison." I was sensitive to the women writing me from prison because I knew what the loneliness was. People are deprived for a long time, you know, and that also requires some understanding.

That deprivation can have an effect on you psychologically. People think that guy's gonna come out like a sexual animal. You know what? Sex is the farthest thing from a guy's mind. Of course he wants to have a healthy sexual relationship, but I'm gonna tell you after a couple of encounters you're not even concerned about that. They do something to a person during that period of time psychologically, unbeknownst to the person who is affected, who's been victimized. Your interest in sex goes away. People think that guys can make up for fifteen, twenty years—it's not even like that, it's not. It's sad because you can really jeopardize a good relationship with somebody who has a sexual appetite, a healthy sexual appetite, and they don't understand why you don't have the same.

Your body has been trained to suppress that urge. Your libido is not operating in the same way. I asked myself this question over and over: "Is there some therapy that's necessary to invoke that passion?" I don't think so. Is there something else that can be done to ignite the desire? I don't know, and I should be able to have an answer to that. But I don't think a doctor has an answer. You know why? Because they have never been in that position before to really understand it. And so many people talk about the wrongful incarceration phenomenon, and all of the dynamics attended to it, but they don't really understand it.

This is something that really needs to be discussed. All women who are in relationships with wrongfully incarcerated men are suffering as a result. They are either gonna want a divorce, to separate, or going to want to cheat. I don't care how well you attempt to communicate it to them, they just don't understand. And then some guys are really reticent, and don't know how to communicate. They want to, but just don't know how.

I want a relationship. I want a good, wholesome relationship. I want to share this money with someone. I really do.

LET'S PUT OUR CARDS ON THE TABLE

In March 2003, Newsome began working for the Center on Wrongful Convictions at Northwestern University, as director of community services, a position that allows him to speak to students and community members about his wrongful conviction.

This is therapeutic, it is. Talking about it, educating people. I'm the expert. I understand what happens to people from here on out after they get out of prison. I want to be of value to those who want to help those coming out of wrongful incarceration situations. You can come out of that situation looking for some kind of vengeance, or some kind of retribution. But you have to move on. This is a short life.

Wrongfully convicted people, as disjointed as they may be, have some value in terms of being able to impart that experience. When we talk about a person who's been wrongfully incarcerated we're talking about a person tortured—tortured mentally, tortured physically. I had to exist in a cell for twenty-four hours a day when I was on lockdown, when we had that ninety-degree weather in July and August. There was no relief. I couldn't go out into the yard and get under a shade tree or walk up and down the gallery to cool myself. I had to actually stay in a cell. That's torture.

You know what? I tend to talk to black folks differently than I do to whites. Don't we all do that in terms of our ethnicity in some regards? Do we understand each other? Let's put our cards on the table. I'll communicate things with black people that I wouldn't communicate with whites. There's always this initial barrier. When I come to a black person there's no barrier, they'll know exactly where I'm coming from.

The hard part is educating people. I do a lot of seminars. I present to a lot of schools. It surprises me how wide-eyed people get. You're talking about Northwestern, one of these elite universities. These kids haven't been exposed to anything. They've been raised in cocoons, closed societies. They don't understand what goes on in the inner cities.

How do you suppose you feel when you've been wrongfully incarcerated, and everybody in the courtroom that has been part of that process has been white? And then you have somebody coming to you after you get out from being wrongfully incarcerated, and saying, "Listen, I understand you." They don't.

This is the first time I really have an opportunity to talk candidly about the differences in understanding with respect to the cultural divide. Basically, a hundred percent of people who are helping people get out are whites, and the people who are getting out are blacks. We don't see anything wrong with that? I see a problem. One of the things that I have attempted to do, with some resistance, is to try to get Northwestern to enlist African American professionals so that they can communicate as best they could the concerns of those who have been wrongfully incarcerated.

The criminal justice system is not perfect. There are going to be mistakes made. And when you have mistakes, you have cracks. And people are going to fall through the cracks. We need people who can resurrect those who have fallen.

Newsome in his Chicago shoe store Heelz (2005.)

GOD DOESN'T MAKE MISTAKES

I just wish I could have those fifteen years back. It's not like I'm over the hill or anything, but I just wish I could get the time back. But *with* the money, I need the money. If I had to have one or the other, I don't know how to answer that. You know what, God doesn't make mistakes. He wanted me to go through this.

I just opened a high-end women's shoe store called Heelz. Women probably have more shoes than anything else. I know women love shoes. I know women.

The store is elegant. I have high heels—what I describe as some of the finest luxury Italian footwear around—with refined casual footwear. It's a high-end salon with glass fixtures. It has a white runway floor that leads to a transaction counter. You have two glass display cases that suspend from the ceiling in the front windows. It's beautiful.

At this time in my life, I no longer have to operate under the dictates of somebody who's telling me when to report to them and when I can go. I write my own checks, I call my own shots, and I follow my own instructions.

What does freedom feel like? These days I'm waking up in the morning at five-thirty or six o'clock, going to the salon— we're ordering our spring line now, and we're on the phones all day trying to get the best products we can into the store so we can get young ladies to buy shoes.

Can I say I really made it? Yes.

Calvin Willis

THANK GOD FOR DNA

NAME: Calvin Willis · **BORN:** 1958 · **HOMETOWN:** Shreveport, Louisiana
CONVICTED OF: Aggravated rape · **SENTENCE:** Life
SERVED: 22 years · **RELEASED:** 2003

In 1982, Calvin Willis was convicted of the rape and assault of a young girl, and was sentenced to life in prison. His story is told in three sections. In the first, Willis speaks about his life before and after his wrongful incarceration. In the second, Janet Gregory, a former paralegal who worked on Willis's case, describes the process of his exoneration by DNA evidence. In the third, Hugo Holland, Assistant District Attorney of Caddo Parish, Louisiana, expresses his doubts about Willis's actual innocence. The name of the victim has been changed.

CALVIN WILLIS:
NOTHING WENT RIGHT THAT NIGHT

My grandparents, they adopted me when I was three years old. My mother had been killed and they took me in. They brought me here [to Shreveport, Louisiana] and they raised me as an only child. They gave me things that my mother at the time wasn't able to give me. They made sure I attended school. They made sure I didn't do without. It was a blessing to have that.

I had reached the tender age of my teens when I met my wife. We went through some hard times, ups and downs in the relationship, but the main thing was that we stayed together until I finally decided to pop the question. She said yes and we got married the day before her birthday: April 4, 1981. From April up until June, things were going pretty good for us as a young couple. June the ninth was when tragedy struck.

My wife was pregnant with my son. My daughter was three years old. That night, after getting off work, I had forgotten that me and my wife was supposed to spend that night together. I had made other arrangements with a friend of mine—I was supposed to introduce him to a lady friend. My wife got upset. She said, "You mean we were supposed to spend this night together and you're going out?" She went on and on. She wasn't the easiest person to get along with, being pregnant and all. She set me a curfew. She said, "If you're not back by twelve, I'm gonna put the night latch on."

Nothing went right that night. First of all, the lady I was supposed to introduce my friend Jerome to, she wasn't home. Next, we stopped at a liquor store, bought a thing of Crown Royal. We left there and we went to a club called the Glass Hat. It was ladies night. There was four ladies sitting at the table. When the waitress came up and asked us if we wanted anything to drink, we said no. She went up and told the bartender we weren't drinking.

The waitress asked Willis and his friend to leave the Glass Hat because they weren't ordering drinks. Later, they went to a club called Little Joe and Strouds.

We came back in this neighborhood and they had a little club on Garden Street at the time. We parked in front of the club and Jerome said, "I can't go in there. They put me out." I said, "Why they put you out?" He said, "I was smoking weed." I said, "I'm gonna go in and see how it looks." So I went in and everything was looking okay. Two ladies called my name. I said, "Y'all want something to drink? Go get your cups and come back out."

A police car pulled up and said, "Oh, y'all have to leave the premises."

It was time to go. One of the first stops we stopped at was [at the house of] Jackie McGee. She didn't want to go out with me because I had my partner with me, but she said, "If you drop him and come back, I'll know you love me."

So anyway, when I dropped Jerome off, I thought about what she had told me. I'm supposed to make a right to go home, but I make a left to go to Jackie's. When I get about two blocks down, I think about my wife, pregnant. I'm supposed to be there, spending time with her, and I'm going to another lady's house. So I went home. I get home and she opens the door and me and her spend the rest of the night together.

The next day, I got off work. I had a friend bring me here to my grandmother's house. When I come through she was at the kitchen sink washing dishes. She turned around and looked at me and said, "What have you gotten yourself into?" I said, "Nothing. Why?" "Two police officers were by here looking for you," she said, "concerning something on Perrin Street." I said, "Okay, I'm gonna walk around and I'll find out and let you know."

I [walked] around. I said, "Man, what went on around here?" Laurine['s] daughter had got raped. It happened at Maxine's house. I said, "What this got to do with me?"

On June 9, 1981, an intruder broke into a home in Shreveport, Louisiana, where three girls—ages seven, nine and ten—were asleep. The intruder assaulted and raped the ten-year-old girl. The mother of the two younger girls was not home at the time of the rape and had left the ten-year-old, a neighbor's daughter, in charge.

The next morning, the younger girls' mother came home to find the victim balled up in pain in the living room. She called the police. The police officers who responded to the call testified that the victim was incoherent and did not provide an intelligible description of the assailant.

The victim was taken to the hospital, where a rape kit, including vaginal swabs and fingernail scrapings, was collected. The police collected the panties and nightgown the victim was wearing, as well as a bedspread and a pair of men's size-forty boxer shorts found on the couch where the victim had been sleeping. The boxer shorts had not been there before the crime and the girls' mother did not recognize them. The victim told police that her rapist had a beard. Willis did not.

I BELIEVED IN THE SYSTEM

That [next] morning when I got up, it was a feeling that I can't really describe. I was like going through the motions. It was like something was going to happen, but I didn't know what it was. I got dressed, I left the house, got in the car, I drove maybe a few blocks down, I turn around, come back in the house, taking my pants off. My wife was laying in bed. She said, "What you doing?" So I made love to her, and the lovemaking between me and herself, it was like I was saying goodbye. It was like for the last time.

I had quit my job and was going to take a test for a truck driving license. So that day I went on down to take the test. The lady said, "You passed all the written tests, you'll be eligible for the driving test the following Monday." Now I feel good. I feel like I'll be able to do some things for my family. I come out and City Hall is right across the street and I said, "I'm gonna go in and put this behind me now."

I go to the desk, and I said, "My name is Calvin Willis. Why are you all looking for me?" He said, "We're not looking for you." I said, "You're not? Well fine, thank you." This detective, he must have had cameras in his office or something, because he comes running out saying, "Mr. Willis, Mr. Willis, Mr. Willis." He named a few names I didn't recognize. Then he named Maxine Jones. I said, "I know Maxine Jones. I been over there."

That's when he told me, "You're wanted for the aggravated rape of Paula Jacobs."

Calvin Willis was arrested on June 12, 1981. He was charged with the aggravated rape of a child.

They took me to Northwestern Criminal Labs, they plucked pubic hair, took blood.

I believed in the system, that it would be corrected. I didn't believe the system had flaws. My lawyer had told me to go before a judge alone [instead of a jury trial]. Because of the age of the child, he said. Nesib Nader was the attorney that had charged my people $700 to represent me, and when he came in the room where I was, he had his briefcase, where he had a manila folder, where he pulled two or three pieces of paper that he had typed something on. Even I had the sense enough to know that getting ready to go to trial, you should have way more paper than that.

The prosecution at Willis's trial presented eyewitness testimony from the victim, and blood typing results from semen found at the crime scene. The source of the semen was blood type O, which matched

Willis, along with approximately 50 percent of the U.S. African American population. Both Willis and his wife testified at trial that they had spent the night and morning of the murder together. Nonetheless, in February 1982, Willis was convicted of aggravated rape. On May 17 of that year he was sentenced to life in prison without the possibility of parole.

I was found guilty. The judge asked me to come to the bench when I come back for sentencing. He asked me, "Is there anything you'd like to say?" I said, "No, except that I'm innocent." He sentenced me to life in a Louisiana State Penitentiary without the benefit of parole.

GOD PUTS YOU IN A POSITION

On the way to Angola [prison] I was, like, tripping. I've always had this closeness with God. At maybe nine or ten years old, I was given a dream. Little did I know it was more like a vision of Angola, and it stuck with me, all through my teen years. If I were to do something wrong, it would always be in the back of my mind, you know.

On the bus ride going to Angola—it's like 18,000 acres, and the view of everything that was coming into focus reminded me of the dream. It was like living a déjà vu. You know, I've been here before. I said, "Man, don't they have a dam around here or something or a big brick wall?" And they said, "Yeah, over by the river." And I said, "And they got some homes and things around here, too, right?" And they have brick homes. So I'm seeing all this shit. Then when I got into the main prison, I went to walk around the yard and there it was, you know, the same dream. I'm like "Damn," you know? How could this be? You know, it was just, it was surreal.

I was scared. Fear is just like a direct hit of the head. It awakens you. Your senses, you become so keen, and you tune in on a lot of things. It can make you or break you. So either you going to be a man or you lose your mind—and everything else that belongs to you.

The first thing you see is a classification man. He says, "Who do you want to contact in case of an emergency?" Well, there was nobody to put on my list except my grandparents, you know, my grandparents and my children.

They only let you have so much stuff. Man, I had like five bags of letters [accumulated while in the Caddo Parish jail] and I only could bring two of them. They trashed the rest. If you got some like important business and stuff stuck up in there, you got some court papers or something, it's gone. I kept letters from my wife. They were like Dear John letters. She was leaving me. She needed to get a house and the people wouldn't give her the loan with her having my name and us being still married. You're already mad when you go into the joint, and here she comes—*bam!* Hits you with this shit.

God puts you in a position. Okay, you're in the streets, you can run whichever way you wish to run, you drinking, smoking, and chasing women, and He says, "Okay, boy, I better slow you down 'cause you ain't listening. You a hard head." So [prison] takes you and puts you in a position where you're locked down, and you can't go out, and you can't rip and run, and you ain't got no smokes, and you ain't got no drink and all that, so you've got to slow yourself down.

Then you sitting in your cell, all quiet, everything, and you start to think about things. You start to think about things that you missed. I missed everything. Shit, my woman. I missed being able to get up and go to the refrigerator, and go the bathroom—use the bathroom privately.

When I first got to Angola it was like the street. When I got
on the big yard, you got guys pumping iron, big old He-Men
type dudes. Cats all playing basketball. Dudes standing up
against the wall with long beards, like something out of a
Hollywood movie. You really have to grow up yourself. It could
really, literally scare you to death. I think if I hadn't had some
experience being raised in the ghetto and getting out into the
streets and mingling with the hustling life, it would have been
that much more difficult for me to adjust.

The homosexual thing there was wide open. When I walked
around the yard, I would see these grown men dressed like
women lying on towels, with these hot pants on. Like real
women. I kid you not. It was a trip. But I've always been the type
of person to have that understanding of other people and what
they going through. Most important is minding your own business and letting other people mind their own business. That's
what really helped me to survive.

When I would try to talk to someone, I would say, "Man,
I don't belong here. I didn't commit this crime." They were like,
"Oh, I heard this so much." You could see the look on their face.
A lot of free people that I would talk to would say, "Man, what
you doing here?" I say, "Would you believe that you have people
in here who are innocent?" They would say, "Man, I hear that
from everybody."

Being innocent and being in prison, that's a hard pill to
swallow. You've got to have an inner energy to push you forward
and make you hunger, searching for different avenues and ways
to get out of that place. You know, as a human being you're used
to being free. No human being supposed to be locked up, and
that was horrible, that was horrifying, being locked up, caged in.

'START TAKING YOUR DRIVING TEST'

There was just things happening in my case. The judge sentenced me and two weeks after he sentenced me, he goes to New Orleans, and they said he died in a motel room doing push-ups, from a heart attack. Nesib Nader [Willis's first attorney] was taken to court on twenty-seven counts of hustling people out of money to represent them and found guilty on seventeen counts. So he was disbarred. Stacey Freeman [the attorney who represented Calvin at trial] was killed in a car accident. When my grandfather was living, he hired Graves Thomas in 1983 to represent me. After he started filing [the appeal], that's when he went out on a boat. He went to the end of the boat and raised up both his hands and said, "Here I am Lord. Take me!" and lightning hit him in the top of the head and come out through his toes. He was killed.

Everything that these lawyers filed in the court was denied. Nothing, it seemed, could strike their interest enough to bring me back on a hearing.

In 1996, I was conversing with another inmate, and at the end of the conversation, another inmate called my name. He called me by my nickname, "Big Hands." He said, "Big Hands, I heard you rapping with the brother. I got an address I'm gonna send you. Write these people. When you write them, don't sweat it. They gonna get back to you." That's when I got the address of Mr. Barry Scheck and the Innocence Project.

In 1999 I got a phone call from Janet [Gregory, a.k.a. Prissy, a paralegal for Calvin's deceased lawyer Graves Thomas]. The Innocence Project had taken the case, made the case a top-priority case. They requested that they [the court] release the evidence.

The DA is saying now maybe I didn't leave behind evidence.

THE PRICE OF PROOF

The high cost of DNA testing prolongs the exoneration process

The DNA tests that led to Bruce Godshalk's exoneration cost $10,000. He paid for them with money he inherited from his mother, who died while he was in prison. After thirteen years in prison, Anthony Michael Green was exonerated in 2001—but only after his father borrowed $3,000 from his retirement account to pay for DNA tests. Innocence projects that represented both men were unable to fund DNA testing.

Anthony Michael Green and his family after a $3,000 DNA test set him free (2001)

The cost of DNA tests depends on who is performing the tests, the type of test, and how many samples need to be examined. State labs may charge a few thousand dollars to perform tests. But when evidence is old, improperly stored, or of minuscule quantity, private DNA labs—which perform painstaking procedures to find and analyze testable DNA— can charge as much as $15,000 for just one set of samples. Often destitute after years of legal fees, the wrongfully convicted may have to wait years to raise enough money to test the sample that eventually exonerates them. Many innocence projects can now afford DNA testing costs.

After thirteen years in prison, Calvin Edward Washington didn't pay a cent for the DNA tests that exonerated him. His tests were paid for by the state of Texas. As of 2001, Texas law requires the state to pay for DNA tests if it believes the results might lead to an exoneration. Many other states, including California, have similar postconviction DNA testing laws. However, these states will only pay for such tests when the court is convinced that they will provide conclusive proof of innocence.

Obstinate prosecutors who tried cases before the availability of DNA technology often argue that the results of a DNA test will be irrelevant even if the results do not match the convicted defendant's DNA. It is not uncommon for prosecutors to fight for years against postconviction DNA testing. Only with the intervention of a judge does DNA evidence find its way into the process of overturning a wrongful conviction.

But he used that evidence to send me to prison. He's saying that this same evidence that you used to send me to prison, now this evidence can't free me?

In 1999, the Caddo Parish DA agreed to release DNA evidence from the rape kit and boxer shorts for testing. Four years later, after Gregory and others raised $14,000 to have the evidence tested, Willis was excluded as the source of the semen and fingernail scrapings from the rape kit. He was released from prison on September 19, 2003.

From 1999, it wasn't until 2003 that I got a phone call. The guard said, "Willis, you got to call your attorney." I called and Janet say, "Start taking your driving test." I said, "What you mean start taking my driving test? I work in a cell block."

She said, "They found fingernail scrapings and the fingernail scrapings match the undershorts and that's not you. You're coming home!" She said, "Aren't you happy? You don't sound happy." I said, "I be happy when I get on the other side of that fence."

September 18th, on a Thursday, of 2003. She [Vanessa, an Innocence Project lawyer] said, "Calvin, they're going to bring you down to Caddo Parish and release you." She said, "Tuesday you got to be in New Orleans to speak at a press conference." I'm like, Tuesday I got to be in New Orleans to speak at a press conference: maybe they're serious. But I still can't let go. I still can't feel the joy.

They came and got me that night. They brought me all the way back to Caddo. I'm like shackled. I'm like laying back on the bench in the back of the van. They stopped and got them something to eat, something to drink. Didn't get me a thing. They got to the Caddo Parish courthouse. When they pulled up there, the first thing I see is this little white lady, Janet. And the cameras, they rolling and everything.

The lady asked me, "Do you have a change of clothes?" I said, "No ma'am." They brought me in a jumpsuit. She goes and comes back and dumps out some clothes. She dumps out a box with tennis shoes. I looking at the clothes. I looking at her and said, "Ma'am, I've been locked up twenty-two years, I don't know how to pick no clothes. Could you pick something out for me?" She laughed and she picked out an outfit and said, "This looks nice." I went in the back and I changed. New socks, new drawers, new T-shirt, new shirt, new tennis shoes. Everything brand-spanking-new. She said, "You look nice." I said, "I feel strange."

I had prayed. I had asked God to renew my mind and put it on my tongue that when I speak, I speak with a level of intelligence and not ignorance, because this was the way that they look at you as being an ex-con. You supposed to be animalistic, you supposed to be vicious. You know, they stigmatize you.

I saw my father, I saw my kids, I saw my grandmother, I saw Prissy, I saw the media, I saw friends. The media asked me, they said, "Mr. Willis, it has been twenty-two years you've been confined. How does that feel? We know that you're angry."

I looked up at the sky. I had a big smile on my face, and I said to God, "What you gone done?" I didn't feel angry. All those people I had planned to reject because they didn't show support towards me, I didn't feel angry.

I said, "You know I'd be lying if I said I wasn't angry when I was there, but anger stagnates a person's growth, I can't allow that to defeat my purpose." My father, he said, "Come on, I'll take you to the store." This was a person who I had planned on being nowhere around. He looked at me and said, "It feel good, don't it?" I looked at him and I said, "Yeah, Dad." That's the first time I ever called him Dad.

He took me to the store and I passed beer and all that and I got an Orange Crush. He said, "Give it to the lady." I said,

"What you mean give it to the lady?" He said, "She's got to scan it." I said, "Scan it, what's that?"

When I got home, they give a little barbecue, a fish fry. I had a telephone call from Vanessa, from New York. They passed me this little bitty thing. I said, "What is this?" They say, "It's a cell phone." It was a happy occasion. That went on for like two or three days. It was one of the happiest moments of my life.

It had been so long since I'd been outside and seen the stars and hills that when I got out and it was nighttime, it scared the hell out of me. Seeing the stars, man, I was like a little kid looking up into the sky.

. The old bed, it was so soft. I was like, "Man, I can't do this, I been sleeping on a hard bunk for twenty-two years." Man, this bed just sucked me up. I slept, but it was totally different.

PAYING THE PENALTY TWICE

I love my grandmother. She's been on her own for a long time. I left home at about seventeen. I was always used to being out on my own. I'm forty-five years old and, really, I feel like I should be on my own. In time I will be, but I want to make sure she's comfortable. In prison I prayed for this, to be able to do some things for her. I think one of her biggest things she wants is to see her house fixed up. I did the two bedrooms. We put new sheetrock up and I painted and got new furniture.

I want to be a professional barber. In prison, I took that to the heart, making people look good. I like to make designs. I like to cut. I like the feeling that you get when you know I'm giving you a good job. You have to like what you're doing.

I haven't looked for a job at all. I've been going to school because I have to get a GED. I haven't wanted a job because I want some time to myself. I didn't want the pressure of being

THE COST OF LOST TIME

Compensation for exonerees varies widely across states

After his release, Kevin Green fared better than most exonerees. California Assemblyman Scott R. Baugh authored a bill specifically designed to compensate Green for his sixteen years in prison. In October 1999, California Governor Gray Davis signed a check awarding Green $620,000. Most exonerees receive no compensation at all.

As of September 2005, only nineteen states had compensation laws. Many of the states that do have such laws have recently adopted them, in response to increased numbers of DNA exonerations. According to Adele Bernhard, a Pace University Law School professor and a leading expert in compensation legislation, even in states with compensation laws, a fraction of exonerees receives payment for wrongful convictions.

Most compensation legislation is neither generous nor easily attained. As of March 2005, Wisconsin offered the least in the way of compensation, at $5,000 per year of wrongful incarceration and a cap of $25,000. California is more generous, at $100 per day or $36,500 per year. In contrast, New York's compensation law specifies neither an annual amount nor a limit. Awards are individualized, reflecting not only the number of years incarcerated but the damages incurred by the wrongfully convicted.

For the exonerated in states with compensation laws, it is not easy to get the money the state is obligated to provide. In California, out of thirty-four claims for compensation filed from 2000 to 2005, only five have been granted, according to the California Victim Compensation and Government Claims Board. Exonerees must, in effect, re-prove their innocence to be paid by the state, and they are not always successful.

In 2003 in California, U.S. District Court Judge Claudia Wilken reversed the convictions of Antoine Goff and John Tennison. After this ruling, San Francisco District Attorney Terence Hallinan signed a court agreement declaring Goff and Tennison's innocence. But the attorney general's office continued to regard Goff and Tennison as guilty.

"Factual innocence doesn't mean you didn't do it," says Deputy Attorney General Michael Farrell. "What it means is that there is no reasonable cause to believe you did it. You might have done it, but there is no evidence [that you did]." In December 2004, California's Victim Compensation and Government Claims Board sided with the attorney general and denied compensation to Goff and Tennison.

"It's really irrational," says Linda Starr, legal director of the Northern California Innocence Project. "The prosecutor and the judge think they're

continued on page 162

Willis and his grandmother, Neralvil Newton (2004)

watched over or being told what to do. After all those years of working under the man for so long, I just didn't need that.

You would be surprised at how many people don't know what exoneration is. The thing of it is that you've been to prison. You've been exposed. Being free is one thing, but you've also experienced being around the criminalistic environment. That right there is like you been contaminated. The most important thing to an ex-con is that he don't be victimized once he's in society. That's like paying the penalty twice.

There is no amount of money they could give me to replace twenty years of my life. I think if they were going to give me anything, they should set me up straight, so I could live comfortable for the rest of my life. I don't think they should come to me and try to give me $25,000, $50,000. Maybe if they gave me $30 million or $50 million.

I missed my kids' childhoods. I always wanted to be a father to them. When I left here, my grandmother, she was strong. Now she's bent over, she's frail. They can't give that back. I missed all

innocent. Why would the board think differently?"

Any admission of guilt, even when false, can make the wrongfully convicted ineligible for compensation. In Iowa, Ohio, Oklahoma, Texas, Virginia, and Washington D.C., if an exoneree has pled guilty, he or she is automatically ineligible. In California, New Jersey, Washington D.C., West Virginia, and Wisconsin, a finding that an exoneree "contributed to arrest or conviction," disqualifies them. This includes false confessions, one of the leading causes of wrongful convictions.

In states without compensation laws, exonerees can either try to persuade the state government to pass an individual compensation bill, or file a civil suit.

Both alternatives present formidable challenges. To get an individual compensation bill passed, an exoneree must find a legislator to champion his or her cause. Bernhard notes that it is often not in legislators' political interest to support compensation for the exonerated, lest they be perceived as soft on crime.

Civil suits in wrongful conviction cases are often extremely expensive and difficult to win, primarily because claimants must show willful or negligent misconduct on the part of police or prosecutors. Law enforcement officials are generally protected from civil suits to protect against frivolous lawsuits that could paralyze law enforcement. In most cases, convictions are based on faulty procedures or mistakes, leaving no opportunity for the wrongfully convicted to pursue monetary compensation through civil litigation. "Somebody gets raped, she doesn't see who it is, and she identifies the wrong person," says Bernhard. "Once that happens, the police have an obligation to arrest that person. And more often that not, he will be convicted. Who's he going to sue?"

In a rare instance of a successful civil suit, James Newsome sued the City of Chicago in 2003 and won $15 million—the most ever awarded in a wrongful imprisonment case. The results of John Lee Duval's civil suits, though, are more typical. Duval was wrongfully convicted of murder in 1973. Both he and his co-defendant claimed they had confessed only after being beaten by the police. After twenty years of maintaining his innocence in prison, Duval admitted guilt and expressed remorse for committing the crime in hopes of being granted parole. It was nonetheless denied.

When a critical witness recanted his testimony, Duval's conviction was overturned and he was released in 1999. He then sued both the city of Rochester and the state of New York for wrongful imprisonment. But because of his statements to the parole board, Duval lost both suits and received nothing for the twenty-six years he served in prison.

See Appendix C for a chart of compensation laws

of that. I wouldn't be going through the things I'm going through right now if it wasn't for the tragedy that they put into my life. So I can't set a limit on how much they should give me. I think it's sad for them to not even have compensation here in Louisiana. If you do wrong, then you stand up and be man enough to admit what you did.

Prison has a way of defining realness. When people say that they're your friend or they say blood is thicker than water, it really tells the truth, how far they're willing to go. My grandfather, he died in 1987, he said, "When I'm gone you're going to actually find out that a lot of them don't mean you no good." He was the backbone of the family. When he died everybody went every which way. When I was in prison my grandmother was there, and Janet Gregory. They were the only two friends I had.

Coming in contact with my inner spirit helped me to realize that there is a God. I've seen people hang themselves. I've seen people commit suicide by cutting themselves. I've seen people take overdoses. I've seen people lose their sanity. That weakness, it may be strange to say, but I gained strength from it. I kept telling myself over and over again that that couldn't be me. I'm not a very religious person, but I think God accepts the way that I communicate with Him. Because I talk to Him regular, when I'm alone. Sometimes I talk to Him like he's my bosom buddy. One time I talked to Him, I said, "God, I don't know what I've done in life to deserve this. But whatever it is, man, I'm sorry. If you could see fit to lift this burden and just let me know what you want me to do, man, I'll do it. If you don't do it for me, do it for my grandmother." Thank God for DNA.

JANET GREGORY:
I WILL GO TO MY GRAVE TRYING
TO PROVE HE DID NOT DO THIS

Janet Gregory, known also as Prissy, was the impetus behind Willis's exoneration. As a paralegal working for Willis's lawyer, Graves Thomas, she became familiar with the details of the case and befriended Willis. When Thomas was struck dead by lightning, Prissy fought for Willis through several unsuccessful appeals. Finally, in 2001, she raised enough money to test the DNA evidence that would eventually exonerate Willis.

I did not meet Calvin until years after I got involved in the case. I worked for a man named Graves Thomas, who got Calvin's case on postconviction. And, for some reason, it was kinda Graves's albatross. You know, we could never quite get things to gel and get together. And in 1987, he was struck and killed by lightning. When I left [the practice], there were two people I just couldn't leave. One was Calvin, and another man, who was executed in 1988—so there's nothing more I could do for him.

The first time I met Calvin was actually in 1987, when his grandfather died, and I had them bring Calvin up here for the family day at the funeral home. He didn't know me from Adam, and he was shackled. I literally ran up to him in the funeral home and grabbed him.

I guess [Calvin] Jr was about five, Keesha about eight, and we were in the lobby of the funeral home, and I remember telling them, "You're going to hear some terrible things about your dad," I said, "but I want you to know he did not do it, and I will go to my grave trying to prove he did not do this."

It was clear that he had just absolutely been railroaded. Just reading the trial transcript, it was enough. That, and meeting his grandparents, who were two of the finest people I know. I knew that they raised him from age three or four, but they raised him up and they did a good job, and it was just clear from the evidence that he didn't do it.

How do you lay your head down at night and go to sleep when you believe with all your heart and soul that this man is not guilty? I never understood why no one else was willing to step up to the plate. When Graves died, all the nonpaying cases, which were the postconviction cases, got kinda put in a hat. Well, a good friend of Graves's got the case and for two or three years, never did anything. Then I talked one of her former law partners into filing something, and he wasn't experienced enough, and we weren't successful. I don't know why we never got success through the courts.

We went through so many years of going up and down the ladders of the appellate courts and such, and in 1994 we first discovered the DNA testing. I said to Calvin, "Sit down and look at me and tell me you want this done because this is it, this is the end of the road." And he didn't hesitate. So then I started going about trying to figure out how we're going to do this. I'd been protecting the evidence over the years. So I started calling labs.

Then Calvin, I guess in 1998, sent me a form he had gotten from an inmate who had told him about the Innocence Project. It took a little while to hear from 'em and then we did; at that time they did not have the kind of funding they do today. In the beginning of spring of '99, they said, "Yeah, this is a go. But we need money."

I asked everybody. I asked the prosecutor, I asked the man who prosecuted him. I called him—'cause he's a private practice lawyer—and I said, "Carey, remember about twenty years ago you prosecuted a guy, Calvin Willis on life charges?" And he said, "Yeah, I do. We have some evidence problems there." And I went,

"Duh, yeah you do, so give me some money." But he didn't.

I wrote the lab a check for a thousand dollars. I'm a poor person. My husband died in 2001. And when he died, I had this huge feature article because these musicians were doing a benefit to help me raise money for the funeral. How embarrassing.

I was able to raise a little over $6,000. We had one contribution from a black person, other than my mother's housekeeper who gave three dollars because that's what she had. She got a thank-you note just like everybody else did, but I was really disappointed in the lack of support in the black community here for Calvin. I contacted the NAACP, the Black Lawyers Association: "Give me fifteen minutes of your lunch, if nothing else." Got nothing.

This is like five years of waiting. It must have been March of 2003 when they finally did say that Dr. Blake had finished his testing. And that the fingernail scrapings and the semen found on the underwear definitely excluded Calvin. So, at that point we knew. And then it just seemed to drag on and on and on and on and on. And you know, I have my opinions about why, and other people have their opinions about why and I know that that was probably the longest five months of Calvin's whole time.

I've been on this like for twenty years. And over the years there were many times when I just wanted to say, "I don't know Calvin Willis, no I won't accept a phone call, I can't talk to his grandmother, not again," because I felt powerless, I felt so helpless. And I was all they had. You know, I was it. And it's a burden. He's always saying, "I owe you this, I owe you that, my whole life." No, all I ever wanted was the gratification of walking through those prison doors with Calvin, and I got that.

September the 16th was the second anniversary of my husband's death, and I had gone to dinner with his mother and sister. And I thought, "My God, I can't bear this. Why am I putting myself through this?" It just wasn't a good day. But when I got home I had a message from Vanessa Potkin, who's a staff attorney at the Innocence Project. And she said that Calvin was going to be released.

He was released on a Friday, the 19th. I was not going to let him walk out in an orange jumpsuit. It wasn't going to happen. I went out with my plastic, because I hadn't worked in almost a year, and bought him white clothes. *The Today Show* had sent a camera crew over from Dallas. And, of course, his family and friends and his daughter had balloons. And his grandmother, who can hardly walk around anymore, was there, and it was just unreal. And his son Calvin Jr. had a friend working [in the prison], and she was keeping him posted. So we hear over the loudspeaker, she's telling him, "Calvin, he's coming out now." I could see him coming in the van, and I'm running across the yard. Waving at him.

Calvin did a great job of saying the things that he needed to say, and then he got a little upset when he started thinking about his grandfather dying, and the things he's lost: his wife, and his children's young lives, and so forth. 'Cause his son was in the womb when he went to jail; his daughter was three.

And then on the way back, his dad had stopped at a little grocery for him to buy something to drink. He got him an Orange Crush. And he paid for it, and he started to walk out the door, and they said, no, no, you've got to scan that. He didn't have a clue. He could've caught a charge, just by simply not knowing what a scanner was. About a week later, his grandmother called and he was fixing to wash his underwear in the toilet. He had already washed the shoestrings, which is what he's done for twenty-two years.

The day after he got out—I go to church on Saturdays because I'm far too lazy to get up on Sundays—and he went with me, he and his daughter, to that service. At the time I was doing the ushering thing, the reception welcome committee or whatever. I didn't do it that night, but the lady that's the head of it spoke to us across church: "How y'all doing? Saw y'all on TV." The next week she stopped me. She said, "Can I talk to you a minute?" And I said, "Sure." And she said, "I know you don't know this, but I'm a rape victim." And I remember her case. She got raped two weeks after getting married. But she said, "When I saw you with him, I knew that I still had this fear." Because he had been convicted of rape. She said, "I've got to get out of my little box."

I don't know what's going to happen to Calvin now. What we're dealing with is a forty-five-year-old adolescent. He was twenty-two, barely nothing, when he went to prison. So whatever ego he's developing is just totally eradicated. He hasn't been able to make a decision. Not whether he can go to the bathroom, not whether he can eat. Not anything. He's been treated like an animal, or worse—it's just horrifying. So he's got a lot of learning. He's a very intelligent man. He's not well-educated, but he's very intelligent. He read the Bible and, I believe, the Koran. He stopped eating pork. I had to lie to him recently when he had Bacon Bits on his salad. I go, "That's not really bacon, it's fake bacon." He'd started eating it. I didn't want him to panic.

He still lives one street over from where the rape occurred. I don't know if they have a lot of the same neighbors. It's kind of a transient neighborhood. A lot of them that are there, they do remember Calvin, but from what I can understand from talking to different people, nobody ever believed that Calvin did that.

It would be the comedy of errors if it wasn't so tragic.

The district attorney's office has yet to admit that this [DNA evidence] has exonerated him. They have said publicly that they cannot solve the crime. I can't imagine a bigger slap in the face. They had gone onto TV saying that this does not mean by any means he was exonerated, he could've done it, dada-dada-da, they could never solve the crime.

In the paper, they had one of the local barber shops, which is what Calvin wants to do. One of the barbers made a statement about so many black males going to prison, which is true. They said, "The one thing is, you can take the man out of prison, but you can't take the prisoner out of the man." Well, with that kind of attitude, what are we supposed to do?

And then this unwillingness of people to even want to recognize the need for him to be compensated. If he went out on our state highway and got hurt, they would give him hundreds of thousands of dollars. We as a community need to take care of our own. We need to hold him up for as long as he needs to be held.

This is society's debt. It's our problem. We need to fix it.

HUGO HOLLAND
THE DEVIL IS ALWAYS IN THE DETAILS

Hugo Holland is an assistant district attorney in Caddo Parish, Louisiana. Though he agreed to release the evidence that exonerated Willis, and would agree that he is "legally innocent," he does not believe that Willis is factually innocent of the 1981 rape.

I've been doing this a long time. I've been doing this for now fifteen years, as a cop for many years before that. And it is extremely rare, in fact I've never seen somebody to be truly exonerated where you can say, "Holy crap, they didn't do it." And this is not one of those cases. There is a reasonable doubt raised by the new evidence that's come forward, and for that reason, people are released. This is not a technicality that we're talking about in Calvin Willis's case. It's not an exoneration in the sense of, "Holy crap, we got the wrong guy." I don't know who committed this offense. I can't say that it was Calvin, I couldn't prove it in court, but I can't say it's not, either, because there's still some evidence that he's the one that committed the offense.

Let me tell you the perspective that I'm looking at here in Mr. Willis's case. Unlike some cases, where there's been some police  misconduct, or prosecutorial misconduct, there wasn't any of that in Mr. Willis's case. There was no police misconduct. The police investigated everything that they could have. The prosecutor at the time turned over everything to the defense lawyer. This is not one of those Southern-lynching white juries. The first African American elected to the

Hugo Holland

district court bench in Caddo Parish since Reconstruction was the one that decided this case. This defendant, Mr. Willis, decided to waive a jury trial and have a judge try his case. So it was an African American convicting. So there was nothing that the system did wrong here. We just didn't have, you know, DNA available at the time. If the system had done something wrong, then there should be some redress, and Mr. Willis should seek that out in court. But there's none of that here. So in that regard, I don't know exactly what it is the government should or could be doing here. I mean, the system worked like it was supposed to. This is just one of those extremely sad cases where you learn something twenty years down the road, that if you knew at the time, you never would've prosecuted the guy.

The fact is that if this evidence had been available twenty years ago, we still would've wondered whether he did it or not. But the fact that he's legally innocent, factually innocent is something different.

The paralegal [Prissy] that used to work for a local defense attorney that kinda spearheaded the paperwork and whatnot here has always believed that Calvin was innocent. I'm still not convinced that he's factually innocent.

I'm sure that Calvin's grandmother is convinced that he's not guilty. Or innocent, because innocent and not guilty are two different things. I'm sure that Calvin's family thinks that he's innocent. I'm sure that Calvin's friends think he was innocent. I've still got a victim here and two witnesses who're convinced that he is in fact the one who did it. So they and their family are convinced that he was guilty, but they didn't want to go through another trial. I don't see how this is any different, although on a much smaller scale, than something as polarized as the O.J. Simpson case. I'm convinced that O.J. is guilty. Most people are convinced that O.J.'s guilty. There's always gonna be people who say, "Oh no, he didn't do it, the evidence was planted, blah blah blah." It's gonna be the same with any case.

I do believe that if you have somebody who's been convicted, and they're granted a new trial because of new DNA evidence, and they can prove by whatever standard of proof that they're factually innocent, and they've been incarcerated, they should be compensated for that.

I don't see any reason in drawing a distinction with people that're exonerated—which doesn't necessarily mean factually innocent—and somebody that's paid their debt, and is coming out, wants to make something of themselves. They both equally need to be eased back into whatever mainstream they came from, or let's say the mainstream they need to go back into, because a lot of them didn't come from the mainstream to begin with, which is why they wound up in prison.

The devil is always in the details. And it doesn't bother me, the fact that Mr. Scheck is saying, "We've got somebody that didn't do it." That doesn't bother me, because when this was first brought to our attention, and my boss said, you know, you were just getting out of high school when this case came around, but you need to handle this. I looked at it, and I couldn't think of any reason why we wouldn't want to do the testing. This one, I don't want to say it was marginal, but if the evidence would've been any more attenuated, we would've not agreed to the testing. Louisiana, a year or two ago, passed the postconviction DNA legislation. And I wrote it. The DAs in Louisiana have a pretty powerful lobby, and the legislation that we drafted was much much better than what was proposed by the Louisiana Association of Criminal Defense Lawyers.

We didn't want criminal defense lawyers to be able to just willy-nilly test any biological evidence in a case. Because I don't care what the evidence is, a good criminal defense lawyer would always be able to make some sort of claim, whether it's colorable or not, or whether it's specious or not, that their guy needed a new trial based on it. What the criminal defense bar wanted to do: if there's any biological evidence in a case, if it hadn't been tested, they wanted to be able to test it. We opposed it.

The reason that it doesn't bother me that the newspaper puts "exonerated," or that the TV mics say it, or that Calvin Willis's family says it, even though I don't think it's the correct word to use, is the fact that nobody can point to what happened in the system twenty years ago and say, "Something, somebody did something wrong." And nobody can point to my boss or me, or this office, and say we did something wrong—we opposed it, we drug our feet. They just called and said, "Hey, will you release this for testing?" and when I looked at it, I went, "Of course I will." I mean, we always did what we thought the right thing was. So regardless of what anybody says out there, nobody can say that we did the wrong thing. So it doesn't bother me how it's put.

Statistically, it's insignificant when you look at the total number of people convicted; it's not insignificant to the people it happened to or their families. I mean, statistically, you don't have much of a chance dying in an airliner crash, but if you're in one of the damn planes going down, then it doesn't make any difference that it's the safest way to travel.

Several years ago we drafted the legislation so that anybody that believes that testing, additional testing on biological evidence—not any other kind of evidence but biological evidence—is going to help 'em, there's a procedure set up in Louisiana for them to file a simple petition to do it. And those guys sitting in Angola have plenty of time on their hands, I assure you. Let's assume that we've got a case that we don't have any biological evidence. Somebody's convicted on four eyewitnesses. What's to keep an eyewitness from taking money and changing their story? Biological evidence, at least, it's not supposed to be corruptible. I mean, if it's stored properly and all that kinda stuff. So that's why we limit it only to biological evidence.

Once we got the DNA test results back, the first thing I did was go try and find my victim, tell her what was going on, and my witnesses. I wanted to explain to the victim what was going on. She said, "No, you know, my testimony would be the same, I don't want to do it again, but if there's a doubt about it, then y'all need to do what you need to do to make it right."

The testimony of the neighbor, living next door to where this offense took place, who testified that she knew Calvin Willis, knew Calvin Willis's car, and at about the time that the victim said the events took place, this witness said that she saw Calvin Willis's car leaving the area at a high rate of speed. But for that testimony, I don't even know if our office would have gone forward if all we had was what the victim said and the two other kids in the house. It corroborated the things that the kids said. Now, is there an innocent explanation for that? Well, sure there is. I mean, Calvin could've been on the street at that time. But

Calvin told the police that he wasn't. He said that he wasn't in the area at all. So it's either believe her saying, "I know Calvin's car, that's Calvin's car," or believe Calvin when he said he wasn't there. Could there've been another car just like it in the area, and they, the kids, misidentify Calvin, and the offender have a car just like Calvin's? Highly unlikely. Yes, it's possible. But, I mean, criminal prosecutions are based on circumstantial evidence all the time. Everybody did their job in the case: the police found the witnesses, the defense lawyer cross-examined on what he should examine on, and it is what it is.

We don't do live lineups here in Louisiana; it's very rare. The [photo] lineup was introduced into evidence. It's not like it was Calvin, a nun, a duck, and a refrigerator.

If he didn't do this, it's horrible that he spent time in prison, absolutely horrible. But out of thousands and thousands and thousands of people I've personally put in jail, me alone, and out of the tens of thousands, or hundreds of thousands that we got in prison now in Louisiana, there are only a couple cases where this has happened. So statistically, it's insignificant.

There's nothing that needs to get fixed. I've been doing this a long time, I write a lot of legislation—there's nothing that need to be fixed, as far as I know, except for a mechanism to compensate somebody if they can show that they're factually innocent. Now, what standard of proof do they use? I don't know the answer to that.

If you can show that you're factually innocent, and you spent time in prison, then you should be compensated for something. That needs to be addressed. We can't leave it up to courts, we can't leave it up to personal injury lawyers, we can't leave it up to people with an agenda; it's something that needs to be legislated, and it needs to be fair, but it doesn't need to bankrupt the state, particularly when, like in Calvin's case, you can't show that anybody did anything wrong.

This is the most powerful thing in Calvin's favor. It's not the sperm on the shorts. That's not it; I can assure that's not it. Not only was there male sperm on the shorts, there was DNA from this victim, but another female on the shorts. I mean, DNA of three people on the shorts? God knows where those things've been. The absence of forensic evidence means nothing, the presence of forensic evidence means everything. So the absence of Calvin Willis's DNA on the shorts doesn't mean he wasn't wearing the shorts. The most powerful thing is that several of the markers in common with the DNA on the shorts for the unknown male were also common with the DNA under the child's fingernail. Now, we still don't have enough DNA to say who did it, but there were markers in common. That clearly raises a reasonable doubt. There're no two ways about that.

The shorts were a size [forty]. One of Calvin's big defenses at trial was, "I'm not a [forty], I've got a twenty-nine inch waist." Well, apparently, Calvin and his lawyer didn't look very closely at the shorts because they had been sewn up to fit somebody with about a twenty-nine or thirty-inch waist. So that evidence kinda cut both ways, as far as he was concerned. It was clear that somebody had sewn them up where a person that was smaller could wear 'em. Now who ever heard of community underwear, I don't know? Anyway, that's the story with the underwear.

At a criminal jury trial the jury never finds somebody guilty or innocent. You don't ever see the word innocent. The only question at a criminal jury trial is, "Has the state proven this person guilty beyond a reasonable doubt or not?" Juries let people go all the time, figuring that they did it, but that the state hasn't proved it beyond a reasonable doubt. This is one of those cases, where if all this evidence was presented to a jury, a jury would clearly find Calvin Willis not guilty, but I don't know how many you'd get to say, "Oh, I think he didn't do it." You might get some of 'em that says he did, and some of 'em that say, "I don't know, those kids were pretty convincing to me, the neighbor was pretty convincing"—you're going to have a lot of questions about it. So, at least in the Louisiana criminal justice system, you never heard anybody referred to as "innocent."

It's a lot of shades of gray. And, you know, if I'm asked by the legislature—which I will be asked, because there's gonna be legislation that I'm working on right now concerning compensation—I'ma have to say that Calvin Willis is legally innocent, but factually, I don't know, I just can't tell you. I think he might have a hard time, depending on the burden of proof that the legislature establishes showing that he's entitled to compensation. Calvin is a maybe… a, a probably.

In June 2005, Louisiana passed a bill that compensates exonerees $15,000 per year of wrongful incarceration. The maximum amount of money an exoneree can receive is $150,000, which Willis calls "an insult." Willis is in the process of applying for compensation and expects to receive it in early 2006. Between 1989 and 2003, there were fourteen exonerations in Louisiana.

John Stoll

IF A FIVE-YEAR-OLD SAYS
YOU DID IT, YOU DID IT

NAME: John Stoll · **BORN:** 1943 · **HOMETOWN:** Bakersfield, California

CONVICTED OF: Child molestation · **SENTENCE:** 40 Years

SERVED: 19 Years · **RELEASED:** 2004

GOOD TIMES

There was nothing growing like Bakersfield. There was just so much money to be made, my God. I mean, they had houses for miles staked out that they didn't even have carpenters to build. I was in construction. Back then, $28,000 to $30,000 a year is good money, and I was making that every year. I started my own construction company. I had it together. I think I could have retired at fifty-five. I wasn't gonna retire a millionaire or anything, but I was doing okay.

The weekends I didn't have Jed, my son, I usually went fishing with some of the guys or something like that. But on weekends I had Jed, you know, it was just a big get-together. It was usually Donnie and Allen [the sons of Stoll's friends] and Jed and

177

I. They were great kids and they were well behaved.

I bought those little water wings, they're the cutest things in the whole world. Jed thought that was great. One day he went running out, and he's halfway around the pool and he said, "Daddy, watch this." And he took his water wings off and jumped into the pool. I just about shit, man! I ran all the way over there and there he was, just going right along without those water wings. He just decided he didn't need them anymore. Little stuff like that you remember.

We would order pizza and rent movies. The kids would say, "Let's have fright night," so I'd say, "Okay." We'd get all these ridiculously scary movies, and they'd stand there halfway through not even watching it because they were scared shitless. You know, kids love to get scared. Jed would look back at me every once in a while, his eyes all big, just to make sure I was still there.

Jed and I had a great time. [Stoll was divorced from Jed's mother, but they shared custody.] I treated him with respect, I talked to him like a man. I never goo-gooed him and gaa-gaaed him, and for a five-year-old he had a heck of a vocabulary because I talked to him like a little man. That's what I called him, "Little Man."

I remember one day my friend and I were in the kitchen and all the kids were outside. Jed comes running in, gives me a big hug, and says, "I love you, Daddy," and runs back out. My friend said, "Wow, wasn't that cool!" I said, "Yeah, wasn't that neat?" He just thought all of the sudden, "Hey, Dad's in there," and he came in and gave me a hug and then went back out to play.

There was nothing but good times and love between me and my son. And then boom.

WITCH-HUNT TIME

Eleven-thirty at night, a knock on the door. The next thing I know the lights to the bedroom are on and there's two people standing at the foot of my bed. Plainclothes, both of them, but they said they were police and they had their badges hanging, you know, and guns.

"Get up. Get up and get dressed."

They took me out and sat me down at the dining room table, and the search warrant was lying there, and Dave and Bonnie, the people that lived with me, were sitting over here. I had no idea what was going on, so I read the search warrant, and it said, "pornographic pictures, videos." I'm going, "What in the hell are they looking for?"

So what do you think at eleven-thirty at night when you get this search warrant? I didn't know. I'm still going, "What in the hell is going on?" I didn't know. I know it sounds strange now, but I never thought, "Oh, here they are to arrest me for child molestation." I mean, it's the farthest thing from your mind. You're not thinking about that, or if you are, you're in trouble. I never, ever expected that. I didn't know anything about it until I went into that interview room and he told me that my son accused me of molesting him.

Two cops in the bedroom eventually come out and said, "C'mon," and we walked out of the house. They take me right out the door, in a pair of cutoff jeans and a T-shirt. That was it. I never again saw my home, I never again saw any of my belongings, I never saw my son, except in court. I still had no idea what was going on. They're saying, "Well, we just need to straighten a few things out here. C'mon, get in the car."

I said, "What's this all about?" They said, "We'll talk about it when we get there." So I just shut up. I just sat there and my heart was racing and my mind was just trying to find some logic in this and it wasn't grasping a thing.

All of a sudden they walk me through [the police station] doors, *bang* and *slam,* and "Sit here." They leave me in a room with a table and two chairs. I'm just sitting there dumfounded. I don't know what's going on. I've sat there maybe a half an hour. There you are, you're in jail, you're scared, you're terrified. What in the world is going on? And then one of the police officers came in and said, "Your son said you molested him."

I said, "What? This is insane, you're crazy." You know, "Give me a polygraph." You do all that, but they're just laughing at you. No matter what you say, you're arrested, you're not going anywhere.

Please let me pass this along to anyone who may read this: shut up when you get arrested. I answered all their questions. I said, "No, no, no, no. I didn't do it. I don't know what you're talking about. That's bullshit. You're lying." They just kept saying, "Jed called you a molester." On and on it went.

That was it. Now I'm booked and fingerprinted and I'm standing there ready to go up to the floor. It's like eight or nine the next morning.

Now I'm going, "Oh my god almighty." But then you start to go, "Well wait a minute, I didn't do this. It'll be okay. This will get straightened out." Because you've got to let yourself know you'll be all right even though you know you're lying. And you just start lying to yourself, you say, "It's okay, everything will be all right. Don't worry." But I was just petrified, I didn't know what the hell was going on. I'm in a holding tank, and I remember I was standing at the bars and there's two cops standing over there.

"What's he in here for?"

"He's a two-eighty-eighter."

Well, I didn't know what the hell that meant. I found out

later that was a child molester. It grew into a ring, a big ring. Some of [my friends] were smart enough to just leave town and I don't blame them. I don't blame a single soul for taking off. You know I would have liked to have them there, standing outside saying he didn't do it. Marching with signs. A lot of them were scared and took off and I don't blame them. I don't blame them a bit.

[Later I saw] my friend Margie Grafton. She just looks like something terrible happened. I realized then that she got arrested, too, because she looked at me as if to say, "What's going on?" and I went like, "I don't know, Margie." Then I realized the scope of this thing.

In the 1980s, dozens of people were arrested in Bakersfield for alleged participation in child molestation rings. At least eight multiple-offender cases were tried there between 1983 and 1986. At one time sixty children were involved in the accusations of alleged molestation and satanic ritual rings.

In a preliminary hearing, prosecutors brought thirty-one counts of child molestation against Stoll. He was officially charged with eighteen counts at his November 1984 trial.

In Kern County Jail, there's forty guys in a twelve-man tank. They're on the tables, they're sleeping under the tables, just unbelievable. I started reading the paper about us.

A man named Rick Pitts had been accused of the same thing. His was a bigger ring, there was seven of them, including mothers and grandmothers, and it was just god-awful. So that was going to trial when I got to jail. Rick [who was being held at the same jail] sat me down and told me all about it, he called it to a tee. He said, "This is how it's gonna happen. They are right now scouring the neighborhoods for kids." I said, "Man, you're crazy.

I don't want to hear that shit." Because you don't want to hear it. He's telling you that you're in really deep trouble. I mean, at this time I'm still thinking, "It's gonna be okay. Jed can't possible say this stuff." We'd compare notes. They were going through the same thing I just started to go through. Rick Pitts had been accused of the same thing.

They charge me with Donnie and Allen. Then they charge me with Victor. Then they charge me with Chris and Eddie. And I'm going nuts. Now my three counts turned into twenty-one. I'm just going, "Oh dear God, what's going on?"

I still clung to the fact that this was America. You can't get convicted for something you didn't do. We'll just have the attorneys take these kids to the doctor. No problem, we'll take care of this.

The first attorney walks in, first time the man ever saw me, he didn't know me from Adam, he said, "Boy, you're in big trouble." This clown had me already. I was already a child molester and I was in big trouble. Not, "What's going on?" or "Did you do this?" None of that. And I fired him. I told him straight-up, stop coming to see me, I don't want nothing to do with you. And then I sold some stuff and my mom sold some stuff and we hired [another] attorney.

The very first day of the preliminary hearing, we thought we were all going home. The first two kids up to bat—*bam, bam*— nothing happened, nothing happened. We were just ecstatic, yee-haw, this is over. This is absolutely cool, we're going home. The next little kid comes in. Victor. Everything's gonna be okay. Here comes Victor. Victor says, "He did it."

I still thought that maybe everything was gonna be okay. I only began to doubt things when my attorney and I tried to put in a motion asking that the kids be taken to a doctor. "Nope, you can't take them to the doctor, it's too traumatic for the children."

That was the ruling. They wouldn't let us take him to the doctor. I mean, they said I was molesting Jed, poking him in the little behind and everything. How traumatic is that? If just going to the doctor is traumatic, then Jed should be a mess by now, just a psychological wreck.

Now here was this poor traumatized little child. Cutest little thing you ever saw. He comes walking in to the preliminary hearing, he walks over and sees me, big smile: "Hi, Daddy." Well, I thought the DA was going to shit: "Your Honor, something's come up." And she takes Jed into the hall. For maybe fifteen minutes he's out there. Here comes Jed, marching back in. He sits down, never ever looked at me again. Never. Every time we went to court he never ever looked at me again.

This is how it went. The lawyers would say, "Daddy put his penis up your butt?"

"No."

"Did he touch you? Daddy touched you here? Daddy touched you there?"

"Yeah."

"Okay, we'll change that count from sodomy to lewd and lascivious acts with a child under the age of fourteen, your Honor."

What did that woman say to my little boy in the hallway? That son of a bitch, what did she say to him? Stuff like that sticks, you don't ever forget it. But there was no jury [in the preliminary hearing], and nobody saw that he wasn't a little traumatized child. Nobody sees the kids, there is nothing written in the paper about them denying a lot of these charges against us. The only thing that's in the paper is we're going to trial for a zillion counts of child molestation. Nobody wrote that Jed looked like an all right kid.

All I'm thinking about is Jed. I can't get over Jed. Donnie and Allen, same way. There's no anger here; there's just great disappointment and sorrow. Because you want your son to tell them, "My daddy didn't do nothing."

In the middle of this we're going on hunger strikes, we're writing to congressmen—House of Representative guys and local community leaders. We wrote hundreds of letters. We went on a hunger strike for the FBI to come.

5 charged with child molesting

By STEVE E. SWENSON
Californian staff writer

Two separate child molestation cases — one involving four defendants charged with 26 felonies and the other involving one defendant charged with 27 felonies were filed late Tuesday afternoon in West Kern Municipal Court.

One case alleges that four persons molested two 8-year-old boys during the past year. Two complaints were filed in this case, one charging three men with 18 felonies, and one charging a woman with eight felonies.

The defendants are John Andrew Stoll, 41, address unlisted; Grant Self, 31, address listed as Highway 178, Walker Pass; and Timothy Palamo, 28, and Marjorie Grafton, whose age is listed as 25 to 30, both of 2301 Mirto

The Bakersfield Californian reports on Stoll's alleged child-abuse ring (June 1984)

Now here we were, twenty-some child molesters asking the FBI to please come in here and look at this! Please. There's something really wrong here.

We said, "Shit, let's just raise hell. Let's just not eat. Let's go on a hunger strike, let's get their attention." And we got it. We all watched me on the 5:30 news. And the FBI came and said, "We can't do anything, it's out of our jurisdiction." I said, "Well can't you just look into it and make a report?" He said, "I might do that." And he left. That was the end of my contact with the FBI.

It was a witch-hunt time. I had read about the McMartin case before any of this happened, but I just thought, "Man, those terrible people." The McMartin case was in '83 and mine was '84. It was just nuts and there was no way to stop it. Everybody was getting found guilty. Everybody was saying the same thing, "We didn't do this shit." But it didn't matter. Because of the charges, nobody was willing to acquit. If a five-year-old says you did it, you did it.

The next case that came up while we were still in trial was a case that involved devil worship. It was so off the wall, it was just nuts. The kids were saying that little babies were burned in the fireplace. Then two weeks later the cops decide to go check the house out and look for the hooks where they supposedly hung kids from the walls, and there weren't any. And there was no fireplace. All those CPS [Child Protective Services] people, they were first on the line making all the accusations. And then the cops just try and find proof for the accusations.

I could never quite figure out what led to the hysteria. It just got legs and took on a life of its own. The story against me just grew and grew. Who even made it up? Who started it? Who is the original person that said, "Well, I got an idea, let's make up this story?" That's a sick person. My son didn't know the word "penis" and he's up there on the witness stand saying stuff like that. I'm thinking, "My God, where did this come from?" There was serious effort from some sick people here.

Their case just rolled right over us, no matter what we proved. If you proved it didn't happen one day, then okay, it was the next day. And if you proved it wasn't the next day, then it was another day. Dates didn't mean anything, nothing meant anything.

The DA just ran over our lawyers. Our lawyers were fighting back, but there was nothing they could do. One of our lawyers got called on contempt and spent the weekend with me in jail. I said, "How can the DA do this, how can the DA do that? Why is the judge letting this happen?" My friend's lawyer said, "Do you know why a dog licks his nuts?" I said, "No." "Because he can!" And that shut me up. Point well taken. The judge is letting him do it, so he's doing it. I'll never forget that.

The lawyers questioned some of the jurors after, and one juror said, "Well, we didn't know what was true. We just didn't know what to do so we just found him guilty of everything." So any defense we had, it didn't matter because—and I can almost understand this—we don't want these child molesters to get away with it, so we'll just find him guilty. They said that something

A CULTURE OF FEAR

A series of child abuse cases in the mid-1980s caused mass hysteria

In the mid-1980s, "Believe the Children" was the rallying cry of prosecutors, investigators and parents pursuing allegations of child abuse charges at the McMartin preschool in Manhattan Beach, California. Ironically, these same investigators, prosecutors, and parents refused to believe the children when they reported there was no molestation.

Peggy McMartin Buckey testifies in her defense (May 1989)

In 1983, Judy Johnson charged that her two-year-old son had been sexually molested by Ray Buckey, a teacher at the McMartin preschool. Two weeks later, Buckey was arrested. The police sent letters to all of the school's parents, requesting that they question their children about other, similar incidents. Parents were also advised to watch for symptoms of abuse, including bed-wetting and aversions to certain foods. Naturally, when these normal behaviors occurred, parents feared the worst.

Many parents, seeking assistance, took their children to Children's Institute International, a child abuse treatment center. There, children were interviewed by Kathleen McFarlane and her colleagues. Though McFarlane was trained in social work, she entered her career in the 1970s, just as awareness of child abuse and incest began to increase. Since McFarlane helped guide the allocation of funds made available through the Child Abuse Prevention and Treatment Act of 1974, she quickly gained respect as an expert in child abuse, though she had no appreciable expertise in psychological evaluation.

Interviewers working on the McMartin case told the students they needed to talk about nudity to help other children, and urged them to be as helpful as possible. Those children who assisted were praised and their intelligence lauded. Eager to please, the children began to tell investigators about games like "Naked Movie Star" or "The Hollywood Game," during which they were fondled, photographed in the nude, and raped by teachers, including Buckey.

Former students were also interviewed, in an attempt to uncover how long the abuses had been occurring. Again, they pressured children to tell

continued on page 188

4 in another child sex ring convicted

By MICHAEL TRIHEY
Californian staff writer

Members of the third child-molestation ring to come to trial in Kern County have been convicted of virtually every charge against them, clearing the way for prison sentences ranging from 14 to 40 years.

The verdicts Thursday in the John Stoll-Grant Self ring makes the district attorney's office three-for-three in the prosecution of child sex abuse rings.

Deputy District Attorney Stephen M. Tauzer won verdicts against:
• John Andrew Stoll, 41, 2423 Center St.
• Grant Gene Self, 31, of Walker Pass. Self was declared a mentally disordered sex offender years ago and was released from the Atascadero State Hospital in November 1983.
• Timothy Palomo, 28, 2304 Mirto Court.
• Marjorie Grafton, 29, also of the Mirto Court address.

Tauzer won the convictions on the strength of the testimony of the seven victims and almost no supporting evidence.

The verdicts, returned in the Superior Court of Judge John D. Jelletich, rejected defense arguments the children had lied or had been brainwashed into making false accusations.

The members of the first two rings to come to trial — the Kniffen-McCuan ring and the David Kelly-David Duncan ring — also were convicted of virtually all counts against them.

Scott and Brenda Kniffen and Alvin and Deborah McCuan were sentenced to prison terms of 240 years or more each; Kelly and Duncan received 60- and 61-year terms and a third defendant in the Kelly-Duncan ring is awaiting trial.

Jelletich set Feb. 14 for sentencing for the Stoll-Self ring.

Stoll will face a term up to 40 years,

Self will face a term of 31 years, Ms. Grafton a term of 16 years and Palomo 14 years.

The nine-woman, three-man jury that heard the four-month case returned verdicts on charges of lewd conduct with children under the age of 14.

Force was not an element of the crimes as charged.

Stoll was convicted of 17 counts, Self of five counts and Palomo of four counts.

Jurors were unable to reach unanimous decisions in one count involving each of the defendants.

The defendants sat behind their defense attorneys as court clerk Marcia Lackey read the verdicts Thursday. Each defendant seemed emotionless as Mrs. Lackey repeated the verdicts: "guilty, guilty ..."

A fifth defendant in the case, Glenda

Turn to MOLESTATION / B2

The Bakersfield Californian *announces Stoll's conviction (January 18, 1985)*

must have happened. Where there's smoke, there's fire.

These children weren't taken to the hospital, these children weren't given any kind of physical examination by a doctor, for God's sake. Jed sat up there on the witness stand and said I sodomized him. He'd just start saying wild shit. He was six. He didn't understand that this was wrong.

It was hard to see those little kids up there, and they were all scared shitless.

DEN FULL OF SNAKES

In September 1985, Stoll was convicted of seventeen counts of child molestation and was sentenced to forty years in prison. He began his term in California's San Quentin State Prison.

San Quentin, that's where it all started. Jesus, I was a forty-year-old carpenter and it was just like kicking me into a den full of snakes. Whew. It was a real scary place. You got five thousand men on the mainline walking around. You just can't keep track, there is so much crap happening. People are getting stabbed,

187

stories of abuse, and unfavorably compared those that did not assist to their more cooperative peers. And again, children came up with stories of Buckey's abuse—even those children who had attended the school before Buckey began teaching there.

Why? In large part because questioners employed interview techniques that preyed on their young subjects' eagerness to please. Using anatomically correct dolls, McFarlane's team asked children to point to where the defendants had touched them and continued to ask the children "where else?" until they finally pointed to the genitals. Eventually, out of 400 interviews with current and former students, 360 led to allegations of sexual abuse.

Children began to claim three teachers other than Buckey had molested them. Their stories became more and more imaginative. One story held that the teachers led trips to cemeteries where they dug up coffins and cut up corpses. In another, Buckey had worn Santa Claus outfits and clown costumes while he molested them. One student claimed Buckey had beaten a horse to death with a baseball bat and cut off the ears of a pet rabbit as a warning not to tell. According to the children, abuse even occurred in hot-air balloons and in underground tunnels.

During the resulting trial, the defense appealed to the jury's common sense, questioning the likelihood these elaborate crimes could have been committed for so long without exposure. The defense also used the tapes of children's interviews to demonstrate the coercive questions of investigators. Their strategy eventually succeeded, although Buckey spent five years in jail before being released on bail. In 1990, after seven years and $15 million dollars—the longest and costliest trial in American history—the jury acquitted Buckey and his mother, Peggy McMartin Buckey, on seventy-two counts of child abuse and molestation.

But the McMartin case represented only the beginning. In the mid-1980s, investigators across the country used these very same flawed interviewing techniques to produce similar results, leading to a rapid growth in the number of cases involving rings of adults alleged to have committed multiple acts of sexual abuse against children. However, a 1994 survey of more than 12,000 of these large-scale child abuse allegations found not one to be physically substantiated—after over a hundred people had already been convicted. Nearly all of these convictions have been either overturned or greatly revised.

there's guns going off and shotguns going off. At least twice a week there was shots fired. Honest to God. Sometimes right in your own housing unit where you lived. The guards would shoot down at a guy on the bottom tier, and those pellets flew everywhere. San Quentin was the craziest place.

Prison was… Man, this is always the hardest because you just can't explain it to people. It's the worst situation you could possibly imagine. You have no freedom. Someone tells you when to shower, someone tells you when to go the bathroom, everything. Some days they just don't open your door, for whatever reason they want. They're in charge, so some days they just say, "Well, we don't feel like letting you out today," so you just sit there.

I went to the hole. Holy shit. That's jail… in prison. That's where they put you when they want to lock you up, in prison. They put me in the hole for nine months. 'Cause they couldn't prove that I had done anything wrong [in prison], and it pissed them off, so they just locked me up. That's how it works. Nine months in the hole. Whew. You just sit for nine months. It's a cell about wide enough to where you can put your hands out, and about eight feet long. There's a light in there, a bare light bulb. So after about two weeks you tape some cardboard up there because the thing's driving you nuts. You get tape off your mail. You get cardboard off the back of your writing tablets. So you have to have enough tape, and you only get maybe a half an inch when your mail comes in. You take it off real careful so it still has some sticky stuff left to it, and you wait until it's long enough to go around. But if the [guards] see it they'll come in knock it off. So you got to start all over again.

I had a real serious shitty attitude at first. I realized that when I went to the hole.

LOSING TOUCH WITH REALITY

Solitary confinement causes psychological problems for inmates

An inmate sent to "the hole"—a.k.a administrative, punitive, or disciplinary segregation—is normally confined to a sparsely furnished cell at least twenty-three hours a day, with near-total idleness and isolation.

No comprehensive national statistics exist on the number of inmates in solitary confinement, but in California in May 2005 there were 10,297 inmates in some form of disciplinary confinement—6.3 percent of the state's prison population. Similarly, in New York, between 1991 and 1996 roughly 10 percent of inmates spent time in some form of solitary confinement.

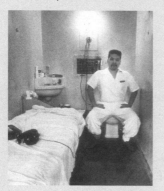

Inmate Jessy San Miguel in the maximum segregation cell block of the Ellis prison unit in Huntsville, Texas (1994)

Inmates may be isolated for reasons ranging from spitting at a guard to instigating fights or riots. The amount of time generally depends on the severity of the infraction and varies across states, from a few days to entire sentences. Nicholas Yarris, an exoneree from Pennsylvania, spent most of his twenty-three years on death row in solitary confinement.

Sensory deprivation causes suffering, as does the constant, random noise from yelling, banging, and gate-slamming and the terrible stench of human waste that can permeate isolation quarters.

Psychological effects of solitary confinement can include perceptual distortions and hallucinations, anxiety, acute confusional states, violent or self-destructive outbursts, hyper-responsivity to stimuli, difficulties with thinking, concentration, and memory, overt paranoia, and panic attacks.

Although some in the corrections world tout confinement as a deterrent to inmate aggression and disruption, little evidence exists to support its effectiveness. On the other hand, many suicides occur in or are a result of solitary isolation. According to one study by the New York Correctional Association, more than half of New York's prison suicides between 1998 and 2001 occurred in disciplinary lockdown, a severely restrictive type of isolation.

THE SAME DAMN BED FOR SEVEN YEARS

I spent most of my time at Avenal [State Prison, about a hundred miles northwest of Bakersfield]. We didn't have cells, we had dorms with fourteen people on double bunks. At five-thirty they'd open the day-room floor. It was a big cement room.

Then at six o'clock, they'd start calling the different workers—the outside workers, the chicken ranch workers. We'd go up to the dining hall and eat in groups. Usually the breakfast really sucked. Very seldom did you get a decent breakfast. Every once in a while the eggs weren't cold so you'd eat them. But it was just hospital food with an attitude.

You'd go from the dining hall to the work site. I worked off the yard. I was a lead cook in the mental health clinic.

We'd be home at noon. I'd go home and change into my sports-walking clothes and try to walk five miles every day around the track. I wanted to stay healthy, I wanted to get out healthy.

After the walk, I'd go back in and take a shower. You were allowed to take a shower from two to four-thirty. So as soon as I'd come home, I'd put one of my ID cards up in the shower to reserve it, so when I came in, that was my shower. They were gang showers. Every once in a while, if you were late, someone would take your shower, and that was your fault because you were late. You shut your mouth and went, "Cool, man, don't trip, I should've been here."

We were allowed to have two pairs of jeans, and strict rules like that. You weren't allowed to have designer clothes. You had to have Levi's or Lee's, nothing with designer labels, or logos. Everything had to be gray or white, and black shoes were okay. To different races, clothes and shoes meant different things. For old white guys like me, I just wore walking shoes. Shoes weren't a big deal, they weren't stolen very often. When I went to work, I had to wear all state clothes, because that was the rule. Once I stepped into my dorm area I never wore another piece of state clothing again, until I went to work again in the morning.

Sometimes you went to the chow hall. I'd say, in a week, if you went four times, that was a good week. Usually three was about it. It was enough to keep you alive, but some of it just tasted awful, it was watered down. Guys' pockets would be bulging with seasoning salt, garlic salt, hot sauce, anything to make it taste.

Then you'd come from supper, and we'd play cribbage until maybe eight or nine, then I'd usually go back to the dorm and get ready for bed, and read some more. I read probably about three books a week, or four, depending on if we were locked down.

There's some people in there that burn every bridge and they never get on the phone and they never have any mail and they never get anything, and out they go and you see them six or eight months later coming in again. Especially at Avenal, I was there ten years, on the same yard for seven, on the same damn bed for seven years.

I hurt my back in prison, and I was in bed for two weeks straight—could not move. My cellie literally had to empty my urine into the toilet, and help me roll over to the side, help me get to the toilet, hold me, practically almost had to feed me. And I asked for them to give me an MRI because I think there was something seriously wrong. They told me, "Well, 602 it." 602 is a grievance. You had to do that. And then they'd either lose it, or write back and say, "It's not that serious, you've already seen the doctor." And how are they supposed to know that? I mean, all they do is give you an X-ray. That doesn't show you your tendons, ripped tendons, tore muscles, slipped discs in your back. It doesn't show any of that. It just shows bone.

Yeah, if your bones are not broke you're all right. This one guy ripped his whole Achilles' tendon. The thing broke, and went all the way up into the bottom of his knee. You know what the doctor told him? He pulled his calf muscle. They sewed it back like a week later, and it was too late.

'WE BELIEVE YOU'

For a while, every time I saw an attorney that did a good deed or something, I'd try and figure out how to write to him. I wrote to hundreds of lawyers. I wrote to [Richard] "Racehorse" Haynes, I wrote to Melvin Belli, and I wrote to Lee—what's his name? That other famous attorney. A lot of the letters came back because I didn't have the right addresses. I really thought it was all over. I thought, this is it. I'm done.

I'm sitting there thinking I'll never get out, and all of the sudden I get a letter. The letter says, "Dear Mr. Stoll, enclosed is a questionnaire. We are the Northern California Innocence Project and we want to look into your case." When they sent me the original questionnaire, I really questioned myself. Did I want to drag this up again? It's just like a scab, you don't want to pick at it again if it's not gonna get you anywhere. Do I really want to tell this same sad story again? Because every time I told it, I got all bummed out. I really did. It starts to hurt. You start to drag out about your child, losing my son. It's just, it's the worst part of this whole thing. Twenty years in prison is kinda disappointing, but losing my little boy? That's devastating.

But Linda [Starr] and Jill [Kent], the people from the Northern California Innocence Project, were so cool. I knew everything was cool the second time they came to see me. The first time, we were feeling each other out. I was leery, I didn't know who these people were. When they told me they believed me, that was enough. Nobody had ever said that in twenty years.

"We believe you." I wrote to hundreds of people, saying I was innocent. But nobody ever said, "We looked into it and we believe you." When they said that, I knew I was okay.

That was pretty cool going back to my cell that night. But you can't be bouncing around going, "Yay, hooray," because somebody's going to say, "What is he so happy about?" So you just sorta kept it inside. I did go tell one friend. I said, "Hey, those Innocence Project people say they're gonna get me out." "No shit?" he said. I said, "Yup, I think I'm getting out of here."

Then I start getting all these letters. You see, inmates don't have anything to do, so they watch everybody else. I've been down eighteen years at this time and I started getting legal mail. "Hey John, you got another legal mail, what's happening?" people would ask.

Beginning in 2002, lawyers and students from the Northern California Innocence Project at Santa Clara University, and the California Innocence Project at California Western School of Law in San Diego, spent two years tracking down witnesses and preparing Stoll's petition for a new trial. During hearings that stretched over five months, five of the six witnesses who testified against Stoll in his trial recanted their testimony. Four of those witnesses testified that they were forced by prosecutors, law enforcement, and social services workers to testify that Stoll had sexually abused them. The youngest trial witness, Stoll's son, Jed, admitted at the hearing that he lied at trial and had no memory of his childhood testimony, yet is haunted to this day by a belief that he was molested.

The *Los Angeles Times* wrote an article about me, then Bakersfield picked it up, other people picked it up. Now it's all over the place. A cop in prison told me, "Hey, look at that newspaper over there. Look at page two." So I grabbed the newspaper and ran into the toilet, a big long line of toilets. And I went and sat in the back corner, where I'd always go sit and smoke. I opened the paper and there it is: "Convicted molester. Seeks new trial."

I tear it out and flush it down the toilet. Because it has my name and it says I'm a convicted child molester. That means other inmates will probably kill me if they find it. Because it is the worst damn crime there is. Taking advantage of a child. It's just the same as a child murderer or any of that. It's a disgusting thing. You're at the bottom of the damn pile, and you're in prison. And there you are at the bottom of this pile of sick people, because of your crime. So if they find out, you're the first one that's gonna get it.

Suddenly my story was out and I was scared someone was gonna stab me. I was a child molester. In the paper it said I was going back to court to try and prove my innocence, but I was still convicted as a child molester. So, to a lot of people, I was a child molester whether I was going back to court or not.

More and more people knew why I was in prison. People I had lied to. So I went to this one real tough son of a bitch, he was from Bakersfield, and I said, "Hey listen, something's coming in the paper, and I want you to know something." I gave him all the information I had, all the letters from the lawyers, the recantations of the kids. He stood right up and said to everyone, "Man, if you touch him, you're dealing with me." And all the Bakersfield car—that's what they call it, a car, it's a group—the whole Bakersfield group just stood right up and said, "Don't touch him, leave him alone."

I never PC'd [went into protective custody], because I knew if I did, I'd be around all of these child molesters. So I would have rather went out on the main line.

In protective custody, you walk up and you say, "Hey, I'm scared." Well, they'll put you with a whole cell full of child molesters. What the hell do I want to be with those people for? I'm not one of them. I don't want to be involved with them. I don't even want to talk to them. So you're out on the main line. And when you're on the main line and you're charged with what I was charged with, it's a damn scary proposition.

And if it pops up, you got to deal with it. You did things that you would never did in your normal life. I have. I had to bust a few heads. I would have never in my life walked across a yard and stuck a man in the stomach with a knife. But I did. If I didn't do that, didn't show my manhood and didn't protect myself, I was the next guy.

I went to the Hispanics, who were the knifemakers. That's who made them and sold them. And a friend of mine came to me, and he said, "You know, John," he said, "this dude bought a knife and it's [meant] for you." And I had made friends enough to protect myself. So I said, "Well…" and I bought a knife for a carton of cigarettes. I bought a piece of plastic that had been honed down about four and a half inches long and wrapped with masking tape around the handle. And that's what I had. And I knew that this man was going to kill me the first chance he had. So I walked across the yard. And he saw me coming, and he gave me a big smile. And I stuck the thing right in his stomach.

He didn't tell. You don't tell in prison. He didn't tell who stabbed him.

All the other prisoners believed in me and they all watched the letters and they saw law students sending me packages. I mean, Jesus, a package is a big deal in prison. Just, "Oh God. Hooray." Because it's a lonely, shitty place. And all of the sudden I got all these friends, and I got all these letters and all these inmates that really believe in me.

I really don't know what would have happened if I had to go back in there and face any of those guys that said, "Hey man,

I thought you went back to court." That scared the hell out of me. The first thing I thought when they took me to court was, "Oh my God, if this doesn't work, I gotta go back to prison." And I really was terrified. To be absolutely truthful, I was scared shitless. And it kept me awake for nights. I would just lay there and think about all the shitty things that could happen to me. Now this was Kern County, they screwed me twenty years ago. There's nothing changed. Here are the cops and everyone saying the same things that I heard twenty years ago.

If I had to go back to prison, somebody would have tried to kill me. Unless they sent me to some faraway prison, but by this time it was on CNN. It was on everywhere. I'm sitting in trial and they tell me, "We were on CNN today," and I'm thinking, "Oh my God, I'm on CNN? They got my name on CNN."

The Bakersfield newspapers are running stories on me and they were getting emails from people in Bakersfield saying how sorry they were that they did such a shitty thing to me. I was absolutely amazed at the way Bakersfield poured their heart out to me, telling me how sorry they were for me. I realized that more and more people realized I was an innocent man.

I remember that second day I went back to court. That was when all the boys came in and said I didn't do it. I went back to jail that day. I hadn't read the paper, I hadn't seen anything about it. I walked into the cell and they locked the door and this guy next to me says, "Hey weren't you in Avenal?"

I said, "Yeah."

He said, "Are you in the paper today?"

I said, "I don't know, am I?"

He said, "John Stoll?"

I said, "Yeah."

He said, "Check this out, man."

He passed his newspaper through the bars and I read about

LESSONS NOT LEARNED

The justice system lacks official reviews of erroneous convictions

After ten years of litigation and nearly three years spent in prison, DNA evidence exonerated Guy Paul Morin of murdering his nine-year-old next-door neighbor. Inquiries found that police investigators had contaminated the hair and fiber evidence found at the scene, and, moreover, that Morin's jailhouse confession had never happened. As a result, the government ordered a top-to-bottom investigation of the national criminal justice system. The investigation resulted in a 1,400-page report with more than eighty recommended reforms.

Morin, however, is a citizen of Canada; his trial occurred in Ontario.

In England, a Criminal Case Review Commission exists specifically to investigate excessive sentences and wrongful convictions. Both the Canadian and the British models have the power to subpoena documents and require governmental responses to their recommendations. Both operate under the philosophy that a wrongful conviction is a threat to the public and a danger that, once recognized, must be repaired.

In the United States there is no mandated federal- or state-level inquiry after a conviction is overturned. The closest thing to an official review board this country possesses are the state-appointed commissions that occasionally study more general justice issues.

Governor George Ryan of Illinois declared a moratorium on executions in March 2000, and then appointed a commission to study reforms to make the state's capital punishment system fair and just. Two years later, that commission recommended changes at all stages of the capital system: investigation, decision making, trial, and appeal. The commission, however, had no authority to enact criminal justice reforms. In fact, the Illinois legislature refused to adopt any of the commission's recommendations until three years after they were suggested.

Advocates of criminal justice reform who have fought for the wrongfully convicted explain that there are multiple factors involved in each wrongful conviction. Yet despite the complexities and wide-ranging causes of wrongful convictions, criminal justice advocates maintain that the steps necessary to effectively reduce the likelihood of such convictions are straightforward. Few states, however, have adopted any of the recommended safeguards.

For a sample of recommended reforms, see Appendix E

how the boys came forward, how one said to me, "I'm so sorry, John." It was all in there. The guy in the cell next to me said, "Hey man, good luck. Good luck to you." A convict. He's got tattoos all up and down his arm, on his neck, he's one of the fellas. So that was pretty cool. That day was pretty cool.

Stoll was not released immediately after his case was overturned on April 30, 2004. He was transported to a holding center in Bakersfield, where he spent several days waiting for the DA to formally announce the state would not retry the case. He was finally released from prison on May 4, his sixty-first birthday, after prosecutors finally dropped charges. He had served 19 years.

When I finally get out and I'm heading towards the door. I walk out and there's probably forty reporters there. There was NBC, CBS, Channel 11, CNN, there was like five motion picture cameras and like five or six cameramen. I never in my life expected that. They had just done so much shit to me, I could not believe I was out the door.

I'm stronger in character than I thought I was. I kept it together better than I thought I would. I thought I'd never get out of prison. Do you know how scared I was when Cookie and Linda [Kathleen Ridolfi and Linda Starr, from the Northern California Innocence Project] offered me the guest room at the back of their house? I actually envisioned people walking around with signs outside their home. And then the next day the neighbor comes over and gives me a big hug and shakes my hand and says, "We're so glad you're out." And the neighbor across the street is waving at me. They were just so nice, the neighbors were great to me. I never had negative feedback, not one single solitary, "Well, maybe he did it anyway."

The Northern California Innocence Project saved my life.

*Stoll walks out of the Kern County Lerdo Detention
Facility in Bakersfield, California (May 4, 2004)*

*Stoll with lawyers Jill Kent (left) and Linda Starr (right) after
Stoll was released on his sixty-first birthday (May 4, 2004)*

I was pretty burnt out. So much stupidity and so much ignorance. I almost got into a couple of fights before I got out because it was just pressing on me and I had just had it. I'm lucky I got out when I did, because I was at the end of my rope. I'd had all the bullshit I could handle. But then, here I am so it's okay. It worked out all right.

Some of the children—now adults—involved in the Bakersfield cases have said that they now feel uncomfortable with children. Some have said that they don't even allow their own children to sit on their laps.

I don't feel uncomfortable at all around children. I didn't do anything, and they just proved I didn't do anything. I get hugs from the kids all the time at home. I don't have a problem with it at all. I'm sorry some of those boys do—that's such a shame, my god. They're afraid to hold their own children.

It all still amazes me. The hardest thing for me to do is to continue to talk about it, day in and day out. I don't have any of the bitterness that I had, but I still have anger. It still makes me mad that they could get away with something like that, and they're all fine and their lives go on and they retire. Nobody has ever acknowledged that there was any kind of mistake made there. I mean, come on. Good lord, something went wrong. How do you get all those convictions overturned unless you screwed up? But nobody even has the balls to come out and say, "Hey man, we made a mistake, let's fix this." They fought me until the day I got out.

John Stoll is currently suing, among others: Kern County, California; the Kern County sheriff's office; the Kern County District Attorney's office; Kern County sheriff at the time of Stoll's arrest; two sheriff's department employees; and a social worker involved in the case. Stoll's lawyers have made a claim for compensation from the state of California.

Everybody says, "Why aren't you bitter?" What the hell do you think I've been doing for the past twenty years? I've been pissed off. But now I'm free. I'm out. I've been exonerated. The court threw it all out. So to just keep beating it does me no good. I've got to get moving here. I've got some life left and I want to enjoy it.

Beverly Monroe

NOW I QUESTION
EVERYTHING

NAME: Beverly Monroe · BORN: 1938 · HOMETOWN: Marion, North Carolina

CONVICTED OF: Murder · SENTENCE: 22 years

SERVED: 7 years · RELEASED: 2002

In 1992, Beverly Monroe was living comfortably near Richmond, Virginia. She had a master's degree in organic chemistry and was working as a patent analyst for Philip Morris. Her companion of thirteen years, Roger Zygmunt de la Burdé, lived on an estate outside the city. He was also a scientist at Philip Morris until a dispute with the company resulted in his quitting and filing a multi-million dollar lawsuit against his former employer. Their families—Monroe's children Katie, Shannon, and Gavin, and de la Burdé's daughter, Corinna—had grown close over the years. Separately from his relationship with Monroe, de la Burdé was carrying on an affair with another woman, which Monroe knew about.

The night of March 4, 1992 was the last time Monroe saw de la Burdé alive.

A TOOTHPICK CASTLE

Roger called me, probably—I don't know—nine or ten times that day at work. He said, "Mouse, get here as soon as you can." You know, "Get here. Leave." I ran by my house, threw on some other clothes. I remember leaving a note for my son, Gavin, on a napkin. Told him I was going to get groceries.

Roger was sixty years old. He was doing a lot of looking back: "What have I done with my life? Everything is a mess."

Financially, everything was a mess. It was one of the reasons I wouldn't marry Roger. He was an unstable person, and a difficult person at times. He was both wonderful and difficult, but my finances were stable. His were not. There was no way I would mix my finances in with that. None.

He was wealthy in the sense that he had accumulated a lot of properties and art. But it was all built on things that were shaky. Not that they were wrong. It's like a toothpick castle. You pull one of those things out and the whole thing can go collapsing down on you. It's a lot of juggling. He got overextended.

He was a research scientist at Philip Morris. A very brilliant person, but not an orthodox person. And he was responsible for some of the major inventions for the industry, not just for the company. He had a suit against Philip Morris for $12 million. They had counter-sued him for $50 million. It was serious. And he was frightened.

That's why he bought the gun. He was afraid—I don't want to say afraid of Philip Morris—but he was. And people close to him knew that. He got a little paranoid about it. It's an area that's not easy to talk about, but it's a fact. It was a huge mess, and it was a tremendous pressure on him.

Roger had all these things going, including this affair with this Polish woman. It wasn't just with her. There were others, too.

I'd been at Roger's that evening. We'd had dinner. While I was there, I was sitting at the piano. Roger had learned a jazz song. I was sitting at the piano and the phone rang. And the message started to come on. He didn't answer it. As somebody started talking, he jumped up and took it off the hook. I had a feeling it was this woman calling him. He took the phone off the hook, and when I left, he hadn't put it back on.

I didn't remember actually driving home. But I remember stopping to get gas because I had rushed to get out there from work. My tank was nearly empty, and it's about a fifteen-mile trip out there to Roger's house. I remember when I was driving into my driveway, the news was on. I keep the station on NPR. I was thinking, it's about ten o'clock. You don't look at your watch when you're doing something, you just have a sense of what time it is. I tried to call Roger. I usually called him, or he called me, Just to make sure that I got home safely, or he did. Well, the line was busy.

Then I went to the grocery store. I always get receipts, and I had written a check. I remember pretty much everything about that evening, including waking up in the middle of the night and realizing that Roger hadn't called. I was uneasy. Not worried. Just didn't sleep very well.

I got up kind of early, and I decided to just go out and see him. There was nothing that you could put your finger on, but he had been kind of sad. He'd been talking about his daughters. He was talking about his sense of failure as a parent. He used to always blame his ex-wife, and I would say it's not all her fault.

I didn't know at that point that he'd made a phone call after I left. Roger called Don Beville that night, a friend, but he was also a publisher and he was working on a book that Roger was writing at the time.

Don said the call was so strange that he had written it down

Monroe (second from right) with her children (from left)
Gavin, Shannon, and Katie (mid-1980s)

on the back of a Texaco bill that he happened to have on his desk. There were three things he remembered Roger saying. One was that tomorrow will be a new day. The weight of the world has been lifted from his shoulders. And everything has been resolved.

But nothing had been resolved. Nothing.

The next morning before work, when Monroe returned to de la Burdé's house to check on him, she bumped into his groundskeeper, Joe Hairfield. She told him she had been trying to call de la Burdé and kept getting a busy signal. Hairfield found a way inside the house and discovered de la Burdé lying on his side on a couch in the library, next to the coffee table where he and Monroe had eaten dinner the night before. Monroe rushed into the room. Hairfield saw de la Burdé's gun and picked it up. Then he replaced it where he thought it had been. Hairfield called the local sheriff's office to report that de la Burdé had shot himself.

THE MEDICAL EXAMINER CONCLUDED SUICIDE

Gregory Neal, Powhatan County's sheriff, arrived at de la Burdé's house at nine o'clock that morning. Treating the death as a suicide, Neal took photographs of the scene, but did not preserve all of the evidence. The one fingerprint found on de la Burdé's gun was his own. The medical examiner also arrived at the scene and called a report in to the state office in Richmond that concluded that de la Burdé's death was a suicide. Upon learning of the death, Don Beville, the last person known to have spoken to de la Burdé, called the police to inform them that de la Burdé had called on the night of his death and had not sounded like himself.

The local investigator, Greg Neal, concluded it was a suicide. He did whatever he was supposed to do at the scene. Took the photographs.

Roger and I had just had dinner on this coffee table. There was an ashtray there, but it was a more decorative thing. There were two cigarettes in the ashtray. Roger didn't smoke. I don't smoke. I would have known if there had been any cigarettes in there [the night before]. He would have noticed.

Greg Neal came that next morning, and he photographed that ashtray and some strange ashes in the fireplace. You know how when you burn papers they leave sort of a structural ash? You can see there were papers. He photographed these cigarettes. He noted them as being Marlboro Lights. He made a specific incident report or evidence report. The cigarette butts were obviously something he took notice of.

That morning and afternoon, people gathered at the home. People later had free roam of the house. The point is, if Neal had believed that there was something wrong, he would have sealed off the area. That's so basic. He would have done something. He

FEMALE EXONEREES:
A LOOK AT FOURTEEN CASES

NAME	STATE	CHARGE	YEARS SERVED	YEAR RELEASED
Lisl Auman	CO	Murder	7	2005
Victoria Banks	AL	Manslaughter	4	2003
Joyce Ann Brown	TX	Murder	9	1990
Sheila Bryan	GA	Murder	3	2000
Paula Gray	IL	Murder, rape, perjury	9	2002
Sonia Jacobs	FL	Murder	16	1999
Gloria Killian	CA	Murder, robbery, conspiracy	16	2002
Margaret Mignano	TN	Murder	<1	2004
Tabitha Pollock	IL	Murder	6.5	2002
Ellen Reasonover	MO	Murder	16	1999
Dianne Tucker	AL	Murder	<1	2002
Betty Tyson	NY	Murder	25	1998
Merla Walpole	CA	Murder	2	1975
Jennifer Wilcox	OH	Child sex abuse	11	1996

Sources: *"Exonerations in the United States: 1989 through 2003." Samuel Gross (2004); The Innocence Project; Truth in Justice; and The Center on Wrongful Convictions at Northwestern University*

would not have just left the house.

Neal concluded suicide. The medical examiner concluded suicide. Roger's ex-wife, who was a doctor, had also called the medical examiner. She said that Roger was supposed to be taking an antidepressant. It was the first I'd ever known of that.

His daughter, Corinna, called the police and said anybody who knew him would believe that this was a suicide. He had a chemical imbalance and this history. He was moody. Unhappy. Ups and downs. Mood swings.

THAT'S HOW IT STARTS. THAT'S HOW EASY IT IS

Virginia State Police agent David Riley became involved in the case the following day. Unbeknownst to Monroe, who assumed that the state was treating de la Burdé's death as a suicide, Riley was convinced it was a murder and focused exclusively on Monroe as the primary suspect.

A state police agent, David Riley, hears about all this the day after Roger's death. It's in the newspaper. It's on the front page. Roger, while he wasn't a prominent figure, he's an interesting person and a lot of people knew him. And he had this aura of wealth. Not real wealth necessarily, but the aura. And he promoted it.

So, for whatever reason, Agent Riley gets involved. He was suspicious because—and I'm almost verbatim quoting—suspicious because, "Beverly Monroe was the only person who ever believed or said anything about suicide."

This is the starting point.

All in all, there were maybe six to ten people who told the police and Agent Riley the very opposite of what he claimed was the premise of his suspicion that it was a murder. That's how it starts. That's how easy it is.

IT WAS MENTAL TORTURE

On the morning of March 26, Neal asked Monroe to come to de la Burdé's house for what was described as a routine follow-up to a death. There, Monroe met Agent Riley for the first time.

I go out there and spent from 9 A.M. until about 11:30 A.M. with Agent Riley. He's very casual, sitting at the kitchen table in Roger's house. Very casual. Not even taking notes that I remember. And it doesn't occur to me that he should, because as far as I know, it was just a conversation. I knew he had a "suicide assessment" form with him, as he called it, and that this was routine. I was the closest one to Roger, and he thought it would be best to start with me.

The entire day was planned and staged, and I don't use that word lightly. He started throwing things into the conversation that were contrary to what I remembered. I'm a person who works in technical information, and accuracy is important—it's in my nature. Accuracy. It's the way I am. I'm a detail person. And I tend to have a good memory.

When I was there at Roger's house [the night of March 4th], we were sitting on the couch and he had this new television. A big television. He was sitting there flipping through the channels and this program came on about Charles de Gaulle. And we watched a little bit of it. But he kind of got edgy and flipped it off.

I remembered that. When you're talking about something like this, you try to think of all of the details because one of the things you think is, "Why didn't I see something? How could I not know?"

Riley told me, "By the way, that Charles de Gaulle program that you were talking about wasn't on that evening. It must have been another evening. But it's normal. You've been through a terrible shock and trauma."

And I'm thinking, from that point on, "How could that be? What's in my mind?" It throws you. So I'm still thinking about that, and then he throws in another one.

He says, "Some people said you told them you were asleep on the couch that night." And I said, "Now that can't be." I did have a clear memory of that night. But I came to question that memory. It was mental torture.

IT NEVER OCCURRED TO ME TO SAY THAT SOMETHING'S WRONG WITH AGENT RILEY

The program about Charles de Gaulle did, in fact, air on television the night of de la Burdé's death on March 4, just as Monroe had recalled. After a two-hour interview with Monroe, Agent Riley, continuing to act like he was conducting a routine suicide investigation, suggested that Monroe come to the police station to take a polygraph test. He told her it was routine.

Agent Riley had said, "We just gotta finish this up." He put it as though it was something that was tedious for him to do. As if he's this police officer, and he has to go through all the polygraphs.

Here I am, a Southern lady. The last thing you do is inconvenience somebody. It's so dumb. It's absolutely dumb, but it's the way you're trained. It's your nature. So here I am. It's not funny, but you have to laugh. I remember trying to call my secretary because I thought I'd be back at work in an hour or two.

It was about noon when I left Roger's house. I had had a cup of coffee. I hadn't eaten anything. I got lost on the way to the police station. I was crying the whole way. Sometimes these floodgates would just open.

I had to go through the whole thing with the so-called poly-

THE RIGHT TO REMAIN SILENT

The innocent often waive Miranda rights—to their peril

In 1966 the U.S. Supreme Court ruled in *Miranda v. Arizona* that suspects must be made aware of their constitutionally guaranteed rights against self-incrimination, i.e., the rights to remain silent and request the presence of an attorney, familiar to every viewer of TV police dramas.

A Miranda warning is only legally required when a suspect is taken into custody. If a suspect is not under arrest and is free to leave, police may question the suspect without issuing a Miranda warning.

Not surprisingly, police prefer to question suspects unhampered by attorneys, in part because a suspect hesitant at the beginning of an interrogation may make incriminating statements the third or fourth time a question is asked.

To encourage suspects to waive their Miranda rights, police employ a variety of subtle strategies. They may issue a Miranda warning in a neutral tone, downplaying its importance. They may precede the Miranda warning with a long description of the police and the suspect as teammates fighting side by side to solve the crime. Or they may merely imply that a suspect will receive some sort of beneficial treatment, either by the police or at trial, if the suspect waives his or her Miranda rights.

An estimated 78 to 96 percent of all suspects waive their Miranda rights, although suspects with previous criminal records are more likely to assert them. Innocent suspects often reflexively waive their Miranda rights after an arrest because they are eager to be as helpful as possible to the police investigation. In doing so, they forfeit one of the major legal protections in place to prevent false confessions.

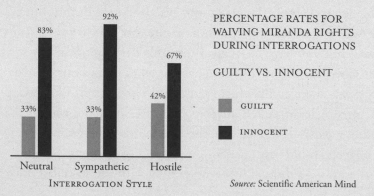

PERCENTAGE RATES FOR
WAIVING MIRANDA RIGHTS
DURING INTERROGATIONS

GUILTY VS. INNOCENT

GUILTY

INNOCENT

INTERROGATION STYLE — Neutral, Sympathetic, Hostile

Neutral: 33% / 83%
Sympathetic: 33% / 92%
Hostile: 42% / 67%

Source: Scientific American Mind

graph examiner at the station. I'm crying. This is that afternoon. I was just sitting there and he [Riley] comes in and he grabs me by the hands. He was somehow trying to impress upon me that there's something wrong, there's something wrong with my memory. He just could see it. He knew it. He had this experience so many times. He is just bombarding me. Over and over and over again. He just can see. He's got to help me. He's right in my face. He had bad breath, and you could just feel his breath.

It's a staged bombardment to try to supplant my real memory with something he's made up so that then he can say that I made some admission or agreed to his theory that I must have been asleep at the house when Roger shot himself.

After one and a half hours with the polygraph examiner, Riley took over and repeatedly insisted that Monroe had been present and asleep in de la Burdé's house when he shot himself. This repetition was a principal strategy of the John Reid interrogation technique [see page 451], a style employed by many police officers in hope of eliciting confessions. The interview room was wired for recording. The tape recorder was not on when Monroe allegedly agreed to Riley's contention that she was asleep in de la Burdé's house when he committed suicide. Only the last seventeen minutes of the interview were recorded—after, according to Riley, Monroe made her alleged statement.

Monroe was also being observed through a one-way mirror. Two secretaries, the polygraph examiner, and Neal all claimed that they were present in the observation room when Monroe agreed with Riley's scenario.

We have no way of knowing whether those tapes were erased, or whether he intentionally didn't turn it on. His version of it was this: that he [told] me that morning that this was a potential homicide, and that I might be a suspect. That was very important because their whole case is that I went to the police station, and that I was somehow boxed in by all of this, and I had to adopt his theory in order to get out of something somehow. They claimed all these people were in this little room supposedly all there just when I made this one statement out of that whole four hours that afternoon: that I remembered being there [when de la Burdé died].

The [police] secretaries put it like this: it was like a light flashed. They said they could see it in my facial expression. That's when Riley claims that I adopted his theory. Somehow I saw this as a way out. That suddenly, I latch on—that is what they said—latched on to this theme.

There's no way that that could have been real. You can see it and hear it on that tape that often I can't even talk—I am so exhausted and so sad and crying. There is no way I am suddenly latching on to this like this is a great idea. I am even on the tape saying things like, "I don't understand," "I don't have any memory of that." And here is Agent Riley saying on the tape, clear as a bell, "Oh, you'll remember. You'll see it, you'll see it in your dreams. Eventually you will remember."

If you look at the transcript itself [of the taped portion], you see I'm utterly confused. I'm saying, "I remember something else." I say at one point, "I don't remember thinking anything like what he's saying." I remember saying, "I don't see how it can be possible." So how could I have just said, "Oh yes, I remember clearly being there, I was asleep on the couch and I wake up?" You don't have to listen to me. You just have to look at the facts. You can look at what's documented and see that that is not possible as a matter of fact.

Never once did I stop and question [Riley]. Somebody talking over you for two hours can make you want to get away from them, just in order to let your brain think. It's so forceful. It's so disconcerting. It's intimidating. Even though you don't think there's anything sinister about it.

That afternoon when I left the police station about four-thirty, I could barely talk—that's how bad the pain was. I could not even walk. Agent Riley had to help me down the stairs and help me with my coat. I was literally a basket case. I really thought something was wrong with my mind. It never occurred to me to say that something's wrong with Agent Riley. I thought, "Something's wrong with me." I thought, "I haven't been myself."

It took us a while even for me to see that one of the techniques he used was talking to me and mixing the events of the evening that I spent with Roger before this happened—the night after I drove home, and the next morning when I went into that room. And particularly mixing my memories of that morning and trying to switch them to some scenario of it actually having happened the evening before. That's how complicated it was. And the way he did this was by talking over me and jumping from one thing to other, from one time-frame to the other, so that if anybody was listening, then they would hear his words and it would sound like it was all that one evening with Roger. But it wasn't.

Then the memories of my father's death were mixed in there, too. My father had taken his life. It had been years earlier. Some of the memories were the same. Some of the feelings were the same. I kept saying—and this was true of my father's death, too—I should have been there. Maybe I could have prevented it somehow. That one phrase, "I should have been there," this police officer took as, "I must have been there."

IT DOESN'T MATTER WHETHER YOU HAVE
A DEGREE IN ORGANIC CHEMISTRY

By May I was really clearer. I'm beginning to get better. I was at work and I got one call from [Riley] in early May, maybe the first week or so. He said, again, "Have you remembered anything yet?" Well of course I hadn't, and I told him so. And we talked about other things, and it was all kind of casual, and I didn't think any more about it.

He had urged me to see a therapist. I'm really embarrassed about that. When you've been a strong person, an independent person, a can-do person, it's very hard to say something might be wrong with me. There is a stigma about going to see a therapist, not as much now, thank goodness, as there used to be. It was a personal thing as well as a societal thing. You just feel, that's not me, I'm a problem-solver. But now the problem's with me, and I don't even know what it is. That's how easily someone can dislocate your sense of being in your mind. I'm clear. I'm a rational person. But it's as close as someone can come to being... a little overwhelmed. And questioning your own memory.

It does happen to rational, clear, strong people. And it doesn't matter whether you have a degree in organic chemistry.

HE WAS EITHER TAKING ME
OR THAT PIECE OF PAPER

Then about a month later, I was at my office. There was a big meeting coming up; I'd finally been able to get back in focus. There were a lot of things that I was working on, trying to catch up. It was June 3rd and it was also my mother's birthday, and I had planned to call her at lunchtime. I got a call about, I don't know, ten-thirty or so that morning. I was really busy, and again, [Riley] was very casual. It's like, you know, "I'm just finishing up the suicide report." And he said, "I just want to talk to you. Are you busy?" I said, "Yes, I'm busy, but of course, you know, if you need me, I can meet you."

I'm just a fairly agreeable person, you know. If somebody asks me to help with something, I don't question, I just do it. And especially someone who is an authority figure. I just told my secretary that I would take an early lunch and be back in an hour or so, maybe half an hour. And so he gave me directions to this park. It was a Civil War park not far from my office, you know, two miles down south of there. I had trouble finding the place. I drove up and it was this deserted park, kind of way back behind a commercial area. I pulled up and he was out of his car, no one else around, and he got in my car.

Just immediately, he started talking about how the forensics showed that this was a murder and, "Everybody knows that you did it," kind of thing. I was so stunned that I probably don't remember all the things he said at that point. I remember my mind was reeling. Again, you can't imagine—it's truly as though somebody has gotten in your car and pulled a gun on you and said, "I'm going to kill you."

He went from making this accusation, this horrible accusation, to trying to pretend to be a friend and saying things like, "You know, oh, I can understand why you did this." These are not his exact words, but it was that kind of feel to it and that kind of tone to it. And I kept saying to him, "But that's not so, that's not true." Then he said something absolutely horrible that I won't ever forget, which was, "Oh, you should get a medal." As if Roger was some horrible person, some terrible person that would have justified any of that. It was just incomprehensible to me.

Then he changed and he started saying things like, "Now listen, I've been a state police agent for twenty-two years and I've never lost a case." He denies saying these things, but I remember them clearly. I don't remember everything he said, but I remember these things because, even though I was stunned, every once in a while something would just pierce through my heart and

SELLING OUT
Snitches provide testimony in exchange for favors

Snitches are informants who testify for the prosecution in exchange for compensation ranging from money to leniency in their own sentencing. These incentivized witnesses are, in effect, the hired tongues of the prosecution.

A 2004 study of the 111 exonerees released from death row since capital punishment was reinstated in the 1970s revealed that 45.9 percent were sent there with the help of testimony from snitches.

Snitch victim Joseph Burrows

In North America, the first snitches were agents of the English crown. Hatred for these English informants was so intense that for many years the U.S. government refused to employ snitches at all. It was not until the creation of city police forces in the mid-nineteenth century that snitches returned to the prosecutorial arsenal.

In addition to monetary rewards, snitches may receive substantial reductions in charges and prison sentences as compensation for their testimony. While being questioned as a suspect in a 1988 Alabama murder, career criminal Ralph Bernard Myers implicated another man, Walter McMillan. On the concocted testimony of Myers, McMillan was sentenced to death and Myers was allowed to plead guilty to a third-degree robbery charge. McMillan was exonerated in 1993.

Not surprisingly, there is longstanding concern over the reliability of witnesses who testify in exchange for personal gain, particularly those who receive sentencing deals. A few states, such as Alaska, have sought to address this concern by prohibiting convictions based solely on an accomplice's testimony.

Concern is warranted. In 1988, Joseph Burrows was sentenced to death for a murder he did not commit due to the testimony of his professed "accomplice," Gayle Potter. Potter was arrested shortly after the crime was committed for trying to cash a check in the victim's name. Although the murder weapon was found in her possession, by implicating Burrows, Potter got her sentence reduced from a potential death sentence to thirty years (of which she would serve only fifteen). It wasn't until nearly four years later, when confronted with new evidence uncovered by

continued on page 220

218

my brain.

He said, "I've got boxes of files and investigation on you. I can twist these things any way I want." And I thought, "What, what? How could that be? I'm just me. There can't be any evidence of anything because I didn't do anything."

Of course all that was not true, but he was trying to make me think that. And he said it, just like this: "If you force me to be your enemy, I can make you out to be the black widow spider of all time." He means, "I can convict you."

I told him, "I probably have a receipt" [from the grocery store], because he was trying to tell me again that I was there that night. I said, "I always get them." He just brushed it all aside. He said, "Anybody can get a receipt," like it doesn't matter at all.

He went back to the original theme of trying to get some agreement to his scenario, as he called it, which was that I must have been there asleep and woke up and was traumatized because Roger had taken his own life.

He pulled out one of these yellow legal pads and he had a pencil, not a pen, but a pencil. I said, "You know, I wasn't there." I said, "I remember Roger telling me goodbye. I know I went home. I probably have the receipt." And he said, "Well this is just a hypothetical." And I remember him using that word, and he wrote it across the top of that page, but of course that disappeared later.

I was still in the driver's seat. The windows were rolled up. I remember that one person had driven up and walked by, and then come back to the car and left, and he had told me to roll the windows up, and he had stopped talking during that time. He didn't want anybody to know, I guess, or to hear anything or to see anything. I mean, that's how isolated it was. It was also blazing hot, it was about ninety-five degrees. He didn't take his coat off. He had a tweed coat on and he didn't take it off the entire time.

Burrows' lawyers, that Potter admitted she had falsely accused Burrows to obtain leniency and to satisfy a grudge she had against him. Burrows wasn't released from death row until 1994.

Prosecutors are legally required to inform the defense about any benefits witnesses may be receiving, thus giving the defense the opportunity to inform the jury of sentencing deals and the like. However, even when a defense has strong evidence impeaching a snitch's character, it may not be enough to erase the impact of a snitch's testimony. Association with the government appears to afford snitches an unwarranted good credit with the jury.

Bribery is a criminal offense. A lawyer can be sent to prison for offering a witness monetary incentive for testimony that helps him win his case. Though federal law prohibits the prosecution from offering "anything of value to any person for or because of testimony," monetary rewards or the promise thereof are still used to entice informants to testify.

Moreover, snitches whose perjury falsely corroborates a prosecutor's theory are rarely, if ever, prosecuted. On the other hand, snitches who attempt to recant false testimony often face serious legal difficulties.

In 1978, Paula Gray, a borderline mentally-retarded seventeen-year-old, falsely confessed to being an accomplice in a double murder and rape. As a result of her testimony, four innocent men were convicted of the crime. When Gray later attempted to recant her false testimony, she was repeatedly threatened by the prosecution and put on trial, both for perjury and the double murder. She was sentenced to fifty years in prison and was exonerated by DNA evidence in 2002.

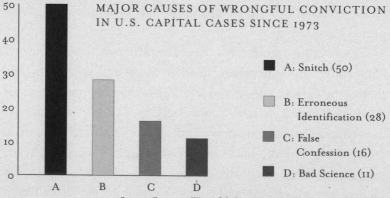

MAJOR CAUSES OF WRONGFUL CONVICTION IN U.S. CAPITAL CASES SINCE 1973

A: Snitch (50)

B: Erroneous Identification (28)

C: False Confession (16)

D: Bad Science (11)

Source: Center on Wrongful Convictions at Northwestern University

He started writing out this so-called statement to the suicide—a hypothetical. He had about three or four sentences down before I said, "What are you writing?" and, he said, "Oh, don't worry about this, this is just a hypothetical," and he said, "I already have this on tape in front of eight witnesses."

He starts writing this down as though I have said it already—that I was there asleep on the couch and that I remember this. And I said, "I don't remember this, I don't think it can possibly be true. I remembered leaving, and I remember him telling me goodbye. I wasn't asleep, he wasn't asleep." But he wouldn't listen to any of it. He just kept writing.

And then he asked me about picking up the gun. He said, "What did you have on?" He never went to a question directly. He just said, "What did you have on?" So I'm thinking, okay, "What did I have on? I had on a long-sleeved sweater." And he said, "Would you have used that to wipe off the gun?"

He's insisting that I go along with this, and I said, you know, "Joe [Hairfield] picked up the gun," because I remember Joe saying it. I didn't see it.

We'd been in that car a little over two hours, and he says, "You have to sign this." And I said, "But it's not true." That's when he got really ugly. His face turned red and he was very angry. He said that all he had to do was pick up the telephone and by that afternoon it would be all in the papers. I would lose my job, I would be arrested, I would not be able to speak to my family, he would drag my family through the mud. That made me realize if I didn't do what he said that my life was going to be over, my life as I knew it.

This person has the ability to destroy you and they're threatening to destroy your life and your family. I wouldn't have a chance to talk to my boss, explain anything. I'm the person that's responsible for my family. I'm a single mother with three kids in college, and what do you do? It's like someone holding a gun to you and saying you have to do it, you have no other way to go. He basically said that he was either taking me or that piece of paper. What do you do? So I signed it.

I thought I would be able to get away, to get back to my office, to be able to think. He said, "Wait here." We got out of the car and he went to his car and he got his gun, a huge gun, and he stuck it in his belt, and he walked me around through the woods. Almost all of that time he was trying to get me to take some kind of plea. He was just threatening me again. It was not till four-thirty that he brought me back to where the cars were.

I remember I asked him what would he do then? He said he would take this to the prosecutor but that I could go back to my office. He said he would call me. This is how strange it all was. You'd think if you really thought someone was a murderer you would arrest them.

No audio recording of Monroe's park meeting with Agent Riley was ever produced. Riley claimed that Monroe requested that meeting and was quite insistent they meet immediately, not leaving him suf-ficient time to pick up the recording equipment at police headquar-ters. On June 10, Monroe was indicted for first-degree murder.

I DIDN'T REALIZE WHAT THE POLICE COULD DO AND SAY IN COURT

On June 3, 1992, I was accused [by Riley]. It wasn't something that could happen to me. You know you're innocent. There can't be any evidence against you. What could there be? At that point I didn't realize what the police could do and say in court.

About two weeks before the trial—the trial was October of 1992—my attorney said this name to me, Zelma Smith, and do you know her, have you ever heard of her. I said, "No, of course not, I don't have any clue." She was in the Chesterfield jail, which is the adjacent county to Powhatan. I'd never known anybody in jail, and I hadn't been in any jail.

She was testifying to this story: that the year before Roger's death, I called Zelma Smith in the spring of 1991. I wanted to buy an untraceable gun from her. We met in the cemetery. She brought this gun, and allegedly I gave her a hundred dollars. That was supposedly the end of the story, that she never heard from me again.

These kinds of informants—false informants I should say— see an opportunity to try to buy some leniency or reward, or it comes from police or the prosecutor in setting it up. It's a horrendous tactic. So anyway, here she was in the jail. My attorney sent our investigator there to try to talk to her, and she refused to talk to anybody. My attorney had no way to prepare, because we had no idea what this was even about.

KAFKAESQUE

Monroe's attorney had no idea what Smith was intending to say at Monroe's trial, which began on October 26. The state's case was built on the theory that Monroe had killed de la Burdé out of jealousy because he was about to abandon her for another woman. The prosecutor presented the jury with the "confession" to Riley's suicide scenario he had Monroe sign in the park. He brought witnesses who claimed that de la Burdé was making plans for his future and was not depressed. He presented forensic evidence that he claimed was consistent with a murder. And he had their star witness, Zelda Smith, testify that Monroe had attempted to buy an "untraceable" gun from her a year before de la Burdé's death. They failed to disclose considerable evidence consistent with Monroe's innocence, including: forensic evidence corroborating the suicide; evidence of Smith's actual background and whereabouts during the time she claimed to have met with Monroe; Smith's prior contacts with state police agent Riley in unrelated cases; and the deal Smith expected in exchange for her testimony at Monroe's trial.

In the opening and closing statements, I went back and counted the times that they used the phrase "Beverly killed," "shot," "murdered." In the space of say a five-minute discourse, it breaks down to almost every thirty seconds. Those are the words the jury is hearing. Kill. Shot. Murder.

The prosecution even had my defense attorneys using the words "victim" and "crime scene" and "murder." There was no crime scene. They were using the term "confession." There was no confession. What there was was Riley's bogus interview to create the impression that I had agreed to a suicide theory that I didn't remember. This is how the murder and conviction comes about. She "must have been there." She agreed to the theory that she must have been there and asleep at the suicide. It wasn't a suicide. It's a murder.

The medical examiner had initially determined that de la Burdé's death was a suicide. After Monroe's indictment, the medical examiner altered the cause of death, labeling it a homicide, and issued a report six months after de la Burdé's death.

As part of his routine investigation, Detective Neal submitted swabs taken from the web of de la Burdé's hands to test for gunshot residue. A handgun releases an invisible chemical deposit, known as primer residue, from the hammer when it is fired. When a suicide is suspected, police routinely swab the web of the deceased's shooting hand. The results came back about three weeks later. The web of de la Burdé's right hand was found to have primer residue, consistent with his firing the fatal shot with his right hand. However, the results from the residue tests were not made available to Monroe's legal defense in their entirety at the trial, leaving her defense unable to use the critical evidence to challenge the prosecution's assertions. Even in the absence of this evidence, the prosecutions' expert witnesses admitted that it was possible that de la Burdé fired the gun.

The real issue, if there was to be an issue and it had come down to it, was this: Was this a suicide or was this a homicide? And that's forensics. And of course the evidence was concealed—the evidence of the invisible chemical residue that was on the web of [Roger's] right hand—that they had since probably before Agent Riley ever tried to talk to me and convince me that I was there at the suicide.

Their theory was that someone—meaning Beverly Monroe—had reached down when he was asleep with the gun upside down in the left hand and pulled the trigger. When the so-called expert tried to demonstrate this in court, she couldn't pull the trigger. She tried three times.

Eight years later we discovered—and it was actually a woman in prison who pointed it out to me—I showed her this photograph. She said, "Oh my god, that's ridiculous. She's [the expert witness] using her right hand, not her left hand." She had done a reconstruction with somebody shooting with her left hand, and it was her right hand. And nobody had even seen that—not my attorney, not anybody. Again, you tend to accept what they say. But these people are lying.

The cigarettes [found in the ashtray the morning after de la Burdé's death] were important because somebody had smoked them and left them there. That meant that most likely, somebody had come after I had left and Roger was still there alive. Obviously the police at the scene thought they were important.

So here we are at trial, and the prosecutor's asking Greg Neal about the cigarettes. And this is where Greg gets extremely uncomfortable. And he says, he somehow didn't think they were significant. How vague can you get? How evasive can you get? What does it mean? It just got left like that.

After Neal was on the stand, the prosecutor stood up and says to the jury, "Look how honest and forthright Officer Neal has been to you folks." They're saying that over and over and over again. It's semantics. It must be Prosecutor 101.

Even if you buy all of this stuff that the prosecution said and forget the evidence, I had a receipt from the store and my canceled check. I was in the checkout line at 10:40.

De la Burdé's estimated time of death was 10:35 p.m.

I didn't remember at the time that I had talked to somebody in the store, but some guy saw the news of the trial on television. He recognized me from the grocery store that night.

The reason I had talked to him—as soon as I saw him again I recognized him and remembered—was because his little kid was with him. And it was late and the child was fussy. I just stooped down and said something to the child. We began a conversation. He said he was a construction worker. He had actually given me his card. I don't remember what happened to it. But if I had been so "cunning," as they said, and set this up, I would have certainly saved the man's card. Come on.

This fellow, Dennis, called and said, "I talked with this woman." He called the prosecutor's office first and, in his words, they blew him off. So then he called my attorney. He comes and testifies. He knows exactly why he was in Richmond that night. He lives about thirty miles away, and he'd been to a counselor. They were going through some family problems. He was unshakable because it was true. Duh. It was true.

[Zelma Smith] appeared on the 26th. You have no way of knowing what the story will be, what she could possibly say, why they would use her, where she came from, nothing. I had never seen this woman or heard of her before. She's very dressed up and obviously very good at this.

So her story is that in the spring of 1991, she supposedly had her business: Zelma Smith's Business Enterprise. She said she'd gotten a message on her answering machine and the person says she's Ms. Nelson. Where she pulled this from, I don't know. [In her scenario], I'm Ms. Nelson. It took me a little while to catch on to that, but I'm Ms. Nelson.

So Ms. Nelson calls her back and says she wants to do some business. We meet at the Burger King. Now I don't mean to sound pompous, but I've never set foot in a Burger King. I probably never will. I didn't even know the place she was talking about. We meet at the Burger King. I'm dressed in a nice suit. I never wore a suit. I am not a fancy person. This is fancy for me: cheap Target slacks, cheap Target shirt, even cheaper Burlington coat on sale. I can dress up, but I've never bought an expensive suit. Never.

That was the first meeting. Supposedly I gave her a hundred dollars and I wanted to buy an untraceable gun. We agreed to meet later. And we met in the cemetery. So I'm there in the cemetery and she brings a .357 Magnum, and I tell her it won't fit in my purse. So I don't take the gun. That was supposedly the end of the story, that she never heard from me again.

If you look at it logically, to make it appear that someone committed suicide, why would you use an untraceable gun when the person has their own gun in the house?

A few times [Smith] had to look at the prosecutor for clues or cues, I guess you could say. In fact, even the judge said something at one point, for him to stop coaching her on the stand. Looking back, I was in this zone of just being in this surreal existence of the whole trial. It was Kafkaesque. I don't know if everyone has read Kafka but they can look it up if they haven't because it's so important to know how these things feel to someone who's being falsely accused and put on trial.

WOMEN ARE THE ROOT OF ALL EVIL

In order to convict me, the prosecution had to do something in the face of all of the contradicting evidence. This is why they used things like, "She went bonkers." They [the jury] had to buy into that.

It's an easy sell that women go bonkers. They used this against me. The other thing is that it's very easy apparently for jurors and people in the public to believe that a woman cannot be independent. That somehow you're not somebody without this man.

Now, it's true that Roger was a fascinating person, and I did care about him and I loved him. But I didn't want to be married to him. I had my own life. I was an independent person with a career, a job, raising a family. You wouldn't say that about a man.

It's very easy for prosecutors to sell what I call this biblical story—that women are the root of all evil.

With as much evidence as there was in that courtroom, there was an awful lot concealed, misstated, perjury that shouldn't have happened. But even so, there were things that were as clear as a bell. Including the fact that I had a receipt. So what does the prosecutor do? He stands up in closing arguments and he says that receipt doesn't amount to a roll of pins. She could have come back later to Roger's house. When? How? Why?

The prosecutor insisted at closing that Smith had no incentive to lie, telling the jury, "Hard as it might be for you to believe, the absolute truth is that she did not ask for any consideration for her testimony from the Commonwealth in this case. And it's absolutely true that the Commonwealth has not promised her anything."

On November 2, 1992, after a seven-day trial and deliberations lasting less than two hours, the jury found Monroe guilty of first-degree murder and use of a firearm in the commission of a felony. On December 22, 1992, she was sentenced to twenty-two years in prison.

I get convicted and the prosecutor stood up and said, "Well, she's no danger to anybody," and the judge said, "You can go home." I went home, after a first-degree murder conviction. Then three days later, they found out that, well, he was in error; he wasn't supposed to do that. So then I called and said, "Well, what should I do?" He said, "Well, why not come in on Monday?" This was Wednesday. You know, this is how they were. It was strange.

THE CAVALRY IS NOT COMING

I went to the women's prison, where they have two cells for Powhatan County at the end of Cottage Three, which is this antique, dungeonlike place. It was cold. I was hungry. There was only one slot in my cell door. If I looked at just the right angle out of my little slot, down the hall to a door that had another little slot, then I could see at certain times the river. The James River.

It was where we used to go canoeing. Roger and some friends of ours used to go. At times, I could actually see the water. And seeing those trees and that water and that serenity was like looking at a master painting that you knew was real. And I cannot tell you how restoring that was.

What I kept thinking right before Christmas was that the cavalry was coming. And that's a strange way to put it, but it's this thing that somebody's going to come out to that prison, a whole group of my friends and family. Somebody's going to come. You know, it's totally unrealistic. And not an intelligent thought.

I was there from November to mid-February. Then I was put in this basement. It was an absolute firetrap. A basement with chains on the exit doors and in front of that about fifty folding chairs. Filled with cigarette smoke, and I was on the top bunk. I could reach the ceiling from my bunk. All the smoke collects up there.

That room held about thirty-five or forty women. At this end were the black women, and at the other end were all the white women. And I was the only white person at this end. I didn't notice that at first. I was sitting with the women that I'd become friends with, and one of the women, I don't remember her name, but her nickname was Red, she had kind of reddish hair. I was sitting on the top bunk, and she said, "Miss Beverly, I have a question for you." And I said, "What?" She said, "How come you're down here with us? And how come you laugh at our jokes?" What could I say? I hadn't noticed. I said, "They're funny."

Maybe if it were men, they're more challenging with each other. But women aren't like that. They were more resilient. They had a sense of humor.

I had just been there a few months. In the evenings we had to mop the floor. And you had to take turns mopping the floor. These women would take my turn so I could work on my case. And they would say—it was noisy as all get-out, unbelievable noise—"Be quiet, Miss Beverly is working on her case." This will stick with me for the rest of my life.

UPSIDE-DOWN AND BACKWARDS

Monroe appealed her conviction to Virginia's Court of Appeals. After nearly six months in prison, she was released on a $150,000 bond pending the outcome of her appeal. She returned to her home, which she still owned. For nearly three years, she and her attorneys fought her conviction in state courts. In addition to getting a $7-an-hour job at a bookstore, she devoted herself, with the help of friends, to investigating the state's star witness—Zelma Smith.

The bond was set at $150,000, which means I had to come up with $15,000 cash for that alone. I still had some liquid assets at that point. The trial cost—just the attorney was a flat 150 [thousand dollars], and then it cost about another $35,000 on top of that. Then the cost of the appeal. You lose track after a while. And that doesn't include the wear and tear and everything else. And the fact that you have no income. It's the hemorrhage of cost.

When I'd gotten out the first time, and gone back to my house, my daughters, Katie and Shannon, and my son, Gavin, and I were on my patio, and the sliding glass doors were open, and Katie had put on a piece by Bach. And for the first time, we could sit and hold hands and just cry. The tears just flood. And nobody can talk. You don't want anything else except to hold on to your children. You really don't care if you never eat again, never sleep again, or anything else.

The appeal process doesn't allow any new evidence, even if it shows there's been fraud or hidden evidence. But I was determined to find out who this [Zelma Smith] person was, it was so out of the blue. I didn't know the forensics, I couldn't stand to look at that, I couldn't stand to think about that. But I could look into this Zelma Smith thing.

I've got to know how in the dickens this was done to me. Where did this woman come from? And how was this prosecutor able to say, "Beverly Monroe is lying and Zelma Smith is telling the truth"? I'd never heard of this woman until she'd walked in that room. I'd never seen her before. You want to stand up and say, "Stop this farce!" And you can't. You're bolted to that chair. Not by bolts but by fifty-five years of dutifulness and civic responsibility. It's all such a weird farce. That's why it feels like *Alice in Wonderland.* Upside-down and backwards. And you're without any anchor except your family and your friends and your sense of what's right, which has been totally dislocated.

Every tiny thing, every name, everything I found led to something else. I was able to determine that she did not have a business. From the time she was thirteen she was committing crimes and committing frauds and perjury and you name it, and she'd been in prison four or five times already, and it appeared from her record that she had gotten out of prison under unusual circumstances.

They have a sentence-reduction hearing for her after my trial. She did get a huge sentence reduction. She got most of the charges dropped before my trial, I learned. I was able to establish that she had been involved in other cases that Riley had initiated at least three years prior to this, in 1989.

At her sentence reduction the judge at Chesterfield did not buy her whole story. When you get the transcript of that sentence reduction you see that he sees through the whole thing. He doesn't know that she's lying about my case, but he sees that she's a repeat so-called informant.

Smith, who had had a juvenile record, was sent to prison as an adult on at least four separate occasions. In 1991, during the time when she was supposedly engaged in operating her own business, she was actually dodging multiple warrants and charges, but was finally caught, charged, and convicted on four felony counts. She was facing a prison term of up to forty years. Out on bond, she left town and went to California, where she was arrested on new charges and then extradited back to Virginia in May 1992.

Smith agreed to testify against Monroe. In exchange, the Commonwealth provided what the U.S. Court of Appeals would later call "substantial consideration to Smith in exchange for her testimony against Monroe."

In August 1992, prior to her testimony at Monroe's trial, the sentence Smith faced before fleeing Virginia was reduced to two years. After Monroe's trial, Smith, who had also faced an automatic five-year sentence for fleeing to California, received another hearing for a further reduction in her sentence.

The sentencing judge at Smith's hearing, in reviewing her criminal record, said, "You know the system as well as I do and as well as the lawyers that are here, and as well as Mr. Riley who testified on your behalf. And at some point, you become as much of a parasite on society as the people that you work to put behind bars." In reference to Smith's sentence reduction, Monroe's prosecutor admitted it was the "cost of doing business." The judge, recognizing Smith's pattern, responded: "I'll look at your record and understand that you're familiar with the cost of doing business." Nonetheless, Smith's seven-year sentence was reduced to three years.

THIS DECISION CAME, AND IT'S ALWAYS A BLOW, A HORRIBLE BLOW

The appeal process has a number of steps—a very expensive and a very agonizing process. There's oral argument and there's your petition, and you have to go through these different briefs and write all of it. After you're convicted, you have to appeal to the state itself. And I know now that had I been selling drugs, I would have had a better chance at appeal than with this case. In a high-profile case, I think the attorney general's office fights much harder and much dirtier. And there's much more reluctance for the courts to overturn that. The last step [in the state appeal] is the Virginia Supreme Court.

This is right after Christmas of December 1995. That's when everything went down the drain. You're never prepared. The opinion that came down was so—you know, I don't have words for it—again, it's the *Alice in Wonderland* thing. It's that Zelma Smith is absolutely credible, that Roger's death occurred at 10:30 or 10:35, and I have these receipts saying I was twenty-five miles away at 10:40, but their statement is this: that the evidence is sufficient to convict. Nothing wrong here. We see nothing wrong. And this decision came, and it's always a blow, a horrible blow. It means that the rest of your life, whatever you have, is gone. Your house. Your future. Your children's future is scarred forever. Forever.

Monroe's appeal argued that insufficient evidence, Smith's testimony, and numerous other errors rendered her trial unfair and unreliable. The lower courts denied her appeal. She then appealed to the Supreme Court of Virginia. They ruled against her. In January 1996, Monroe was taken back into custody to serve out the remainder of her twenty-two-year sentence at Pocahontas Correctional Center in Chesterfield County, Virginia.

Katie, Monroe's daughter, quit her job as a lawyer and dedicated herself full-time to fighting Monroe's case. Katie began the federal appeals process by filing a habeas corpus petition.

'WHEN ARE YOU GOING TO GET
YOUR MOTHER OUT OF HERE?'

Katie was my attorney, my daughter. Suddenly the warden calls
me in. She gives me this two-hour lecture about how my daughter can't come visit me on weekends, because she's my attorney.
And so this went on for days, and I sat there and I took notes,
and I said, "What do you mean?" She's my daughter, but she's
also my attorney. And I'd never had any problem before. So this
went on and on, and of course nobody outside knew that this
was happening.

And so finally the warden calls me in, they have about three
or four people in the room and she says, "You have to make a
choice. She's either your daughter or your attorney." And I said,
"You know, I'm sorry, she's my daughter, she's my attorney. I can't
say she's not my daughter!" But they weren't going to let her visit
me as my daughter if she came on a legal visit.

So this went around and around. So we ended up having to
take it to court, sort of tagged onto another case, and force them
to admit that it was all something made up. Next day the warden
smiles at me and says, "You know, there was never really any
problem."

So you have these strange things that happened in prison;
they can make up the rules any time they want. They can say if
you have a family member, you can only visit one family member. I knew people like that who had sisters, the family could
only visit one, not the other twin sister. They'd have to take turns,
you know, just crazy stuff.

At that time, even when I would have on the jeans and the
uniform, I would have people come up to me, women come up
to me, as though I was not a prisoner, but as they put it, a "professional." Not only the women there, but people from outside,

would come up to me and start talking without realizing that I was a prisoner. I can't tell you exactly why. Some of it may have to do with the way you speak or you carry yourself. And it always took me by surprise. It made me uncomfortable.

The most bothersome thing was that they could take me and put me in there and label me like this: convicted killer; murderer. But the second thing that bothered me was that you could label these women as felons. Convicts. Inmates. I despise the word inmate. I don't like labels. What it does is ostracize you. You're not a person.

The only way women could get to the dentist, they put you in chains and drag you over to the men's prison. You sit there all day. I went twice in seven years. The one time she nearly butchered me. But the women, almost all the women there, they couldn't believe I had all my own teeth, because they were so used to having their teeth pulled. And I would tell them, "Don't let them pull a tooth. Don't let them pull your teeth out." That's all they wanted to do. I saw women with abscessed teeth. They're women in pain. They wouldn't get there for weeks.

Monroe was tapped by other inmates as a resource and by prison officials as a teacher. On her own initiative, she set up an informal program teaching English, spelling, and math. Later, she was assigned to teach in the general education program and then in the prison's business program.

There were women who had mental illness. Severe. Lack of education. Women who had—for one reason or another—killed their child. They were not ostracized because there were always reasons. Everything from postpartum depression to some other circumstance involved. And a lot of physical and emotional abuse. I knew these women. They were not bad people or evil people. It changed my views, because I grew up in a conservative, traditional crime-and-punishment kind of atmosphere.

If people came in from, say, the Department of Corrections, into the classroom where I taught, the first thing I would do, just like I would in any business setting, I would go up and shake their hand. But it had an edge to it because I was determined to do it. I was determined that they would acknowledge me as a person and acknowledge all the women in the room as people at work. You feel like it's a very small way to fight.

One visiting time, Katie was there with her son—my grandson, Asher, who was just four. I could feel him kind of tugging. I stooped down, so I could be right on eye level with him. He said, "Mimi, you've got to come home. We've fixed a room for you, and we painted it green. And there's a really comfortable couch and there's art on the walls." It was a little prepared speech that he had in his mind. "You've got to come home. It's ready for you."

He never lost faith. And it was a different kind of faith. Anytime they were at a wishing well, or he would point to a star, anything, it was always, "Bring my Mimi home." He had that belief that I was coming home.

People working in the prison were not supposed to be personally involved, but they were. And they were all supportive. They were supportive of Katie. When she came in for a legal visit, they were ecstatic. She was that representation of hope.

There was one officer in particular. When Katie had come on a visit, he kind of whispered over to her and says, "When are you going to get your mother out of here?" That tells you that people understood.

In 1998, Katie Monroe began to receive assistance, pro bono, from Steve Northup, an attorney at the Troutman Sanders law firm.

MOST PEOPLE DON'T HAVE A TRUE
APPRECIATION FOR FREEDOM

Major Hill, who was the assistant warden, came in to the prison dorm and I think it was one of the few times in my life where I felt my knees were like rubber. That I couldn't walk. She said, "You've got a phone call." She said, "You've got to return the call."

I said, "The phones are right there"—there were three in the dorm—"can I just make it right here?"

She said, "No, you've gotta come to my office."

She was acting funny. So I had to walk, and that thirty yards to the warden's office seemed like forever. 'Course, everybody is just on pins and needles. It was a big topic. Everybody was aware. And so I get down there, and first she talks to my lawyer. She has tears everywhere. She's getting the Kleenex on her desk. I was watching her on the phone talking to him, but still no real clue. Then she hands the phone to me to talk to my lawyer Steve Northup, and Steve doesn't say right away that we've won. He kind of hesitates and says, "Well, the opinion has come in." I'm about to die. It's not on purpose, you know, I think he couldn't get the words out.

And I hear Katie in the background, crying and screaming, hysterical. I still don't know exactly what the news is. So when my lawyer finally tells me, I can't really be sure. You're just afraid to believe.

On March 28, 2002, U.S. Federal District Court Judge Richard Williams vacated Monroe's conviction on the grounds that prosecutors concealed material evidence at trial. He called Monroe's case a "monument to prosecutorial indiscretions and mishandling," criticized the management of the death scene, described the forensic evidence as "unclear and contradictory," and called the state police's interviews of Monroe "deceitful and manipulative." Williams described the prosecution's case as weak, especially given Monroe's "unrefuted alibi for the time of [de la] Burdé's death."

I don't even remember the words. It was more about the opinion. That it's in our favor. That we won. After all, all this time. And then I'm hugging Major Hill and she's hugging me, and we're dancing around, and I got a chance to talk to Katie. And we're so emotional we couldn't even talk.

Walking back into the dorms was just amazing. Amazing. It was pandemonium. I took those steps coming back up the landing and I don't think I even hit a single step. I was flying. I was literally flying. Then it occurred to me that there are all these people there, locked in. Normally, during the day, those bars were unlocked.

I gave the thumbs up sign, and it was just... it was like everybody was being released. It wasn't about me. It was just about that somebody could win, against the system. When your daughter and your family fight and win, there's this other dimension to it. It brings out the best in human spirit, it really brings out the best of what you're capable of doing.

I go down the aisle, and everybody is just reaching out. It's just like this huge victory line.

It takes about a week for me to be released, and every day it's the same kind of bedlam. Every day, people would watch the news and leave a note on my bed: "Have you heard anything yet? Have you heard anything yet?"

By that time, reporters were coming. And again, the prison was very accommodating. It's a surprising sort of dichotomy going on. They were joyful, but at the same time, they were doing things to promote the prison, and some of the publicity was about them. Which was fine. The only thing I resented about that was when I learned that they had women up all night waxing floors because people might see or come in. That bothered me.

I was released in April of 2002. When I walked out of that gate, the sun is different and the air feels—it just feels different from inside. Even that perimeter wire fence. It was a whole different world. A whole different sun, a whole different feel. You actually feel the touch of the air on my skin now that I didn't [before]. And it's a joy. Every nuance of awareness like that is an absolute joy.

ABSOLUTE DREAD

After Monroe was released, the state appealed Williams's ruling.

In March 2003, nearly one year after Monroe's release, the state lost its appeal. The U.S. Court of Appeals for the Fourth Circuit unanimously affirmed Williams's decision to vacate her conviction. Noting that Monroe was "by all accounts a calm, gentle, and kind person" with "an impeccable reputation as an honest and law-abiding citizen," the court went on to list numerous items of potentially exculpatory evidence that the state had suppressed. The court found that "Smith's testimony was the Commonwealth's major evidence of premeditation," portraying Beverly as a calculated killer. The court stated that the case against Monroe "can be fairly characterized as tenuous."

After losing the federal appeal, Virginia's Attorney General decided not to contest the decision from the Fourth Circuit Court of Appeals. After the state bowed out, the Powhatan prosecutor still had the option to retry or reindict Monroe. Under the threat of reprosecution, Monroe spent thousands more on legal assistance. By that point she had already lost her home, and had spent hundreds of thousands of dollars on legal fees—even with the pro bono help of attor-

Monroe's hope for freedom hangs on prosecutor's choice

Appeals court backs overturning conviction, but state could seek new trial

By BOB DAVIS

Katie Monroe (left) and her mother, Beverly, are celebrating news that the U.S. Court of Appeals for the Fourth Circuit issued its opinion upholding last year's federal court decision overturning Beverly's conviction on the grounds of prosecutor misconduct. (Mary Franks photo)

The Hanover, Virginia Herald-Progress *reports on Monroe's exoneration (2003)*

neys at the Troutman Sanders law firm and the assistance of investigators and friends.

We still had to fight this battle for almost two years. We had this sense of momentary relief at times, and we tried to take advantage of it, but I wasn't allowed to travel, to visit friends. I wasn't really free. I didn't have my independence back. I didn't have any real freedom back. I certainly didn't have my life back. The thing wasn't over.

During that year and a half, I stayed with Katie. [Asher] could come down in the morning and jump in bed with me. So there were wonderful parts, you know. I could read to him, I could hold him.

I tried to give Katie some space by moving around. I did some housesitting for my ex-husband, and I stayed with my other daughter several times. And so I moved—packed up computer, files, clothes and everything—I think thirteen times during that year and a half, back and forth, so I felt like gypsy.

It was good and it was terrible. It was wonderful to be free, to be home, to be able to help out with things, to have a sense of freedom and to have sense of vindication. The most important thing to me and to my family was clearing my name and then beginning to come out of this morass of legal process and dread, absolute dread that somehow something could be done to us again, or we could be just buried in this process because of this resistance and refusal to acknowledge the evidence and the truth. I mean, even when the court adjudicates it, the vindication, it isn't over. And so there was this horrible dread, and I think it was worse for Katie than for anyone because she has worked so hard and given up so much of her life that she wanted it to be over. Once you win, you don't want to have to start battling again.

AS A TAXPAYER, I FIND [IT] SO HORRENDOUSLY WRONG

In June 2003, prosecutors dropped all charges against Monroe.

I have to really give credit to the state here, meaning the state of Virginia, the attorney general's office, for dropping everything. That was a great, great feeling.

After you've been exonerated, after a case has been overturned and vacated, there is no investigation and nothing to prevent this from happening to someone else. You know, it's wrong. And they know it's wrong. If it were a medical situation, if it had been a car accident, you can demand records. You have some mechanism for getting to what happened. But in cases where somebody has been falsely accused or wrongfully convicted, you have no access to the same kinds of information. Or accountability. As a taxpayer, I find that so horrendously wrong, on top of what happened. There needs to be some way to correct it. But everyone wants to move on, you know. There's war in Iraq, many, many more horrendous things than what happened to me. It's not about me. It's about accountability in the system. About making things right. Making things work the way we think they're supposed to be.

This is not something that has just happened in the '90s. Or the '80s. Or the '70s. It's been going on since the beginning of time. Power is the problem. And lack of accountability. One person cannot do it. It takes the entire system. To go along with it, or to contribute. And I know this from personal experience. And that doesn't mean these are necessarily evil people. But something happens in the mentality to allow them to think that it's justified. Or to look the other way. And that's what the result is. People's lives are ruined. And it's beyond that. It's our whole system that becomes untrustworthy. And once you lose that, it's very hard to get it back. And that's where the media comes in.

I agonized over how people in our case, who came from the media and who were interested, did not do an accurate job. Accuracy. I mean, if you have a scientific question, you work very hard to get the facts right. And you check those facts. And you question. You don't try to turn it into something sensational or entertainment. That is part of the problem with the public. The public doesn't want to have to think. They want emotional answers. "I think he's guilty." "Oh, I think he's not." What do you know? My first question is, "What do you know about the facts of the case?" And it turns out it's zero! Zero. And you wouldn't do that if you had a medical question. You wouldn't do that if you had a question about your automobile. If you have a flat tire, you don't go and say, "Well, I think it's... this." No! You want to know. Does it have a nail in it? What caused it to go flat? I mean, how simple can that be? Well, we don't do that. With these kinds of issues it becomes sheer emotion. And some kind of internal satisfaction that, "That can't happen to me. Look, that person must have been guilty." And there is a comfort in that. I don't understand it because I get no comfort seeing anyone accused, arrested. I don't even get a feeling of safety. Now I question everything. I have to admit I didn't before. But I question everything. And we need to teach that. Not just question authority, but question facts. And know what you're talking about.

I understand it takes years of education to have systemic reform. But change can come. Reform can come. With a lot of media exposure. And encouraging the police and the prosecution to see that it's in their best interest.

NOTHING FEELS NORMAL ANYMORE

I took off to visit some friends, and I just drove, I drove all the way up, visiting friends all the way up to New Hampshire and back, and probably saw a dozen or so people who'd been particularly supportive, and that was a sense of freedom. These are the feelings and the turning points for me personally, and once I got the apartment I began to do some restructuring.

I had a good education, a super job and career. Somehow it didn't feel like I was sixty-five years old. I didn't feel that age. I didn't think about it being a factor, and I had wonderful contacts, people who were head of human resources with corporations, people who were CEOs, people who I knew through other people, people whom I knew personally.

So I started the job [hunt] thinking, okay, six months I'll be back in reasonably good shape. It didn't turn out that way. You know what it's like to send out résumés—first you get one together and you update it, you go for interviews. It's an extremely time-consuming process, and you can put a week or more into one application, and then other weeks if you have to follow up and keep that process going, and it ends up being a total waste of time. You don't make any progress. Mostly you just get rejections.

It's been a very, very difficult and discouraging process. I'm not an easily discouraged person and I'm not discouraged now; I know I can get something. But the realization is that I will not

Monroe celebrates her release in Washington, D.C. with her daughter Katie (2003)

be able to earn a half, maybe not even a third, of what I was making fifteen years ago, or have the same sense of responsibility and enjoyment of my job and my career.

When I think back, since I had my first job at age five, I've never been rejected for a job, never, or anything else that I've applied for. So the times have changed, and between that and all these other factors it is extremely difficult, and I didn't expect it to be so.

I lost my home and all of the equity that we had in that. So it was the need to rebuild in the sense of not just having a place of my own, but doing it in a way that's sensible. I don't like the idea of renting, I like the idea of building equity. I'm fortunate enough to be able to get a mortgage without a job.

Monroe relocated to Williamsburg, Virginia, and bought a home in a community on the James River.

The house is great. I've got a lot of work to do, and I like doing

Monroe (center) with her daughters Katie (left) and
Shannon (right) and grandson Asher (2003)

work. The real strain is not having the financial means to do what
I would like to do here or to get it in shape. So I spend a lot of
my time doing things the hard way, trying to do as much of the
work myself as I can. But that's nothing to complain about
because again, I'm so fortunate.

It's beginning to feel like my home, but not really—not the
home that I had. Nothing feels normal anymore, and when you
meet people, they want to know why you moved here. Well,
I have the standard thing, that my daughter [Shannon] lives here.
You don't want to just slap them with this whole sad story, and
yet you don't want to evade the issue either. I've talked to my
neighbors, because they want to know why I'm looking for a job
at sixty-seven. People are just naturally curious. You have to
explain to them that you're not a normal person.

It's not my nature to be secretive, and I want to educate people about the dangers of wrongful conviction. I want people to

know, number one, that this should never have happened, and number two, it should have never have taken this long to correct, and three, it can happen so easily and so quickly to anybody. It doesn't matter what your education is, it doesn't matter what your status in life is, it can happen to you in a heartbeat, and once it does, it's so difficult to turn around, and then your life is changed forever.

This is a community with its own little police force. One of them had come by, just to be helpful, really nice guy, and he, without my saying much of anything to him, he went and checked the website FreeBeverly.com. The very next day he came back and said, "Oh my god, you were framed!"

TALKING TO THE RIVER

Where it's hit me hardest is in losing people. I lost the person that I loved, who took his own life, and I've never really had a chance to grieve, or even be sad. And so those memories have been tainted a lot. Even the things that they said about him, which were untrue, at trial. They had to make him out to be a bad person in order to make it look like I would be somebody who would want to do something to him. They destroyed my relationship with his daughter, his family. Those are things that you can never get back.

My mother, that was hard. Granted, she was in her eighties, but she suffered through this. She went to trial with an oxygen tank. We didn't know she had congestive heart failure. There was never a more gentle, wonderful lady than my mother, and I lost her. She died five months after I was released. And I lost a brother while I was in. He had diabetes, he became blind; he couldn't come to visit. Two months after my mother died, my other brother died. You have these losses that are irrecoverable.

You learn to move on. I've spent a lot of time with the day-to-day things, and doing what I call talking to the river. During prison, to free my mind and to separate myself and to transcend a lot of the pain and dread and anguish, I remember I read poetry. My daughter Shannon had given me some in German and some in English, by Herman Hesse. There was a lot of poetry that other people would send me, even when they didn't know that this was one of my favorite subjects, something that's vital to my existence.

I have a lot of these things and I take them to the river with me and recite and remember and read. That's so restoring. The other thing is music. I listen to music, particularly to opera and particularly to Domingo, who was always my favorite. For seven years I only heard his voice twice. Those were the most, oh gosh, intense and transcending moments that can take you out of any prison.

Michael Evans   *Paul Terry*

SHEEP AMONGST WOLVES

NAMES: Michael Evans and Paul Terry · **BORN:** 1958

HOMETOWN: Chicago, Illinois · **CONVICTED OF:** Rape and murder

SENTENCE: 200 to 400 years · **SERVED:** 27 years · **RELEASED:** 2003

In 1976, Michael Evans and Paul Terry were sent to prison for the rape and murder of a nine-year-old girl. Both men were 17 years old. Terry's twenty-seven years in prison were extremely debilitating, leaving him unwilling to speak about his experiences. Evans emerged well-spoken and optimistic.

This narrative is split into two sections. In the first, Evans speaks about his experiences. In the second, Terry's sister Pamela Hawkins speaks on Terry's behalf. At Evans's request, the name of the key witness in the case has been changed.

MICHAEL EVANS:
WE COULD BE ANYTHING WE WANTED

I grew up in Chicago. It was a neighborhood of poverty. It was a neighborhood of minority people of all types of backgrounds. I never was rich and I never was poor because my dad, who was a country boy, he was a workaholic. So he always did his best in raising us up, him and my mother, to the best of their knowledge and leading us in the right paths and giving us direction. We could be anything that we wanted to in life if we put our minds to it.

My dad worked until he died. He would always try to teach me good qualities and values about work. My father instilled me, he said, "Son, as long as you educate yourself and keep a job, you will always be able to hold your own and be able to support yourself."

My mother is a very strong woman. She were a very religious woman. She was raised and born in Jackson, Mississippi.

I never seen my mother and dad actually fight. Matter of fact, even argue. Growing up with them, there was no alcoholism where they got drunk and then wanna fight and fuss. They was always in harmony and unity with each other.

I was a family man, being surrounded around my family. I have six sisters. We had a lot of fun. I love my sisters very much. I believe that my sisters, deep in my heart, love they brother. We was a family that prayed together, stayed together. Prayed and supported and loved each other.

I was the type of guy to play sports. I loved to play sports. I played football, I played softball, I played basketball. I was a church-going type of boy. I sung in the choir. I went to church events and I just were one that loved the sports activities and who wondered about things, about life in general.

When [Paul Terry] first moved in the community, he didn't know anybody, so I was the first one who embraced him and welcomed him to the community. Paul always had been shy and quiet but he were a type of person who could fix things, almost like a carpenter. He had a twin sister, he have several sisters. Later on we became like homeboys and homegirls in the community. My eyes kind of captured his sister Beverly who were a real close friend of mine. She died since I was incarcerated.

I BELIEVED IN THE AMERICAN DREAM

My son name Tyrone Burnett. I was fourteen when his mother was fifteen. I got her pregnant at fourteen. We were schoolhouse sweethearts at the time. What they consider as puppy love. I didn't really understand. Only thing I do know was that it felt good. She was more mature than I were, so she knew more of what she was doing. As matter of fact she instructed me, directed me as to what to do. But I guess I got too good. 'Course, I didn't have a child by myself. It took two.

Her mother and them moved to Detroit at the time. We stayed in touch for about two or three years. She called me and told me what she was naming him and all that, saying as long as she had the child, she had me with her. That I was there with her.

At the time I believed in the American dream—my country, the land of the free, land of the brave. Land of opportunity. The land of equality. But then I felt that I had been betrayed after they had wrongfully incarcerated me. At the time when they took me off the street, I was just seventeen years old.

MY INNOCENCE WAS BEING RIDICULED

In 1976, a nine-year-old girl was raped and murdered in a southeast Chicago neighborhood. Five days after the crime, a woman named Nancy Tammler told detectives that she had seen two black youths struggling with a young girl on the night of the crime. She and a police artist produced sketches of two men.

After a $5,000 award had been offered for information, Tammler implicated seventeen-year-old Michael Evans, claiming that he was one of the youths involved in the struggle. Police arrested Evans the next day and he was indicted for rape, kidnapping, and murder.

The [crime] happened in 1976. My niece had seen it on TV and she said, "That's the young lady lives down the street from us about a block." The police at that time were desperate. They were going house to house to see if anybody had eyewitnessed anybody or seen anybody.

The police came to our house. They wanted me to show them which way did I come back home and what time did I get home—I was at my auntie's house—and what was I doing at my auntie's house.

The lady named Ms. Tammler, who bear false witness against me, proclaimed that she knew all the time who the murderers were. Forty days later she decided to come forth. She seen in the newspaper that there were a $5,000 reward for anybody who had information.

She made a statement that she has seen myself as well as Paul Terry, [who] never had a driver's license, never had drove a car—she had seen us jumping a car and, you know, [abduct] a girl and threw her in the car.

One day I was going down the street. [Ms. Tammler] had called the police department and said the guy who committed the crime is walking down the street. A plainclothes detect[ive] arrested me and handcuffed me. My niece, who was with me at the time, ran home and told my mother, "You know, the police just arrested Michael."

And from there I was taken down to the police department to be questioned. When I got down there they put me in this interrogation room where I was constantly cross-examined.

Some come in play the bad guy, others play the good guys. They took turns, teamed up and cross-examined me.

I felt that I was being like humiliate[d], my character was being assassinated for a crime that I had no knowledge of. My innocence was being ridiculed.

I couldn't even perceive a thought in my mind or heart of ever committing a crime that they accused me of. Not only was I heartbroken, I was, I mean, can they really do this in the land, in the country that I so-called believed in? Can they really do this? Now I know that I was the perfect candidate. I had a clean record, no criminal record, never accused of anything, so they wanted to mess it up. So at the same time by me being Afro-American they wanted to frame me.

Evans's first trial was declared a mistrial after prosecutors failed to reveal that they had provided "financial assistance" to Tammler in exchange for her testimony.

Before Evans was retried, Tammler also implicated Evans's friend Paul Terry in a police lineup. Based on the lineup identifications, the Cook County State's Attorney's Office obtained indictments charging Terry with rape, kidnapping, and murder.

Evans and Terry were tried together in April 1977, with the prosecution relying almost entirely on Tammler's testimony.

According to the Center on Wrongful Convictions at Northwestern University, "After six hours of deliberation over two days, with the intervening night in sequestration, the jury sent a note to the judge, Frank W. Barbaro, saying, 'We are deadlocked unalterably. What shall we do?' Barbaro responded, 'It is your duty to continue to deliberate.' After further deliberation, the jury sent a second note saying, 'In almost four additional hours of deliberations we cannot reach a unanimous decision.' The defense moved for a mistrial, but Barbaro denied the motion and directed the jury to 'continue to deliberate.'"

At the conclusion of the trial, Michael Evans and Paul Terry were convicted of rape and murder and both were sentenced to 200 to 400 years in prison.

I were ignorant to the justice system because I'd never been accused of any crime. I were always positive that I would be found not guilty. I did not have an education with the prison system. I was very much unaware of the agendas and the way the system operates. I was seventeen. I was young and dumb. Immature when it come to the way of society and injustice and crookedness.

I were always optimistic that they would come to their senses. As time went [by] I got pessimistic and I began to think if they were going to let me go, they would let me go by now, but they didn't. I were very, very, very... you know it was unbelievable. It was a shock.

My first trial was a bench trial. I was pleading for mercy on the court. The judge granted me a new trial after he found that my witness [Ms. Tammler] had been bribed, who bear false witness against me.

The second trial, I was tried by twelve peoples. But the jury, my understanding, were hung. They could not make a decision. I don't think they wanted to make a decision. But they was misinstructed by the judge, who made prejudiced statements. I believe the jury got tired of deliberating. You know in those jury seats it be hot and they was fed up and uncomfortable. They went in and came out with a verdict of guilty.

IN PRISON YOU DON'T HAVE FRIENDS, YOU HAVE ASSOCIATES

Prison were a horrible, terrible, negative place. Very lonely, horrible, depressed place. It's not for me. With people that were there who were seasoned criminals, I always say I felt like a sheep amongst the wolf.

The negativity of prison, of being incarcerated, if you have any principles, you try to separate yourself from the negativity, but it's hard because you in an environment where there's violence every day. Every day is something different and then you wonder what's gonna happen today. Am I gonna get stabbed in the back or get my head busted in or...?

In prison you don't have friends, you only have associates. That same person who say they're your friend might try to stab you in the back, you know, when you walk out the door. Out of jealousy or envy or if you got more commissary or something than he got. I never had friends. I had associates.

I had a couple of fights. I had to beat down a couple guy[s] that got in my way. After they seen that I wasn't no punk or that I could be pushed around, the word finally got around. And then when they found out how much time that I had, they said, "Well, this man over here, he can actually kill us or hurt. He got 200 to 400 years, what he got to lose?" After that, I never really did have no problems.

I was in a place where I knew I shouldn't have been there. It was hard but with encouragement—a mother, a little sister who always believed I was innocent, who believed I was falsely accused—it gave me hope and I prayed to God. I read the Bible. Even when I was stressed or in pressure, the words of the Bible will comfort me and uplift me. I stayed prayerful, read my Bible. I was involved often into religion activities—churches on Sunday mornings and church in the afternoon, Bible classes and things. I give all praise unto God, Jehovah Jireh, El Shaddai, who was always there, who gave me the strength to continue and to keep on keepin' on. To continue to believe that somehow, someway the truth would manifest itself. That somehow I would be able

FREEING THE INNOCENT

Innocence projects fight for the wrongfully convicted

In the mid-1980s, hope arrived for many innocent inmates with the emerging availability of DNA testing. Such tests have led to steadily increasing exonerations over the last two decades. According to a 2003 study by University of Michigan Law School Professor Samuel Gross, exonerations averaged six per year during the '90s. From 2000 to 2003, there were eighty recorded DNA exonerations, an average of twenty per year.

These numbers do not tell the entire story: nearly half of all exonerations are based on evidence other than DNA. Gross's study found an average of forty exonerations overall per year from 2001 to 2003. Many experts believe that the total number of exonerations may be much higher.

Jim McCloskey of Centurion Ministries

The growing number of innocence projects across the nation has played a large part in the increasing number of exonerations. In 1980, after working as a student chaplain in a New Jersey prison, Jim McCloskey founded a small nonprofit called Centurion Ministries; it was the first organization devoted to freeing the wrongfully convicted. McCloskey's group exonerated twenty-five people from 1980 to 2000. In 1992, Barry C. Scheck and Peter J. Neufeld founded The Innocence Project at New York's Benjamin N. Cardozo School of Law. Scheck and Neufeld, both former public defenders, created the Project to handle cases where "post-conviction DNA testing of evidence can yield conclusive proof of innocence." Innocence Project lawyers and students have assisted or been the counsel of record in most of the 162 successful DNA exonerations to date.

The Center on Wrongful Convictions at Northwestern University, begun in the late 1990s, has enjoyed similar success. Its work focuses on non-DNA cases that require years of investigation. The center also holds conferences to assist law schools in initiating their own innocence projects.

There are at least forty innocence projects operating independently, without assistance from law or journalism schools. They are inundated with inmate requests from every state, leading to difficult decisions about which cases to take on and long waits for those seeking help. Still, the contribution of innocence projects has been significant. And according to Neufeld, the larger goal of such projects—beyond the exoneration of individual clients—is "nothing less than the complete overhaul of the criminal justice system with a new awareness of how to make it more reliable."

to prove my innocence. I were always prayin' that they would catch the guy or guys because I always wanted to see who, what type of creature or character that will commit a crime like that, you know.

I never had patience but I had to learn patience 'cause patience is a virtue. Many of us want it. Don't many of us have it. It began to make me see a lot of things and just hold fast and just believe that where's there's a will there's a way. I never knew how I would be delivered out of prison, but I always knew that I would be delivered out of prison.

I had 200 to 400 years, which is an indeterminate sentence, where you have to go before the prisoner review board for parole. The parole board would decide if you ready for society or not.

I would see the parole board. I would go up there in good faith, hoping. I always said that I was innocent of the crime I was accused of, but the parole board, they weren't really interested. They would always say, "Yeah, well if you innocent you need to try to prove you're innocent." They ain't never planned on releasing me out of prison until I was an old man, walking on a cane.

THE ANGELS WERE DANCING IN HEAVEN

My family always knew that I were innocent. It was something new for them, because I had never had no one in my family that had ever went to jail or prison for a horrible terrible crime like Paul Terry and Michael Evans were accused of.

My family were my strength. My mother and my sisters, who always believed in me, who was always by my side from beginning to the end, from the moment that I went incarcerated back in 1976 all the way to May 2003 when I was released. They have done they best. They have been there for me.

My niece had written the places like the wrongful conviction centers and lawyers to try to get this case vindicated, where her uncle could prove his innocence. My niece and my mother got these letters written out and to the people who would look at the matter. And when they did, they decided from the evidence that something was truly wrong with that case. I mean, professionals who studied law. Deans who know when a case is right, it's right, if it's wrong, it's wrong. And they found a lot of wrong that was done in the case of Paul Terry and Michael Evans. A lot of technicalities and a lot of errors.

In 1994, the lead prosecutor in the 1976 trial, Thomas M. Breen, began to have doubts about Evans's and Terry's convictions. Breen expressed these doubts to Northwestern University Law Professor Lawrence Marshall. In 1999, when the Center on Wrongful Convictions at Northwestern University was established, Marshall and his colleague Karen Daniel began the legal process that would lead to DNA testing. Prosecutors fought Northwestern's request for DNA testing. They claimed that even if the test excluded Evans and Terry as the source of the semen, it was possible that the semen came from a third, unidentified accomplice in the crime. Defense attorneys call this the "unindicted co-ejaculator" theory.

In 2000, after fighting the state's attempts to deny testing, Northwestern lawyers convinced the Circuit Court of Cook County to allow the semen sample from the crime to be tested. In September 2002, the DNA tests excluded both Evans and Terry as the source of the semen.

Prosecutors requested additional testing of the semen sample in hopes of identifying an "unindicted co-ejaculator" who committed the crime along with Evans and Terry.

When the prosecution's tests failed to implicate anyone, the state grudgingly agreed that Evans and Terry should be granted a new trial. Evans and Terry were released on May 23, 2003, and the

Evans talks to reporters in Chicago (May 2004)

charges against them were officially dropped on August 22 of that year.

I knew that once my DNA came through that I would be out of prison. Most of all that's all I was waitin' on, for my DNA for to come. 'Cause I had no doubt in my mind that I was innocent. When the DNA come, I'ma be out there, out of prison. Was something I had prayed and hoped for a long time.

The judge reviewed [the DNA]. The state's attorney reviewed it, but then they had to check it with they people. And the same results came back saying that no possibility could Paul Terry and Michael Evans have committed this crime, because the DNA does not match for the crime that they was accused of. From what I understand, whoever committed the crime, their semen was shot in the girl. That was not my semen, not Paul Terry's semen, not any of the homeboys I was affiliated with's semen. It was not theirs. It was someone's semen but they know not who because the person who committed the crime either he's already locked up in a prison out of state or in another country or he are

LIFE AFTER EXONERATION

Many exonerees leave prison with little help and nowhere to go

Earl Truvia and Gregory Bright were seventeen and twenty years old, respectively, when they were sent into Louisiana's prison system. They were released twenty-seven years later, each with a $10 check and a bag of

clothes. Exonerees are not entitled to housing assistance, employment, financial aid, or health care. After being freed, they are essentially left to fend for themselves. For many, that means finding a job and a place to stay. Though they have effectively had much of their lives taken from them, exonerees are in most cases given nothing in return. Following are the problems they face and the ways exonerees have addressed these issues:

Gregory Bright and Earl Truvia hold pictures of their release from prison (2003)

WORK: In 2003, Lonnie Erby returned to work at the same Chrysler plant he had left in 1986. Erby spent the intervening seventeen years in prison, serving a 115-year sentence for a rape he did not commit (he was exonerated by DNA). Among exonerees, Erby is an anomaly, not because he was able to return to his former profession, but because he has a stable job at all.

George Rodriguez is more representative of employment prospects among exonerees. Freed in 2004 after serving seventeen years of a sixty-year sentence for rape, he dreams of starting a car-repair business, but has failed to find any sustainable work since his release. Life After Exoneration Project (LAEP) director Ernest Duff says, "[Exonerees] usually find jobs that are temporary and that don't necessarily lend themselves to upward mobility—if they find jobs at all." In a survey of exonerees conducted by LAEP, a majority cited employment as their most urgent concern. According to Duff, "The desire to work is there—the means to get there is the issue."

The time lost in prison, where educational opportunities have dwindled, can leave released prisoners unprepared or with obsolete job skills. During the 1990s, vocational training and educational classes were largely

continued on page 262

deceased now.

When I went to court, Judge Porter had to know that something wasn't right. After getting the DNA back from the laboratory, which he evaluate himself, he seen that it was negative and that we had did enough time, that they had held two innocent men in prison too long for a crime that they did not commit. So we were released on May the 23rd of 2003.

That were a glorious day. I will never forget. It was a day of a lot of joys. Rejoice and love. My sister, my nephew, mostly family members, my immediate family, who showed their love and embraced me. I felt so good. I felt like I was on top of the world because after over two decades, I got a chance to exhale and inhale the fresh air again. I felt truly blessed. It was a day that I would say that the angels were dancing in heaven.

I went to South Holland, [Illinois], where my sisters and my mother were staying.

Even though my mother's paralyzed, when she seen me walk through that door, she forgot about that. 'Cause she was sittin' in a chair in the kitchen. She forgot about that she couldn't walk. She jumped up and stood and I ran over there and hugged her and things. She always believed that the truth would come to light, that God would let her live to see her son return back to society. It was a blessed day for her, too. Not just for her but for all my family members and loved ones.

'MY DADDY HOME'

My baby sister called my son. And he called me on the three-way over to my sister's house and he was crying on the phone. He was crying. He said, "I just talked to my daddy, my daddy home." He ran out in the street hollering, "My daddy home, my daddy home!"

phased out of prison programs in the U.S. As a result, it is nearly impossible for inmates to keep their skills current. Many have never written an email or used a computer.

Exonerated prisoners must also address the void in their employment histories, and their explanations for those missing years can be offputting  to potential employers. States may take years to clear exonerees' official records; often, exonerees are compelled to pursue lengthy and costly legal proceedings to fully expunge all wrongful charges and convictions. If they are unable to afford expungement or unaware that their records still bear charges, employment applications which ask about criminal records can become awkward stumbling blocks. If exonerees claim they have no criminal history and an unexpunged record reveals otherwise, they are caught in the embarrassing position of having to explain the discrepancy. If they reveal their record, whatever its state, applications may be rejected before that record is checked.

Ernest Duff

Many exonerees carry newspaper articles or letters from their lawyers to demonstrate their innocence to skeptical employers. But the mere fact that exonerees have spent time in prison causes many businesses to reject them. According to exoneree Herman Atkins, "They don't know what expungement means."

HOUSING: When Atkins was released from prison in 2000 after serving fifteen years for a rape he didn't commit, he had no place to stay. So, at thirty-nine years of age, he moved into his grandmother's house. Each morning he awoke on a recliner in her living room; he would then neatly fold the sheets and blankets, tuck them away, and head off to school. And each evening his grandmother waited up for his return.

Ironically, if Atkins had actually been guilty of rape and on parole, he would have been eligible for some—albeit minimal—transitional services under California's prisoner reentry program. Atkins is also barred from federally funded "Section Eight" housing because his record still carries his conviction. In this way, exonerees are caught in a gray zone: both their criminal records and their innocence can prevent them from receiving government-sponsored services.

continued on page 264

[My son] have two kids. He very happy. He just kind of angry that they took all of the time out of his dad's life when he was growin' up. Everybody else had like a father figure to look up to. And he knew where his father was at, but his father wasn't nowhere around to help raise him up. He was just kind of angry about that.

I did try to reunite back with my son's mother, to replace back the lost years that I had lost or that [my son] had lost. It didn't work, but at the same time, the experience was wonderful. We were schoolhouse sweethearts. She was my first love. But I didn't realize that as the years go, people change for the better or for the worse. They get better in they thinking. They get better as far as career. They get better as far as being a person or they get worse as being a person. I know it must have been hard on her, tryin' to raise a son up, my son, by herself, because a woman can only play like a certain role. A boy still needs a father figure, just like a daughter still need their mother figure, in being raised up. It takes two to raise a child. I kind of missed out, too, as being a parent and watching a child grow up into being a man.

It would've been different because I would've been able to play football with him and baseball. I would've been able to walk around in the park with my son, you know, go to the park, go to the beach, you know, do a lot of things and maybe instill some principles in him that would be very valuable to him in the future. But I'm grateful to God that he turned out to be a pretty good boy. Even though he's a man now, he turned out.

I treat him more like my friend than like my son, because I was away for a while. He love me, there's no doubt in my mind, as much as I love him.

It's estimated that one-third of exonerees are dependent on friends or family for basic necessities like food, clothing, and housing. One study found that at least 44 percent of exonerees lack adequate housing; some are known to be homeless.

Many end up living with family members for years at a time. But even living with well-intentioned relatives can be stifling for someone who has spent decades under the watchful eye of prison guards. After serving eighteen years on a false charge of aggravated rape, Clyde Charles left prison to live at his sister's house. Three years later, having found no employment and having received no compensation, Charles chose to live in his car. He said it gave him a measure of independence.

Even after exonerees are able to afford a place to live, there's no guarantee that landlords will rent to them. Exonerees typically have little in the way of a rental record, and their credit history is often problematic; if convicted early in life, they might have no credit history at all. And increasingly, private landlords are checking applicants' criminal histories, which can disqualify an exoneree who has not been able to get his or her record corrected.

THE LIFE AFTER EXONERATION PROGRAM

During the initial rush of DNA exonerations in the 1990s, little attention was paid to the needs of exonerees after their release. That changed in 2003, when a Life After Exoneration Program study revealed the plight of sixty exonerees surveyed nationwide. The LAEP study showed that:

- 48 percent lived with family members
- 34 percent were financially dependent on others
- 30 percent had lost custody of their children
- 28 percent suffered from post-traumatic stress disorder

Duff observes that exonerees must cope with the psychological and physical consequences of torture even as they are attempting to enter a community ignorant of their experience.

"Like political asylum seekers who have been victims of a highly personalized yet systematic process of injustice," says Duff, "the future of exonerees hinges on how supportive an environment they land in is, and on the resilience within each exoneree to avoid despair and take their newfound freedom as an occasion for growth."

CONVERSATION, EXONERATION, VINDICATION

I stayed with my mother and my sister in South Holland, several months. It was different living with them. After a while, I said that I felt that they had been with me all this time and stuck by my side, and it's about time for me to accept my own responsibilities and be somewhat constructive, like earning like my own money.

I were given a job working for Harold's Chicken Shack. My girlfriend is a manager and my son is assistant manager, so those are the first jobs that she introduced me to, where I have some money in my pocket, and I feel that I'm being more responsible as a man. I was cashier, I took call-ins, like the orders, I also fixed the order. My specialty were mostly taking the call-in orders and like wrapping the food and putting whatever sauce I needed to put on.

I left Harold's because it was low payin,' you know, minimum wages. I felt like I wasn't making enough money that would fit my standard of living. It worked good for a while but then there was things, like other things that I need to support myself like food, clothes, and shelter. You got to make the money that fits your standard of living. Money is a necessity to support yourself or be able to support your spouse, your girlfriend. To be helpful or supportive to anyone else, a friend or a family member who need your help. It's hard, because they does not give a person who were incarcerated for twenty-seven years anything to be able to support himself and live successful out in society. It's hard to be able to readjust to a society where there's no benefits and no programs.

I was living with my girlfriend at the time and we was trying to make ends meet with two joint accounts. It worked for a while, but it was time for me to move and to try to expand my education and get some job training while I'm waiting to be compensated.

There oughta be a law that compensation should be more expedient. If I didn't have any family members, where would I go when I was released? The halfway house? Who would want to stay in the halfway house? That's just like prison. They need to raise it up to like $250,000. Even though that couldn't pay for the damage that had been done, it be something to help you get on your feet until you received employment or something. But I won't be compensated until the governor have pardoned me.

To be compensated for a wrongful conviction in the state of Illinois, an exoneree must be granted a pardon from the governor. Michael Evans was pardoned in January 2005. He will receive approximately $160,000.

If you are guilty, then a person should accept the consequences for they transgression. But if you are innocent, a person should be treated like a citizen and should be righteously granted everything that him or her deserve through conversation, through exoneration, through vindicat[ion].

Even compensation cannot bring about, cannot change the hands of time of the years that I spent incarcerated, for a crime that Michael Evans and Paul Terry never did commit. It's not going to bring about them years of being a boy, no matter what. It's still not gonna bring about the sorrow and the heartache and the pain and the suffering that they caused my mother and family members and sisters and loved ones.

I WAS IN PRISON, BUT THE PRISON WAS NOT IN ME

You know, society have changed a whole lot since when I went to prison in 1976. I was surprised at the way peoples, this whole new generation does not have morals or principles. When I was raised up, what was instilled in me was to respect my elders, and nowadays this generation here don't have no respect for they elders or for even humanity. Crack cocaine got a lot of people strung out, out of sight, out of mind. They walkin' around like zombies. They don't know if they comin' or goin.' So that was one of my big surprises.

What's been hard about the transition is that there's no benefits for wrongful conviction, peoples who was locked up, no programs, no jobs, no trades, no conversations. I was very surprised. That's been hard.

What's been easy is being able to learn about the new technology, with CDs and tapes. When I was put in prison, there was mostly like the records, like forty-fives.

It's not hard to make the transition, because I was in prison but the prison was not in me. It remind me that in prison I considered myself dead, and when I come back to society I consider myself back to life again. It's like being reborn back to life again. It almost like you have to start off from being a baby again. A lot of things that we might have missed out on, things you would have been able to achieve.

Most of all, I missed being with my mother and my dad and my sisters. I missed out on just life in general. And those were precious years, precious years that I cannot capture. It's long gone. Who knows what I would have accomplished or became? Become, I should say.

The way I look at the world, if I could turn back the hands of time, I don't think I would let it happen again. Because I'm a little bit more educated now, I encompass a lot more wisdom than I did when I was seventeen.

I CANNOT LET THEM DESTROY MY MIND

[Me and Paul Terry] was together for like over two or three years. Paul was always in Unit D, I was in Unit E, so we was in different cell houses. People would keep me informed on how he was doing—you know, "He's not coming out to eat," "He's not washing up." And I would go over there sometimes, you know, being [observed] by my captain in my unit, he would let me go over there and talk to him. [Paul] had stopped going to the chow hall and he had stopped taking care of hygiene, he had stopped doing a lotta things. So I would go over there from time to see how—was he comfortable with the cellie that he had? Or should he talk to the superintendent of his unit to move him?

I had tried to get him, you know, moved in the same unit, to be an inspiration to him and encourage him to keep the faith— and that everything's gonna be all right, you know, as long as he continue to try to not lose his mind. I often expressed to him that I realized that he are innocent as well as I was, but it's something that he got to be strong, for now, until we prove our innocence.

[A prison] officer called me "Smiley." That was my nickname, because I never really did go around all sad or cocky or trying to be a bully. I was just myself. I was just actin' normal. I kept it simple and I kept it real 'cause I am a realist. The way I carried myself, a lot of them thought that I just had just three, four, five years.

Paul was not as strong as I were. He took it harder than I did. He was going through a lot of emotional stress—depressed, oppressed, being repressed by just being around those type of peoples and that environment. When I did see him in the tunnels or in the chow hall, I would try to encourage him, but he would always tell me, "Yeah, Mike, you know, I shouldn't be here. I don't know why I'm here." And I would just tell him,

"You know, I ain't supposed to be here, neither. Ain't neither one of us supposed to be here. But you gotta try to make the best out of a bad situation. Until brighter days comes."

But he took it hard. He was put on medication, which was called Thorazine. Then later on he was sent to Dixon Correctional [Center] and he was placed in the psych unit. I would always try to hold on to my mind. I said, "I cannot let them destroy my mind." I didn't want to lose my mind because I know if I'da lost my mind I'da lost everything.

PAMELA HAWKINS ON PAUL TERRY:
SOMETHING WAS MISSING, AND IT WAS HIM

Two years after his release from prison, Paul Terry is extremely soft-spoken. He is hesitant to speak at any length about his arrest, conviction, or time in prison, where he deteriorated mentally. His twin sister, Pamela Hawkins, who has been extremely close to Terry throughout his life, including his twenty-seven years in prison, speaks in his place.

WE DID EVERYTHING TOGETHER

We grew up in the Englewood area on 61st [in Chicago]. We're the youngest. Paul is nine minutes older than I am.

We was very close, always have been. We did everything together. When one got the measles, the other got the measles. We was just close. There was times we'd come home and had to cross this big street. We would close our eyes as we ran across this big street and he was supposed to have been my eyes and would tell me when to run and I'd run. And then the next day, it was on him. Things like that, just growing up very close.

He was quieter than I was but a little bit more outgoing.

Quieter but outgoing, you know. Paul didn't do a lot of things. Paul didn't do a lot of reading. No basketball.

I remember our Christmas together. How my mom would buy the toys and place them in different places. Paul always seemed to be the one to find them. We had a very good Christmas. A very good childhood. My mom was there for us. My father was there for us until he died.

I wanted [Paul] there. I wanted him there for my high school graduation. I wanted him there for all those things. Every time we would do something, I would think, "My brother supposed to be here, be a part of this." These are the things you think about. You're twins, you graduate together, you know, your prom. He wasn't there for any of that. I thought about each occasion, "My brother's supposed to be here."

I felt when I got married that maybe I shouldn't. Not that I shouldn't get married but my brother's supposed to be getting married, too, someday. I did think about little thoughts like that. The day wasn't completed. I guess I don't know what I'm trying to say, but I know what I feel. Something was missing and it was him.

A THIEF IN THE NIGHT

I remember the night the police said the little girl was killed. The detectives stopped door to door, saying something had happened in the neighborhood and how they was going from door to door asking people had they seen anything. Later on, they started pickin' up.

They didn't pick up my brother until eleven months later. I figured he was another one they pickin' up. It's been this long— they still going around pickin' up people, they can't find anything. And when they picked him up I just knew he'd be home within a few hours, a day or whatever. We was young. Seventeen years old.

Pamela, Beverly, and Paul Terry at home in Chicago (1964)

Never had to go through this. He's scared. I'm scared. Everybody's scared, you know. We didn't know what to expect. We just know he was innocent and he was coming home. We thought he'll be home in a day or two. Twenty-seven years later…

My mom used to always say, "That's funny how they can just come and take your child from you and nothing you can do about it." She used to say that all the time. They can just come and take your child from you and there's nothing you can do. And that's what they did. They came and took him. He supposed to start a job the next day at Sears, for the holiday season. He had his little blue jeans ironed up and red turtleneck laid out on the couch. Very happy. Had ate about four or five boiled eggs. Knock on the door. Took him. Just like that. Like a thief in the night. That's what it was. A thief in the night.

After Evans's first conviction was vacated, Terry was implicated in the crime by Tammler, the same woman who identified Evans. The two were tried together and convicted. Had they been tried eighteen months later, when Illinois restored the death penalty, they would have been eligible for death row. Instead, they each received 200- to 400-year sentences.

My other sister told me, she say, "Pam, I remember that day they

sentenced Paul and I was at home with Mama and they broke in on the television with the news and they say they sentenced them, found them guilty. They was sentenced 200 to 400 years." She said my mama just beat the wall. And screamed. My mama, she just couldn't take that. She broke down at home. Broke down when she heard the sentencing on television.

Terry shortly after his trial (1977)

I cried. I cried. I knew my brother was innocent. I just couldn't believe that it could be real. I can still see him walking. I do remember seeing him walk towards the back [of the courtroom] and it was so heartbreaking.

See, my brother lost so much. Almost thirty years of his life. Teenage years, all of our twenties, all of our thirties, and half of our forties. That's a lot to do when you didn't do anything. That's a lot to swallow.

THE LETTERS GOT SHORTER AND SHORTER

I have letters that Paul wrote [from prison] and phone calls. It was terrible. I cried for my brother many, many, many days. When I would go see him, I hated to leave. I hated to leave my brother. You know, it was terrible. He would write letters, really long, asking about the family. As time went on they got shorter and shorter.

It was five or six different institutions Paul went to: Stateville, Menard, Pontiac, Graham, and Dixon. Dixon used to have a picnic every year for the inmates. Every year, my mom, my sisters, all of us would go to this picnic. And he wouldn't get involved with the games, and they had a band out there, but he was talkative. We'd get ice cream.

Terry in an undated photo from the early 1980s

I'd go there, we'd eat, sit there and talk and have a decent conversation. Paul would have a conversation, initiate a conversation. It was okay starting off. I would always say, "Paul, you know, you're going to get out of here. You're innocent." The same thing. "Hold on." He was hopeful. He was holding on for a while and then they started transferring him to like Pontiac, Menard. You could see the change in him.

Then as the years went on, he got a little dimmer, dimmer. The visits got so that Paul wasn't talking, we'd just eat. If you asked him a question, he'll answer. You just start seeing a change, a physical change in his appearance, you know. His clothes wasn't neat. His hair wasn't combed.

I figure if he want to talk, he'll talk. Even today, he won't even discuss certain things. A program might come on TV and he say, "Oh yeah, I seen that when I was locked up." But as far as everyday things or things that happened, he won't really get too involved.

He would write on a piece of toilet paper and says, "I need a hundred dollars soon. Please send it soon to me. Paul." Or it was a piece of brown paper. He started calling his mother Fannie instead of Mama. It was always Mama. Said, "Send $250 when you put in the letter. This is Paul Terry." Then it says, "Hurry." Little things like that, you know. It went from paper to toilet paper to I guess whatever he could write on. He had to get the message out. I would send him $25 here and there. I guess when he needed new shoes or things like that. Winter come, maybe a heavier jacket.

GOD KEPT HIM

And I believe God kept him. He kept him alive. For twenty-seven years. He made it possible for them to use this evidence, to free Paul and Michael. We prayed hard. We would get in a circle and we would pray. I'm sure he had very, very, very bad days but I believe the Lord was in the midst of them.

We were praying for him. I have no doubt in my mind that the Lord did this. How did they preserve the evidence they did have for so long and were able to use it? I know beyond a shadow of a doubt that the Lord was

Paul Terry and Pamela Hawkins (February 1993)

responsible for that. Ain't nobody can tell me no different.

Nothing positive was happening. The lawyers my mom would get, seem like after they take her money, work a little bit, and seem like they vanish. These lawyers, they promised everything. But when the money's gone, you can't have a lawyer. That's how it seemed to me. They would vanish. We wouldn't hear about that lawyer anymore. You know, it got slimmer and slimmer and slimmer and slimmer.

We'd tell him, "You going to get out one day. You going to get out. There's a light at the end of the tunnel." That would be our word. There's a light at the end of the tunnel. We had to believe that for ourselves. More so for Paul, but we had to believe it, too. I do believe that if you don't have a dream, you might as well die. You had to have a dream. I guess Paul slid down so much and so long that he lost the faith.

They did the DNA testing, which we had no doubt in our mind was gonna come back like it should have. I said, "Lord, this is what you promised us."

I THANK GOD FOR THAT JUDGE

I knew Michael [Evans]. But once they was in prison, after the trial, and everything was over with, we didn't stay in touch. Michael's sister and niece came over one day and said they had received a letter from the Northwestern clinic, saying that they're going to look into Paul and Michael's case, we have to pay for the DNA, things like that, and that's what got the ball going. So we really got excited and happy. 'Cause we knew they was innocent, but just, you know, start getting busy now. We were thinking that something going to start happening now. Once [Northwestern] took the case, it must have been something they'd knew or seen or thought it was worth the effort to even put into it. We knew they were in process of whatever they was doing. That was December.

Then we went to court May 23rd. They brought Paul up about five o'clock in the morning. We all went to court. Prior to that we had started preparing, you know, fixing up the bedroom. That morning we tied two big yellow ribbons around the tree. It had been the spirit of God leading us. We all wore yellow T-shirts to go to court. As we was sitting there in court, there was some things we was understanding, and some things we wasn't understanding and we hear Judge Porter saying, "We'll start preparing the papers." We getting excited now. They said, "Well, this is the weekend, it's four o'clock in the evening." They said, "We have to get the papers from Dixon, you know." And the judge said, "Fax them." We're really getting excited, tears are running down our faces. We holding hands. At this point, Paul didn't even

know it. Paul said they went in the back and told him he was going home. He couldn't believe it. My husband, he was wearing his yellow shirt, but he had a black shirt under it so he took off his yellow shirt and gave it to Paul so we could all be together. We was really happy about that.

Pamela Hawkins and Terry (May 2005)

I thank God for that judge. He could have easily waited for Monday. He took the time and compassion, which we didn't have for the last twenty-seven years, and told whoever was supposed to do what he was supposed to do to process the papers and get it done. It was a couple of hours until all the papers were processed. Then we went home.

It was very sunny. Everybody was excited because Paul rode home with us. We had the famous one with us. They called on my cell phone and said, "Where are you? Come on, come on!" Paul got off the truck and walked to the porch and this is when he saw his mother. Face to face.

A VERY DIFFERENT PAUL

You have to put certain things behind you, if that's possible. You have to let certain things go. When my brother first came home, he would get to the door and stop, because being locked up, when you get to a door, you stop. I said, "Go to the door, open the door now." Little things that you see, they've been conditioned for so long. That's what they are, conditioned. It takes time for that, and you might need a little help.

I'll never forget when I went and got him a set of keys. He was just like a baby with a sucker. I took him up to Ace Hardware and got him a set of keys for the house. And I said, "Paul, try your key to make sure they work," and he was so happy about it. He was just working that key in that door. And I said, "Look at my brother." The little things. Playing music. When he came home I took him right up here at 87th Street. He wanted to look for records. They don't sell records anymore. Things like that. Some things it made me sad.

HE COULD HAVE BEEN SOMETHING

But the Paul that came home almost two years ago is a very different Paul.

We asked Paul, did he want to come and live here or with another one of my sisters? [My sister] was buying a new home, so he went there. He loves to sit on the porch, he smoke cigarettes and we want him to be comfortable as far as doing these things. He's not doing anything as far as trying to get out there and be constructive, and he say he don't want to. Not now. You know, I think he just want to enjoy freedom. And not be obligated to a job or just being obligated to certain things. Certain situations. Just want to be free. I really believe that's the state of mind he in right now. Just want to be comfortable and enjoy freedom.

I'd like to see him to be able to take care of himself and be comfortable with the decisions that he makes. I want him to be where he in that state where every decision he makes is his and he's comfortable with it. I want him to be at that point in his life where he's free to make his own decisions. If he makes a mistake, okay, then we move on. That's the main thing I'd like to see.

I can't choose for him. I can't tell him to do this or go to school or get a job. He have to make that decision. They done made so many decision for him for so long so whatever makes him comfortable, if it's sitting at home being comfortable, then let it be. We can't dictate what's for someone else's life. Now, I think if he hadn't of ever got locked up, Paul really could have been something. What, I don't know. But I know he could've been something. Easily.

Paul is a very strong man. I don't know if I could have gone through what Paul did. God knows who can go through what. He's still here. He survived. I look at my brother and I think, "He all right." You all right, brother.

David Pope

I'M STILL TWENTY-FOUR

NAME: David Pope · **BORN:** 1961 · **HOMETOWN:** Dallas, Texas

CONVICTED OF: Aggravated sexual assault · **SENTENCE:** 45 years

SERVED: 15 years · **RELEASED:** 2001

FLOWERS IN YOUR HAIR

I was born in Dallas. My parents were both going to college. They became hippies involved in the counterculture that was going on in the country then. [In Dallas] in the '60s, there were campus demonstrators, people smoking pot out on the lawn, and "Everybody's going to San Francisco, that's where you wear flowers in your hair." There was an innocence about that. Young people were going to turn on and change the world. My dad was a little bit more down to earth. He didn't want to leave Texas. He was afraid of pot—back then you could go to jail for a seed, especially in Texas.

My mother left him when I was nine. My mother came out here [to California] in '71. She had three sons; she brought two.

I stayed behind. Maybe I bonded more with my father, or maybe I was more like him. Maybe I knew it was a little too abnormal out here [in California] for me at the time. My father was just more partial to the South. He was raised in an old one-room cabin out in Alvarado, Texas, and is more of a country boy. He

had a tendency to hook up and marry women that didn't make very good stepmothers. I wanted to be with my father, but I couldn't be around some of the women that he was [involved with]. So ultimately I opted to come out to Marin County and go to school. That's how I became split between Texas and California.

I came here to be with my mother and my brothers Daniel and Paul. My mother was still a part of the hippie

David Pope at age 17 in Texas

scene; it was reggae music and pot almost every day. All her friends smoked pot—this was Mill Valley in the '70s. Everybody encouraged me to grow long hair even when I was little. I did it to please them. It seemed like Texas had more normal family values, and that most kids came from a functional household. When I came out here I thought it was much more dysfunctional. The kids were really neurotic. There's a lot more ostracizing, more bullying, cliques, economic stratification, "my parents have more money than you" stuff going on out here. And I never liked that. I was kind of a shy geek until I turned twenty-something. I really wasn't popular. I was a loner who stayed to myself. I would come home after school and stay in my room. I got heavy into science fiction and *Star Trek*. When *Star Wars* came on the screen, I'd never seen anything like that, so I wanted to do special effects. I collected books on special effects and tried to re-create them myself on home movies. I thought I'd like to go work for George Lucas.

I'D BETTER JUST LAY LOW

I went to school in Mill Valley from fifth grade until ninth grade. Right when I was going to reach fourteen, fifteen, starting to think about trying to become an adult and getting a car, I realized that I didn't want to be in Mill Valley. I wanted to go back where things were a little more normal, so I did. In my freshman year of high school my father had divorced my stepmother. I went back to Dallas to live with him for a while and finish school. I stayed with my dad until I was nineteen. At that point, he met his fourth wife. We were the exact same age. It was causing a little bit of awkward tension in the house, so I needed to move out.

I had a job working at a Target automotive center. I mounted tires, I did oil changes. I lived in the Eastgate Apartments. They had three swimming pools, an athletic field, and a little gym. Eventually, I just couldn't make the rent. I couldn't really survive, so I got evicted from the apartments. I really didn't have anywhere to go. In Dallas, you can't be homeless—you're just as good as being in jail. At that point I still had my job. Then I changed to another job: I went to paint houses with my friend Craig. I was sleeping in my car on the weekends, and during the work week I was with him.

In the early morning hours on July 25, 1985, Sharon Lemke was sleeping in her Garland, Texas apartment when a man with a knife broke into her room, raped her, and fled. Several days later, the rapist began making threatening telephone calls to Lemke. She alerted police, who then taped a telephone call from the assailant.

Pope had been evicted from Lemke's apartment complex earlier that year and had been living out of his car. He often parked his car in the complex parking lot to sleep. On August 28, more than a month after the crime, police who were staking out Lemke's apartment complex arrested Pope on suspicion that he was the rapist. He was leaving the complex parking lot, on his way to work.

That night I was sleeping in my car. I parked it on the property of the apartments that I was evicted from, because it was a large complex, and I knew it well enough. I thought, "Well, at least I used to live here." I was lying down. I rose up and I looked over and there were two police cars doing their little morning ritual. The cops would park together, drink coffee, and kick it back and forth. I thought, "This is a bad time. I'd better just lay low." In Dallas, and in many parts of Texas, politics create a lot of fear in the public. So they hire more police, not always very well-trained— a lot of them are just out trying to find somebody to harass. I kept looking at the clock and thinking, "When are they going to leave?" I had to get to work painting with Craig. I thought, "I need to get on going to work. I'm going to take a chance." So I rose up again, and started the car. Sure enough, I don't know if they were aware that I was sleeping there, but now they saw there wasn't anybody in that car, and now there's somebody there.

The sun was just coming up when I pulled out of the parking lot onto the main street. One of them drove up behind me, put his lights on, and came up, asked me for my driver's license. I didn't have it, because one night I stayed out at the apartment swimming pool and fell asleep and someone broke into my car and stole my wallet out of the glove box. I had an old car, so you could break into it pretty easy. So here I am, in my car, with no proof of identification, and that's an issue. And then I have no proof of insurance. He asked me to step out of the car and arrested me. I became pretty belligerent because I thought, "I might have lost my wallet, but they didn't have to arrest me." This is very early—I think those cops had been up all night, working the graveyard shift. None of us was in a very good mood.

They put me in the back of the police car. They wanted to know what my story was. Instead of saying that I was living out of my car, I said, "I was just visiting a friend here." They asked me, "Who's your friend?" and I named one apartment. They drove around and got out, went up there, knocked on the door. This girl that lived next door to me just must have left early for work, so there was nobody to vouch for me, to say, "Hey, I know this guy." I was hoping I could talk them out of taking me to jail, but the cop was determined that he was going to take me downtown. I thought, "I have to be at work. I might lose my job with my friend. I don't know how much it's going to cost to bail me out." I cussed one of them out from the backseat.

At the police station, Lemke failed to pick Pope's photograph out of a photo lineup, but later selected him from a live lineup.

At the police station in Garland everything's below ground level, so you drive down to the booking area where they take mugshots and fingerprints. Some detective in a suit came up and took a Polaroid of me but didn't say anything. I thought it was a mugshot, that maybe the big camera is broken, or they're just harassing me. I waited. I was being real patient, because they were letting me sit outside—at least I wasn't in a cell. The detective comes back forty-five minutes later, and he does the same thing: he takes another Polaroid. It was then that I thought, "Something's a little weird; something's strange about this." He wouldn't say anything, either. I'm trying to get him to tell me— "What's this all about? Why are you taking Polaroids? You already took one. Why are you taking another?" Fifteen minutes later they put me in a jail tank. I was in there together with maybe five or six others. They give you a mattress. It's so dark and smelly. It's just a dungeon. The only thing you can do is sleep.

Some time later the bailiff came in the door and said, "Everybody up. We're going upstairs." Some of the guys had been through this before, so they knew the routine. I said, "Where are we all going?" and the bailiff said, "We're going to the lineup." I thought, "Okay, whatever, I'll do what they want me to do." I was put in a lineup in which I was the only one that had blond hair. All the others had dark hair and all were shorter than me and Hispanic. We walked in a circle in a room about eight feet by eight feet. One by one, we would pass by this two-way mirror. After that we all filed out. "This whole thing is so unprofessional," I thought. "Just so hokey. Why are they leaving the adjoining room door cracked where I can hear a woman's voice?" I heard a woman in there talking as if the officer's with her and she's saying, "Well, I don't know, maybe…" and "I'm not sure," with doubt and indecision. From there they separated me. I was put in a single cell with no windows. There's nothing—you have a light, a mattress, and that's all. They told me that I was being charged with aggravated sexual assault and aggravated robbery. They put me in there and then gave me my phone call.

'I CAN'T MORTGAGE THE HOUSE
TO HIRE ANY LAWYERS'

I told my dad on the phone, I said, "[This is] the craziest thing. I don't know what's going on, but I got arrested for no proof of insurance. I have a valid driver's license but I don't have it with me. They got me down here in the jail and they are accusing me of some kind of rape with a knife." My dad said he didn't know what to think. I said, "Dad, I may have done some things before, like not paying tickets. I shoplifted once when I was fourteen, but I don't know what's going on." I was going before the judge the next day for a hearing; the bond hadn't been set yet. He said, "Look, you shouldn't have anything to worry about, just call me tomorrow." I called him the next day and said, "They got two charges, a hundred thousand dollars each." He said, "Well, I don't know what to do. Are they going to give you a lawyer? I can't mortgage the house to hire any lawyers." I come from a very middle-class family, which means we're almost poor people. My dad was still paying on a $47,000 house. It took him about thirty years to pay it off.

I got my court-appointed attorney, Curtis Glover, a couple of days later. The first thing he asked me was, "Well, are you guilty or not?" I said, "Hell no." And he said, "Well, okay, so you're claiming you're innocent. Oh, and by the way, the state has told me to tell you that even if you plea bargain, they want sixty years." It might as well have been two thousand years. He told me that he was an ex-DA, and now he's working as a public defender. I signed some paper, and he left; it was real quick. At the time he didn't have any basis for knowing whether I was innocent or not.

Some time later, he told me that he wanted to give me an assignment. He said that he wanted me to write a little bit about myself: my background, leading up to my arrest, and the whole arrest. I wrote out about ten pages and mailed all this to his office. Then we talked on the phone and he said, "I really don't think you did this. From my time talking to you in person, and from listening to the tape of this crazy guy, I don't think you're this guy at all. You don't articulate like the guy." He said, "They're saying that you broke into this woman's apartment and then harassed her over the telephone. They got these recordings. I got them on tape. I'm going to bring them so you can listen.

We'll listen to them." And we did—he had a little cassette player in his briefcase. We sat there and he played it.

The first thing that stuck in my mind was that this guy, the real assailant, was going on and on. He wasn't really getting to any point. When he calls her, he's not just saying something and then hanging up, but talks as if he's seeing her around a lot, or he knows a little bit about her, or maybe she knew him. They have a long drawn-out conversation which goes at least fifteen minutes. It seems very stupid to me that this guy would be doing this. Why stay on the phone for a really long time if you're threatening somebody, or if you're guilty of a crime? It didn't really make a lot of sense. He said things like, "I'm really smart for eighteen. You better not call the police because I've got a really fast car, so you're never gonna catch me." He gave his age. He gave the name of a junior college that he had attended. He mentioned what kind of car he had. Those things did not match me by age, by the college, or by the car. So I thought, "If I'm this guy, why in the hell am I going to call her up and manufacture a story?"

In late August 1985, police had Pope read aloud a transcript of the previously recorded conversation between Lemke and the assailant. These two recordings were compared and analyzed by now-defunct voice spectrograph technology. This spectrograph was used to help convict Pope.

My lawyer said, "Well, they still think you're guilty, and they want you to make a voice tape." They had me say what the assailant said. They wanted me to read a printed script, word for word. I'd pick this telephone up and they were going to record me over the telephone. By now I'd been in jail for so long, I was trying to do just about anything if it was going to help me get out. They actually had this woman, Sharon Lemke, on the other

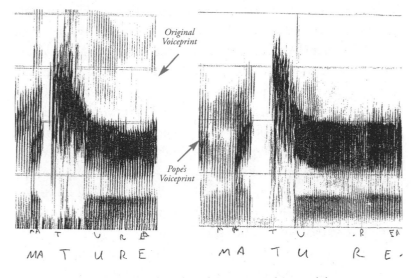

*Voice spectrograph readouts from Pope's trial (state exhibits
26 and 27,* State of Texas vs. David Shawn Pope, *1986)*

phone. I was reading this crazy guy's words, things like, "I know
you liked it, and you'd better not tell anybody. Do you have a
boyfriend?" First it was very dry. Then it started to get more and
more sick: "I really love you, and you'd better not tell anybody,
because I can come up from behind you at any time and you
never know where I'm going to be, but I really love you, and you
were my first." He had called her, and then she called the police.
The police came to her apartment, gave her some kind of recording device, and said, "If he ever calls back, I want you to press
this button." He called back at least twice, maybe three times,
and she taped these conversations.

I WAS THE FIRST PERSON IN TEXAS TO BE
PUT TO TRIAL WITH A VOICE SPECTROGRAPH

My first trial was five days. Craig Firch, my friend who I was working with, let me use his suit at the courthouse. The first day was a hearing without the jury on the admissibility of voice-prints. The state had to convince this judge to rule to allow voice-prints to be used for the first time. The state's witness got up and he was a spectrograph examiner, and a polygraph examiner, and had been in a war, and had been around. He would guarantee that this was a sound science. This guy gets up there and says, "A voiceprint is like a fingerprint. Everybody in the world has a dis-tinct, unique voiceprint. Therefore, if we record Mr. Pope's voice and I run it through my spectrograph then we know it's him." The judge allowed him to use it. I was the first person in Texas to be put to trial with a voice spectrograph.

The next day the jury is there and this woman named Sharon Lemke, and a news guy from *The Dallas Morning News* in the audience. Neither one of my parents were at my trial, so you can see how that can really hurt your case. When something's hap-pening to you like that and ain't nobody gonna stand up for you —you know, family—you internalize a tremendous amount of rage and anger. There's also some of this, "This isn't really hap-pening, it's not happening to me." You're emotionally shut down. There's a lot of fear that if you do jump up, flip the table over, go over and try to grab the judge, that obviously that's going to play right into what they want, isn't it? So you just hope your lawyer's going to do something. I thought it was going okay, I really did. I believe my lawyer knew I was innocent. I thought he was doing a pretty good job.

Sharon Lemke went on the stand and my lawyer asked her in cross-examination, "Miss Lemke, were you examined by any doctors or a female police officer or anybody?" And she said, "No." Then he said, "Do you know what a rape kit is?"—that's where they gather evidence that was left, blood or hair or semen—and she said, "Yeah." They went over that pretty quick.

On Friday, it's been going for four days and the jury's tired, trying to get this over with. They reached this point where they're like, "We're going to deliberate and we'll come back with a decision." It was an hour, hour and a half, and they came back and they found me guilty. They told me to stand up and they read the verdict, and yeah, I was outraged. I didn't yell or scream. But then the judge told me to sit down and I was like in defiance, "No, I'm not going to sit down." I didn't know what else to do. Finally the judge had to get his hammer and he yelled at me and slammed it—"You sit your ass down!" So finally I sat down.

On February 7, 1986, a jury found Pope guilty of aggravated sexual assault and he was sentenced to forty-five years in prison. The prosecutors' main evidence against Pope was Lemke's voice and face identification, and a spectrographic analysis of the phone calls. Curtis Glover, Pope's attorney, filed an appeal on February 27, 1986. The appeal argued that the spectrographic evidence should not have been admitted and that the judge gave unconstitutional instructions to the jury prior to Pope's sentencing. On May 16, 1988, the Dallas Court of Appeals reversed Pope's conviction on the basis of the unconstitutional jury instructions. However, in a rehearing, prosecutors fought the appeal and convinced the Court of Appeals to withdraw its opinion and uphold Pope's original conviction.

YOU DON'T CARE ABOUT HIM, HE DOESN'T CARE ABOUT YOU

The first five years in prison it's really a lot of psychological pressure. You're still new to all this; you haven't seen and done everything in prison. One time, I think there was probably a hundred people in the day room. A black guy was sitting on a Mexican's bench. He was probably new, just like me. I walked in and sat

FLAWED EXPERTS, FAULTY EVIDENCE

Defunct technology and incompetent experts obstruct justice

*A technician works in a Houston crime lab faulted for
scientific ineptitude and mishandling of evidence (2004)*

In 1927, the well-known phrenologist Edgar Beall testified against Ruth
Snider, who had been accused of murdering her husband. Beall—whose
expert witness-testimony was treated as fact—noted that Snider's chin
"tapered like the lower face of a cat," and based on the shape of her face,
pronounced her a woman of "murderous passion and lust." Though times
have certainly changed in the decades since, for the thousands of innocent
people imprisoned as a result of bad science, forensics still has far to go.

"The premise is interesting that scientific evidence is more reliable
than other evidence," says Simon A. Cole, assistant professor of criminol-
ogy at the University of California, Irvine. "It would be nice if it were
true." In fact, according to a recent study of sixty-two cases of DNA exonerations, one-third involved "tainted or fraudulent science."

Forensic science can fail in two ways: flawed technology and flawed
human behavior. In the first instance, it is usually the science itself that is
bad, as was the early science of phrenology that used physical features to
determine character and mental ability. Other forensic techniques that
claim to be scientific, but lack any substantial validation, include microscopic hair analysis, handwriting identification, bite mark analysis, voice
recognition, microscopic carpet fiber analysis, and tire track analysis. Hair
analysis alone—considered reliable a generation ago but now highly dis-
credited—played a critical part in implicating twenty-six of the first sev-
enty-four exonerees cleared by DNA tests.

In twenty-five years of criminal defense work, Peter Neufeld has not

continued on page 292

down, and it just happened to be the black guy's bench. I didn't know that. But they told me. They come up and tell you, and then you move, or if you're stubborn, you say, "I'm not gonna move," and then somebody come up and start a fight. They start swinging. A lot of prison is game plan. There's some fighting, but more than anything it's trying to perpetuate fear.

It's all a game. I'm not saying I'm glad I'm not black, but to be black and be in prison is really hard. Mexican also. Because you can't be your own man. It's been easier for us, because there's more white people running the prisons. We're more likely to have some kind of power. If all the guards were black or Mexican, it would be different. But they're not.

I talked to all kinds of people. They may not be your choice of really good, quality friends, but you do it, maybe in kind of a superficial way. I mean, you can be sitting in a dayroom on a bench, and there's a movie on, and the guy next to you, you're talking to him. But you don't really care about him, he doesn't care about you.

I think I called my dad every few weeks. I would give him updates, but we had a really dysfunctional relationship at that point in my life. My father was passive; he wouldn't stand up to women. Usually, the women he got involved with were somewhat mentally imbalanced. They were threatened by his children, or his first marriage. So he didn't get involved financially with me, and he didn't visit me. He did come to the jail at one point in my stay there. But I don't know that it really helped any just having a parent stand there and say, "Well, I don't know what to do, son. I hope you get out."

Then he didn't come to visit me until eight years later. He wrote letters, but I just think a large part of it was not having the resources to help. It's really hard to come to prison and see somebody you care about, love, and not have money. He lived about

tried a single case without forensic evidence being presented by the prosecution. Just by virtue of their sheer prevalence, unsound scientific practices continue to influence court decisions.

In the courtroom, expert testimony has a profoundly persuasive effect. "Study after study shows that juries put a great deal of faith in the testimony of expert witnesses," writes Sheila Berry, director of Truth in Justice.

But in many cases, members of the jury (not to mention lawyers and judges) do not have the scientific literacy to understand expert testimony, and are therefore not appropriately critical of evidence. The science itself can then assume the force of "mystic infallibility." To protect unwitting jurors from expert testimony that is without scientific basis, the 1993 United States Supreme Court decision *Daubert v. Merrell Dow Pharmaceuticals* obligated judges to act as gatekeepers to prevent unsound scientific practices from being used at trial. Still, defense attorneys virtually always lose their *Daubert* challenges of the prosecution's evidence.

It is often not the forensic method itself that is the source of concern, but rather the people and system through which the results are produced. Experts can ignore contradictory data or distort the significance of their findings, as did Arnold Melnikoff when he testified that the likelihood that a hair from the crime scene belonged to anyone other than the defendant was one in ten thousand when the known error rate suggests at least a 10 percent likelihood that any microscopic hair match is wrong. Labs can be poorly managed and tests sloppily run. No one knows how frequently forensic evidence falls prey to an incompetent lab or to distorted testimony by an expert. But a detailed examination of 138 DNA exonerations revealed that 33 percent of the cases entailed misleading expert testimony, suggesting such occurrences are not rare.

The lack of supervision in the government's forensic labs allows the work of scientists and their testimony to go unscrutinized. Both inadvertent technical mistakes and deliberate falsifications are difficult to detect without supervision, and the consequences, as Fred Zain's twenty-eight-year career as a forensic scientist demonstrates, can be catastrophic.

In college, Zain was a below-average student, failing chemistry courses and otherwise disqualifying himself from becoming a forensic scientist. Nevertheless, for thirteen years, Zain was employed as a medical examiner and forensic expert by the West Virginia State Police, rising to the position of chief of serology (a course he failed in college) at the West Virginia Department of Public Safety.

According to Berry, "Fred Zain became something of a forensics 'star,'

continued on page 294

a mile from the police station, but he was probably afraid. He didn't want to go down there and stir anything up with the police. He didn't visit or get much involved with me. He'd write me a letter every once in a while, every Christmas.

And then, about eight years into my sentence, he decided he was going to change, and he wanted to be a better father, so he was going to start coming to see me. My dad is a passive person; he's not a real stand-up kind of guy. In fact, he didn't even teach me much about defending myself, so I had kind of a crash course on that in prison. In there you don't walk away. You see that person everywhere you go, and it's never going to be over. If you do win a fight, then he'll have a friend, and you'll have to fight that guy.

My dad made a comment during the O.J. Simpson trial. What he was trying to tell me was that he had seen for the first time the inner workings of a courtroom, and that he could see how it really can get twisted around. And that, "Yeah, maybe they did that to my son. If O.J. was probably guilty, and they let him off, then maybe my son was innocent and they made him out to be guilty."

My mother was still out here in California. We wrote a lot of letters from jail and prison. She's a writer. I talked about the books I was reading, and history. If you're in jail or prison you measure history through what you see on TV. You have the news, and you're gonna talk about what's going on out there. I remember there was that earthquake in '89. That was a big thing. We got to see it on the news. My mother was in Bolinas, but there was no damage to her area, fortunately. I called my brother Paul. He's four years younger, and he's the closest. I have a normal relationship with him. He's pretty stable. He's not on drugs, he's married, they have a baby. My older brother has been a mess since the late 1960s. It's just that he has an addictive personality. I have

sought after by prosecutors who wanted to win convictions in difficult cases." "Zain was a prosecutor's dream," agrees George Castelle, a senior West Virginia public defender. "If he needed blood or semen to match, Zain matched it. If the prosecutor didn't want to match skin or hair samples, they didn't match."

Zain was involved in thousands of criminal cases held in a dozen different states. But then, in 1992, following the exoneration of Glen Woodall—a man who Zain's testimony helped sentence to 203 to 335 years in prison—Zain's house of cards collapsed. A court-ordered investigation and a report by the American Society of Crime Lab Directors confirmed that Zain had "fabricated or falsified evidence in just about every case he touched," including 133 murder and rape cases, some of which resulted in death sentences. So far, at least seven convictions he was involved in have been overturned.

Bad science, however, is not simply about corrupt, renegade "experts." Sometimes the system itself becomes infected. In December 2002, a Houston Police Department crime lab was shut down following an audit. Ensuing investigations revealed scientific ineptitude of considerable proportions, involving every single lab technician and affecting hundreds of individual cases. So far, two men have been exonerated. Hundreds more, including several death row inmates, currently await DNA retesting.

"There were two different problems with the crime lab," says David Dow, a University of Houston law professor, "scientific incompetence and corruption. That's a deadly combination." Harris Country, where Houston is located, leads the nation in sending people to death row.

While most agree that the fiasco at this laboratory was exceptional, many also believe that such problems are not unique to Houston. "Similar troubles are evident in other crime laboratories," observes an August, 2004 *New York Times* article. "Standards are often lax or nonexistent, technicians are poorly trained and defense lawyers often have no money to hire their own experts." Currently only three states—New York, Oklahoma, and Texas—require crime labs to be accredited by an outside agency.

Some believe the real problem with bad science—at least unintentional bad science—is deceptively simple. "It starts with an analyst who has a name," says respected forensic scientist and DNA expert Ed Blake. "That's where it starts. Somebody who was hired to do a job, who was not competent to do the job. It starts there and it ends there. That's what the criminal justice system is all about—individual accountability. I mean, that's part of the irony."

two brothers and we're all different, and they'd maybe not have been able to survive in prison. I guess you just got to be stubborn to survive it.

I MIGHT AS WELL READ THE BIBLE

When you first go to prison, you have to do fieldwork. You're called a "New Boot." You do mostly a lot of flat weeding, which means you go down a row where there's little weeds growing up around the crops, and you flat weed it. You do that for a really long time, and then you pick vegetables and cotton. Sometimes you go out and chop down trees. A lot of times you like it, because at least you're getting outside the fence. And then other times you actually cut grass, where you line up, everybody's got a hoe, and you hit the ground at the same time. They do a counting: "a-one and a-two and a three and a four, stop." Sometimes they do a little military singsongy thing.

Traditionally it's a chain gang, but they don't chain you together anymore. But they do have a lot of shotguns—a lot of the field officers are dressed as cowboys on horses with guns. Then later you're offered a job to come inside and work in the kitchen. When you have a long prison sentence, like ten, fifteen, twenty years, you think, "Texas is not paying me to work, so maybe if I work in the kitchen there's some benefits there, which is the food. You'll always be able to eat good."

I was in Ferguson Unit [a prison in Midway, Texas] for eight years. I developed a good relationship with the chaplain. He was new and pretty young, only like thirty-eight. He told me about when he found the Lord. Most of the prison chaplains are Baptists. The Baptist thing for me was interesting, and it was new and it was good in the beginning. But it's their emphasis on getting saved over and over again, that's what I didn't quite reconcile with. The message was that if you believe and if you come to the altar and humble yourself by getting on your knees and saying the sinner's prayer, then you're saved. Some people have some kind of emotional lift off their shoulders.

I always thought I was different because I was innocent. I think there are a lot of guys in prison that are having to live with a lot, carrying a lot of guilt around with them. I was interested in finding out why this happened to me. I was interested in the Bible for that reason. In jail, I said, "I might as well read the Bible, I never read it, I might as well," so I did. And then something started to open up to me and I thought, "Well, wait a minute, look at Joseph." His brothers sold him into slavery. And then he got put in prison. When he was in prison, he was still a righteous man; God was in his favor. He found out that the king was having bad dreams. Nobody could interpret them, so Joseph interpreted his dreams somehow. One of the dreams was about these cows that were fat and these cows that were really skinny and they represented something about famine. The king was going to have many years of famine. So the king let Joseph out and then exalted him to a prince.

When famine comes on the land, his brothers have to come back to ask for a handout, and Joseph's the one that's owner of the grain. They have to come back to their brother. They don't even recognize him, but he recognizes them and he has compassion on them. He had compassion, even though—I mean, they really did a cruel thing—they threw him in a pit, then some slave traders came and took him away as a little boy. They were jealous of him, because he was so righteous and he was a beautiful boy. He had a multicolored coat that the father bought him. He was the father's favorite. They took his coat and they ripped it up and put blood on it, and told the father that he had been eaten by a lion.

Another story is Job: Job has all kinds of bad things happen, everything you can imagine. He lost everybody in his family, they died. He loses all his property, and he swells up with these boils, and he's sick. But he's the most righteous man in the whole land. Everybody came to him and said, "How can you worship God when he's doing all these bad things to you?" No matter what would happen, Job would still continue to worship God, and praise God. So it was then that God finally gave him back everything. He restored his health, he gave him another wife, and he had all kinds of children, and he gave his property and his cattle and everything back. So through these kinds of stories I somehow identified with that. I thought, bad things happen to good people, and somehow something good is going to come of this. And I did give my life to God.

YOU'RE INNOCENT, BUT NOBODY UNDERSTANDS THAT

Prison is a crazy place, because it makes you live for the future, with this idea that there's this day that you're going to get out. And so what you do is you start living to prepare for that day. The free world in the United States is structured. We have a holiday every month here, and people get drunk to relieve their stress, to get their ya-yas out. In prison, the youngsters in there are really acting out and trying to get ahold of drugs and whatever they can.

But people can mature into something that means something. You get really, really into college or religion because you have to—you need something. If you're doing a lot of time you want to be with other guys that are also doing it, so that you have a lot more things in common. I did have friends in the religious community, guys that had given their lives to Christ. I believed in that for a while. I don't think of it the same as I did then. It's

NO ONE ELSE TO TURN TO

Exonerees embrace religion when the justice system ignores them

For the wrongfully convicted, religion is often their last hope. Innocent but behind bars, they are all too aware of the imperfections of secular institutions and often experience spiritual conversions or renewals of faith.

Roughly 70 percent of U.S. prisons offer some form of religious counseling, either via chaplains or outside ministries.

Marvin Anderson

Marvin Anderson, who was exonerated by DNA evidence after serving a fifteen-year sentence for crimes he didn't commit, describes the role religion played in his prison life. "From the time I was able to walk, run, you know, my mom and dad told me, 'Always believe in the police department, trust in the police department, fire department—these are people that are trained to help and protect you.' These are the same people that sent us to prison. So who do you trust? My experience—trust in God."

And in many cases, prisoners have nothing else to turn to. As funding for educational and extracurricular programs in jails and prisons has dwindled, privately funded religious organizations—Christian, Jewish, Muslim and others—have risen to take their place. Participation in organized religion has yielded positive results for prisoners and prisons. An evangelical Christian group called Prison Fellowship Ministries was shown in a 2003 study to effectively reduce recidivism rates for Texas inmates who participated in religious activity. Inmates who graduated from the program were less than half as likely to return to prison as a comparable sample of convicts who did not. In Florida, thousands of prisoners are on the waiting list to transfer to the faith-based Lawtey Correctional Institution. There, they seek both a more religious environment, and a far safer one. Despite the positive effects of many of these programs, some experts fear that the line between church and state is being blurred, and that many services prisoners need, such as educational programs, are being slashed by administrators who see religion as an acceptable substitute.

"It's not singing 'Amazing Grace' that keeps you from going back to jail," says Barry Lynn, executive director for Americans United for the Separation of Church and State in an interview with ABC. "It's having a job when you get out, and Florida has cut the funding for those kinds of programs."

kind of like foxhole religion. If you're under fire—if I was drafted today to Iraq, and I was out there being fired at—you're going to draw close to God. It is about having some kind of hope. If you lose hope, then you lose your sanity. I think we all acted crazy in there. Craziness is the stress and tension that comes from the abnormality of living in that kind of environment. It makes you blow up and get angry.

My worst memory was getting the letter that said I'd lost the second appeal. I went to the rec yard and I ran. That's what you did: you just ran and ran and ran until you were exhausted. It's kind of like the effect of screaming or crying, because screaming and crying is not really cool to do in prison.

It's kind of like being in a black-and-white world. You can be so numb emotionally that you can't appreciate anything. You can't feel much, you can't see beauty. I tried some therapy. There was one lady that I told my story to, and I don't think she really believed me. But there's another one that did. Her opinion was that I needed to move forward with this and put it behind me: I'm still in prison, but I've got to let it go. I've got to make amends with the police officers, the complainant, this woman that accused me. Don't carry a vendetta around with you for the rest of your life, even if it means not fighting this anymore. I exhausted all my appeals already. I know the truth and God knows the truth, and that's what is important.

During the first five years, I spent all my time and effort in the law library, filing appeals and doing everything I could. It's very difficult, it's a lot of let-down, a lot of despair. So I had to move forward. It gets easier. You just stay in school and have a routine, somewhat like in the military. I had to let go of a lot of the anger. I had it, and it was only going to hurt me. You've got to find a spiritual awakening; you've got to do something that's going to allow you to survive prison. Because you carry around a lot of hate, you're either going to kill somebody in there, or you're going to get killed, or you're going to self-destruct—you're going to kill yourself. You're dealing with that kind of anger. You have a right to it, you're innocent, but nobody understands that.

THE NATURE OF THE CRIME

I came up for parole in October of 2000. I go to the interview. I think, "I've done all you want me to. I've served fifteen years. You're supposed to let me out." I had all my family write parole letters: "We still love our son. We're going to stand behind him. He can come live with us." By the time I get in they barely even look up, and they say, "David Pope. Okay, you've been through college; you've done this program; you've done AA; you did cognitive intervention, okay, yeah, yeah, okay, next!" I assumed that I would be released, because I fulfilled all those requirements.

Then I get the letter that says: "You're denied parole. Nature of crime." I was just going to have to wait for my next parole interview which would be a year later.

I was very angry. The main thing in there is that when you get a sentence, you want to be able to take a calendar and mark a day when you're going to get out. They're messing with your mind. They tell you, "You do fifteen and you're going to get out." It's a problem in Texas. Texas prisons are really bad. They say, "Mr. Pope, in the year 2001, you'll make parole if you stay out of trouble." They tell you that so that you won't be a problem inmate. But then when you come up for parole, they say: "It's the nature of the crime."

HEY, THIS GUY'S INNOCENT

In 1999, after receiving an anonymous tip, the Dallas County dis-

trict attorney's office decided to perform DNA tests on the rape kit from Pope's case. Pope contends this anonymous tip came from one of the case's original prosecutors. The evidence matched an incarcerated sex offender, James Milton Roberts. However, he could not be tried for the offense because the statute of limitations had already expired.

Pope suspects that aides in Texas Governor George W. Bush's office knew that he had been cleared of the rape, but intentionally left him sitting in jail for more than a year. Pope also suspects that Bush's office was reluctant to sign his pardon because Bush was running for president at the time and didn't want to create any negative publicity. After Bush won the presidency in 2000, the new governor of Texas, Rick Perry, pardoned Pope on February 2, 2001.

A real strange thing happened one day. I get a call from the guard office that says that I have a visit. Well, visits only come on the weekends, so why would I have a visit during the week? It can only be one thing: a religious volunteer, that's happened before. When I went out there, there was two men in suits. They were with the Dallas Police Department. They introduced themselves, they were detectives. They didn't say anything about why they were there. They just started interrogating me about the crime from fifteen years ago, and I just went along. I said, "I'm telling you the same story I did from the very beginning. I guess you all want to know if my story's still the same." I thought, maybe this is part of parole: they came here to check out my story, and to see if I was still claiming to be innocent.

After that little interrogation, I was very bewildered, and I ask them, "Why are you here? Why did you all call me out?" One of them gave me his card, and I said, "Am I going to hear from you again?" He said, "Yeah, we'll be in touch," and that was it, they turned around and left. And I just felt like something's going on. It's got to be good, because what's the worst thing they could do?

They're not going to put another charge on me. I didn't know what to think, so I went to sleep.

The next day the warden calls me. It's a female warden in this unit, the only unit I've ever been in that had a female warden. She calls me up there to her office, and that's big. I mean, I've been in there fifteen years, and the warden has never called me to the office. She looked at me, with kind of a strange look on her face. Later I learned that she'd never heard of anybody being innocent before in her prison. She said, "Look, I've got a call from this reporter, this guy named Bill Brown. He's a journalist with Channel 8 in Dallas, WFAA News, and he wants to come here and interview you. Do you know anything about this?" And I said, "No, I don't know." And she said, "Well, you have to sign this consent form, which says I'm giving him the right to interview you, but you have to agree to it. If you don't want to do it, you don't have to." I said, "Well, sure, I'll sign it." I signed it and that was it. I went back to the cell block.

The warden had said, "He'll be here tomorrow, at one o'clock in the afternoon. So try to be ready, and wait for your call-out." And so I was real anxious. All kinds of things were going on inside of me, so I went outside on the rec yard, because I didn't want to just be sitting around. I was out there walking around the yard from twelve to one. It's one o'clock, it's one-fifteen, and it's one-thirty and what's going on? So I went back, checked with the guard, and I said, "Have you heard anything? I was supposed to be called out to the visiting room," and he said, "No, I ain't heard nothing." Next thing I know, it's probably about 1:45. A guard said, "Pope, pack it up." Now, "pack-up," that's one of your favorite words to hear, because that means you get to move and go somewhere. And he said, "Yeah, you're on the chain," and I already knew they don't pull no chain in the middle of the day. They do a chain bus at the night time. And so I knew at that very moment I was going to get out.

It takes me ten minutes to get all my personal possessions, mostly books and a couple of little duffle bags, and from there I carry them all the way to the end where the fence opens and they have a bus that comes. Well, there's a holding area, and I was sitting there, and I sat there for about an hour in that holding pen, and there was guys I knew, they were walking by and saying, "What's up? They don't have no chain bus in the middle of the day," and I said, "Yeah, it looks like I'm getting out." I can guess that somehow my case got overturned, because I'm not going out on parole. And most everybody is wishing me luck, because a lot of guys never see anybody get out of there that's innocent, and it gives them hope: "This guy got out; maybe there's hope for me."

And so, instead of a bus coming, it turned out to be a van. There was two guards, and it turned out they were off-duty, but they were called to work overtime to come special escort me, to take me to Huntsville. The new governor had stepped in, and heard about this, and he wanted me whisked out of there so fast that it didn't give time for the reporter to even show up. They didn't want this reporter coming in there—they wanted me out of there. Because the reporter was going to go right back out there in the news the next evening and tell everybody, "Hey, this guy's innocent and he's still in jail."

The two special escorts drove me to The Walls [Unit] in Huntsville. It's about a fifty-foot-wall-type prison. When you first come to prison that's where you go through first, then you're dispatched to the unit you will be assigned to. When you get out of prison, you also go back there, so I rode in this van. I was in the back, kind of like chauffeur-driven. I still had my handcuffs on. Of course they knew I was innocent, but they had to get me back to go through all the formalities to release me properly.

I think it probably took at least three hours to get there.

It was dark now, like nine o'clock. They said, "Well, I don't really know what I'm supposed to do, but I know you're innocent"—they told me I'm innocent—"so you can go." And they let me go, right? I said, "Well, I can't. I don't have nobody to pick me up." So I literally walked out, and then, as I'm walking, the guard says, "Well, look, why don't you come on back, and I'm going to put you in a cell but I'm not going to lock the door. And I'm going to go get you a tray from the officer's dining hall and some fried chicken. But for all practical purposes, you're innocent. I'm going to have to wait until the building captain is here in the morning to get this thing worked out."

So he got me that tray, and I'm in that cell, right? Some other guard comes through and slams and locks the door. I knew I was going to get out eventually, so I didn't worry too much. I went to sleep. The next morning I'm waiting and waiting, it's going way past 10 A.M., and nobody came to see me. Finally the guard comes and says, "Get your stuff," and he walks me to the major's office. The major's sitting behind his desk wearing a cowboy hat. He says, "I got the phone right here. Governor Rick Perry's holding a press conference right now, and he's signing your pardon. I'm talking to him right now. They're going to fax a copy over in about fifteen minutes, so when I get that, we're going to let you out the front gate." And that's how it happened. He shook my hand and said, "I think you're the first innocent man to be released like this, and I want to shake your hand."

THEY KNEW I WAS NOT THE ASSAILANT

This story I'm going to tell you now wasn't all together when I first got out. The only reason I'm actually able to tell all this is because I learned it over a period of a few years. Around 1995, prisons started to look at, "Maybe we better start keeping a DNA bank of everybody that's incarcerated." They took a little blood sample from everybody in prison. So when they did me about 1996, I didn't think anything of it because everybody else is having it done.

This district attorney, now retired, decided, "I'm going to go back. Something's really bothering me about this case with Pope." He got my blood. He knew that there was a miniscule amount of DNA from this woman who accused me. She had had a rape kit done on her, but I was never told [about it]; in fact, when she went on the stand, she said that she hadn't had one done. It was so miniscule that in 1985 they couldn't do anything with it. It was kept on file, though. This district attorney knew that. When he got my blood, he went back and opened up her [rape kit] and tested it. At that point, between 1996 and 1997, he knew without a doubt that it was not me. From 1997 to 2001, they knew I was not the assailant. But they didn't have anybody else. So, they just wanted to sit around and wait and see if maybe this guy [the true assailant] will do something stupid and get arrested again. He did, eventually, but it took some time. And in that time, I came up for parole. If I were guilty, they were supposed to let me out. I served time. I not only was denied parole, I didn't know why. It was very strange, because I was a model inmate: I went to school. I did everything that was required of me so that I could get out. And they wouldn't let me out. I was very traumatized by that. I only know now, it was because if they would have paroled me, then I would be a "guilty man," an "ex-convict," a "registered sex offender," out on the streets.

George Bush was running for president. He was still residing as governor. Now it's, "Okay, we know it's not Pope. Oh my God, not only is it not Pope, it's this other guy, James Milton Roberts. He's over here in the Darrington Prison Unit." But George Bush is running for office—you know how they try to get dirty laundry on different candidates; it would really look bad if they painted a picture that George Bush had somehow known I was innocent and had left me in prison. So they kept me in there three or four more months. They had no choice but to keep me in there a few more months until after the election when George Bush was going to leave to become president. As soon as he did, within that day, the new Governor Rick Perry was notified of the series of events. He found out that they left me in there, even when they knew it wasn't me, that it was this other guy. And he was outraged. I've never met [Perry], but he did sign my pardon.

The only reason I ever found out the name of the actual assailant is because I wrote a letter to Governor Rick Perry's office and asked him for any reports, or press releases, or anything he could tell me. He sent me a press release which disclosed the name of this rapist [James Milton Roberts]. I already knew that the statute of limitations had run out, because it had been fifteen years. They know it's not me. And they know it's him, but they can't charge him with it. They can't do anything. I found out that this guy was in prison for indecency with a child, and he didn't get very much time. He did a couple of years in that sentence and they let him back out. He's out there on the streets now. Whether or not the statute of limitations is right or wrong, I feel there should be closure for me. He has to apologize to me, and he has to apologize to the woman that he raped.

Sharon Lemke should have to at least write me a letter to say that she's sorry that this happened and "I was wrong; there's no question that I identified the wrong man." There hasn't been any of that accountability. I think that's wrong. It has really bothered me a whole lot to find out that there was evidence, that she had a rape examination and that the kit had been kept in storage for all those years.

My lawyer—his name is Randy Daar, and he works in San

Francisco—actually found her. We got an address, and I composed a letter that just said, "Look, it wasn't me; it was this other guy. We're not trying to get you in trouble. We don't want anything. We just want some acknowledgment." She didn't give us anything back. We don't know if she even received the letter or not. It was about that time that the restitution became available, so I just kind of left it at that. Still, this may be ongoing. Before I die, I may decide I really need closure with this, I need to try to get a lawyer to contact her, see if she'll meet with me someday.

THEY GAVE ME FIFTY DOLLARS, AND THAT WAS ALL

When I began my incarceration, every parolee was entitled to $200, and that was all you ever got. The parolees were supposed to buy a bus ticket, which is about fifty dollars, and get on the bus to Dallas or Houston. As soon as you get off the bus you're supposed to report to your parole officer. Over the years they found that a lot of these guys were going right to the liquor store with the money, or going to buy drugs. Then he never would show up at his parole officer. They felt like $200 was too much money to give an inmate. So then they decided, "We're going to give them fifty dollars, and that's just enough for a bus ticket." Then when he gets to his parole officer, they'll give him another fifty dollars. I didn't have a parole officer. They gave me fifty dollars. And that was all.

I didn't know if anybody was going to be there to pick me up, but my dad was. The reporter called him and told him when I was going to be released, so my dad was prepared. He was able to be there, right when I was released. He picked me up at the Walls. He was in a Jeep. His fourth wife was in the car, and I thought, "Why did you bring her? She ain't somebody I wanted to see. She didn't write me one letter. She didn't support me when I was in prison." He got me that late afternoon and by the time we got back to downtown Dallas it was dark. I didn't ask him to, but he took me to a steakhouse and put a beer in my hand. He thought that's what I wanted, or needed. Like that would be the most important thing to have when I got out—a beer? But it wasn't. The steak really wasn't what I wanted either, because we used to have some steaks in prison, so I had it before. What I wanted was a guitar.

I spent the night at my father's house. The next day my mother's plane arrived at the airport in Dallas. My father took me there and we met her and my brother. I was real happy. Not 100 percent, because they never visited me the whole time I was in prison.

When I was released, a reporter ran up to me as soon as I walked out of the door. Then there was media waiting for me at Dallas, so I did three or four interviews within twenty-four hours of being released. When my news interview ran on TV, a guy called in to the news station the next day and said, "Hey, I have this guitar, and I want to give it to David Pope."

I didn't have any time to think that I was going to have a normal life because I was rushed out so fast. I assumed that I was going to be a paroled sex offender registered with the police, that I would be full of anger for the rest of my life. Can you imagine what I would have been like? People would be looking down on me forever. I don't know how I would have dealt with that. But I think maybe, somehow, God, or whoever your higher power is, had some way of knowing that, look, I'm not going to be able to deal with that. I had enough bad karma as it was because of what happened to me. And so maybe now I'm not going to have any more. Maybe I had enough already.

DAVID POPE

Man freed by DNA evidence starts new life in Sonoma

By CECILIA M. VEGA

THE PRESS DEMOCRAT

The last time David Pope lived in the "free world," VCRs were the latest craze, U2 topped the music charts and $6.50 an hour made for a pretty good paycheck.

That was 1986.

Pope was 24 when he was sentenced to 45 years in a Texas prison for breaking into a woman's apartment in a Dallas suburb and raping her at knife-point.

Fifteen years later, DNA evidence proved what Pope claimed all along: He was innocent.

It has been only five weeks since Pope was released. Since then, he has moved to Sonoma, where he lives with his brother and his sister-in-law and tries to adjust to life on the outside.

"I don't relate to the new music that the youngsters are listening to . . . I was raised on the Beatles and oldies," he said while rocking comfortably in a chair in his living room. "I never heard a CD before."

Making up for the lost time will not be easy.

"I'm 39 going on 21. At my age you should have a wife and kids. I don't have any of that," he said. "I'm just trying to put my life back together."

While he was in prison, Pope said, "I used to tell a lot of people about my story and they were like, 'OK, yeah, well, sure.' When you're in there for sexual assault, it's a real bad stigma. You can say you're innocent but people don't really know."

Thirteen years into Pope's sentence, an anonymous phone call to Dallas authorities prompted them to reopen his case. DNA tests not available when Pope was convicted proved police had the wrong man.

Authorities have since linked the rape to a registered sex offender who is in prison for another crime. He cannot be charged because the statute of limitations has run out.

Even now, however, Pope, a mild-mannered man who parts his hair, wears pressed shirts and talks with a southern drawl, is not angry.

He said he's not angry that he never received an apology from

TURN TO FREED, PAGE B2

David Pope served 15 years in a Texas prison for rape before he was pardoned when new DNA evidence proved he did not commit the crime.

The Santa Rosa Press Democrat *announces Pope's release (March 2001)*

I WANTED TO FIND OUT WHO
I WAS IN THE FREE WORLD

We're talking about being institutionalized. It's one thing, being in there and thinking it's all bad, but in some ways, what happens in institutionalization is that you don't concern yourself with things like finances. All your food is cooked for you, all your laundry's done; you're being taken care of. Over a period of years, you just don't realize it. All of a sudden when you get out you have to do all these things for yourself. And you're usually alone; you don't have the camaraderie; you're not in an environment where there's hundreds of people around you.

[When I first got out] February 2001, [I lived] with my mother in Bolinas. I commuted to work in Corte Madera at Nordstrom's for four months. My brother had been at Nordstrom's a long time; he got me the job. I wasn't released from prison with a way to plug back into society, other than I did get some college credits. In prison they do have programs, but it's not the same. I got an associate's applied science degree in electronics, but it's not state of the art. I didn't get out of prison with a way to plug into a decent-paying job. It was basically go into fast food or retail, and that's what kids do when they get out of high school. That's the kind of job I was destined for.

309

When I got out, I had the option to go back to school if I wanted to, but I decided I didn't want to immediately. I just wanted to find out who I was in the free world. It's like having a midlife crisis, but in a lot of ways you're still twenty-four. Socially, you're locked away from society at the age of twenty-four, so all things that you should have been able to do, that most young people would do, you didn't get a chance. But now you're forty, you're having this midlife crisis: "Oh my God, my life is running out; I've got to hurry up and do these... What am I... ?" So the prospect of going back to school didn't thrill me too much. I wanted a life right now.

It took a while before I got my driver's license. I was just very paranoid about being in moving vehicles. I just felt too vulnerable. I had this fear hanging over me that something bad was going to happen. [I avoided cars] also because of sensory overload. One of the reasons that [prisoners] usually become good at things like art is because they are sensory-deprived—you tend to become more acute in other areas, like a blind person. If you're surrounded by a gray wall all the time and you don't have all these colors around you, or all this variety and change, it just makes you go inward. My memory became really acute. And then you spend a lot of time reading and contemplating, which is not the same out in the free world, where you're so bombarded and overwhelmed by all the media.

Some of my closest friends in Texas were involved in prison ministries. Judith was one of those who had always stood behind me. She would write me and then come visit when possible. She wrote me sometime after I was out and said, "I've heard you've gotten out—you've been in the newspaper. By the way, there was a Senate bill passed in Texas granting restitution. You probably don't know about it." There was a website I could go to and find out about it. So I did, and I printed this thing out.

The new governor signed a bill that would grant some money for however many days you lost if you would have been working. But there was no money granted for anything like mental anguish.

In 2002, a year after his release, Pope received $390,000 from the state of Texas—$71 for each day he spent wrongfully incarcerated.

When I got restitution, I quit [my job at Nordstrom] and lived off the money for about three years. It was like winning the lottery, pretty much, because nobody in my life had ever had enough money to do anything, really. I felt like for the first time I could hold my head up with the rest. There's always this element here, that you're not good enough because you don't have enough money. [I moved to San Francisco] because I could afford it. I chose the Marina because it was close to the water, and it had the athletic field. I felt like I could probably handle that at least I'd be halfway grounded to nature; the Marina is not as claustrophobic as other parts of the city. I signed a year lease, and I paid it all up front. I was going to live there for a year, and that's what I did. After a year, I wasn't able to commit to another year—it was a lot of money to throw away. I'd never been anywhere before like this, where it's all about prestige, and wining and dining, and foreign cars. We didn't much see things like Beemers when I was coming up in Texas.

I drove a really old Honda. Then it started giving me problems. My mother cosigned on a new car, and I started paying on it. When I got some restitution I traded that one in, and I got a real car, a 2001 Mustang. Later I traded that one in, too. I went through that phase of my life which means experiencing those things. When I was in high school I couldn't afford one of those cars. I had the opportunity now to live out that little dream for a while. I thought it'd be a good conversation starter. I'd make friends—it was going to be maybe even a babe magnet, but it really wasn't. It's a superficial thing. I had to go through that and realize that I'm a more mature person than that. I'm not a teenager anymore, trying to get attention based on what kind of car I've got. Now I don't even care. I don't want that car, I like what I've got; I'm not interested in that, I got it out of my system.

I had paranoia about staying in Texas. I was a free man, and I made the choice not to stay in Texas. With that choice, I came to extreme culture shock in San Francisco, Silicon Valley, and all the Internet tech, satellites, cell phones, all this technology that's changed society. It's very materialistic. I didn't even know what the word *jaded* meant until I came here. I still wasn't quite sure I got the concept, but I think I understand it, because jade is a very hard stone, and there's a certain hardness about some of the people.

I have issues with feminism and women that want to kick you in the balls. I feel like, well, damn, a woman put me in prison, right? A lot of white women here don't allow a man to feel like a man. So therefore a man feels threatened. It's just different in the South: a lot of the women there feel more comfortable with being [women]. When you turn on country music videos, what do you see? You usually see women that wear makeup; they say in Texas that a woman doesn't go out without her makeup. It's still part of that family values that you're supposed to find a man, get married, and have babies. Out here, not everybody's interested in that.

Even though I was resistant to some of the culture when I arrived here, I've been here long enough now that I've established some memories. I'm finally getting to know my way around San Francisco, and to start over. In Dallas, I don't have any friends. I don't have anybody there. My father, but he didn't even come to my trial; he didn't get involved.

DAVID POPE

BACK TO TRIVIAL EVERYDAY LIFE

In Texas they told me if I agreed to stay and be a resident, they would give me free mental health [care of] any kind. When I came out here [to California], I didn't have that option; I had to pay for it. It was helpful but expensive. One of [my problems] is female interaction. I mean, can you imagine being labeled a rapist?

Having been in so many interviews, I got to thinking about modeling, acting, that kind of field. I was not in any school plays as a teenager. At some point, after I got my restitution, I had a little money to experiment with this.

Method acting is often a lot like therapy in that things from childhood that shape who a person is, create problems in life later, create neurosis, create attacks of the superego. When you're in prison every man has a lot of attacks, things that the mind plays on you: I must be here for a reason. I'm cursed. God hates me. Why did this happen? I'll never get out of here"—hopelessness, despair. Method acting is a way of getting in touch with the truer self, or what we really feel.

One of the qualities that I do admire about the Bay Area is the likelihood of finding enlightened or artistic people interested in truth, honesty. I got a callback from Rob Reese method acting. What impressed me was that when I did talk to Rob one-on-one was that he was very open about himself. He was being vulnerable and honest, and that's what I needed: somebody that was willing to be a mentor. He had been drafted to Vietnam. He came back, he was a part of a lot of the same problems that are happening now in Iraq: Men are going over there and they have a duty, a tremendous responsibility, a purpose and a role. Then they come back to the world, back to trivial everyday life and all of a sudden they don't really know where they fit in anymore. Because something's happened to you. You've been changed by new experience. You can't stand certain things anymore. Things really bother you. You want to know where you fit in, and what you have in common with people. I began to see through reading and watching films about Vietnam that [I have] a lot of things in common with [a soldier]. Somebody that goes into prison is exposed to elements of war, intense emotions—anger, fear, threats every day. You learn to survive in prison. I think there's a lot of similarities.

The first day [in acting class] I sat and observed what was going on. I thought it was the weirdest thing I'd ever seen. It was like looking at some psych patients—I thought this was crazy. I didn't quite get it. In one of the exercises, a girl and a guy got up, and Rob calls out the "Love-Hate Exercise." I don't know what that is. They start right into this exercise, and I'm going, "Wait a minute. What's going on here?" The guy and the girl are just two people, they don't love each other or hate each other; they're just called to get up in front of the class. They have to express love for each other, so they stand apart and say, "I love you"—the guy says, "I love you," the girl says, "I love you." Then Rob says, "Switch." The guy says, "I hate you," she says, "I hate you," and they do this more and more intensely, more and more, "I hate you," "No, I hate you," "No, I really *hate* you," and try to express hate. Of course, there's no physical contact, no pushing or hitting. After ten minutes, he tells them to stop. Then he asks them, "How do you feel?" They express how they feel. I think, "Hey, I'm starting to get this." The purpose is to be affected by the exercise. I felt like this person hated me, and I didn't like that feeling. But I really felt like this person loved me, and I really liked that feeling. It takes a lot of courage to do some of these exercises.

The workshop can be an acting stage, and it can also be a nuclear living room where we all sit and we talk. Well, when it's like that, I feel like it's a family: We are all vulnerable—this student did something embarrassing, but so did I. We all did this thing together, we're not judging each other, and that's a nice feeling. But when the class is over, everybody is off in different directions, and we don't often bond outside of class. We're living all over in different places, we got things we've got to do, we've got a job, we don't have time.

I tried Great Expectations, a singles party cruise around the [San Francisco] Bay. I talked to this woman, and it seemed like we had a lot in common. We kind of connected, and she gave me her number. She was a veterinarian. She lived up in Sonoma County. Something happened where her number

Pope, a year after his release (2002)

changed. She moved, or something, and I never did get back [in touch] with her. At the time, I think I was thirty-nine and she was forty-something. I didn't know what I needed or wanted in a woman; maybe I thought she was too old. A woman my age can't really have children. I think I thought I wanted children when I got out; now I'm beginning to be careful about going into anything too soon, because it's a lot of responsibility. I'm still working on trying to help myself now. I don't want to go into a marriage or raise kids when I'm not really ready yet.

I really believe that dating is a lot easier if you have a job or you're on campus. People need to see you consistently; that's how you make friendships. I didn't ever spend any time on a college campus. If I go down here to Telegraph or University or Shattuck [avenues in Berkeley] I see all the young people out, and they're just at that age when it's all about partying. I've really matured past that. But a part of me is kind of sad, because I missed out on most of my twenties and all of my thirties. I was forced to grow and mature in other areas when I was in prison. Every Friday and Saturday night you're sitting in a cell. You're not out partying, going to clubs, watching movies.

RESPECT

I wanted to leave the country. I thought, "White people are really screwed up." Well, damn, white people disown each other, they break up, they don't stick by each other, they're arrogant. If something like this happened to somebody in their family, Asians and Hispanics would be much more likely to do all they could for that person. It's white people that came over here, that started this capitalism, this greed. A lot of the most neurotic people are white people, if you ask me—maybe it's from the Puritan values that were brought over here. The word *penance* comes from the Catholic Church. In Texas obviously it's "an eye for an eye," which is the Old Testament, and Don't Mess with Texas, and "If you hit me, I hit you back." Texas has always wanted to be about, "Well this is America, goddamn it. I'm a Texan, I'm a white man, and we don't like niggers and gay people." They've never really been very tolerant of people that are different. I'm sure it's changed, and it's trying, but it's very hard because of the Old West pulling it back.

Asian people seem like they have it together. I ended up going to the Philippines—I was going to try to meet some eligible single ladies. There's all kinds of services in the Philippines that'll [help you meet ladies]. If you just say you're American, they'll say, "We're going to set up an interview for you over here."

When I went over there, I was pretty vulnerable and a little bit fearful, being an American and because of 9/11. Can I just walk the streets, and go out on my own? They already told me

Manila wasn't really a safe place. And you're real close to the Arab world over there. If you're an American you don't really want to be advertising it.

So I was involved with this service that booked me a hotel, and were going to bring over some eligible single ladies that were marriage-minded. There was fifty, I think—more than I ever thought they'd bring to the hotel. The average age of them was eighteen, and I saw real fast that it's just too young. Over there a lot of girls can't go to college because they don't have money. In that part of the world, they think in terms of if she can keep a good house, and she can cook, that's important, and that's what some men who go there want: they just want someone to take care of them. With me, what I wanted was a soulmate, somebody I could confide in. I'm the one that likes to cook and take care of the house, because I've been doing that. I'm just an independent person.

What I had to do, because it's really hard for me to hurt anybody's feelings, is I had to date as many of them as I could. I'd meet them at the mall, and we'd go to lunch. I realized, there wasn't much we really had to talk about. Then there were some others that were older, and one girl—she was twenty-three—she kept calling me at the hotel, being very persistent. She was the kind of girl that liked to be a companion. Whatever I wanted to do, she wanted to be there. And I liked that, because I never really had anybody like that. So we're compatible, but she wanted me to marry her. I'm the kind of person that, I'm not going to marry unless I know that it's going to be for a lifetime.

But, see, I'm forty-three, right? I've seen a lot of this world, and money, materialism doesn't impress me anymore. When you're twenty-three, it's different. You haven't experienced anything yet; this is all Disneyland to you. It's hard to understand, but people there have lived, often in one room with several family members, their whole life. And you're going to transport them all the way here and they're going to have no family, they're going to be around all this? I would have to be her whole world. I just don't know how I could do that. But they're very, "Oh, I want to go to America." I don't know how I feel about it; I just think it's risky. I'm not going to say it couldn't work, but I don't want to bring her over here and have her be isolated. And I'd say, "I want you to go out, I want you to go to the college, meet friends… " But then, the risk is that she's going to realize, now she's plugged into the Filipino community, that "I've got nothing in common with this American guy, and in three years I can file for divorce." Their culture, their family is very much about, they want to marry another Catholic. And I'm not a Catholic. I am accepting of anybody's belief system.

They have a large extended family in which they don't use babysitters, because the grandmas and the aunts and everybody is in one place. When you show up at the door all the kids come out, and they're excited and the young ones take your hand and touch it to their forehead, which is a blessing, and it's really sweet. All through Southeast Asia they respect people that are older than them. It's a really nice quality because white people don't do that.

They were just really, really nice. I've never seen that before. They weren't like, "Oh my God, you poor thing, a bad thing happened to you." It's almost like they can't really believe that there's any corruption in the U.S. They think it's only in their country, because over there they've had a history of that. The presidents are usually corrupt; a lot of money's not used to feed the people. When I was in prison, I was way better off than them. I mean, I was healthier. A lot of times, all they got is rice. I was taken care of a lot better than they are. They look at me, I look totally healthy. They're feeding me three meals a day in prison. I don't look like I went to prison, and it's almost like, "I don't think I really believe him, but I'm not going to say anything."

I stayed five months in a pension house, which is the same thing as a boarding house. When I got there, I didn't want to come back. I didn't have anything to come back to. I felt like I was getting validated by people treating me with respect over there. Part of it is because you're white. I was feeling like I was getting what I should have gotten over here when I got out of prison. I feel like when I walk down the street here, I'm invisible. People don't acknowledge you. Over there it's not like that. Everybody smiles. Here you assume bad intentions. You walk by me, I assume you have bad intentions until you prove otherwise. Over there everybody is assumed to have good intentions first.

WHERE I AM NOW

That pretty much brings me to where I am now. I've been out for three and a half years. Six months ago, I was looking for work, but I was being very selective. It's mostly about retail, but I need hard work. I want to be outdoors. I want heavy equipment, construction, something like that. I really need work, not just the hard physical [aspect] of it, but the social. I actually found out that I do like helping people, and maybe that means that whether it's retail, or something, but interacting with people, they come and they need something, or somebody has a problem—that humanitarian aspect that fulfills a need in me.

I've never really looked for a job since 1984. Back then, it was pretty much before the Internet, so you either saw a sign, or you walked in a store, or you got a newspaper. I've always been kind of annoyed at doing job résumés over the Internet where I can't really see a person and I don't know that I'm actually making a connection with a real person.

In Bolinas, a town made up of people that are, you know, very eccentric—drifters, hippies—a landscape supply business is always advertising. [The owner] puts out her Help Wanted sign, it seems every other month, because there's a high turnover. I just happened to catch her one morning with a sign. I thought, "Might as well go in there and give it a shot." I was lured in by the $13 an hour. I worked there for three months. These people are somewhat wealthy, and they have a tendency to want servants. People that have money, they can go, "So what? If this one don't work out, we'll just buy another person," and that's what happens.

I composed a cover letter that I started to pass out to employers before an interview. Sometimes they wanted an explanation why I hadn't worked in so long. I had to explain that I had some money to live on, and how that came about. Prison sticks in people's mind, and then they really want to be convinced that this is not an ex-convict, this is not a guy that was guilty, but somebody that something really bad happened to. Some people don't have the capacity to deal with something like that. It's like if a guy came back from Vietnam and said, "I've been in Vietnam," you don't know how to deal with him or his issues. If somebody comes out of being exonerated, there's not a lot of people standing in line with open arms to nurture this person, to help him, really.

Joseph Amrine

I'M A DEAD MAN WALKING

NAME: Joseph Amrine · **BORN:** 1957 · **HOMETOWN:** Kansas City, Missouri
CONVICTED OF: Murder · **SENTENCE:** Death
SERVED: 17 years · **RELEASED:** 2003

I NEVER THOUGHT THERE
WAS GONNA BE A TRIAL

On October 18, 1985, inmate Gary Barber was fatally stabbed at the Missouri State Penitentiary, where fellow inmate Joseph Amrine was already serving a fifteen-year sentence for burglary and robbery.

I was in the room where the murder happened. I didn't actually see the murder. I was playing poker when we realized something was going on. Everybody immediately turned around and seen someone lying on the floor. We didn't have to get up because eventually someone was gonna come over where we was at and tell us what happened. You been in prison so long, when something like that happens, you get to a point where you see it and

321

you just turn around and finish doing what you're doing. Everybody had their speculations.

The warden and the investigators came, one of the officers who did see something, they asked him, "Did you see something?" He went over and pointed to [inmate Terry] Russell and asked a few questions. When the sheriff gets there, they takes the guard out and asks if he seen anything. Eventually they come back in and everybody had to be searched.

I went back to my cell. I think I had been there five minutes when four guards come down there and say, "Amrine, they want you downstairs." It was the investigator, the sheriff and the warden down there. And when I go in, the investigator says, "Joe, guess what. Terry Russell says you killed Fox." I said, "Yeah, right." He said, "That's what Terry Russell's saying."

What ended up happening was I denied killing him and denied seeing who killed him. I never thought there was gonna be a trial. I know the guard seen it. The administration know these guys [Barber and Russell] had a fight. It was the first time they'd been back around each other. Plus the prison snitches was there.

One day they came and got me and took me out of town and charged me. I was saying to myself, "I got the guard. The guard seen it... I'm just gonna ride this one out."

Prison guard John Noble originally identified inmate Terry Russell as the perpetrator. When questioned, Russell implicated Amrine, saying Amrine had admitted to the stabbing. After a preliminary investigation, Amrine was charged with Barber's murder.

The state's case against Amrine relied on the testimony of inmate witnesses Terry Russell, Randy Ferguson, and Jerry Poe. Mirroring what he had originally told investigators, Russell testified that Amrine admitted to the murder. Ferguson testified that Amrine was

*walking next to Barber for several minutes before pulling a knife out
of his waistband and stabbing Barber. Poe testified only that he wit-
nessed Amrine stab Barber.*

*Amrine introduced evidence showing that he was not the killer
and that Terry Russell was. Prison guard Noble testified that he saw
Barber chase Russell across the recreation room before Barber pulled
the knife from his back, collapsed, and died.*

*Six inmates testified that Amrine was playing poker in a differ-
ent part of the room at the time of the stabbing, and three of those
inmates identified Terry Russell as the person that Barber was chasing. None of them implicated Amrine.*

MR. AMRINE, YOU HAVE A LAWYER.
I DON'T TALK TO YOU

When the trial first got started, I was like, "I can't believe this.
This has gone on long enough now." The second day of the trial,
my lawyer told me, he leans over and says, "We're halfway home."
I'm looking at him saying, "Halfway to death row," because what
I'd seen of the trial so far, it didn't look good for me. Because they
had two guys who claimed they'd seen the murder, and I'd committed the murder. They had Terry Russell, who claimed I told
him I committed the murder. The main thing I was thinking was,
"How they going to believe inmates over the guard?" And that's
one point I could never get past, that they actually took the
inmates' word over the guard. So that was going through my
mind. The guard was in the room when it happened. And the
guard identified another guy as the one who committed the murder. And the guy he identified as committing the murder had just
been released from the hole, solitary confinement, for fighting
the guy that was killed thirty minutes earlier, and the guard did-
n't even know Russell and Barber had a fight.

323

They had this blood that was on my pants, which was five, six, seven years old. They didn't say it was his blood. They just implied it was his blood. That hurt me. My lawyer wasn't cross-examining witnesses properly. I knew what the outcome was gonna be. If I was a juror sitting there I would have convicted me, too.

By the time of the trial, Amrine's court-appointed lawyer, Julian Ossman, had gained notoriety as an incompetent capital defense attorney. Each of the previous four clients he represented in capital trials was sentenced to death. Ossman had been a lawyer for Ferguson—a key prosecution witness—on a pending weapons charge until two weeks before Amrine's trial. That charge was dismissed in exchange for Ferguson's testimony. Amrine's appellate attorneys later argued that this created a conflict of interest, particularly because Ossman failed to effectively cross-examine Ferguson.

Furthermore, Ossman failed to present exculpatory information from prison guard Noble, and overlooked a number of witnesses who would have significantly contributed to Amrine's defense, including one witness who saw Barber's murder and identified the murderer as Terry Russell.

The representation which my lawyer was giving me was very, very poor. We was going back and forth about that. He was a public defender, also known as a "public pretender." He was just pretending to be a lawyer. I knew going in that he wasn't a good attorney because he had represented [four] different people and gotten them all the death penalty. I knew he wasn't that good, but I didn't know he was the type that just didn't care and was just there for the paycheck. He said, "We got to think about what we're going to do about the penalty phase." He had never brought this issue up before. And you know, any lawyer knows that that's part of the initial investigation—prepare for the penalty phase. If the medical examiner was on the witness stand, he would come over and say, "You want me to ask him anything?"

I said, "You know, I really ain't got nothing for you to ask him. All he's doing is telling you what the cause of death is. He's just the medical examiner. It's really not important, we all know what the cause of death was, there's nothing to be disputed."

But then when one of the inmate witnesses gets up there, the lawyer wouldn't even look at me. He wouldn't come nowhere near me. Naturally I'd have some questions for them, but no. He would keep his back turned away from me, and say, "No more questions, Your Honor."

Actually, I had kind of like a 101 in law right there in the courtroom. Because I ended up writing stuff on a tablet—things I didn't like when he did, things I didn't agree with and stuff like that. Like I said, I didn't know much about the law, but I did know this much—common sense. I had good common sense. Anybody with common sense could see that he wasn't doing the things that he should do. I'm thinking to myself, "What can I do to try and make sure this stuff don't go unnoticed or make sure this stuff don't get lost in the wash?"

We got into it right there in the courtroom 'cause I had asked him to look at [the tablet]. He looked at it and said, "What do you want me to do with this?"

I said, "I want you to sign it, to say that these are my complaints and you were made aware of it right here during trial." And he wouldn't do it.

He had a paralegal there, and me and her had been talking, and she's the one who suggested writing it down. She didn't like him at all. Every chance she got, she'd talk bad about him. It got really bad because I ended up trying to bring it to the judge's attention. I say, "Your Honor." He don't say nothing. I say again,

DEFENSELESS

Ineffective counsel places the innocent at risk

In 1963, the Supreme Court ruled in *Gideon v. Wainwright* that indigent defendants must be provided "effective assistance of counsel." But in the forty years since the *Gideon* decision, poor legal representation for indigent defendants continues to plague the U.S. justice system.

In 1987, Jimmy Ray Bromgard was convicted for the rape of an eight-year-old girl in Montana. His lawyer, nick-named "Jailhouse John" Adams for having such a high number of clients sent to prison, failed in almost every aspect of Bromgard's defense. An Innocence Project report claims that the lawyer "did no investigation, hired no expert to debunk the state's forensic expert, filed no motions to suppress the identification of a young girl who was, according to her testimony, at best only 65 percent certain." Adams also failed to give opening and closing statements and did not file an appeal after Bromgard's conviction.

Calvin Burdine

After serving fifteen years in prison, Bromgard was exonerated by DNA in 2002. Others haven't been so lucky.

"No constitutional right is celebrated so much in the abstract and observed so little in reality as the right to counsel," according to an article by Stephen B. Bright in *The Champion,* a publication of the National Association of Criminal Defense Lawyers. In the 2003 article—a sweeping indictment of the U.S. indigent defense system—Bright detailed some of the most egregious cases of ineffective counsel:

• In Texas, defense lawyer Joe Frank Cannon fell asleep several times during the 1984 trial of his client Calvin Burdine. Burdine was found guilty and sentenced to death. Despite this, judges continued to appoint Cannon to other cases, including capital offenses. "Most people caught sleeping on the job in any line of work are fired," Bright writes, "but Houston judges continued to appoint Burdine's trial lawyer to capital and other criminal cases." Eighteen years later, Burdine was granted a new trial from the Fifth Circuit Court of Appeals, but not before two lower courts

continued on page 328

I say "Your Honor." He looks at me, he say, "Uh, Mr. Amrine, you have a lawyer there. I don't talk to you. You got something you want to say to me, you say it to your attorney." I said, "But Your Honor, it's about him." He said, "I don't care," once again. "Now if you got something to say to me, you got to say it to your attorney." He said, "Now if you make another outburst, we're gon' hold these proceedings without you." Now what can I say?

I was stuck with him, because I didn't have no money to hire an attorney in Jeff City [Jefferson City], where I was at. Their public defender's office was, like, maybe three people, and he was the only one who had any experience in capital murders. So I really didn't have no choice.

I DID NOT WANT TO SPEND
THE REST OF MY LIFE IN PRISON

On October 30, 1986, Amrine was convicted of the murder of Gary Barber. After intentionally campaigning for the death penalty in hopes of attracting attention to his case, Amrine was sentenced to death the same day by an all-white jury.

I knew I was getting convicted. I gotta come up with my own plan now. Luckily for me, each day at the end of the trial, they would take me back [to jail]. And there was other guys who was down there on murders and kidnappings, and we would talk. I didn't know nothing about the law. Only thing I knew about the law was they shouldn't have me handcuffed and shackled in front of the jury.

I tried my best to get the death penalty. I had already been down a long time and I'd seen a lot of other guys there who had life and fifty years without parole—they didn't have no lawyers

concluded that "sleeping counsel" did not violate the Sixth Amendment.

• Between 1987 and 2000, four of the thirteen people exonerated from death row in Illinois were represented by attorneys who were later disbarred or suspended.

• In Georgia, a group of lawyers contracted with several counties to handle felony cases at an average cost of less than $50 per case.

In many states, public attorneys are saddled with caseloads far too great for their experience, time, and talent. According to the National Legal Aid and Defender Association (NLADA), public defender caseloads are commonly three to ten times the suggested maximum of 150 cases per year. In Washington, the American Civil Liberties Union found that for one county, a single public defender was responsible for nearly 40 percent of all felony defendants—350 cases per year.

Death penalty defense lawyers, in particular, are often poorly compensated for their work. For example, in Mississippi in 1995, court-appointed lawyers in death penalty cases earned an average of $11.75 an hour. Furthermore, prosecutors typically receive three times the amount of money from state governments than public defenders do. An NLADA report found that "underfunding affects the quality of representation by limiting resources for essentials such as trainings, investigators and experts, and technology."

In the United States, simply being represented by a public defender is often perceived as an indication of guilt. A survey by the NLADA found that 54 percent of the American public assumes clients represented by public defenders are guilty. Theoretically, this puts the 80 percent of American defendants represented by public defenders at risk for wrongful conviction.

Despite modest efforts from some states to address serious inequities in public defense, most poor defendants are represented by underfunded, time-strapped lawyers who cannot mount the caliber of defense that better-paid lawyers can.

Bad legal representation can cause not only unfair sentences and wrongful convictions, it can increase the chances that an innocent person will be executed. In Georgia, 97 percent of death row inmates could not afford a lawyer. Steven Hawkins, executive director of the National Coalition to Abolish the Death Penalty, says, "We know that the death penalty is not reserved for the worst crimes, but rather for people with the worst lawyers."

or nothing. So I'm thinking, rather than spend the rest of my life in prison, I'm gonna take my chances getting the death penalty for a murder I didn't commit. If nothing else, I'll have a lawyer throughout my appeal, and unlike a life sentence, the death penalty in itself adds a lot of attention. People would give notice to me being on death row, more than if you have life or fifty years without parole.

At the time when [the conviction] happened, me running the risk of being executed really didn't matter to me. I think the thing that played a part in it was being mad. Just, "I wish y'all would give me death for a murder I didn't commit." Because the way I was looking at it was like, if my appeals run out and they execute me, then they just doing me a favor. The only thing that really mattered to me was that I knew that I was not gon' spend the rest of my life in prison. Before I do that, I'd rather be executed.

I don't remember talking to anybody before them as far as me trying to get the death sentence. Now, after I was convicted and after I got the death sentence, I had said it to certain people, including my family, and they were shocked. They were saying that that didn't make sense—"Where there's life, there's hope," stuff like that. And I was trying to explain to them that being in prison the rest of your life is not life. You just walking dead, you know?

I DIDN'T HAVE TO MAKE NONE OF IT UP

I went back in there and he [the attorney] put me on the witness stand. I started off telling them that they had found me guilty, and I wasn't mad at none of 'em, in fact that I believed in the death penalty, that I think the death penalty is appropriate in certain situations. If I'm not mistaken I think that's how I started my testimony. And uh, I went on to tell 'em about how I was raised, my family, my father, my mother, and about trouble with the law. I just did everything I could to make sure I got the death penalty. I told them my father used to beat us, my father didn't work. We was poor, lived in the projects. My older brothers and them had some run-ins with the police and went to prison before I went to prison.

My goal was to make sure they gave me the death penalty. I didn't know the law back then, but actually when I got on the witness stand, it was like a plea for mercy. That's probably the way they took it—a plea for mercy by me telling them about the way I was raised and being in trouble, my brothers being in trouble, me being in trouble. It was like a plea for mercy. I was on the stand for probably about forty-five minutes. I talked about my prison life—I'd been in trouble in prison, been involved in stabbings, gambling, I ran with a gang. I didn't have to make anything up. Pertaining to me and my life before I went to prison and when I was in prison, and my family life—no, I didn't have to make none of it up. It was the truth. No exaggeration at all.

[The jury deliberation] was quick, maybe like an hour, forty-five minutes. It was really quick. I just wanted to get the proceedings over with. Get me where y'all gon' take me and let me start doing whatever I need to do.

Soon as the jury recommended the death sentence, the prison officials escorted me to death row.

I WAS RIGHT, THEY ACTUALLY WAS WRONG

They put me in a cell and a white guy come to my cell and he say, "You just get here today?"

I said, "Yeah."

"You got the death sentence?"

"Yeah."

330

He say, "Do you know the law?"

I said, "No."

Said, "Do you want to learn the law?"

I say, "Yeah."

Said, "All right." He left. Came back with two law books. And he put 'em in my bunk.

He said, "Read these."

His name was Doyle Williams, and he was on death row. He had come down there in '82. He was in college before he came on death row. He was going to be a corporate lawyer, so he had a lot of knowledge about the law. So when he came on death row, he turned into a criminal lawyer. He helped everybody.

When he brought me the books I probably had mixed emotions as far as being able to learn the law, you know, 'cause how am I going to learn the law just by reading the books? But the bottom line was, I'm locked in a cell, ain't got nothing to do, no reading material, no TV, no radio, and I just got a death sentence. And I think I started off reading the law books from having nothing to do. I was trying to keep my mind occupied.

Actually, I got kind of caught up in it—not only the law, but also, they have brief synopsis of the guys' cases and stuff. So I would just read all about the cases and all about the issues and stuff like that. That's all I did. The books were like three thousand pages. They were like novels and I enjoyed that.

By the time two years was up, I was basically an expert on my case, my issues—what law applies, what case to cite, because that was the only thing I was looking at, was my case. A lot of issues jumped out at me: being handcuffed and shackled in front of the jury; bringing all the witnesses in front of the jury handcuffed and shackled. I felt it was a violation for them, introducing this blood that they claimed they took off my pants when they couldn't say whose it was. I think that prejudiced me. They tested it and said it was human blood, that's all they could say. But yet, the jury left with the impression that it was the victim's. There was quite a few things that I felt was wrong. And actually, when I did start learning the law, I was right, they actually was wrong. Like one of the guys, he testified that he took a polygraph test. That's illegal, that's against the law to say that on the witness stand. But he did it.

I started talking to some of the other inmates about me being innocent. Most of them were convinced that I was guilty—just another person claiming to be innocent. They didn't care. I stopped talking about it. I only talked about it to people who knew the law, and people who wanted to know about it.

THE WHOLE PLACE WAS INFESTED
WITH ROACHES AND RATS

You wouldn't believe it. I was locked in my cell twenty-four hours a day. We was in a dungeon. We lived in what was called "The Basement," which is literally where you at, it's the basement. You're basically underground. The air was just so stale; ventilation was really bad. The whole place was infested with roaches and rats. Not mice, but rats. The food was terrible. The food was always cold because our food had to be brought in from the main kitchen. And because we was on death row, for instance, we might get breakfast at four-thirty in the morning. We might get lunch at nine-thirty in the morning. We get our last meal probably around twelve-fifteen, so now we gotta go from twelve-fifteen in the afternoon all the way to four or five the next day before we get some more food. And that was wrong.

Our safety was an issue because at that time when you would go on visit or to the hospital, all they would do is have a guard take you over there and you would be in handcuffs. And the whole general population would be right out there. So if I'm coming through there and I'm in handcuffs and it's a guard with me, and there's a guy in general population, he could be standing right there with two knives, and just commence to killing me. The guard ain't gon' do nothing.

The recreation facilities was just a grass, fenced-in area. The walls was tore up, peeling. The toilets stayed flooded up, and they were, like, so old where they just—you'd be scared to sit on it. I mean it was just that bad down there. The lighting was real bad. You only had one light bulb, and the ceiling was like fourteen, maybe fifteen feet high. And the cell is like 9x11, 9x12. You take a 9x12 cell, you got a fifteen-foot ceiling, one thirty-watt light bulb—they don't make too good conditions for reading.

Amrine (April 1995)

I had one particular friend at Missouri State Penitentiary, young white guy. They had made a homosexual out of him and everything. And he ended up killing somebody there, and he had come to death row. At this time he was on the walk that was mixed up with some whites and some blacks. Some of the black guys on there took advantage of him and everything, so the administration moved him off that walk and they put him on a walk with all the white guys. I think he lasted about two weeks. I mean, they just straight-up sexually and physically abused him. I mean, as far as they were concerned, he was a homosexual, and that's what he's here for. So he ended up getting moved off that walk and getting placed in what they call protective custody. And in protective custody you in that cell twenty-four hours a day.

I happened to see him one day and I said, "You know, you could move over here with us."

The walk I was in, it was all black, 'cause they refused to put any white guys over there—and I told him, I said, "You not gon' have no problems. Ain't nobody gonna mess with you, unless you—if you want to have sex with one of the guys on the walk, that's on you. But as far as somebody taking some from you, or taking anything from you, or just abusing you, that's not gon' happen over here."

So I went out there and I told the lieutenant, I said, "Hey, I don't feel anybody on death row should be placed in protective custody because they're facing execution."

It just made me feel bad thinking that this guy might have to spend the last days of his life in protective custody, locked in a cell twenty-four hours a day simply because other guys want to take advantage of him. He has enough on his plate right now to be worrying about you trying to take advantage of him.

So I went in there, I told the lieutenant, "I give you my word: You move him on the walk with us, he will not have a problem. Nobody will mess with him or nothing."

He said, "I got your word on this?"

I said, "Yeah."

He said, "Write the warden. Tell the warden that."

I wrote the warden. The warden wrote me back. He say, "We will move him on the walk with y'all in the next twenty-four hours." And they move him on the walk, and he never had a problem.

TALK CRAZY, TALK TOUGH, SELL THREATS

The biggest problem down there was there was a lot of racial tension. When you have whites over here and blacks over there, that's gon' be a racial problem. Especially when they separated like that. They gon' always be talking, you know. They gon' talk crazy, talk tough, sell threats, from both sides. But once you get 'em together, equally, then it's no problem no more.

When I first come on death row, around May of '86, two white inmates on death row had killed this black inmate down there. And that's where the racial problem was really created at. So what they ended up doing, they had all the whites in one area, all the blacks in one area. The problem the administration was running into was, they was running out of space to put the rest of these white guys with the rest of the white guys or the rest of the black guys with the rest of the black guys.

You'd feel it a lot of different ways. And not so much through the inmates, but I felt it mostly through the administration. It was obvious every day you'd see the difference in the treatment that was being handed out between the white inmates over here and the black inmates over there.

It was different on every level. When the food comes down—even if it was hot when it came down—by the time it got onto the black walk, it was cold. Because they would bring the food down there, they would immediately start serving the white walks. Or when it comes time for recreation, we know they going to get the white guys and take them to rec first. When the canteen come, they go over and they give them their canteen first. I remember one occasion where, it was the holidays coming up and they had told everybody we would not be receiving canteen for like, another week. Everybody was mad, but the white guys on the other side, they didn't like that at all. So they flooded and burnt the cells, and banged on the bars, everything. And the administration come back there and ended up making a special trip, going over there, getting their canteen, passing it out to all the inmates over there, and didn't bring us ours. I guess they had

Missouri State Penitentiary, also known as "The Walls,"
where Amrine was taken just after his conviction

figured as long as we at each others' throats, we could never try
to get together to go after the administration itself.

I talked to the lieutenant and I explained to him when you
make it even like that, when you make 'em have to live around
each other, a lot of the racial slurs they hurl out their mouths,
whether it be whites or blacks, they not gon' be so quick to hurl
that out their mouth. Because now, we're in contact with each
other. So you gon' use a lot of restraint. I said, "You know, a lot
of these guys just talking because they know that they're never
going to come in contact with each other again." And the lieutenant said, "Yeah you're probably right, but we can't take that
chance." They really didn't do nothing.

*In 1989, Amrine and his sixty-nine fellow death row prisoners were
moved from Missouri State Penitentiary in Jefferson City to the
newly built Potosi Correctional Center, about 120 miles to the southeast. The construction of the new prison was prompted in part by a*

federal lawsuit declaring that MSP's death row conditions were so bad that they violated the Eighth Amendment and were considered "cruel and unusual punishment." MSP's death row was housed in the rodent-infested basement of a century-old building with inadequate plumbing and ventilation.

At Potosi, death row inmates were merged with the general prison population.

When we went to Potosi what ended up happening was, say, within two to three weeks, all the whites and all the blacks was all in there in one housing unit where we come out every day, be around each other in the day, be around each other in the yard. We go to the dining room together, and there was no tension because now we on even terms.

It was sixteen of us on death row that had prison murders. And we was all cool. We was all close. Six or seven blacks and nine or ten whites. We didn't hang out together every day all over the yard, but anytime somebody had a problem, if ain't nobody else coming, these fifteen here are coming. These fifteen here are coming. And we had an understanding that nobody coming on death row is gon' be taken advantage of—whether it be sexually, financially, or whatever. And if they're not strong enough to stand up on their own, well then we got some people here on death row who is strong enough. We decided that amongst ourselves. And at first, everything was going along real nice because the guys was like, "Oh no, he's on death row. He's off limits. You better leave him alone." Regardless if he's sixteen and cute as Madonna, you better leave him alone cause he's on death row. And that lasted for a while, until the group of people at Potosi changed, and it was a little bit more of a prison as time went on.

337

PREDATORS AND PREY

U.S. inmates face dangerous, even guard-sponsored sexual abuse

Prison rape victim Hope Hernandez speaks to a San Francisco
meeting of the National Commission on Prison Rape (2005)

In 2004, the U.S. Justice Department reported at least 8,210 incidents of sexual abuse and rape in U.S. prisons and jails. Often, victims are young, nonviolent, shy, gay, effeminate, or in prison for the first time.

"Predators looking to rape someone tend to pick people without close ties or a gang affiliation," said prison rape expert and psychiatrist Terry Kupers, in an August 2005 article in *The New York Times.*

In 2003, Congress passed the Prison Rape Elimination Act to address the long-ignored ramifications of sexual abuse in prison. However, prison rape remains a pervasive and often unaddresed problem.

Since the victims of sexual assault often fear retaliation, many prison rapes go unreported. Prisoners must prove "deliberate indifference"—that officials had actual knowledge of a potential risk but consciously disregarded it—to get help through the courts. This is a difficult task at best.

In some cases, prison officers actually encourage rape. As one veteran corrections officer puts it, "Prison administrators use inmate gangs to help manage the prison. Sex and human bodies become the coin of realm… '[Y]ou and Willie and Hank work him over, but be sure you don't break any bones and send him to the hospital. If you do a good job, I'll see that you get the blondest boy in the next shipment.'"

Kendall Spruce was infected with HIV after he was raped at knifepoint in an Arkansas prison in 1991. He claims he was raped twenty-seven times in a nine-month period, according to *The New York Times.*

IF ALL THEM BOXES WAS TO OPEN UP AT ONE TIME, I'D PROBABLY LOSE MY MIND

Before I came on death row, I didn't have nothing or nobody, nothing good to say about nobody. The change in my life was formed from death row, from the people I came in contact with— just the people I started associating with. In population [before I was convicted for the murder], I'm around the guys who was on the same level I was on, the guys who liked beating people up and stabbing people, playing poker, smoking marijuana, running in gangs, fighting the guards. That's the crowd I ran with.

Then I came on death row. By me being interested in wanting to learn the law, that put me in the company of a lot of white guys, or black guys who had their head on straight. They was thinking about working on their cases, and suing the state, and bettering the conditions on death row. And so I found myself in their company a lot. And then I found myself saying, "Damn, this is kinda fun, learning the law."

It might sound crazy, but being on death row actually saved my life. It did. The murder went down in '85; if I'da got out in '86, I know for a fact, my state of mind in 1986, if I'da gotten out I'da probably gotten killed, or killed somebody. Because I still had that, "I don't care" mentality. Or that, "I wanna be bad" mentality. So if I'da gotten out at that time, I probably would have gotten killed on the streets. And then, not only that, maybe if I hadn't have gotten out, I probably would have gotten killed in prison, you know, from the life I was leading. Or I would have ended up killing somebody and ended up on death row. So I felt like, for real, that saved my life. Even my sisters and brothers say that today: "That's a tragedy, being on death row seventeen years, but you know what, Joe, that saved you." 'Cause I was out of control.

I think what I had to learn how to do was place things in certain areas. I couldn't just sit here and be thinking about my case, and then at the same time be thinking about, "Aw, my sisters and brothers and family and the changes I been going through with them," and then thinking about these guards harassing me, and then think about this lawyer that I don't like, and then the jury, and all these different problems that I got, different things that are just bothering me. And I realized, "You can't do that, Joe. You ain't strong enough."

So I had to learn how to put stuff in different areas. It's like, if I got my problems with family over here, and right now I'm dealing with the problem with my lawyer or my case, well then, my situation with my family don't even come into play. It's locked in a box. And these are all in little boxes. Now, if all them boxes was to open up at one time, I'd probably lose my mind.

'I AM SO SCARED THAT I'MA LOSE MY FIRST CHILD THROUGH AN EXECUTION'

[When I was in prison my mother and I] had lots and lots of conversations. Just name it—when we was coming up, why things were certain ways, about my father, about my sisters and brothers when we were coming up, how they're doing now, and their kids. And not just at visiting time but on the phone, cause I'd talk to her for two and three hours on the phone at a time.

My mother was soft-spoken. She was half-Indian and half-black. She spent time on a reservation and spent time in adopted families, then distant cousins, and was shipped from home to home. She didn't have no sisters and brothers and my father didn't have no sisters and brothers, so my mother said she basically was not raised.

She told me that when she started having her kids, basically she didn't know how to go about being a mother, you know, far as the motherly love, and all the different things. And my father didn't, either. And so I think that had a lot to do with it 'cause I never once remember my mama ever saying, "I love you," or hugging up to me when I was young, or encouraging me in school, or anything that a mother would do.

If I'da been on the streets, I probably wouldn't have time to sit down and even have a conversation. Because the conversation we had about her childhood, the thing about the way we was raised and why it was like that and everything—I'da never thought about that stuff if I'da been out.

I guess through the years we might have talked about certain issues as far as my appeals and stuff like that, and witnesses, little things like that. I'll never forget the time when we was sitting there. Think I had been on death row about thirteen years. I had been denied in the district court, in federal court, and she said, "Now that you done gone this far in your appeals and everything, and you ain't got no reversal or nothing," she say, "do you have any regrets?"

And I looked at her, I said, "Nope."

She said, "You mean to tell me you rather be executed than life in prison?"

I said, "Yeah."

She said, "Well, you know, where there's life there's hope."

I said, "Well, Mama I understand that. But I been locked up too long to even think about spending the rest of my life in prison, when I just spent all what life I had in prison."

Then she told me one time, "You know, I got five sons and five daughters. We grew up in the projects, all y'all been in and out of prison, always in trouble."

And she say, "I am so scared that I'ma lose my first child through an execution." Aww man, that just, that floored me. That really floored me, not necessarily how painful it would be,

but just how painful that thought is. Just the thought of you losing one of—your first child—or even any child, through an execution. And it'd really been pain for her 'cause it was ten of us.
And coming up in Kansas City—ten kids, five girls, five boys, we
all in the projects, we all ripping and running, doing different
things, robbing banks, you name it, we was doing it. And she has
not lost one yet? And then, you know, here we are up in age now,
and she scared she gon' lose her first one through an execution.

All while I was in prison, one thing I always liked to do was
smoking weed. And she never came to see me not one time out
of twenty-four years that she didn't bring me some. She would
smuggle it in to me.

My mother was like, "I can't do nothing else for you, it's the
least I could do." She would drive all the way from Kansas City
to Potosi. That was a six-and-half-hour ride and she would make
that ride by herself—six hours there, six hours back. She was like
sixty-seven years old, still driving all the way up here by herself.

I DIDN'T EVEN TELL HIM BYE

A lot of people had the opinion that, even though we sentenced
to death, [the state] ain't killed nobody yet, so it's really nothing
to be worried about for real, not right now. When they executed
Tiny Mercer, that changed a lot of things down there.

He was a friend of mine. He was a white guy, a good friend
of mine. Once Tiny was executed, you could actually see the difference in a lot of the guys on death row. It's like they just had a
reality check. It was real noticeable. A lot of the guys ran around
there laughing and playing. And when they had that first execution, them guys started thinking, "This is real. This is real."

But the main thing that I didn't like about that particular execution was that the administration, they had locked down the

whole institution. They ended up showing an X-rated movie. They had never done that before. The execution was at twelve, they started showing the X-rated movie at eleven-thirty. It worked. But I think it would have worked if they hadn't have showed the movie. Because there really wasn't much inmates could do. You could riot, you could do whatever you wanted to do, but when you get through, that person still gon' get executed.

With Tiny's execution, it really didn't move me one way or another. The way I looked at it was, he was sentenced to death, they executed him, nothing I could do about it. My attitude toward the executions changed as time went by. I started staying up on nights of executions, because you never know if the person will be actually executed, and he might win a stay of execution.

These was the first guys who had been sentenced to death. There was a lot of instances where a guard would come and take a guy to where they execute you. Say you're going to get executed on the twenty-first. And then the next thing you know, on the twentieth or twenty-first, you get a stay of execution, and then you come on back. This happened all the time. So I would stay up till however long it would be until the news say, "This person was declared dead or this person has received a stay of execution." And I would do this just about for every execution. And it was taking its toll. I had one, two, three, four friends who I was really, really close to that was actually taken out of the cell with me, and executed. Them was the hardest situations I have been confronted with.

And I think probably my worst experience being on death row was one I had with a guy named Tony Murray. Me and him was really close. He loved playing basketball, I loved playing basketball. He loved playing poker, I loved playing poker. He had to be about thirty, thirty-one, maybe six years younger than me. And he had a death sentence.

A CONTROLLED TYPE OF CHAOS

Sexual assaults, vendettas, and gangs wreak havoc

In 2000, sixty-eight inmates were killed in U.S. prisons, but that number does not tell the whole story. In the same year, 8,094 inmates required medical attention as a result of inmate-on-inmate assaults.

Typically there are three types of inmate-initiated prison violence: individual, gang-related, and collective.

Officers stand watch at Florida State Prison, where guards assaulted Frank Valdez.

Like sexual assaults, individual acts of inmate violence often occur as punishment for snitching or failure to pay debts. Weapons are usually fashioned out of metal objects within the prison: silverware, razors, and forks. Even toothpicks can be sharpened to slash and stab.

Most gang violence is carried out in the name of business. Gangs that engage in drug distribution, prostitution, and extortion often seek to maintain or expand their territories. And because gangs are politically useful to the prison staff, many large prisons attempt to contain and direct gang violence rather than end it. It may be preferable to some prison administrators that prisoners fight among themselves rather than with the outnumbered guards.

While most prison violence occurs among inmates, the incidence of guard-initiated violence is difficult to determine on a national scale. In 2000, a county jail in Oregon paid an inmate $1.75 million to settle an excessive-force lawsuit. An inmate had been strapped into a restraint chair, pepper sprayed, and choked; as a result, he lapsed into a coma for seventy-one days and suffered permanent brain damage. Also in 2000, four guards from Florida State Prison were indicted on murder charges in connection with the death of inmate Frank Valdez. The autopsy revealed ribs broken from severe beatings. There were boot marks imprinted on his body.

Former Pennsylvania prison official Charles Graner—convicted in 2004 for playing a major role in the abuses at the U.S.-run Abu Ghraib prison in Iraq—noted, "The Christian in me says it's wrong, but the corrections officer in me says, 'I love to make a grown man piss himself.'"

Tony came down to the end of his appeals. And I was in lock-up, I was locked in my cell all day. And where I was being held at, the bottom tier was lockup, the top tier was general population. He was in general population. His vent and my vent was connected and we used to talk [through the vent].

And he comes in one day and I said, "Where you been all day?"

He said, "I been up in the visiting room taking a lie detector test."

I said, "Oh yeah?"

He said, "Yeah, I'm getting my clemency papers put together." He said, "Now I took the lie detector test. I took it five times, Joe. I passed it all five times."

I said, "Aw yeah?"

He said, "What do you think about that?"

I said, "That's good."

He said, "What do you think that ol' governor gon' do when he see I passed the test five times?"

I said, "I don't know."

He said, "Do you know anybody else who took the lie detector test and passed?"

And I wanted to tell him the truth. I knew lots of guys who had come to the end of their appeals and took three and four and five lie detector tests. And passed them. And was still executed. So when he asked me, I said, "Naw, I don't think so."

He said, "What do you think my chances are?"

I said, "I think you got a real good chance." But in my heart, I'm saying to myself, "You're through." Because you passed the lie detector test, that don't change nothing.

What ended up happening with me and him was, he was in his cell, and I was up walking my floor and I seen these white shirts—the guards with the white shirts, the ranking officers—

they come in, and they look right up to his cell, and I see them walking up the steps. So I get up in my vent and I'm trying to listen, and I heard them say, "Murray, we have a warrant here for your execution."

And he said something, he tell 'em, "Let me get my property and stuff together, I'll be ready in a few minutes."

They said, "All right, take your time." They go back downstairs and leave out the housing unit. Next thing I know—other people who'd seen it, they hollering out the doors, hollering at him, "What's going on? They just read you your warrant?"

Well, I'm laying down there, he jumps up in the vent, he said, "Joseph!"

I don't say nothing. He keep calling me. I don't say nothing. Well, I guess he think maybe I'm asleep or whatever. So they come back to take him out of there. They bring him down the steps. I got my lights turned off, I got it where my cell is pitch dark cause I cannot stand to look at him. I couldn't stand to look at him.

When they brought him down the steps, I couldn't even look him in his face, I couldn't even tell him goodbye. I didn't even tell him bye.

MY TIME HAD RAN OUT

After Amrine's direct appeal to the Circuit Court of Cole County, Missouri, failed in 1987, his lawyers filed a motion for postconviction relief in 1990. This motion also failed. Shortly thereafter, Amrine acquired new appellate attorneys who were unaware that Amrine had intentionally campaigned for the death penalty.

When I come in that room, [my new attorney] said, "First question I got to ask you…"

I say, "What's that?"

He say, "Was you trying to get a death sentence? Look like you were going out your way to get a death sentence."

And I looked at him and I said, "Actually, I was."

He looked at the other lawyer, my lead counselor, and said, "I told you he was trying to get it on purpose."

He said, "Why?"

I said, "Because if I didn't, I wouldn't have no lawyers. Y'all wouldn't be here."

She was shocked. He thought it was really smart, but she was disgusted by it.

She looked at me like I had shit in my face or something, and from that day on that's the way she played me. And she was the lead counsel. She wouldn't accept my calls, wouldn't answer my letters, wouldn't do nothing. She's for the death penalty. What happened between me and her was, we already didn't have no actual rapport whatsoever. I would have to call somebody else to call her on a three-way to talk to her, and even then it was just nasty.

And when I got denied in federal district court, normally what the lawyer would do is call the prison, tell the warden, "Look, can you tell Joseph Amrine he needs to call his lawyer?" Then you would call your lawyer and they'd say, "Look, I got some bad news for you, the district court just denied you today." And then you might talk about the next step. Well in my case, I got denied. She didn't bother calling, she didn't bother writing, she didn't do nothing. It was fourteen days later when I found out. And they got where you can file a motion for reconsideration. And you have fifteen days to do it. Well, I couldn't file mine because she didn't call or write me and tell me I had been denied.

My time had ran out. I was so mad behind that, I wrote a letter to the Eighth Circuit Court of Appeals, and I wrote a letter

AN IRREVERSIBLE MISTAKE

Death row exonerations expose the risk of wrongful executions

As of April 2005, there were 3,452 inmates on death row in the United States. As of September 2005, there had been 981 executions in thirty-eight states since the death penalty was reinstated in 1976. Since then, 120 inmates on death row have been fully exonerated.

The number of executions nationwide has generally increased each year, reaching its peak in 1999 with ninety-eight executions. In 2000, Illinois Governor George Ryan made a historic decision to declare a moratorium on executions in the state, after thirteen people were exonerated from death row in a three-year period. "There is a flaw in the system," Ryan said, "and it needs to be studied."

Other states have tried to adopt moratorium legislation. In 1997, Florida successfully halted executions after thirty-nine-year-old Pedro Medina burst into flames while being electrocuted. The state resumed its executions less than a year later.

One of the mainstays of death row prisoners' attempts to fight wrongful convictions is their ability to file habeas corpus petitions—a request by a prisoner to appear before the court, to ensure that his or her imprisonment is legal. This right suffered a severe blow in 1996, when the Anti-terrorism and Effective Penalty Act went into effect. The act, which makes it difficult for inmates to file habeas corpus petitions by creating one-year deadlines and limiting successive petitions, has been criticized by Amnesty International as "a blatant attempt to accelerate the frequency of executions in the USA."

U.S. EXECUTIONS
(1976-SEPTEMBER 2005)

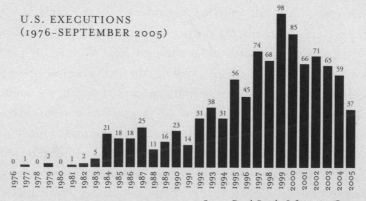

Source: Death Penalty Information Center

to the American Bar Association complaining about her, telling them how unprofessional she was by not having enough common decency to call me to let me know I had been denied.

I'M DEAD

From 1989 to 1996, Missouri executed twenty-three people by lethal injection.

After the Eighth Circuit Court of Appeals denied Amrine's post-conviction petition in February 1996, Sean O'Brien and Kent Gipson, Kansas City attorneys from the Public Interest Litigation Clinic, took on Amrine's case. They located a key witness in the original conviction, Jerry Poe. Poe recanted his testimony, admitting in a sworn affidavit that he did not see Amrine stab Barber, and had falsely implicated Amrine. Both of the other original trial witnesses had also recanted their testimony, claiming they lied as a result of threats or promises made by police and prosecutors. The Eighth Circuit Court of Appeals ordered the case back to district court for an evidentiary hearing to determine if Poe's recantation could be considered new and reliable, thus warranting habeas corpus relief.

Amrine presented new testimony from the jailhouse informants and Officer John Noble to the district court. Noble testified that Terry Russell was the actual perpetrator and that Amrine was in another part of the room when the murder occurred. However, the district court held that only Poe's testimony was "new evidence" and that his statements were unreliable. The Eighth Circuit Court concurred and the U.S. Supreme Court refused to hear the case.

In November 2001, the attorney general asked the Missouri Supreme Court to set an execution date for Amrine.

Well, Doyle went on and got executed. After that, my mother died and my mind really wasn't on the law.

Sean [O'Brien], my attorney, said, "You know what you need to do is you need to write a letter to the Eighth Circuit telling them you want me to represent you. Then I'll write them telling them I want to represent you."

I said, "Sean, you don't know nothing about my case."

He said, "Yes I do. I been keeping up with it."

I give the credit to two college students up here at Webster University [in St. Louis]. They read an article about my case. It was on *20/20*. They came to Potosi to see me. We sat down and talked and they were both interested. They went out and did a real investigation. They talked to jurors, witnesses, prison officials. They went down and talked to Terry Russell. They came back and said, "We know you didn't do this." They was 100 percent certain. So they go back to St. Louis.

I had just been denied by the U.S. Supreme Court. So they're looking like, "He's gonna get executed." Nothing they can do. They sent a copy of their article down to the University of Missouri, Columbia, and this professor got ahold of it and he read it. He walked away with the clear impression that I was innocent. He decided to do a documentary about my case. He told me they did the documentary because they'd either be documenting the execution of an innocent person, or documenting the exoneration of a person. That's why they wanted to do it. That got me a lot of publicity.

The first big word I got came April 15, 1997—a month after my mother passed away. The Eighth Circuit ordered my case back all the way to the district court. Which was a really good sign. They said they need to send my case back. But that judge ended up denying me. I was right back where I started.

I said, "I'm dead. I'm a dead man walking. I don't have any more appeals."

WHO'S GONNA GET THE FIRST DATE?

They locked me down, solitary every day, twenty-four hours a day. You can't smoke, you can't drink coffee, you can't buy food and items from the canteen. You can't get exercise. Basically, you just locked in your cell all day. You get a shower every other day. You use the phone once every ninety days. It's very hard. What you gonna do? There's only one thing you can think about: being executed.

When I got denied by the Supreme Court, there were a total of nine of us who got denied at the same time. I talked to Sean that night and he said, "You know, the attorney general's office has already filed a motion with the Missouri Supreme Court to set your execution date." I said, "Damn. That was quick." I asked the other guys if [the state] had asked to set their execution dates and they said, "Nope." Turns out they did. But these guys didn't know. They didn't know nothing about the law.

Now there's a total of nine of us who don't have no appeals, and they only set one execution date at a time. Now that's the thing. Who's gonna get the first date? I felt so bad. I'm already in solitary confinement. And there's about four or five other guys in the same predicament in solitary. Everybody knew they set execution dates the first Tuesday of the month. That's when they come to get somebody.

Here we are the first Tuesday. I'd holler to somebody, "Hey, you heard anything yet?" He'd say, "Well, I heard they got such and such." And I'm like, "Phewww. Glad it ain't me." Because I know that if they came and got him today, then his execution got to be at least thirty days later. And they won't set another date until after he's executed. I'm saying, "That leaves eight more of us. Wonder who's next." That went on for a year. It was really wearing on me.

'EVEN IF WE FIND MR. AMRINE IS ACTUALLY INNOCENT, HE SHOULD BE EXECUTED?'

Amrine's lawyers continued to press his case by petitioning the Missouri Supreme Court to reconsider Amrine's conviction based on the new evidence they had uncovered. Arguing against Amrine's effort to reopen his case, an assistant attorney general contended that the court need not stop the execution of an innocent person, as long as the prisoner had a fair trial. In a hearing on February 4, 2003, the following exchange occurred:

Missouri Supreme Court Judge Laura Denvir Stith: "Are you suggesting even if we find Mr. Amrine is actually innocent, he should be executed?"

Assistant State Attorney General Frank A. Jung: "That's correct, your honor."

The Missouri Supreme Court rejected that statement, declaring that a "manifest injustice" would occur if an innocent man was executed. The court agreed to review Amrine's conviction and considered the recantations of all three witnesses who implicated Amrine, as well as new testimony from prison guard John Noble. On April 29, 2003, the court overturned Amrine's conviction, ruling that he had presented clear evidence of his innocence. The court ordered Amrine conditionally discharged within forty-five days unless the state refiled charges.

In February of 2003, the Missouri Supreme Court decided to look at my case. They argued my case in March and rendered an opinion in May. In the opinion, they told him to conditionally discharge me or retry me within forty-five days. I'm telling myself, "I'm going home."

On the forty-fourth day, I'm lying in bed asleep. They said, "They want you in medical." I wash my face and everything, taking my time. Next thing I know, there are three guards in my cell. They say, "They want you in medical right now. We are to escort you over there." I say, "I'm going home."

I get sent to medical and I see two transportation officers. They shackle me up, handcuff me. Where we going? Nobody will tell me. We're on the highway. I still think I'm going home. We're up in Jeff City. Took me straight in there and charged me with the murder again. One day before the forty-five days are up. That was a hell of a blow to me. Took me up there, refiled the charges, took me up to county jail.

At the jail, they had me on TV, had my picture. One of the guys said, "Hey that's the guy back there." They hollered back, "Is that you?" I said, "Yeah, yeah." I did fifty-nine days at the county jail. Everybody was floored. Sean was floored. He said, "Joe, I don't know what to do."

In an attempt to prevent Amrine's exoneration, the state filed new charges against Amrine two days before the Missouri Supreme Court's mandated release. Contending that they had blood evidence from Amrine's clothes that could implicate Amrine in the murder, they asked for a ninety-day stay of Amrine's release to analyze it.

Improperly stored and degraded, the evidence failed to yield a meaningful result when tested. On July 28, 2003, Amrine walked out of prison a free man.

One of the guards I got real cool with came up to me and said, "I supposed to be cutting your hair on Monday but I don't think I will." I said, "Why?" He said, "You ain't gonna be here. You going home." I'm sitting there. I got a phone in my cell. So I said to myself, "He don't know what he talking about." I said to him, "All I'm waiting on is the DNA test and it ain't come back yet." And he said, "It came back."

Amrine at a press conference after his release (July 28, 2003)

Then Saturday night, this major come up to me and he said, "You didn't hear it from me but you're out of here. The DNA test came back." I stayed up all night thinking about it. I decided to stay up as late as I could so I could sleep all Monday. I didn't even have to.

It was eight-thirty in the morning, on the 28th of July, 2003. I went to lay down and they came up and said, "Pack your stuff. You're out of here." I'm just looking at him and he said, "You don't want to go?" I go downstairs and the sheriff was there and he said, "Would you like to smoke a cigarette?" Then I thought this might be real.

I get on the phone. First I call my brother because I knew he had a bunch of clothes for me. He not there. I call my lawyer. He not there. Then I call a guy named Mark Thomason. I said, "I need someone to come get me." He came back and said, "Sean is on his way."

So he's on his way. He called a guy in Columbia who came over brought me some clothes. He had me looking crazy. From

K-Mart, you know. He brought me an Ironman watch that cost three dollars. Some blue-and-white flip flops. Finally the back door opens and Sean comes in. All the media's out there.

They asked what I wanted to do, and I said, "Go to McDonald's and get a mosquito bite."

WHAT ARE YOU GON' THINK
ABOUT YOUR UNCLE?

After returning home, Amrine began to reestablish ties with his estranged family members, including a son, who he had lost contact with while he was incarcerated.

Everybody always ask me [what it was like going home] and I can't describe none of that. I can't describe what the feeling was, what the mood was, I can't describe anything. I actually have it all on tape. And my youngest sister is the first person who grabs me. She was fourteen when I got locked up. During the time I was in prison I might have seen her two times, back in '77, '78. But after that I never seen her.

I have five sisters and four brothers and I think in the twenty-six years in which I was locked up, I probably fell out with each and every last one of 'em with the exception of one of my sisters. In twenty-six years not one time did me and her ever fell out, never had no words, never was a time when she had a block on her phone, or when I couldn't call her and say, "Vanita, I need you to send me some money," or "Vanita, I need you to come and see me." And she had no problem with that as long as—if she was coming, she wasn't bringing no drugs. That was her policy.

As far as me having problems with my sisters and brothers, things kinda fell apart in 1983 after my father died. Right after that our family just kinda drifted apart. My father was never really an important piece of the family setting. Whatever transition [my brothers and sisters] made, they made it during the time I was in prison, when I was on death row. Because prior to that, they was good at making money, hustling. And I guess they all grew out of it because now they all don't get in no trouble. They all got good homes and good jobs, money, and it's kind of surprising.

Now [my youngest] sister's a grandmother and everything and she's weighing about 275 pounds, look like a little bitty baby, and got her hair dyed blond with dreadlocks. I'm looking at her like, this my baby sister. And then she standing there with her two daughters.

The house is so packed. And everybody standing around like, "Do you know who this is? Do you know who that is?" And in actuality, all my nieces and nephews, I knew who they was. I just didn't know their kids.

They didn't know what type of person I was. [When] everybody knew I was getting out, they had what they call the family meetings, and sure enough, that was a big issue. They was uncomfortable. They was concerned about being around me or how they should act around me, am I crazy, stuff like this. My nieces and nephews had some concerns. My sister was telling me about it. She said, "Man, they was worried. They didn't want to come around you, talking about you were crazy, may even try to attack them."

They were hearing these stories. From being in prison, to staying in a lot of trouble, to ending up on death row, there was a lot of stories that could be told, and they was hearing them all. So you grow up hearing these stories about your uncle, an uncle you ain't never seen. He's in prison, and next thing you know, you a teenager and you still hearing these stories about your uncle and he's still in prison. Now you in your twenties, and you still hearing these stories about your uncle and he's still in prison. What are you gon' think about your uncle?

HOW IS IT THESE KIDS CAN THINK OF THE MOST EXPENSIVE THINGS TO ASK THEIR GRANDDADDY FOR?

When he was released, Amrine was given nothing by the state of Missouri—only the $14 in his inmate account. The Public Interest Litigation Clinic in Kansas City obtained a two-year grant that pays Amrine $30,000 a year to talk about his experiences. He is currently suing the officers who investigated his case.

My biggest problem getting out was not being able to say no. I could not say no to nobody. No matter what it was, I could not say no. I couldn't see something, and not buy it. I don't know what it was. They told me, "That's one of the symptoms of post-traumatic stress disorder." I've been through four budgeting classes, counseling about how to budget your money. It hasn't done any good at all. And now the only time I can go anywhere, especially out of state, or to a grocery store, I can't have no credit cards on me. I can't have no money in my pockets. If I do, I'm going spend it.

I got four grandkids and all the grandnieces and nephews. I mean I looked at it like this here—when I was coming up my parents would buy me stuff for Christmas. The stuff that they would buy me, nine times out of ten, it would be something that I really didn't really care for. I would've wanted it but I probably would've preferred to have something else, and most of your best presents probably came from aunties and uncles. I didn't mind the gifts I got on Christmas from my family but I wanted to see what my uncle gave me. I wanted to see what my grandmama gave me. And that's the way it was with them.

One of my granddaughters, she's seven. I bought her a $169 Barbie doll. It was one of the life-size ones. Three days before Christmas I had one of my other nieces over there, and I was telling her about it and she said, "Well, that ain't goin' work."

I said, "Well why not?"

She said, "Because she got to have clothes to change clothes."

I said, "Aw man, well what's that gon' cost?"

Well, it cost me another $162. Just for the clothes and that was only four sets of clothes. But I bought her that and a bunch of other stuff. My grandson, he's eleven. He wanted a motorized scooter that cost $300-something. I had told their grandmother, my son's mama, "You know what I don't understand? How it is these kids can think of the most expensive things to ask their granddaddy for? Are their mamas telling them this?"

But I bought one of my other granddaughters a motorized little scooter, like a little car, with the batteries. She's only two. My youngest grandson, he's three, I bought him a car, with a remote control, that he rides in. Then I got so many grandnieces and nephews, it's quite a few of 'em. Some of 'em I bought stuff for, but the rest of them, I gave 'em $50 apiece.

And then like we had pulled names out of a hat. And whatever name you get that's who gift you buy.

And I pulled one of my nephews—one of my youngest sisters' grandson. I went and bought him a big ol' remote control Hummer. He's only two. Do you know what ended up happening? I played with that thing for two weeks while it was at my house. And it was funny because on Christmas, we was all at one of my other nieces' house. And they was opening up and gifts and everything. So little Jordan, he go and gets my gift and he opens it up and this big ol' remote control Hummer in there. And they hooks it up and you know what? It won't even move. The batter-

Amrine with his niece, Ronnaica Gray (August 2004)

ies ran down. I had actually ran the batteries down.

Everybody knew it. All my sisters, all my brothers, and all my older nieces and nephews they knew 'cause they would be over my house a lot. And they'd be talking about, "Man, put that thing up!"

I'd be sitting there on the couch and the remote control car might be in the back bedroom. And I'd get the remote and next thing you know here it comes coming out the bedroom. I would leave my cigarettes and my lighter on top of it and I'd be in the front bedroom and we'd be in there talking and playing cards and stuff, and next thing you know here come the Hummer coming through the hallway with my cigarettes and lighter on it. So they all knew what had happened, why the batteries was down.

WHAT I WOULDN'T GIVE TO HAVE A DAUGHTER

Boy, I wish I had me a daughter. Not no son, a daughter. I want me a daughter so bad. 'Cause a daughter, she don't never grow too old, there will never come a point in her life where you will not be able to grab her and hug her and kiss her. Whereas with a son, it's, "Come on man, come on Pops, get up off a me." Shake hands. It's totally different, you know. I'll tell my sister all day long, "Man, what I wouldn't give to have a daughter."

I have a grandniece. I bought her a big gift over Christmas, too, but she didn't get it. She wanted a PlayStation 2. I had seen her grade card, she had all F's. She hadn't went to school at all.

I said, "If you go to school, and get good grades, don't get no F's, I'll get you the PlayStation for Christmas."

She said, "All right."

Right before Christmas, I go and buy the PlayStation. So right before Christmas she gets her grade card. I said, "What's up with your grade card? Let me see it."

I look and she got three F's on it. And I kinda talked crazy to her but nothing serious, no big deal. And that was it. Well, that evening my girlfriend gets home and Shapunkin's there, and she said, "Shapunkin, where your grade card at?"

'Punkin goes and get her grade card, and gives it to her. She said, "Shapunkin, you know what you need to do? You need to figure out something else that you want for Christmas, 'cause you got three F's on your grade card. I don't think this the type of grade card warrants a PlayStation 2."

Well, I been in jail all my life—I didn't even think about that. But when I heard her say it, I said, "Oh my God, she's right. How can I give her the PlayStation?" And so that was all that was said. About three days later, I asked her, "Can you think of something else you want me to get you for Christmas?"

She say, "Yeah."

I say, "What?"

She say, "Two outfits."

I said, "What else you want?"

Said, "That's enough."

"Are you sure?"

She say, "Yeah."

Well she's under the impression she's gon' get two outfits *and* the PlayStation. Because I never said that she didn't have it coming. I said, "Well wait a minute baby, you know you ain't got that PlayStation coming, don't you?"

She said, "Uh-uh."

I said, "Didn't Carmela tell you you didn't have that coming?"

She said, "Yeah, she said that, but you didn't."

I said, "Now, baby, you ain't got that coming, that's why I asked you what else do you want."

After that, she didn't want nothing. So I didn't get her nothing for Christmas. I had a friend in prison who has a nephew in Iowa, they been asking about a PlayStation. So I told him, "You know what? I got one here. Get their grade cards, see what their grade cards look like, and if their grade cards look good I'll send it overnight delivery." Sure enough he got their grade cards, and they was nice, and I sent it to them overnight delivery, and signed his name on it.

For a long time she actually thought the PlayStation was still at my house, and I was holding it for her, or whatever. And the last time she was out there she tore it up and she did not find one.

I ended up telling her, "'Punkin, you blew that."

But I ended up getting her one. Her mama done moved to Leavenworth, Kansas, and that's pretty far from here. So I don't see her that often. As a surprise I bought one and mailed it to 'em.

YOU BEEN OUT EIGHTEEN
MONTHS, YOU LIVED A WHOLE LIFE

When you in prison for a long time, it's kinda like an act, because you got to act like you ain't scared. You got to act like you ain't got a whole bunch on your mind. You got to act like that guy didn't make you mad from what he said. You got to act like this guard didn't make you mad. It's an act. And so you're so used to being hard, you don't show compassion in prison—I ain't got nothing for nobody. If I give you something, you gonna give me something in return.

And all these years in prison this compassion is held in. But then when you get out here, you ain't got to put on the front. You ain't got to act. You just be yourself. Well, what come flooding out? All these emotions that you sheltered, all this just come out— all this compassion 'cause you ain't got to hold it in anymore.

It makes my day when I give my niece or my granddaughter or one of my sisters or brothers some money. That makes my day. I don't care. I could buy me a new Cadillac or anything else. Or get a new girlfriend or anything. It would not stop me doing something for somebody else. And I know it's wrong. Like for Christmas. Six thousand dollars for Christmas. In January, I couldn't pay my rent. I couldn't pay no bill at all. How's that possible? But I know where that comes from.

But one good thing about it is I've gotten better. I've gotten a lot better. A few weeks ago my car broke down. It cost me $4,300 to fix. My apartment manager told me I had to move.

They turned my lights off. They just told me about my hepatitis—I had two of them. So I was really straight down. And I was so mad and disappointed with myself and I said, "I'm going to deal with this myself. I'm not calling nobody. I'm not asking nobody to gimme the money to get my lights back on or nothing. I'm not moving in with nobody. I'm stayin' right here, in my apartment, even though I don't have no heat, no nothing. And that's what I did. And it got so bad that I ended up going to a homeless shelter for one night because I didn't want to go to none of my brothers' or sisters' houses, because I wanna be on my own. I'm so bad. I wanna be on my own. But my brother ended up coming out there—we hadn't spoke probably, in maybe nine months. We had fell out. He told me, he said, "Man, you just done did a turnabout. You done reached the bottom of the bottom, and you ready to go back up. And what you did, Joe—and I knew you was going to do this—you lived a whole life in the eighteen months you been out."

Peter Rose

FAMILY MAN

NAME: Peter Rose · **BORN:** 1967 · **HOMETOWN:** Lodi, California

CONVICTED OF: Rape and kidnapping · **SENTENCE:** 27 years

SERVED: 10 years · **RELEASED:** 2004

REALITY HITS ME

I've only been out a week and a half.

It's like I just got out yesterday. The feelings and everything are still real new. I'm learning how to use a computer from my nine-year-old daughter. It's really fast out here. A lot of technology is different. There is a whole new, different world out here—being away from prison. I don't think it's really hit me yet.

Coming home to a strange house that I've never been in before with my family made me really nervous. It was really hard to just sit still and do nothing, just sit there. In prison when you're in lockdown or in a cell or something, you're always walking back and forth [in front of] the door. Because that's your only view. I caught myself pacing the living room floors and not having anything to do and being really nervous all the time and not eating that much. My mom was talking to her friends about it. And it was real funny, because she's calling all her friends, "There's something wrong with him: he's not eating and he's pacing the floors and he's going crazy I think."

Prison is real easy. Everything is paid for. You don't really have the worries of having to be real responsible because they make you be responsible. You have a program that you do. You get up, you go to breakfast, you go to your work, you come back, and the rest of the day you have time to yourself to study. Just time by yourself to think. And since I've been out, I haven't had no time to just sit down by myself and think. Because someone's always present. From the [minute] that I get up in the morning till at night. I mean, I have to put the kids to bed at eight o'clock at night. Then I have time for myself, but I'm still sitting with my mom, talking with my mom. And then I stay up later than that, a little later, and I'm only by myself for half an hour of every day. Not having time to myself to just accept being out. I still feel like sometimes when I wake up in the morning, it was just a few minutes ago that I was in prison. I do not miss prison. Not one second. But I was there for so long—ten years.

Now I'm my own person, and I have all these children and mother and things that need to be done. Now I just have it all thrown on my back all at one time. And to be successful, you've got to have some money to spend to fix things up or take care of things that the children need, like clothes, shoes, basketball clothes, football stuff. I'm totally broke. I don't have nothing.

My mom is supporting me as of right now. That's why I want to get back and go to work right away. But I'm still adjusting to being around a lot of people. A lot of people make me nervous. I'm still stuck there a little bit. I still feel like I'm there sometimes. But then reality hits me and I'm here. And my kids keep me so

Rose and his children (from left to right) Ashley, Brittney, Pete Jr., Tanner,
and nephew Joey at Mule Creek State Prison in Ione, California
on the day of his release (October 29, 2004)

busy that the hard stuff is just gone right away. The kids are just great. They're helping me through every day. To have them there with me in the morning is the best gift ever.

I NEED TO STEP UP

What I've been thinking about is just how am I going to get a roof over my kid's heads and be the father that I need to be to take care of them and give them a good life. It's really hard because I have nothing right now. And I haven't started to work yet, but I'm getting ready to. That's been my worries. How am I going to support my kids and the responsibility of going to school when they get in trouble, teachers' meetings and the sports that they're involved in? I'm still learning what they do, who their friends are, where they're going. I'm still learning.

Out here now, my kids, my mom, I'm all they have. And

SO MUCH TIME LOST

Exonerees struggle to reestablish relationships with their children

---

The day he got out of jail, Peter Rose found himself wiping makeup off his sixteen-year-old daughter's face. When Joseph Amrine was freed after seventeen years of wrongful imprisonment, his son was thirty years old and had developed a drug habit. When John Stoll was released, his son, Jed, refused to have any contact with him, still holding lingering doubts about his father's conviction for child molestation.

More than ten million children in the United States have a parent incarcerated during some point of their childhood. Children suffer that imprisonment, too. The consequences for them are considerable, including depression, withdrawal, antisocial behavior, poor school performance, low self-esteem, anger, aggression, guilt, and general emotional dysfunction.

Compounding the burden of a parent in prison is the shame their parent's crime might bring them. Vincent Moto's daughter, Millie Strickland, had a difficult time coming to terms with her father's wrongful conviction in 1987 for rape and robbery. "It was hard for my father to explain to me, 'I got convicted of raping somebody, but Daddy didn't do it,'" Strickland says in the documentary *After Innocence*. "I was like, 'How you not do it Daddy if you been in there for all these years now?'"

Children with parents who have been incarcerated are five to six times

continued on page 370

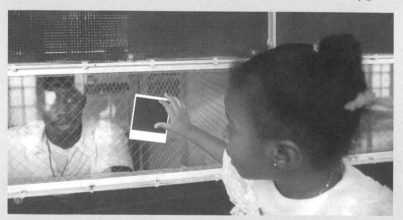

Inmate Randy Greer visits with his two-year-old daughter in the visiting room of the Ellis prison unit in Huntsville, Texas (1994)

I just don't want to let them down. But tomorrow, they can be all dependent upon me and expect me to do all these things for them, and tomorrow I can go out on a boat and have a boating accident and drown.

It's a lot of pressure, but I know that I'm going to be able to do it. I didn't think there was going to be [pressure], but there is. And there's all these things that I need to do, and I haven't done none of it yet. And I feel really uncomfortable with that because I need to step up.

I feel like I owe my family more than I could ever pay them back. You just cannot pay back giving somebody their life. I've been away for a long time. And they kind of grew up without me, and I haven't been a father to them, really. Like when they were little, tucking them into bed. When they'd fall down and scratch their knee, I wasn't there to attend to it. When they get hurt they still run to their grandma for the hugs and stuff instead of coming to Dad and letting Dad help them or give them a hug. I feel really out of place right now. But I know that I'm welcome and I'm wanted there.

My kids are already dealing with problems with Dad being gone for ten years. If it wasn't for my mom raising them, they'd be in foster care. I don't think they even understand that. But they've been through so much. They were free, but they're still in prison in their heart.

I don't think they're angry at me at all. I'm sure that the children have doubts about stuff. But they don't think rash at their age. They're just happy-go-lucky. They're being taken care of, and that's all they care about. They get what they want and that's all they care about. My mom doesn't feel like that. She's just happy that I'm home. Same thing with my brother and family. And everybody's willing to help.

I'm still learning every day to wake up and just do it. Taking

more likely than their peers to serve time in prison when they reach adult-hood themselves. Even after a parent is released, problems may continue: the release itself often creates family crisis, requiring difficult learning and readjustment to life on the outside.

Visitation is one way of bridging the distance between children and their imprisoned parent, but rules governing visitation and the distances separating prisoners from their children can be daunting.

In many prisons, schedules are often inconvenient and irregular, and visitors may arrive, only to be denied contact for reasons ranging from dress code violations to lack of identification for children. Children must undergo frightening, often intrusive body searches and may have to wait for long periods in facilities lacking seats, toilets, and water.

Prisons are often located in remote areas, making visits difficult for those with limited resources. In state prisons, over 60 percent of inmates live more than a hundred miles from their last place of residence; in feder-al prisons, almost half are held more than 500 miles away. The auctioning off of prisoners to privately run prisons in distant states has worsened this problem. As the private prison industry has increased, states seeking to cut costs will often send prisoners to the lowest-bidding private facility, regard-less of its location. More than ten thousand inmates are held in jails or pris-ons outside the state in which they were sentenced.

Most parents in prison today have never received a visit from their children. Tough visitation limitations and exceptionally long distances often make visits from family members difficult or impossible. This can have an especially traumatic effect on children of the wrongfully con-victed.

In 1995, Ulysses Rodriguez Charles and many of his fellow prisoners were transferred from the overcrowded Walpole Prison in Massachusetts to a jail in Dallas County, Texas. Charles, who had been wrongfully convict-ed of a 1981 triple-rape, was 1,500 miles away from home when his daugh-ter Denise was suffering mental and emotional problems.

"I was no longer around for her to lean on," Charles says. "She had nobody. She was having a nervous breakdown."

Denise, a senior at the University of Massachusetts, had frequently vis-ited Charles when he was in Walpole Prison and depended on him for sup-port. But while Charles was in Texas, unable to see or console his troubled daughter, she committed suicide by jumping off a bridge into traffic. When their connection was severed, Charles believes, Denise was simply unable to cope.

PETER ROSE

every day just one step at a time and just do my best. And I know
I have to because that's life. Especially after you have children,
your life is no longer yours no more. It belongs to them. And
your time is spent taking care of them, making sure they are safe.
Kind of like how it was when I was in prison: getting up in the
morning, having to go to work, being told what to do. The kids
have to be told what to do. You got to make sure they do their
homework. I want to be their dad, their friend. It's really hard to
just get out after not being their dad for ten years and then
just show up. I don't want them to think I'm ordering them
around. I'm trying to figure out their little personalities and their
daily routine.

Kids these days just… it's like they have their own personalities. You've got to know them. If you don't know them, you can't
communicate with them. And it's like my teenage son, he's only
in seventh grade, but, he's got his own little personality, and if
you treat him a certain way, like a little kid, he's going to act like
one. And he doesn't want to be treated like that. And little Pete,
he's happy all the time. He's easy. Brittney, she wants all my attention. And if I don't spend most of my time with her and not with
the boys, then I don't love her and she hates me. My sixteen-year-
old [Ashley], I was there raising her. I got to change her diapers
and all that when she was a baby, and was there for a lot of her
life before I went to prison. But I really didn't get to spend time
with my other children, so getting to know them again is a big
thing right now. I want them to know who I am.

I think the best teacher is just the parent being an example to
their children. Kids these days cuss. My kids cuss like they're
twenty-year-old cowboys out in the cow pasture. My son is using
the F word and all this. And I always tell him, "Do you hear Dad
cuss? No. You'll never hear Daddy cuss." I think we are the example to everybody around us, and if we don't show a good example,

then they're going to fall right into the world.

It is a different generation. Like the clothes that we see people wearing walking down the street is just—you don't wear clothes like that. Before I went to prison, the girls never wore hip-huggers. The guys never wore baggies. You know, that's gang stuff. I don't like to see my daughter wearing clothes like that. She's only sixteen. That's like showing way too much. Some people might get the wrong idea. But that's just the way the kids and stuff are these days.

I NEVER DID NOTHING TO NOBODY

On the morning of November 29, 1994, a man approached a thirteen-year-old girl as she was making her way to school in Lodi, a small town in Northern California. The man grabbed the girl and forced her behind a house, where he sexually assaulted and raped her. The perpetrator escaped and the girl walked back out to the street, where she flagged down a passing motorist, who took her home. When she was interviewed by police, the victim maintained that she was raped by a stranger. She said she did not get a good enough look to identify him.

The case received a good deal of publicity in Lodi. A composite sketch of the perpetrator was published in the local newspaper. The victim's aunt, Wendy Neri, told police it resembled Rose. Neri knew Rose. She was friends with Tammie, the mother of Rose's younger children. Rose was living with Tammie at the time.

Because of Neri's call, police included Rose's picture in a photographic lineup shown to the young victim the day after the rape. The victim looked at all of the pictures and could not identify the perpetrator. Nonetheless, Neri believed it might be Rose, and repeatedly suggested this idea to the victim.

Three weeks later, two detectives brought the victim in for a grueling interview, in which they repeatedly accused her of lying. They claimed that she had consensual sex with the perpetrator, and only afterward claimed it was rape. They promised that if she admitted to lying, she could avoid more serious consequences.

The victim repeatedly denied that she knew the identity of the attacker. After three hours of interrogation, the victim finally said, "I'm not sure, though, because I don't wanna say if it is or not... His name is Pete. He lives on Sutter Street and my [aunt] Wendy talked to his girlfriend and his girlfriend said that he wasn't home... that morning... and he's been... acting [inaudible]... ever since."

The police browbeating continued. They asked the victim if it was possible that Rose was her attacker. She said, "I don't know. I... can't say it is or not. What if it's not?" (See Appendix B for a longer excerpt of the interrogation.)

They need to learn how to do it better, to teach the police how to communicate with victims. It just amazes me how the police treated her, and I don't think that was right. That's a victim. It's not somebody that you're supposed to interrogate; it's somebody that you're supposed to give a hug to. You're talking about a thirteen-year-old girl who is probably scared out of her mind, sitting in a police station. I got a little girl. You don't just say, "Why did you do it?" or, "You need to say you're a liar." I mean, that would just traumatize her. That's a crime in itself, I think.

How I got caught up in it, I don't have no idea. I know that her family never really cared for me too much because of my girlfriend. To this day I still don't know why they would do that. I mean, to them maybe they don't have no conscience or feelings of what they did. I don't know if it was just the police hating me for something. I never did nothing to nobody. I never violently hurt a police officer in Lodi. I wasn't a drug dealer. Of course, I drank and hung out at the bar every once in awhile, but I don't

A VICTIM AGAIN

Harsh interview tactics re-traumatize crime victims

During questioning, victims must often endure substantial pressure from family members, doctors, police, and prosecutors to identify a suspect or provide specific details of the crime. This pressure can escalate to the point of threats and coercion, and in the face of such duress, many victims falter and offer inaccurate testimony.

Because most police training is geared toward handling suspects and obtaining confessions, police often lack expertise in questioning victims. And although some states and counties are beginning to offer victim interview training for their police forces, most don't have the resources to implement such new procedures.

In the 1994-95 Wenatchee, Washington child abuse cases, one young woman testified that she was forced into a psychiatric facility by a police detective, where she was given mind-altering drugs by a therapist, with the aim of convincing her to falsely accuse her parents of abuse.

Prosecutors, too, may go to questionable lengths to obtain details or accusations, often forcing victims to undergo extended and repeated interviews. One of the two young children who wrongfully accused James Rodriguez of sexual abuse later revealed that his aunt and the district attorney had coerced him into testifying against Rodriguez. The prosecutor had forced the children to participate in grueling interviews, denying them access to a restroom. As a result, one of the victims said, "I was like a tape recorder, that's how much they drilled it into me. I knew it line for line, verse for verse."

Authorities may also subject victims to suggestive language. Such tactics are particularly successful in cases with child victims. According to Mark Chaffin, a child development specialist, "Even in situations less stressful and coercive than a stationhouse interrogation... substantial numbers of children will agree to things that are factually inaccurate."

Relatives also wield extraordinary influence over testimony. In cases of abuse, relatives may willfully direct a child's accusations away from the real culprit if that culprit happens to be a family member—shifting the blame to an innocent bystander, as in the case of Sylvester Smith.

Smith was dating the mother of a four-year-old girl. The child and her friend, six, were molested by a nine-year-old cousin. Upon learning of the abuse, the grandmother of one of the girls persuaded both of them to accuse Smith instead. Smith was sent to jail for twenty years and was exonerated in 2004 after the two girls recanted their testimony.

See Appendix B for a partial transcript of the interrogation of Peter Rose's accuser

understand why they did this to me. I don't. To this day I don't.

I really didn't hang out with many people, but the kids' mom's friends just weren't good to be around. I didn't like them around me, and they didn't like me because I didn't put up with their little kid stuff because they were playing games. They're doing drugs, and you never know what they'll do, shoot you, shoot your house up because they didn't like me.

The aunt, Tammie's friend, didn't like me. She never liked me from the beginning. She came over to my house with a couple of her friends, and they were real rowdy. I don't know if they'd been drinking, but I told them to leave. I didn't want them around in my house. But Tammie always used to, while I was at work, go down to their apartment and sit and talk with them, or have coffee or whatever. And anytime we'd argue or fight she'd go crying to her and just spill out her guts to her, her feelings and everything. The aunt just didn't like me. And I believe that she also had a lot to do with me going in prison. I believe she convinced her niece to say it was me. I believe that.

A NOVEL OF LIES

Peter Rose was arrested on December 21, 1994.

I remember the day that I was arrested really well, like it was yesterday. I had my son on my shoulders. We were going to the store to get some chips and soda. And the next thing you know I have police officers rolling up behind me in a police car, telling me to freeze. Put my hands up. And I don't remember what my son did. I don't know if they took him back. I can't remember that part. I was still in shock because I'm being arrested. They don't even say why I'm being arrested; they just arrest me and take me down to the jail. And for one full day and a night I didn't know. They left me in a jail cell for a day and a night not knowing why I was there. And then the next day I think they started asking me questions about this crime.

They brought me into a little room and started to ask me questions. And I told them that I knew nothing of this crime. I knew the girl. I wasn't guilty. I did not do the crime. And so I kept being persistent about it. And I kind of got angered with them a little bit, too. I told them, "You know, you guys are on drugs!" I mean, that's how they were acting, like they were literally on drugs, interrogating me. I even think they turned the heaters up. I remember being real hot and sweaty. They made me really uncomfortable by antagonizing me, trying to get somebody to confess to something they didn't do. And I didn't confess. And I would never confess because I'm innocent.

Rose was held at the San Joaquin County jail for more than a year, as preparations for his trial were made.

I thought it was just a matter of time before I was going home. But to top it all off, I had a [court-appointed attorney] saying that he needs a year to prepare. And the trial shows up and he comes into the courtroom with a yellow legal pad—a piece of paper—and a pen. It's like, "What did you prepare?" I knew at that moment that I was going to be in big trouble. But, I still didn't think that they were going to convict me, because when you're innocent you don't think about that part of it. You think, "Well, I'm innocent, they've got to prove that I'm guilty, so I'm going to be okay with this lawyer." They got to convince a jury that I'm guilty, and I know they can't do it, because I didn't do it.

Then again, I didn't know how the district attorney was going to bring his case to court. He basically wrote a novel of lies. That's what I felt like—everything was a lie.

They said that they had a pair of boots. And they got a pair of black sweatpants out of my house, which were not even mine, they were [Tammie's]. They bring all this stuff to court that is not even evidence, but they present it as being evidence when it's not. How can it be? So what? You have a pair of sweatpants and my boots.

What I don't understand, also, is how the judge can allow things into evidence that is not evidence. It's not factual evidence. Period. It's just so amazing how they can just bring whatever they want to court and say, "This is evidence," and present it to a jury. When all it is, is my girlfriend's sweatpants, my boots. What does that have to do with the case? And my girlfriend's sweatpants—who doesn't have a pair of black sweatpants in their house?

When you're at home and you're totally innocent, you're sitting there and all of a sudden you read in a newspaper about a crime. Three months roll by and somebody asks you, "Where were you in 1846?" You just don't really know unless you sit down and think about it, and look back at the calendar and try to pick specific times and dates, and you can remember. So when you're asked that question right away by a police officer, "Where were you at back in the 1800s?" It's like, well, I wasn't even born yet; how am I supposed to remember?

But going over the calendar, I remember that I was beekeeping off and on, and working here and there in construction. I remember being home on that day with my girlfriend. My girlfriend came and testified that I was at home with her. She figured it out on her calendar, and sure enough I was home. But it didn't matter after that, because at the time when they asked, "Where was he at?" it was like, "How the heck am I supposed to know where he was at three months ago?" And she said, "I think he was home. I'm pretty sure he was home on that day."

I did not take the stand because my lawyer told me I shouldn't because I was hot-tempered at the time. [I might] easily speak up and say, "Well this is a bunch of crock." I believe the lawyer just didn't care to do a good job. No one is that incompetent. I'm not smart at the law. I could have done a better job myself if I would have had somebody guiding me. I could have done it. But when you're innocent I don't think you really need to have a great defense—you just bring up the truth. If you can find the truth you're going to go home. You're going to convince a jury that you're not guilty.

I believe the victim getting on the stand and saying that I did it is the only thing that was damaging in the trial. I think that the jury believed her instead of the defense that my attorney had brought forward. Here you got a thirteen-year-old girl up on the stand. If I'm sitting in a jury I'm going to believe her just to be safe, you know? Just to be safe, so I don't let somebody like that go back out on the street, because I got four kids. And if I'm not sure and they don't present the case and convince me that he's innocent, you're going to prison for the rest of your life, basically. In my book, anyway.

So while I'm fighting my case and going through all this, my girlfriend and our kids were homeless. Then she got the kids taken away by Child Protective Services because she didn't have nowhere for the kids to live. All those factors coming together at once was just overwhelming. I'm really blessed my mom stepped forward and took them and raised them like they were her own, like they was me when I was little. And I'm really lucky for that.

After the trial was over, I thought I was going to go home and win my case because there was no evidence against me. All there was, was one person's word against mine. It took the jury two or three days to decide. I ended up getting the maximum sentence at twenty-seven years.

After I was found guilty, I kind of lost it for a minute. This is impossible, this didn't happen. And when I did get a hold of my family, they said, "Don't worry, we're going to get you an attorney and he'll get you out of there as fast as possible." I didn't realize it was going to take ten years.

Rose's trial rested primarily on the victim's tenuous identification and testimony. Rose was convicted on April 5, 1996 of kidnapping a child under the age of fourteen; kidnapping with the intent to commit rape; kidnapping for a lewd and lascivious act; rape by force and fear; and forcible oral copulation. On April 15, 1996, he was sentenced to twenty-seven years in prison.

EVERYTHING BROKE

Rose was sent to Mule Creek State Prison in Ione, California, to serve his sentence. During the first few years of his incarceration, Rose's mother brought his children to visit. In the mid-1990s, California passed a law that prevented convicted sex offenders from visiting with their own children.

A person's mind, your thoughts, your emotions, you just change. You're just not the same person no more after that. It's like getting hit in the head with a two-by-four and not really coming out of the daze. You're still dazed. And to this day, I still feel like I'm dazed. You know, I lost everything when I left. But I was more worried about my kids because their mother, when I left, it kind of also had the same effect on her and she kind of went crazy and then was unable to care for my kids.

When I was taken away, everything went to shambles, everything broke. Lives were destroyed, including my kids, my ex-girlfriend. From that point on it's a feeling of helplessness, worry for your family and your children. And everything that you own is going to be gone—you know it's gone. You're already gone. You're already on a bus. Away. And you don't know what's going to happen. I was just dropped off in the middle of a world that I knew nothing about. It was scary. I even wrote home and told my mom, "I'm never going to make it in here. Just pretend I'm dead and just go on with your life, because I'm not going to make it; they're going to kill me in here." I thought for sure that was going to happen.

With a charge like what I had, going to prison is not a nice thing. You're looked at being the worst of the worst in prison. And people would like to take advantage of that and really try to harm you in prison. I was attacked a bunch of times. Sometimes they weren't reported, sometimes they were. The tension of being there—I thought, "I'm never going to make it out." Even though I have an out date, I'm never going to make it out of prison because of the crime that I was in there for. And as a father, I can't blame those guys. I know what I would do, probably, to somebody if they ever touched my child. I would probably do something I would regret later. I don't know if I would be sane enough to hold myself back as a father.

I was always a problem in prison because of my crime. I got stabbed in the side when I went to chow. I acted like it never happened. I went back to my cell, and I just duct-taped it up. I just taped it up because you don't want to tell on the person stabbing you. You just bang their head a couple of times up against something and give them a nap.

And so that was my thing. I used to say that, "I guess they're feeling sleepy." And usually the word will get back to them: "He said you're feeling a little sleepy." Well, this guy means business. He's not going to just take it. I just didn't feel like being a victim. I was already a victim by the district attorney.s

I grew up real fast. I made it a point to let them know that if you're talking about me, you're feeling sleepy. And then, if you're approached and they come within arm's range, you give them a permanent nap, knock them out. Give them a nap—this is a nice way of saying it. I let it be known that, if somebody was going to come at me, they were going to be feeling a little sleepy after a little while.

It got really bad for a little while. And then finally when [prison officials] were convinced that I could no longer be on the yard without getting in trouble, they sent me to a protective custody yard.

I ended up at Mule Creek on the Level 4 yard, which was mostly everybody there for life. They were never going to go home. I ended up being Level 4 because I had so many years, so they gave me a lot of points, which is like a high maximum-security prison. And the violence wasn't as bad as it is in a lot of other prisons, I've heard. I'm really lucky to be where I was at.

Mule Creek is a very good program. You can get up in the morning and go to breakfast, and then you can go to work. The yard closes at 3:30 and then they have a night program on the Level 3 yard from 6:30 to 9:00, so there's really a lot of time to play sports, walk in the yard, exercise, stuff like that.

[Once,] we caught a goose on the yard. Somebody threw a rock and hit a goose on accident in the head—a Canadian honker. And we grabbed it, and took it and stuck it in our jacket, and carried it back in the cell and plucked it up and tried to figure out how to build a fire. We got firewood, a little bit off the yard at a time, from the Indian lodges.

We got wood and we built a fire in our toilet and cooked him in the toilet—those things are cool, stainless steel. I'm just saying our toilets are that clean. I mean, they're like mirrors. Let me put it this way—how clean would your toilet be if it was right in the middle of the living room? It'd be one clean toilet, wouldn't it? We cooked a goose in the toilet and had goose. We ate the goose.

I wrote my kids all the time, drew them things for their birthday, sent them letters constantly, called them on the phone twice a week. I ran Mom's phone bill up to 180 bucks, just me alone, every month. That was important, just to stay in touch with the kids, because it kind of helped me through where I was at, too. When we think of ourselves, we start wanting to feel sorry for ourselves, and that's just not a good thing, because a lot of people in there, they really lose control of themselves and go crazy. So I've always kept my mind focused on my family and my kids. They really helped me through it.

To receive a letter from my child telling me that they love me and they miss me gives me life and hope while I'm in my worst mental state ever. Being by yourself, thinking about them all the time. And just to receive the little things from them like a letter with an "I love you," it just helped me get through it. It helped me get through every day that I was in there. And they didn't send me letters because they had to. They did it because they loved me, for the same reasons why I write them back.

YOU FIND THAT HAIR, I'M GONE

After the rape, the police had retrieved a small amount of semen from the victim's underwear. They were able to perform simple serological tests—a blood-type test and an unsophisticated genetic fingerprinting technique called PGM marker status—but the quantity of semen was insufficient for DNA analysis techniques, which, at that time, required a large amount of biological evidence. The blood-type test of the semen did not match Rose. The PGM marker status did match Rose, along with 30 percent of the population. The jury was never informed that the blood test did not match Rose's blood type.

In postconviction proceedings, Rose's appellate attorney argued that his trial attorney was ineffective, failing to introduce this evidence at trial. In those proceedings, experts testified that that test excluded Rose as the source of the semen sample. The prosecution's expert testified that the blood type mismatch was due to the fact that the victim's blood type (which matched the results) could not be separated from the perpetrator's. The state appellate court denied Rose's petition.

In January 2003, lawyers from the Golden Gate University School of Law in San Francisco, in collaboration with the Northern California Innocence Project, took Rose's case.

GGU Innocence Project Attorney Janice Brickley and students met with Rose and explained that a DNA test would be damaging if the results confirmed Rose's guilt. He insisted that they perform a DNA analysis on any evidence they could find.

My family hired me an attorney, a private attorney, Charles Bonneau. He'd been working really hard on my case. He got me an evidentiary hearing on the blood type that was never presented at the first trial. That wasn't enough to get me out. They denied that, finally, after going through many years of denials and stuff like that.

I'[d] been trying to contact the Innocence Project. I think I wrote a couple letters to different innocence projects and never received a response. But I think my attorney contacted them to help with the DNA.

While I was sitting in the prison I get a legal visit. And I'm thinking that it's just my regular attorney. So I go out there and here's Janice and the [GGU] law students. And they asked me if they could take my case over. And I said, "Sure, I need all the help that I can get."

I asked about the DNA because from the very beginning, I have always believed DNA was going to get me out. I hear that

Rose hugs his son Pete Jr. on the day of his release (2004)

technology has gotten a lot better, and they're saying back then they couldn't get the test results that they needed—it had come back inconclusive. And I also found out that they could now do DNA on hair, without the cuticle on the end of it. And so the first thing I thought of was that hair—there was a hair that they had found. And so the first thing I said to them was, "Look for that hair. You find that hair, I'm gone. It'll prove my innocence."

And so they immediately took my case. They talked to me. And I felt real good. We're going back, and I told them everything. But I didn't want to get my hopes up too much. And they told me, "Hopefully we'll have you out by the end of the year." That was kind of exciting. It gives you hope. For a year I had hope.

At the time, California had a law requiring that prisoners and their lawyers be notified before any biological evidence from their case was destroyed. Without notifying Rose, the state destroyed all the evidence collected from the rape: the underwear, pubic hair, and rape kit.

After learning this, attorneys and students working on the case discovered that one tiny piece of biological evidence had been retained by the California Department of Justice: semen that had been extracted from the victim's underwear. The Northern California Innocence Project then filed a motion in San Joaquin County Superior Court for DNA testing. They requested that the remaining evidence be sent to a private lab for DNA analysis.

The test excluded Rose and he was released from Mule Creek State Prison on October 29, 2004.

I don't know who was holding on to the rape kit, or whatever they have. I don't know who was hanging on to that, who had it, or who put it away. But they ended up doing the DNA testing on the old sample that was tested before, that they had tried to get a reading from before and said that they could not get it. So they ended up retesting that.

I got a letter from Janice saying, "Great news," that, "you have been exonerated." So I immediately went and called her and she said, "You're exonerated. It's not you. We have a male profile, but it's not you." I'm just so overwhelmed. Everything is going through my head. I'm thinking of my kids, my family. Man, I better be out of here pretty soon! And that's when Janice told me that I'd be going home, on a Friday. I don't know what happened in the courtroom, because I wasn't there. They just told me I was going home.

'ROSE IS GOING HOME TODAY'

The officer showed up at my work and told me they had to escort me from here to my building because I was going to go home. And so that now that I'm a civilian they had to watch over me, and took me in to get my stuff.

THE MAGIC BULLET

DNA technology is often the only hope for the wrongfully convicted

---

From 1992 to September 2005, more than 160 prisoners were exonerated by DNA evidence.

The exoneration process usually involves testing old physical evidence using technology not available at the time of the trial. The results can be a magic bullet for those who have fought unsuccessfully, sometimes for decades, to prove their innocence.

Dr. Edward Blake in his Richmond, California laboratory (August 2005)

Despite the almost miraculous effect DNA-based results can have for those convicted of crimes they did not commit, biological evidence receives little protection by state and federal legislatures to ensure that it is preserved after a conviction. By the time help arrives from innocence projects, biological specimens, like rape kits or stained clothing, are often lost, destroyed or degraded beyond repair.

The federal Justice for All Act, passed in 2004, makes it easier for inmates to petition for DNA testing and provides incentive grants for states that adopt measures to preserve evidence after a conviction.

These grants are an encouragement, not a mandate. Legislation governing the storage and maintenance of evidence remains uneven. Although eighteen states have statutes concerning the retention of evidence after conviction, the form and substance of these laws vary considerably, and none are backed by any enforcement measures. In addition, most laws that do exist say nothing about the conditions under which the evidence must be stored. And if not properly maintained, DNA evidence risks being contaminated or ruined entirely. Biological evidence can turn up in detectives' desks or ordinary filing cabinets, long forgotten and often degraded.

"The standard of practice with regard to these preservation issues is very, very poor," says forensic scientist and DNA expert Ed Blake. "Do you know what most of these laboratories do? After they're done with their DNA analysis, they take their DNA preparation, and they ship it back to a police department. And they expect some cop that runs some evidence room to know what to do with that."

Standards for evidence rooms, also called property rooms, vary widely. Although some are situated within police precincts, others are located off-

continued on page 388

There was a big disturbance out front that somebody was being released. They knew it was me. "Rose is going home today." When I walked into the gym I heard a lot of guys cheering, "Yeah, right on! Go home, take care of your family and those kids." Because we share pictures of our families and stuff.

No words can speak about a person's feelings and emotions at that point. Your heart just wants to burst. You get a warm sensation. You get tingly and lightheaded, almost like you're going to throw up. Like being carsick or seasick, you're going to throw up from the excitement.

And when I seen my kids, when I come through the front gate, I felt them watching me through a window, but looking at the window all I seen was like a mirror. All I seen was myself, standing between the fence of the inside and the outside. And I'm standing right in the middle, waiting for the gate to open up. Being asked my name, CDC [California Department of Corrections] number, making sure that I'm the right person they're letting go. You got to go through all these little steps, like an airport. I felt my kids looking at me. I felt it right away, without even seeing them.

And when I come through the door little Pete was the first one that come running to me. My son. And he came and give me a big old hug. And my mom walked up. I was just so overwhelmed. It wasn't real.

And then I see my daughter, my sixteen-year-old and my boys. It was just great. I even tried taking the makeup off my daughter when I seen her, because she was wearing all this makeup at sixteen years old. And when I grew up sixteen-year-olds just didn't wear makeup, even in high school they just put a little eye shadow on, and that was it. So I was freaked out. I'm like, "Oh, God, I'm in for it!" I've got a lot of stuff I see I'm going to have to do. And right then I knew that I was just going to have to just

site—which can create security concerns. And there are no mandates governing how property rooms are to be constructed or maintained. "There are 18,000 police departments in this country and you won't find two [property rooms] that are the same," says Joseph Latta, executive director of the International Association for Property and Evidence. "They vary from a locked file cabinet in the corner of the sheriff's office to a Costco-sized warehouse, and everything imaginable in between."

Additionally, there are no general standards for training property room personnel on how to preserve the potentially exonerating evidence.

In August 2004, police investigators stumbled across 280 boxes of evidence crammed into a 24th-floor property room in Houston. The mislabeled, overpacked, and degraded boxes—previously thought lost or destroyed—involved some 8,000 criminal cases and included bloody clothes, human body parts, and a fetus. Two men have already been exonerated as a result of the discovery, and hundreds more, including several death row inmates, presently await DNA testing.

Even with proper storage and maintenance, the testing of biological evidence can be problematic because of resistance from district attorneys to allow testing to proceed. According to Barry Scheck, co-founder of the Innocence Project at the Benjamin N. Cardozo School of Law in New York City, some Innocence Project clients have had to wait for years, fighting the district attorney every step of the way, to get permission to perform a DNA test. Even when exculpatory DNA results are returned, district attorneys can continue their battle. Wilton Dedge, who had already been in prison for nineteen years, spent another three years there as prosecutors quibbled over DNA tests that conclusively demonstrated he was innocent of the rape for which he was sentenced to life.

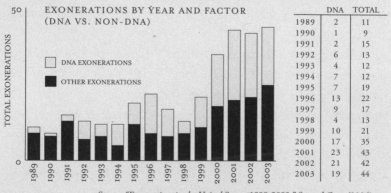

	DNA	TOTAL
1989	2	11
1990	1	9
1991	2	15
1992	6	13
1993	4	12
1994	7	12
1995	7	19
1996	13	22
1997	9	17
1998	4	13
1999	10	21
2000	17	35
2001	23	43
2002	21	42
2003	19	44

Source: "Exonerations in the United States: 1989-2003." Samuel Gross (2004)

continued on page 390

adjust real fast and just take one day at a time. Don't rush into nothing because everything is going to be okay. Nothing from here on out is going to hold me back from what I want to do.

I'M NOT GOING TO CRY ABOUT NOTHING

Five months after his release, Peter Rose was still living with his four children and his mother, who was diagnosed with bone cancer after his exoneration. To make money, Rose had begun salmon fishing on his brother's boat.

It doesn't even seem like five months. That went fast. I never really slowed down long enough to think about it. It was a shock just to get out.

I think the rape victim would be twenty-four years old now. Right after I was exonerated, she called the newspaper [*The Record*, in Stockton, California] and said that the police made her say it was me, and she never said it was me [until the trial]. If she never said it was me, then why was I put in prison? Or why did the cops even pursue it? It was unjust, it was wrong.

Now the truth's come out, and I don't feel any better about it. I sat in dang prison for ten years, my life being threatened all the time. Even the girl now is saying it never happened. She says, "They made me say it was him. No, he didn't do it. I told the police he didn't do it, they made me say it was him."

She spoke the truth ten years late, but I don't blame her. I mean, she was a kid, she was thirteen years old. I've got kids myself, a child like mine, they're not grown-up, they don't understand what's going on. I'm not mad at her, I'm just a little upset she didn't try to say something sooner when she got a little older, but I'm thankful now that I'm out. And I can't keep no anger built up inside me for anything, you know. I just let it all go.

Post-conviction DNA analysis is seen as a threat to the finality of legal judgments and a particularly ominous threat to those that value finality more than the protection of the innocent.

In 1982, Roger Coleman, a coal miner from Grundy, Virginia, was arrested for the rape and murder of his sister-in-law, Wanda McCoy. Coleman maintained his innocence throughout a trial riddled with controversy and error. He was sentenced to death and executed May 20, 1992.

The DNA tests available at the time of the trial were rudimentary when compared with the technology available nearly twenty years later. Those tests pointed to Coleman but would not be considered conclusive by the standards of 2000 when several newspapers, including *The Washington Post*, requested that the physical evidence from the trial be reanalyzed using more advanced technologies. The Virginia Supreme Court refused to authorize retesting in 2001 and instead ordered the sample sent back to the state from the private lab that had conducted earlier tests. A similar request was denied for the case of Derek Barnabei, who was executed in Virginia in 2000.

"Virginia has done everything in their power to destroy the sample," says Blake—in whose Richmond, California, laboratory freezer sits a vial holding one-fifth of one drop from the twenty-year-old sperm sample from Coleman's case—"and I've refused to give it up."

Blake's fear that Virginia intends to destroy the last remaining biological sample from Coleman's case is not unfounded. In 1986, Joseph Roger O'Dell was convicted of the rape and murder of Helen Schartner. His conviction rested heavily on circumstantial evidence provided by a jailhouse snitch, who later admitted to giving false testimony.

O'Dell spent a decade petitioning the state to have the biological evidence in the case retested using more advanced technologies. His appeals, which were backed by Mother Teresa, Pope John Paul II, and the Italian government, were repeatedly rejected. As then-Virginia Attorney General Mary Sue Terry flatly stated in reaction to one of O'Dell's appeals, "Evidence of innocence is irrelevant." On July 23, 1997, still maintaining his innocence, O'Dell was executed.

The fight to have DNA testing continued. The state of Virginia rejected the requests and then, in 2000, ordered the remaining biological material sent from a private lab back to the state and destroyed it.

As of August, 2005, post-execution DNA testing has not been permitted in any state. Virginia is the only state that has had three separate opportunities to confirm the accuracy of its executions. It has declined each one.

Life's got to go on. I'm not going to cry about nothing. I try to forget that ten years of my life was wasted.

WE'RE NEVER GUARANTEED TOMORROW

I hope someday to have my own boat and catch sea urchins, do crabbing, commercial fishing, and salmon fishing. Be able to have my own crew, go out and work for five hours a day and come home and spend the rest of my time with my family. I picked a job that I will have time to spend with my family. If the ocean's rough, we don't go out. I spend time with my family. As long as I make it out twice a week, I've earned enough money in a week to support my family. And it's not a lot of money to support the children and the things I like to do for them, but we still have each other to spend time with, and the money really isn't that important to me no more. I hope to have a house for them or some property that they'll always have somewhere they'll always be welcome. A home. Somewhere they'll always have so that they don't have to worry later on in their life.

I don't know what ten years being in prison, what my life would have been otherwise. I could have been successful. And maybe I would never have been successful. I just don't know. And I try not to think of that, because it's depressing. And the things that you don't know will drive you crazy if you try to figure them out, or wonder what could have happened. It's not then, it's now. So you got to just move on.

Point Arena is quiet, peaceful, with not a lot of people. I go down to the pier and drink coffee at the coffee shop with the fishermen. We wait for the ocean to get calm and as soon as the ocean gets nice, we all decide what to do that day—fishing, hunting, making money. It's fun. I go out, I do what I like to do and in two days I made 600 bucks. I couldn't work five days a week and make that much money, just getting out of prison, at another job. And now urchins are coming back, we're going to be doing urchins, so I'm going to be really busy making a lot of money. I just got an ATM card.

Work and making money has helped me getting used to being out, but it's also giving me a headache. I already got my oldest daughter's mom wanting me to pay child support. I mean, she's took care of her for the past sixteen years, you know, and I never once gave her a dime. Well, we helped her here and there, my mom has, but I never have. So I really don't have no say so, it's my daughter anyway, my responsibility as a father.

It's been hard. They're little kids, and I just come home after ten years. My oldest son had a little smart remark. He said, "It's your fault why you haven't been here for the past ten years." I'm totally innocent and I'm home now, but still, [he said], if I wouldn't have been hanging around with the wrong crowd, you know, I would never have been, you know, sent to prison. So it's tough. It's hard. But it's life, you know, you get through it.

I'm supporting my kids, and I help out with Mom now with money for groceries, and I give her a couple of extra hundred dollars every time I get paid to do what she wants to do.

I hope to be compensated for what happened, to help me get started. If it doesn't happen I'm not going to cry about that either, I'm just going to go on. No money can pay back for what happened, for what my kids have been through. They suffered so much.

I think that me being away and them not having their mom has been really hard for them. It's caused problems in school and the way they treat each other. They're really insecure with life and things around them because it could be taken away from them real fast. We're never guaranteed tomorrow, so the time that we are with each other, we have to make it special every day and just try to let them know that you love them no matter what.

I'm working now, and I'd probably feel better if I made my own way, but some money would be cool. But I will fight for compensation. I'll get a hundred dollars a day for every day I was in. It'll be 300-something thousand. I think that, by now, within ten years, I would have had a house for my kids, some property, and I think that they should help at least pay for that, for my kids—put a roof over their heads, in case something ever happened to me, they'd have their own home. That's all I really want. After I get that I'll be happy, whether I have to work for it or get compensated for it.

Rose is currently awaiting compensation from the state of California. According to California compensation legislation, Rose can only be compensated for the eight years he spent in prison, not the two years he spent in jail awaiting trial.

You need a certificate of innocence, which I got in the courts, and now I guess the law firm is taking care of it. It can take up to, like, one year or something like that.

I ain't waiting around for a year, sitting on my butt. I can save money right now. I hope to have my own crabbing boat. No. I *will* have my own boat. I don't care if I get compensated or not—in two years I'll have my own boat. I'll just save money, put a down payment on it, and buy it.

Kevin Green

BAD THINGS HAPPEN
TO GOOD PEOPLE

NAME: Kevin Green · **BORN:** 1958 · **HOMETOWN:** San Diego, California

CONVICTED OF: Second-degree and attempted murder and

assault with a deadly weapon · **SENTENCE:** 15 years to life

SERVED: 16 years · **RELEASED:** 1996

YOUNG AND DUMB AND FULL OF IT

I went to high school in Missouri, in Jefferson City. I was raised
Lutheran and attended church religiously, not willingly. Mom
and Dad drug me to church and made me wear a tie. You know,
I thought I understood what faith was about and how it worked
in your life and that good things happen to good people, bad
things happen to bad people.

My brother and I and another guy had a job at a country
club. After a football game one night, we went back to that club
to buy a case of beer. It was closed. We knew where they kept it,
so we went in and took a bunch of beer and whiskey and stuff
and got caught by a cow. This is a story I got to tell in prison a
lot because I tried to impress upon people, "If you think I'm

smart, I got caught by a cow."

We went there to buy a case of beer. We couldn't buy it, so we broke a window. I shoved a guy through the window, and he brought stuff out. I had a '56 Chevy. You know how big the trunk of a '56 Chevy is? It's huge. I had it full of stuff. We drove away from there saying, "Now what?" So we drove around, drove around. We drove down this path at three in the morning, took everything, set it on the side of this little path, and left.

The next day one of my friend's family's cows got out. His dad went looking for the cow and finds this pile of beer and whiskey and stuff. He calls his next-door neighbor, who happened to be a county deputy sheriff, who happened to be in charge of the investigation at the country club. The sheriff had four names on his short list of idiots smart enough to pull this off. And three of us were on his list.

I was given five years' probation. I joined the Marine Corps to stay out of jail. I turned eighteen in boot camp. I was young and dumb and full of it.

I FELT LIKE I WAS GETTING AWAY WITH SOMETHING

Marine Corps boot camp is as hard as it comes. They definitely produce people who will accomplish the mission. It's a brain-washing kind of deal, but at the end you are completely and totally prepared. [The] first phase is set up to take away who you thought you were. There's a lot of reinforcement that the person who you were—the slimy civilian puke—isn't you, that what is emerging is who you really are and who you really were meant to be. When you graduate from Marine Corps boot camp, there is no doubt in your mind that you are the baddest, the most pre-pared fighting person on the planet.

The first month of boot camp, I was miserable. Beyond belief miserable. It wasn't anything like I expected. As far as the drill instructor saw, I did what they asked me to do. But I manipulated my way to where I could get on the phone and say, "Dad, get me the hell out of here. These people are crazy." My dad was a Marine Corps drill instructor for three years, and his first question was, "How in the hell did you get on the phone?"

In [the] second phase, we start doing things like infantry training and using weapons. And as soon as they stuck an M16 in my hand, I was like, "Hey, I can do this shit. This is fun. Because I get to shoot it, and I can hit the targets."

From that point on, I was the leader of my classes going through the

Private First Class
Kevin Green (1976)

schools. But I didn't feel comfortable. I did the job. I led the people. I encouraged the people, but when I walked away from the job, I felt like I was getting away with something. I didn't feel like I had proved or earned it.

When it was off-duty time, then I would go about trying to prove that I deserved the kind of recognition that I was getting, and the only way that I found that was go out and drink and party hard and be rowdy and all that kind of stuff. Play pool and beat everybody. Do all this young kid stuff that I was kind of unleashed and allowed to go do.

I was a raving alcoholic. I had to be the first one there, the last one to leave, and drink more than anyone else because I was a hoo-rah Marine and I was good at it, and I had to prove it all the time. It basically was a big insecurity, and I didn't have any other reason to have self-esteem but to prove that I could do this.

PIE-IN-THE-SKY IDEAS AND DREAMS

My first wife [Tina] and I were in high school together. After boot camp, that's when we really started dating. Tina had never been out of the state until we got married. We got married after she graduated, then we moved to California. It was a lot of pie-in-the-sky ideas and dreams that weren't really based on a whole lot of reality in terms of being able to handle a relationship.

I did really well on duty, but I couldn't get it through my head that I deserved it. I kept thinking, "One of these days, they're going to figure me out." Off duty, I would drink and party. Tina didn't want to do that.

I wanted to go our separate ways and get divorced. In trying to do that slowly, I started going out with my friends and ended up meeting Diane at a place called the Handlebar Saloon in Santa Ana, California. I actually left the bar at one point to pick up Tina from work and take her home. When I got back to the bar, I sat down next to my friend. I was there watching the band, and the seat next to me opened up, and a girl sat down. A couple songs later, she was tapping me on the shoulder. As I turn around and look at her, she was saying, "You don't like to dance much, do you?" I took one look at her, stuttered, and grabbed my beer, took a drink, and said, "No. Do you want to dance?"

When Diane and I got together, she was eighteen. I was nineteen. Diane's dad was ex–Air Force and was very much opposed to her dating anyone from the military. And then marrying somebody in the Marine Corps was like, "Oh God." It was a tense relationship. We got along just because we had to. Her mom liked me, though.

After divorcing Tina in March 1979, Green married Diane D'Aiello a month later.

On August 29, 1979, Tina gave birth to my daughter, Desiree Sunshine. Tina and Diane were both pregnant at the same time. See, there's parts of this that kind of make me go, "You stupid..." but anyway, it is what it is. It was way too much for being young and dumb and full of it.

It was tense with Diane. I'd leave the base and go home and get in a fight with her. I couldn't balance it right. When I went home, I was not the boss. I couldn't figure that out. I was the leader of men. I could command somebody to go die. I could shoot someone if they refused my order. To go home and walk into the household that I didn't run, that I didn't own, that I didn't command. We had a really stormy relationship. We had tempers that matched. We had the immaturity to allow those tempers to be exposed—a lot.

We had been married for less than a year by the time all this happened.

At 1:30 A.M. on September 30, 1979, Kevin Green left his apartment in Tustin, California, to get a cheeseburger at a nearby Jack in the Box. He noticed a man walking alone in the apartment complex as he left but didn't think anything of it. When Green returned minutes later, he found his wife Diane unconscious in their bedroom. She had been beaten so severely in the head that Green believed she had been shot through the forehead at close range.

Diane was nine-months pregnant when she was attacked. She suffered brain damage and lost their unborn daughter, Chantal Marie. That night at the hospital, local police told Green they suspected the attack was the work of a serial killer in the area, who would later become known as the "Bedroom Basher."

GRIEF AND SUSPICION

Wrongful conviction doubles the pain for victims of spousal murder

On the evening of November 18, 1990, Richard Dexter left his home in rural Missouri to pick up groceries. When he returned, he found his wife of twenty-two years lying dead in pool of blood. She had been shot several times and bludgeoned with a hammer.

After investigating the crime scene, police arrested Dexter. Reeling from the trauma of discovering his dead wife, Dexter refused to answer

Richard Dexter after his release (1999)

questions about her murder and requested an attorney. To achieve a conviction, the state used Dexter's reticence against him. They construed his refusal to answer questions after his arrest as an indication of guilt. "It seemed right away they zeroed in on me. They didn't do anything else, didn't look anywhere else," Dexter said. He was sentenced to death in October, 1991.

After murders involving spouses or couples, the surviving partner often becomes the focus of the investigation, and not without reason. In 2003, according to the FBI, 32.3 percent of murders against women were perpetrated by a husband or boyfriend. In cases of alleged spousal murder, juries are much more likely to convict a defendant based on "intuitive profiling"—using stereotypes of spousal murderers to make their decision. This makes it all the more likely that an innocent person will be mistakenly convicted.

Greg Wilhoit was falsely accused of killing his wife in 1985. He describes the dual emotional blows as being "sucker-punched." "I was emotionally bankrupt, devastated," Wilhoit says. "You spend all of your emotional energy on the death of your spouse; you've got nothing left to fight with when the other shoe drops." He was exonerated after spending more than four years on death row.

For Dexter, the shoes kept on dropping, even after his exoneration in 1999. After he was diagnosed with a terminal form of cancer, he bemoaned the absence of Carol, his long-deceased wife. "I miss having her around, especially now with the shape that I'm in. They had a funeral and everything, but I was locked up and couldn't go." Dexter died in April, 2005.

At the time of the attack, everyone pulled together and everybody was very supportive, because the police told them, and I told them, and they knew me well enough that they knew I hadn't done this. I may have been sporadically loud. But just not to that level. It couldn't happen.

Diane's family and I worked together in what little ways we could to help her survive the surgeries that she had to have. And then when she was released from the hospital, to help her start to learn how to talk all over again. The amount of brain damage that she suffered was just tremendous.

And then one day, the police officer—Steve Foster, who's the chief of police now—told my mother-in-law that in spite of everybody else's conclusions, he thought it was too convenient, and that I was his suspect, he was investigating me, and for her not to tell me.

Why he felt it necessary to do that, I don't know. The facts told a whole lot of other people that it was somebody else, but once he focused in on me he was able to get things past his supervisors who, if they cared at all anyway, let things keep going and keep going and ballooning.

So the relationship between me and Diane's family immediately deteriorated to a them-against-me, me-against-them kind of thing.

Green was first arrested on November 30, 1979, two months after his wife's attack and the death of his unborn daughter. Although he was arrested on charges of first-degree murder, attempted murder, and assault with a deadly weapon, he was released five days later.

On March 25, 1980, Green was arrested a second time on the same charges, with an additional charge for spousal rape.

Diane divorced Green in the summer of 1980 while he was in jail in Orange County.

By late September 1980, Green's trial was underway. The charge of spousal rape had been dropped, and first-degree murder charges were reduced to second-degree murder. The defense took two and a half days to argue Green's case.

On October 2, 1980, the jury found Green guilty of second-degree murder, attempted murder, and assault with a deadly weapon. His conviction was based primarily on Diane's testimony that Green bludgeoned her with a key retractor and a ring of keys. There was no corroborating evidence. On November 10, 1980, Green was sentenced to fifteen years to life.

On December 10, 1980, Green was taken from the Orange County Jail to the Department of Corrections reception center in Chino, California. He entered San Quentin State Prison on January 29,1981, to serve his sentence.

IN SAN QUENTIN, THEY SHOT FIRST AND FIGURED IT ALL OUT LATER

My family had lived in Jefferson City, Missouri, off and on all my life. We visited every year. There were people my parents' and grandparents' age, and some my age, who knew me growing up and, for the most part, didn't know I was in prison. They knew I was in the Marine Corps, and whenever the subject came up with my parents, they would usually just say, "Kevin's working in California," and change the subject.

It was rather difficult for my family to say, "Well, he's in prison, but he didn't do it." The reciprocal thought to that is, "Well if he didn't do it, why's he in jail?" Then you'd have to explain that. It just became easier not to talk about it, which, you know, I completely understand.

That society in prison, there are certain types of people—types of crimes—that are not tolerated by the general prison population. I was targeted in San Quentin for being in jail for the death of a baby.

I was tested, to see what I was going to do as far as standing up for myself. They don't necessarily go after you immediately. They want to figure out what you're about. If they figure there is some justice they can give to the victim, that's why they're doing it.

I did not run around and tell people I did it, and I did not run around and try to convince people that I was innocent. I knew my case was common knowledge. It was pretty much headlines in Orange County. There wasn't any keeping it secret.

After several months of being in general population in San Quentin, I got a food package from home. Troy, one of the guys I walked the yard with, came by when I was waiting to put the stuff in my cell. He reached in the box, grabbed a jar of coffee, and walked away. It totally caught me off guard. I didn't know what to do. In that society, my requirement was that I had to go and kill him for what he did to me. For taking that jar of coffee. But I couldn't see any sense in somebody dying over a $4 jar of coffee. I went to go deal with it my way.

Troy was standing in front of the cell waiting on me, and his cell partner was standing in the open doorway as his backup. I started poking Troy in the chest and yelling at him about what a fool he was to pull such a stunt. He had a padlock in his hand to use as a weapon, so I was just waiting for him to move. As soon as his back hit the bars of the cell, I heard the guard on the gunrail behind me cock his shotgun and yell for us to stop. We both froze because normally in San Quentin they shot first and figured

Green at San Quentin State Prison (1981)

it all out later. As I turned I noticed there were three other guys who had followed me down the tier to help Troy. If the guard had not been doing his job that day, I would probably be dead now. The guard called for more officers, and I told them why these guys were about to pound me to a pulp, but correctional staff don't care much for "baby killers" either.

They threw me in the hole—administrative segregation—for about three months. I awoke the first night in that cell with hundreds of cockroaches all over me. The sewer backs up into that block when the tide comes in and the cockroaches have to have someplace to go. They finally decided after three months to put me in protective custody. I spent a month or so there in San Quentin in protective custody, and they transferred me to Tracy, California. I was there for about ten months before they decided that I didn't need to be in protective custody and let me back out into mainline. I got to Soledad, California, on August 4, 1982.

I KIND OF FLEW IN UNDER THE RADAR

The main problem is that once somebody goes to protective custody for any reason at all, then you qualify as every single child molester, rapist in the world. Mainly that you were a rat and you cannot be trusted and you do not need to be breathing the same air as everyone else.

When I arrived at Soledad in 1982, the last thing I wanted anybody to know is that I had been in protective custody in San Quentin. Coming out of protective custody to a mainline institution, I mean, that put me up as a humongous target. I was doing what I felt I needed to do to avoid detection.

Fortunately for me, when I got to Soledad, the institution was on lockdown because of a killing. For the next three years, the institution was on lockdown on and off, for different violent occurrences: murders, staff assaults, riots.

I kind of flew in under the radar. Within the first week of my being there, my cell partner told his bosses that I could type. They pulled me out so I could type disciplinary reports and other documents. While all this lockdown stuff was going on, they would bring people through this office where I was sitting at a typewriter. I would go to their disciplinary hearings and counseling sessions. At some point in time, if anybody asked, "Hey, where'd that guy come from?" Somebody was apparently responding, "I don't know, but he works over in the unit office." It was just dumb luck.

I had this job, and I was out of the cell. When I would come out of the cell to go to work or I would come back from work, they would let me take a shower. Everybody else was locked down twenty-four hours a day, with a shower every two or three or four days.

OKAY, GOD, HOW DO YOU LIKE THIS ONE?

I had to do things that caused them not to be suspicious. Inmates wanted to get messages from one cell to another, to send coffee from one cell to another, or tobacco, and then occasionally send some marijuana down. Somebody would say, "Hey man, I need you to take this package over there." I don't care if they're white, black, Mexican, or whatever. You just gotta say, "Okay, look, dude, lemme check and see where the Man is." And you drop it off. The reputation I ended up getting was that people could trust me. Whoever they were, they knew they could trust me. My fear of being discovered was paramount.

This one guy I knew named Dave somehow hooked up with a guy from Riverside, on the outside. The guy was bringing Dave a quarter pound of marijuana a week in balloons that weighed two ounces apiece. They were secreted in an orifice where things are only supposed to go one way.

Dave would come back from his visits, and I would package things up. I broke it down and packaged it into the amount that was distributed. We called it a cap. You know the cap on a ChapStick container? You filled that with marijuana, and it was ten dollars' worth. I didn't have to buy anything and didn't have to charge anybody anything. My payment for helping this guy out was that I got a percentage of what he was doing.

This was during my "I hate the world" days. I was kind of self-medicating during that time. God and I had a major falling out over my understanding of faith and my understanding of prayers getting answered. I had a lot of bitterness and anger and hate in me for three or four years. It drove me, honestly, to the brink of suicide. I wanted to kill myself because I was a mess. I just wanted to die.

I had occasion one day to be sitting at a typewriter, and I couldn't get my hands to quit shaking. That was the last straw for me. I felt I had no control over my hands. I had no control over being in prison, over getting people to listen to me, over the pain that my family was going through because of me.

I just decided, you know, I can control this. I can get control back. I can make this stop. I decided to get up and go back to my wing and climb up to the third tier. Climb up on the railing and see if I can fly. God never came into my thoughts. It wasn't like, "Okay, God, how do you like this one? Try this on for size." It was like, "I can make this stop."

I got up from my desk. I left work. I was walking down the hallway in Soledad, and I got right to the middle of the prison, and my feet just stopped. I thought, "God, I can't do this anymore. I need help." And right then, I got calm from my head to my feet, a physical feeling of calm. And then, the lights kind of went on in my head, like, "Oh! That's what faith is. That's what this is all about." I asked for help. I got it because I wanted it, I needed it, and it was there in just that little way. Subtle. These things that are happening, my being here, my parents being in pain, all these things are happening for a reason. It's part of something else.

SHE DIDN'T REALIZE SHE WAS
TALKING TO A PRISONER

I got a job working for an organization called Friends Outside. At the time, out in California, they had conjugal visits where families could spend two days and two nights together in a series of trailers they had set up there. These people help visitors and prisoners have a better visiting experience. They make sure everybody knows what's allowed and what's not allowed.

So I was working for Friends Outside to try and have a little money in prison. As part of that, I got to help coordinate a Christmas party in 1984 for the prisoners and their families at the free facilities at Soledad. I had to coordinate the inside paperwork, had to coordinate with the employees outside the fence. I had to call this one lady and just verify that she got stuff, I got stuff, just go back and forth as we coordinated this party.

Her name was Darlene, and we talked every day for four months. It started off as a five- or ten-minute conversation. Then it would be an hour, and over time it turned into three or four hours at a time because I was in this little office in an area that was not patrolled by anybody very often. So we eventually over this four-month period just got to know each other.

Never laid eyes on each other during that whole time. In the beginning, she thought I was staff. She explained to me that she used to sit at her office and watch the officers as they left for the day and tried to pick me out of the crowd. But then one day,

I said that I had to get off the phone and get back for count. And she was kind of caught off guard. She didn't realize she was talking to a prisoner. I wasn't trying to hide the fact. I just figured she knew because our common boss worked in the office with me.

She was twenty years older than me. I was twenty-five. Actually, the very first time I laid eyes on her was at the Christmas party. We only got to talk for three or four minutes, but she was attractive. She was obviously older than me, but I didn't know she was twenty years older than me. I thought she was in her thirties.

That's when I got thrown in the hole for the drug thing. In 1985 they finally decided to drop the net on us. They threw twenty-nine of us in the hole and fired four staff members.

During this time, Darlene had no idea whatsoever what I was involved with inside. It was not something I wanted to talk to her about or share with her. They were able to identify very quickly that she wasn't involved in any of this because she wasn't coming into the institution, no direct contact or anything like that. No way she could be involved.

Darlene decided one day to quit her job. It was December 1985. She said, "I want to start coming in and visiting this guy." Totally shocked me because I knew she had no money. She had actually got the job on a vocational-rehab deal.

As we got together, her grown daughters were like, "Mom, are you out of your freaking mind?" She had to go through those issues with her kids and convince them one at a time to come and meet me.

Darlene and I were married while I was in prison, in July 1985. So I became Dad. As her daughters came and met me and we developed relationships that way, I became Dad. And I became Grandpa. And over the years, it was a very healthy experience.

We had a couple of visits in the very beginning, where it was just Darlene and I. And, of course, she was nervous. And some of these ladies would come out after the family visit battered and bruised—just come out in worse shape than when they came in. Many would come out, you know, it's just another day in paradise, an opportunity to be with their husband. But there were the few that had not-very-good experiences.

I had had one family visit before, with my parents. My parents came out, and we had been able to have those days together where we could sit and talk, and I'd stick my head out the door every few hours to be counted to verify I was still there. The trailers were actual mobile homes. They had four apartments that were just one building, that were two-bedroom apartments, with a very big living room, color TV. Fully furnished and stocked kitchen as far as utensils go. And they had a couch and decent beds, that type of thing.

Our very first family visit, when Darlene arrived and moved all the food into the trailer, we ended up talking until three in the morning. We continued to do what we had been doing. We were communicating and talking and going over things before consummating the marriage.

But Darlene asked me, "Well, why didn't you just throw me down on the kitchen floor when I walked in the door? You haven't been with a woman in all these years." I said, "Well, honey, is that really what you wanted me to do?" She said, "Of course not."

So she was able to get over that kind of self-consciousness about things. And then as the girls came in, we hardly ever had another family visit where it was just the two of us. One or two or three of the daughters would come with their kids, and we would have actually a family dinner. We actually had an opportunity to do family-type things. Take ourselves mentally into what would our world be if it weren't for the guard tower and the razor wire and all that stuff.

AN IMPERFECT UNION
Marriages in prison present challenges for exonerees

Maintaining a marriage can be particularly difficult for exonerees, both during their time in prison and after their release. "Coming from a position of being heart-hardened for so many years, I can't actually say that I even know what love is anymore," says exoneree Frederick Daye. "I'm still feeling like I'm being victimized each and every day of my life."

Daye's case is typical. Convicted of a rape he didn't commit, he spent ten years in prison. During his last few months in prison, he began to exchange letters with his high school sweetheart, Mary Bell; after his release, they married. However, Daye was emotionally damaged by his time in prison. He felt tremendously angry, depressed, and betrayed. Unable to find steady employment, he began disappearing for months at a time, taking drugs, and cheating on his wife. Five years after they married, Mary filed for divorce.

For most inmates who form relationships while incarcerated, courtship consists of long letters, phone calls, and brief visits. Couples who seek to marry face a number of legal obstacles, which vary by state. Some states bar inmates from marriage on the basis of their crime, or require counseling to obtain permission to wed.

Maintaining a marriage behind bars is difficult: roughly 36 percent of exonerees became separated or divorced while in prison. Visits between partners are of paramount importance, but it is difficult to maintain quality contact when the prisoner is sent far from home and when long lines and humiliating searches make visitation traumatic for the partner. Still, the marriages that do last become a vital part of an exoneree's support network.

Even years after exoneration, trauma suffered during a wrongful conviction can impact relationships, particularly in regard to matters of trust. And while spouses tend to want to put the past behind them and move on, exonerees often feel a need to share and explain their experiences.

But exonerees' marriages don't always end badly. Steve Linscott's wife stayed by his side through his arrest, trial, and wrongful conviction for sexual assault and murder. She even relocated to be closer to him while he served his sentence. And when he was exonerated and released three and a half years later, they were still together.

NO VACATIONS. NO TIME OFF. NO TIME-OUTS

One of the ways to describe being in prison is like being a police officer: it's long, excruciating periods of tremendous boredom, punctuated by moments of sheer terror. You know people get stuck in a rut? When you're free, you can somehow change your rut. Change your scenery. Change something. Go do something else. When you're in that rut in prison, you just sometimes look forward to those moments of sheer terror.

Those are the moments that are interesting to people. But the rest of it—get through the day, get through the week, get through the year—it's kind of hard to capsulize it.

Go sit in your bathroom. Close the door. Shut the window. Get rid of all the nice smelly stuff. Let the toilet overflow a couple of times and then sit in that bathroom for a month. And never leave. Eat your dinner. Eat your food. Sleep in the bathtub. Then imagine that never ending. The smell, the noise. If you have people outside making noise and stuff and you can't go participate in that. You have to stay in that bathroom, in that little enclosed space. And then add to it another person that you may or may not like. And they don't leave either. Over and over and over. No vacations. No time off. No time-outs. You don't understand how long a minute is. Just a minute. Watching that second hand tick around.

I just tell people, "What did you do in the last sixteen years of your life? Everything. Go back and remember. Who have you met? Who did you fall in love with? What jobs have you had? What schools have you gone to? And then take it all away. None of it ever happened. None of it. What was your life like?"

Most people don't have a block of time where nothing happened. Their life is full of things. But if you can wrap your mind around the concept of taking everything that you've known, everything that you've done, and take it all away, and fill it in with nothing—fill it in with a big blank—you start to get an understanding of some of the suffering that is intended with prison.

You do start to relish routine. At a certain time of day, they're going to release the housing unit to go to breakfast, and they're going to have another release to go to work and maybe another release to go to the yard. So people get into their daily routine. If there's a delay for whatever reason—there's been an incident in the chow hall and maybe on a given day—instead of going to breakfast at seven in the morning you don't go till ten. Those sorts of interruptions in the routine are frustrating. It's just another sign you have no control over anything. So the smooth routine of things is sought after and protected as much as possible.

Some guys will go out and do weights. Other guys will go out and play basketball, play handball. Some get into doing artistic stuff—hobby crafts, stuff like that. There's opportunities for people to vent.

I added to my day by getting involved in other people's business and listening to people and advocating for people. I felt like I could do something about it. I didn't have a lot of dead time to think about the things that would drive me up a tree.

The last two years that I was in prison, I was a politician. My parents always used to say I should be a lawyer when I was little because I argued about everything. I was the president of the Men's Advisory Council in Soledad prison and had to give presentations and explain things to people, not just so they would have the information, but to prevent people from dying. I had to actually convince them that my ideas and my way of doing this and putting my reputation and really my neck on the line was really what they needed to trust, because the alternative is they go their way and people get hurt.

I filled my administration in the prison with gang leaders, or their seconds in command. And I'm not affiliated with anything. I'm just a Marine from Missouri. The administration could not have asked for better. We didn't have a killing for years. We didn't have a major riot. We didn't have any major incidents between the gangs or between the ethnics, because when there were tensions I would know about it and I would go to my resources before it became a problem.

I achieved a certain level of respect through time. My opinion was sought after. My direction was listened to, and some of it was fear factor. I think people didn't really know what to think. If they didn't do it the way I wanted them to, something bad might happen. As long as you can baffle them with bullshit, then go for it. I'm not the biggest, baddest guy on the walk. I'm just not, but I encouraged people to do it my way. Don't be the biggest, baddest guy on the block—just get things done.

Rumors were the biggest problem. My whole administration, if you want to call it that, was on rumor control. When rumors started flying, it was my job to get answers, and when I couldn't get those answers, it increased the frustration and the tension. You'd be surprised how victimized people in prison feel. They're the ones doing the victimizing, but once they're in there then they become the victim just by the circumstances. You know, human in a cage.

One time, rumors came down that conjugal visits were going to be negatively affected by rule changes. So inmate discussions had reached the point of a determination to take over one of the housing units, take the guards hostage, and generally cause a lot of attention. I pointed out to them that if you do this, it's going to get you killed. You will die, and so will other people.

My solution—the solution that I suggested and really kind of stopped them in their tracks—was that what we should do to demonstrate our solidarity across racial lines, across gang lines, all of that, was that on a Saturday when everybody's out on the yard, at the stroke of noon, everybody should stop doing what you're doing, walk toward the center of the yard, get in a really big circle, do three jumping jacks and go back to doing what you were doing. I said, "If we could pull that off, you don't think they would see that as power that they can't control?"

So the plan to take over and hurt guards went away. I went to the administration and told them exactly what I just told you. We still didn't get answers about whether conjugal visits would be affected. But we got some promises, enough for me to go back and relate to these guys that we had made progress.

YOU AREN'T GOING TO BELIEVE THIS, THEY TURNED HIM DOWN AGAIN

My first parole hearing was just three years after being busted with an ounce-and-a-half of marijuana. I had been waiting for over nine years. As it gets closer and closer and closer, there's a lot of nervousness and anticipation, trying to make sure that you've covered everything that you can and any documentation from the institution about behavior or accomplishments or whatever.

And then I got to the parole board and, especially the first time, I didn't know how sarcastic they would be and how demeaning it would be.

As far as my in-custody behavior, I'd been involved in one fight that they had documented, I had been to protective custody, and I had this drug bust. I didn't have a lot of hope. They were able to very easily say, "Well, it doesn't look like you're adjusting well." I couldn't just sit there and say, "Look, I haven't stabbed anybody!" So I was hopeful but still reserved about it, and when they said, "No, we're going to deny you for two years,"

I understood.

I still had hope that things were going to relax and that they were going to get back to what the judge said when I was sentenced. He told me, "You're going to do nine years, eight months, and you're going to be paroled. I hope you have time to think about this, and blah blah blah. I hope you have a good life." At the time I was sentenced, nobody expected people doing second-degree-murder time to do any more than the minimum unless they were very bad people. and did more very serious physical crimes in prison.

So the second and the third and the fourth time I went to the parole board, I did have much more hope, because I had by then achieved each time more of the criteria that were supposed to be used as judgments. The psych reports of course were always glowing. They were as good as or better than you could expect. The education—I finished the degrees. I had participated in every self-help group. I had started them. I had run them. I had become a politician. By the time I went to the parole board the fourth time, I had gone ten years without any kind of disciplinary write-up. As my lawyer pointed out to the parole board, I had gone without so much as a parking ticket. How many people on the parole board could say the same thing? In an environment where your every breath can result in a disciplinary write-up, I was able to avoid write-ups for over ten years.

If anybody could earn a parole, it should have been me.

My parents flew to California for every one of them. The system in California does not allow people to testify to the parole board who are in favor of your parole—only the people who are opposed to it. The people in favor may submit letters. I had plenty of letters.

Well, the parole board would start explaining that, you know, you're not showing any remorse and blah blah blah. My ex-wife

A DOUBLE-BIND

Maintaining one's innocence makes parole nearly impossible

For the wrongfully convicted, the parole process can be one of the most demoralizing and frustrating aspects of their time in prison.

Parole standards vary greatly across states. In California, for example, inmates serving life sentences are allowed to plead their cases after serving approximately 85 percent of their minimum sentence. In Tennessee, anyone serving a life sentence with the possibility of parole must serve at least fifty-one years before parole can be considered.

Often, in cases such as murder or rape, statements from the victim or their next of kin are considered. Boards also consider an inmate's counseling, behavior, and participation in prison programs.

In addition to statements from victims and family members of the inmate, parole decisions often hinge on the degree of remorse an inmate expresses. During the hearing itself, they gauge an inmate's attitude and responses to questions and accusations. The most daunting challenge for exonerees is admitting to and expressing remorse for a crime they did not commit. At parole hearings, the wrongfully convicted inevitably face a showdown between their assumed guilt and their actual innocence.

Some innocent prisoners have admitted guilt and expressed remorse in hopes of gaining parole. For many wrongfully convicted inmates, abandoning the truth to satisfy parole boards—much like plea bargaining for a lesser prison sentence in exchange for an admission of guilt—is too high a price for freedom.

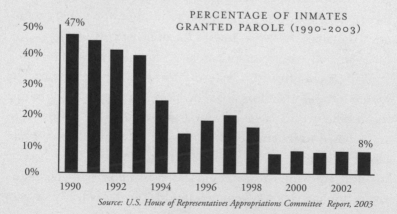

PERCENTAGE OF INMATES
GRANTED PAROLE (1990-2003)

Source: U.S. House of Representatives Appropriations Committee Report, 2003

and her mother, who went to every parole hearing, were sitting there, and they would use their pain as evidence that I'm not helping them by still denying things.

[It's against parole board regulations] to consider whether you admit or deny guilt. It has to do with after-incarceration behavior. One of the parole board members said, "I don't think you're ready for parole. I think you have a serious psychosis that you're not amenable to therapy for." I said, "Yeah, I'm innocent." That kind of pissed him off.

As far as somebody being remorseful for something, there's nobody that could be more sorry for what happened that night than me. I should have stayed home. It's a freaking cheeseburger. I should have stayed home. What would be different? Everything. I took parole hearings as an opportunity to let Diane know that this was our daughter, and to me, this responsibility of my not being there is why this happened. Even with the parole board chastising me up one side and down the other, like they're supposed to do, I did get that opportunity.

Then I had to walk back down the stairs and out into the hallway, and the world was still revolving, and everybody's still going on about their daily routine. But my world has just crashed again. And it means absolutely nothing to anybody else in that hallway. So it's kind of like a slap of reality. And you don't have time in there to mourn, even for a moment, to lose your focus and your attention. Because prison is a dangerous place. You can think about it like a construction site, and things are falling about you, and if you're not paying attention, you're going to get seriously hurt.

[A day or two] after the hearings, my parents and I would sit and talk about what happened. That was the thing that helped hold me together, because then I was able to help hold them together. That's what kept me going. We were sharing this experience, and they needed me to do what I could do. This was after God and I had reunited, so I knew that if I took care of what I had to take care of, God would take care of the rest.

We weren't happy, but we were okay to wait till the next two years came along. Then once the next two years came along, it was the same process all over again. The months of preparing and anticipation and great confidence—here I have accomplished all these different things and surely this was going to impress the parole board—and then it's the same process of humiliation. Them kind of poking me in the eye with my accomplishments, saying, "Ohhh, so now you're a college graduate? You know, your daughter can't do that. Your wife can't do that."

By the fourth time, there was no individual in the prison that was not confident that I would be walking out of the room that day with a parole date. Nobody achieved what I had. There was just no doubt in their mind.

And, of course, before I could actually walk back from the hearing room back to my office, the word was out because the officer sitting at the desk there also just knew that I'm going to get a parole date. And as I walked out and he knew that they'd turned me down, he was on the phone: "You aren't going to believe this. They turned him down again."

Darlene and I tried to be very, very real about our future. We went ahead and talked about that pie in the sky: "What if?" And then each of us recognized, and usually it was me bringing it up, "Okay, all that sounds good, but here's the reality." And I encouraged her always, "If you have friends you want to go out and do something with, just go. Male, female, I don't care. Because I'm here. We don't know when I'm coming home. We don't know when I'm getting out. And there are aspects of your life that don't need to stop." And every now and then, she'd go to Nevada, and she liked to dance, and when she came back we'd talk about it, and she was able to share that with me. In that sense, it was a different type of relationship. It wasn't an open marriage but it was… we could, I don't know, enjoy the sharing of it. And the trust.

I talked about if and when I do get out, I made it clear over the years that I want to be in Missouri. That's my goal. I'm going to get out of California, and we're going to be in Missouri. At that point in time, it was like, "No problem, that's exactly where I want to be, with you, and we'll make a life. Cardboard box is fine." All those kind of comments.

And I was still trying to be real about it, too. More brutally real and say, "If that doesn't work out, we've got to maintain the beginning. We were friends. We could count on each other, we could talk to each other. And let's let that be paramount. Don't screw that up." And I told her, "If I can't go with you, if you can't go with me, let's just let it be that way." So we were married for eleven years by the time, and then all of a sudden, with no warning and no notice, I'm let out.

MAN, I'M GOING HOME

In 1996, using a new DNA database, the California Department of Justice matched DNA evidence from Green's case to serial killer Gerald Parker. Parker, who was serving time in California's Avenal State Prison for a parole violation, was also linked to several other rapes, beatings, and murders in the Los Angeles area in the late '70s and early '80s. When pressed about the case by investigators, Parker eventually confessed to assaulting D'Aiello and murdering five others. Shortly after Parker confessed in 1996, Kevin Green was exonerated and released after spending more than sixteen years in prison.

Three days before I was released in 1996, an investigator from Orange County came and asked me for blood for a DNA test.

I had no idea there was any investigation going on around my case. They were trying to solve unsolved murders by using DNA on these old cases, and the DNA of the girl who was killed a week after my ex-wife was attacked was the one that had identified the serial killer. They came to me asking me for blood. I believed they were going to try to charge me with other murders. I'd been to the parole board four times over an eight-year period, and all they wanted me to do was say, "I'm sorry, I did it," and they would let me go. And, of course, I wasn't going to do that. My daughter is the reason I maintained my innocence throughout. All I could give her was the truth about how she died, that it was not at the hands of her father.

The next day an investigator [Tom Tarpley] from the Tustin Police Department came and told me, "We need to talk, and when we're done talking, I'll tell you what's going on." We went over the case again, we went over every prison I'd ever been in and all the black guys I could remember. And then he showed me a photo lineup of eight faces.

I'm doing the math now. I'm figuring out that something really has happened. I had seen [Gerald Parker] twice the night of the attack, but I told him I never saw the guy's face. I just saw this person and I described him to them. They said, "We have his confession. We have his DNA, and you're getting out of prison." He said, "You can't tell anybody."

I about fell out of my chair. The deal was they were already getting the DA's office behind this. They came to Soledad prison on June 20, 1996, and told me to gather my stuff. I'd been in for sixteen years and three months. Up to that point, over those three days, I wasn't able to call my parents.

When they finally said, "Time to go," I was still very, very distrustful of this. I didn't believe it. Not 100 percent. I went back to my housing unit, and the laundryman was filling up a big laundry cart. I said, "Man, I'm going home. I'm doing fifteen to life, and I'm going home!" He started crying. This guy helped me load everything up. We went up the hallway, and the officers were opening the doors to these different offices and wings and coming out, the word was going out, "Kevin's leaving, Kevin's leaving." They were coming out into the hall to say goodbye. The receiving-and-release officers were coming in from home, calling in from home, to say goodbye.

Even with all that, I still was in prison. When it came time for me to actually leave, those waves of expectation that I had built up with the parole board and being denied... I'm going up the hallway to leave, but there are still a lot of gates, a lot of fences, and a lot of guns between me and outside. When I got up to receiving and release, there were two officers from Orange County there. Both of them kind of looked at me like, "We're here to pick you up *why?*" They had their marching orders.

They took me out to the car, opened the front door for me, no handcuffs, no nothing. I'm like, "Okay, I'm getting in a car." We drive over to a sally port, and it's routine. But when we get in there, they said, "Everybody get out of the car."

And I'm like, "Lying sons of... They're taking me back."

But we got out of the car and, the officer in the sally port, he's like, "Man, Kevin, this is cool."

We got back in the car, and we head out on the highway. We're heading from Soledad prison to Salinas. And we went to the Salinas airport. They've got this little four-seater plane, and they're gonna take me in that down to Orange County. The judge is waiting.

While we're waiting for them to fuel the plane, the homicide detective is like, "You want lunch?"

I said, "Okay, lunch. Cool."

I'm sitting with three officers. There's three guys sitting

behind us, business guys traveling someplace, all drunk. And there's a waitress with a very, very distinct Southern drawl. These business guys were disrespecting her. They said something that was disrespectful. And I started to get up. And it wasn't because I was gonna defend her. It was because I was conditioned that when you hear something—any kind of disrespect—in prison, something's gonna happen. I would always try to stop it before it started. The waitress handled it. It was a really quick example of… where I was isn't where I'm going to be. I'd been conditioned, more than I wanted to believe. I tell people, if they want me to talk like a convict, I can go there.

The officer asked me if I wanted to make a phone call. He went over and dialed the phone for me. Dad answered the phone.

I said, "Dad, guess where I am?" He'd always been worried that I was gonna try to escape.

He said, "I know where you're supposed to be."

I told him, "No, I'm at the airport. I'm on my way to come down and be released, and I'm coming home." And silence for a second or two.

He said, "Do you have handcuffs on?"

I told him, "Nope."

That's when he realized. He started crying.

AFTER WHERE I'VE BEEN,
TRY TO MAKE ME NERVOUS

When I got out, I of course came here to Missouri to reunite with my family. Then I went to live in Utah for the first year I was home. Darlene was living in Salt Lake City, managing a forty-unit apartment complex. I don't have any money. I don't have a job. I don't have nothing. And all of a sudden I'm dropped in her lap.

Darlene liked to play bingo. We went to the bingo parlor. It's open six nights a week. The owner asked what I was doing for a living. I said, "I'm not doing anything else," and he said, "Do you want a job?" I'm like, "Okay." Six or six-fifty an hour to come in and call bingo. He had his best employee train me. It wasn't that difficult to catch on to, so I called bingo that night.

When I got done, the ladies came up to me and said, "You are so good. Your voice is so wonderful. Where'd you do this before?"

I said, "I ain't never done this before in my life." They said, "Well, you seem so confident." I said, "Well, after where I've been, try to make me nervous."

I got the job calling bingo six nights a week. I went from being arguably the most powerful inmate at Soledad prison to calling bingo six nights a week. And loving it.

I did not assume I would still be the shot-caller. I'm no longer that person. I'm now a free man, but I'm a married man, a father, a grandfather. Those priorities are much more important than being what I used to be. When I asked God for my life back, I did not mean I wanted to be twenty-one and in the Marine Corps again.

I prayed for many years to get my life back, the good, the bad, all aspects of it. The bad things happened, but the good things happened, too. We had weddings, and we had births. When I got out, soon after being home, I went to the funeral of a step-grandson who died on his way to visit us. And I went through a divorce.

Darlene and I ended up getting divorced on what I consider to be good terms. It wasn't pleasant. It wasn't the adult conversation that I wanted to have. I actually came home from work one day and she had left. But I wanted to be with my family in Missouri, and that's where we were.

I'M STACKING LIGHT BULBS AND
PAINT CANS, I'M NOT A CELEBRITY

When I was released, there was a lot of press. There was a lot of notoriety. The Bedroom Basher case, a serial-killer case, brought in a lot of press, and there was a lot of interest from local and national TV shows. There were headlines everywhere: "Innocent Man Set Free at Last."

Old family friends were caught off guard and shocked. It's taken some people a long time to figure out how to approach me about it. They don't know if I want to talk about it. They want to talk about it. So those are strange moments.

I make it easy, I think, really easy on people, because I explain to them as soon as I can that I tried talking about it for sixteen years and nobody would listen. Try to shut me up now. You got a question? Ask it. Let's get it discussed. I feel what happened to me can help.

The good headlines helped me personally get into interview situations for jobs. I would go in, and I'd have zero job history, and I'd fill out my résumé and put that I'd worked for the California Department of Corrections for sixteen years and I'd got paid $48 a month. It would raise an eyebrow, and I'd pull out the headlines with my picture on the front. I'd say, "I'm that guy." I'd have to be able to explain to them that I can do the job, I'm not institutionalized, I'm not shell-shocked, and all that. Let's have a conversation and get on with it.

I went to Wal-Mart and started at $6.15 an hour, and I was in the process of doing an interview for *20/20*, so I told people in personnel that *20/20* might want to come here and film me. After I was on the floor for three days, the manager called me in his office and said, "Well, I didn't know we had a celebrity working for us."

I said, "Wait a minute, dude, I'm stacking light bulbs and paint cans. I am not a celebrity." He said, "Well, it looks here as though we've hired you at an inappropriate rate due to your age and experience and education." They gave me a dollar-and-a-half-an-hour raise.

MY NEXT SIXTEEN YEARS NEEDED TO BE BETTER THAN MY PREVIOUS SIXTEEN YEARS

The attorney who was representing me when I got out was a really, really high-dollar guy working for me for free at the request of the district attorney and the police officer [Tarpley] that got the confession from the real killer and really got the ball going. They looked at it like, "If I was in this situation, who would I want representing me?" and they approached him, being the best in the area. He really jumped right on it.

Now, I was out of prison for two years, and I hadn't seen a penny, not a dime. My attorney found this fifty-eight-year-old law in California. It said they could give me $10,000. Total. They went through the process, and it went through all the committees. A year-and-a-half later, they funded it, ten thousand freaking dollars.

The process brought the issue to the awareness of the lawmakers themselves. They looked at it like, "This man did sixteen years in prison, and all we can do for him is $10,000? It ain't right." They made a necessary change. They said, "We gotta do something better." They started off, "Well, let's give him a million dollars." Then they whittled it down to $100 a day, based on another existing law that has a provision in it for failure to parole somebody in a timely manner. Under this law, though, it was $100 a day for every day I was in prison.

On October 5, 1999, California Governor Gray Davis signed legislation authorizing the state to pay Green $620,000 for his sixteen years of wrongful imprisonment.

The next day, the legislature introduced another bill that would allow future people coming out of prison to apply for compensation under my law. I understand there have been four or five people able to apply for that compensation, and it has become a bureaucratic pile of crap, taking up to three years for people to actually see any money.

That's wrong. That's just wrong. I think one of the hurdles that somebody faces coming out of prison is not being able to establish themselves: have a place to live, have transportation to have a job. All those things need to be immediate. Somebody coming out with a finding of factual innocence should be immediately handed something and then go through the process of getting the rest.

After his conviction in 1980, Green was sued by his ex-wife Diane and her family for $1 million in a civil suit. In 1984, a judge ordered a $6 million default judgment against Green, as he could not be present in court to defend himself. After Green was exonerated, he had to deal with the suit and the people behind it.

After I was released, my lawyers approached my ex-wife and her family, and still they said, "No, we're not gonna drop it. The police got it wrong." They had eight, ten, twelve million reasons to want there to be a civil judgment. As far as my ex-wife's mother is concerned, the world rotates the other way. She's a nut. She would parade my ex-wife in front of any camera. Diane still has a lot of problems with memory, speech. But her biggest problem at that point was her mother.

Even though I'd been found factually innocent of all charges and allegations on the criminal side, this default judgment stands on its own and doesn't go away unless they say, "Oh damn, you're right. Got it wrong. Go ahead and drop that suit." They weren't dropping it. They figured I'm going to get compensation from the state in some shape or form.

We found that there's only two ways to have civil default judgments thrown out. One is to show that fraud was involved in gaining the judgment and to appeal it in six months. The other was that to allow the judgment to stand would cause a grave injustice. We had that hands down, but we didn't have judges with gonads enough to say, "Okay, let's explore this." It took us a long time to find a judge to hear the case.

This time, I'm the plaintiff, and Diane's the defendant.

After I testified, the judge ended it right there.

It's unfortunate that Diane's mom was more interested in money than helping Diane get on with her life. My relationship with Diane's family sucked. And there has not been a relationship since. In a sense, I care to know how she's doing, but I'm not going to go out of my way to ask questions that may then be relayed back to her and cause any kind of trepidation in her life. I'll just let it go.

After Green was awarded $620,000, he voluntarily contributed $50,000 to cover Diane's legal costs in her failed suit against Green.

When the state gave me the check for $620,000, I had to turn around and pretty much the same day pay the attorneys. My attorney got a third. I came home with over $400,000 for sixteen years of my life. Eventually, I set aside $50,000 with the civil judge, gave my parents that much and more, gave some to my sister, bought a car, spent some more, and ended up investing a little over $200,000 in late 2000. The stock market took a dive in early 2001. My problem was that I had put most everything I had into the market, not realizing that I was going to need to spend more money than I made at Wal-Mart. I would sell bits and pieces of the stock off at a loss until it was all gone. In the end I sold off what I bought for a total loss of $58,000.

The experience that I've had and that other people have had when you've been handed a bunch of money: My family said, "Don't do this, do this, don't do this." I did follow some of their advice, and I didn't follow the other parts. They knew better than me. So I kind of screwed myself.

The experience left me with an idea of what would have been better. It was kind of like my dad said, that my next sixteen years needed to be better than my previous sixteen years. Making that money stretch out over those sixteen years in some way.

IT WAS MY TURN

Kelly, my wife now, was my sister's best friend in high school, so she was like a member of the family. She was always around. After high school, she got a job at the Missouri State Bar Association and worked there for fourteen years. Got married, had a daughter and all that, got divorced.

On my 40th birthday, she called. She and her brother called me to go out to go for a drink and knew that I wasn't doing anything else. I met up with them that night. She only really intended to satisfy some curiosity that she'd had for many, many years. But she hasn't been able to get rid of me since.

Green married Kelly Watson on August 11, 1999. Two years later, they renewed their vows in a formal wedding service in front of family and friends.

[In 2001] we planned a big church wedding in my family's church where my parents married, my uncle got married, I think my grandparents got married, my brother got married there, my sister got married there. It was my turn.

When we got married, I was in dress blues so I didn't have to rent a tux. We had the fellas from the Marine Corps League waiting outside the church to do canopied swords, and we got to walk under. And the last guy got to slap Kelly on the butt with the sword, and say, "Welcome to the Marine Corps, hoo-rah!," and everybody says "hoo-rah." It's kind of like a Klingon thing.

For Kelly, even though she knows the family, she knows what they've been through, she's the kind of person that wants things, once they're done, to be done. And move on. Not to keep revisiting them. Because I think, for her, it's a safer way of getting through the rest of her life.

She still has somewhat of a naive belief that the police, prosecutors, and all those people are, by and large, not out to hurt people. And that we're making too big of a deal of the times that it does go wrong, because she doesn't want to understand that it does go wrong a lot more than we do talk about.

Since his release, Green has become a popular speaker at various conferences and group meetings. These speaking engagements have forced him in part to relive the traumatic experience of his arrest, conviction, and sixteen years of wrongful incarceration.

In a joint interview, Kevin and Kelly Green speak about the effect of Kevin's story on their marriage.

KEVIN: In the early part of our marriage, it bothered her that I was going to have to go through it again. You know what I mean? And she wasn't sure how to handle that… how to help me through that. It took her a while to understand that she did-

Kevin and Kelly Green renew their vows (2001)

n't have to help me through it, and I think that bothered her.
I didn't want to have it be something that she would then have
to be burdened with. She could go to these speeches, participate
in it, go see the sights, or whatever, but don't think that I'm going
to be mentally in need of, you know, restoration after this. And
maybe it bothered her—"Why did we have to talk about that?"

KELLY: I don't wanna say I get sick of hearing it, but I've heard
the story over and over and over again. You know, there's a lot of
people who still call. They want him to go here and go there. I'm
glad he gets the opportunity to do that. It could be a "we" thing.
I have a daughter, and she's to the age now where it doesn't
matter.

To me, it's the past, let the past go. But that's something that
it's not like… he's not a person who went to prison and got

released. He went to prison for something he didn't do. He's been a very long time there. I try to be understanding about it. But sometimes it's hard, 'cause you know, it's like… there's a lot of prison stories. To me it's like it's nothing to be proud about.

It's something I don't feel everybody in the whole world needs to know, that you've been in prison. He just doesn't think about things like that. When we're out and talking about something, he's always throwing something in like, "When I was in prison…" I'm like, "You're not in there anymore." He's all, "My cell…" And I'm like, "You don't live there anymore."

KEVIN: She wants life to be normal and it's helpful because I don't dwell on, "I was in prison all this time." I have to dwell on, "I have bills to pay. I have a yard to maintain. A wife and step-daughter who really need my attention."

What does become difficult is the need to pass on what I've experienced.

KELLY: There's a lot of talk about the past, about when he was married to [Diane], and that's kind of hard for me. I met her actually when she was pregnant. What happened to her was awful. And I guess in my opinion, there are certain things I'd like to say to her. He deserves, maybe not an apology, but something from her, because it was his child, too. I don't think the things that have happened have been fair to him. I would like to see her apologize.

He's not your stereotype prison people. He's educated. He knows how to talk. [At an exoneree event in New York,] they weren't very educated. They came out here and it was basically like, "Society owes me." Talking about being broke, can't do this, can't do that. Well, you know, I'm sorry. Yes, you got a bad deal, but it's time to get over it and get on with your life. There were very few like Kevin that were educated and came out like, "This happened to me," and got on with their life.

KEVIN: One of the comments that she made that brought perspective to it was, "They had to have done something."

KELLY: They had to. The police don't just come to you.

KEVIN: But they do.

KELLY: No, they don't.

KEVIN: But they do.

David Pope   *Beverly Monroe*   *Peter Rose*   *John Stoll*   *Ulysses Rodriguez Charles*

PEOPLE DON'T KNOW HOW LUCKY THEY ARE TO HAVE THEIR LIBERTY

[AN EXONEREE ROUNDTABLE]

NAMES: Peter Rose, Ulysses "Bubba" Rodriguez Charles, John Stoll, Beverly Monroe, Scott Hornoff (not pictured), and David Pope

SERVED: 70 years (combined)

The following is an excerpt from a series of informal roundtable discussions held from November 12 to 14, 2004 in Berkeley, California. The discussion was attended by six exonerees, the editors of this book, and several UC Berkeley graduate students.

FREEDOM

PETER ROSE: When I got home, like the first couple of days, I started pacing the floor in the living room. [In] a cell, you'd hear things going on and you'd get up and go to the door because that's your only window—the door—to see what was going on. And so I caught myself, when I got home, pacing the floors. And I guess I wasn't eating. My mom was all worried about me. She called all her friends: "He's not eating. What's wrong with him?

Something is wrong—he's pacing the floors." My aunt told me, "You know, your mom is worried about you. You're acting strange. You're pacing up and down the floor. You don't eat barely nothing. And you'd think somebody that didn't have all that food would eat, you know?" And it's like... it was weird, you know? Kind of a claustrophobic thing. I noticed it myself right away.

JOHN STOLL: To me, my biggest thing—it still is—is get outside. Every chance, I got to get outside. I want to go outside. I want to be outside. I'm going outside. Because you couldn't go outside. You went outside when they said to go outside. Now you can go outside when you damn well please!

ROSE: You will never catch us walking counterclockwise again in a circle.

STOLL: Never! I will never walk in a circle.

ROSE: That was one thing. I said, "I'm walking straight! I'm not walking around the block." I am not doing it. I am walking a straight line.

STOLL: For years I walked five miles a day, every day. But I didn't walk a straight mile anywhere, ever. For twenty years. Because it's only a quarter mile around the track. So here you are with this damn circle—walking in this circle. Day in and day out. Passing the same thing. And past the same inmates. So there will be no more circle-walking for me.

ULYSSES RODRIGUEZ CHARLES ("BUBBA"): What I find myself—you just raised this here, something that I never really paid attention to—but when I come home I go straight to the bedroom every day. And it was brought to my attention one time. You don't realize—I have a living room, I have a dining room. I have kitchen, right? I have a hallway. I have a little office space with my computer. But I always go straight to the bedroom and I close the door.

STOLL: You gotta quit goin' to your cell, man.

CHARLES: That's what my wife, she be telling me, "What's wrong with you?" But I do that to this day.

People don't know how lucky they are to have their liberty. And what are they doing with it? People have their liberty and they're not doing anything. They don't know how fortunate they are. So since I got out, now I'm trying to do like a million things at one time. And it's not good. It's not good.

I went to prison when I was thirty-four years old, and I'm in my fifties now, okay? And I'm realistic, you know? I don't have much quality time left. But what I'm saying is now, each day, I'm going to have to live it to the fullest. I'm not able to reconcile my current age with my age that I was at the time I went to prison. It's a lot of confusion there. I'm still thinking I'm thirty-six, thirty-five.

STOLL: You know, my body is telling me, "What are you doing?" I'm thinking I'm forty and doing shit that I did when I [was] forty. And my body is going, "Whoa, dude! I'm not doing that anymore!" But it was really hard for the first couple of weeks because I went out and worked in the garden like I had always worked, and I damn near killed myself. I could hardly get out of bed the next day. You stop living and then this little shitty area took over in your life. And then you got out again, and now you're living again. So all that crap didn't count. I didn't want to take that off my life, so I just didn't count it.

CHARLES: I'm saying your mind doesn't account for all the time you spent in prison. It's like you went to bed and you got up the next day. But it's not a day, it's years! Your mind doesn't allow to account for all that time.

STOLL: One bad dream.

MONROE: I had been outside, some. There were months that I didn't get outside at a time. Partly because of the job, partly because they just didn't let us out. And being an outdoors person, that was hard. So when I walked out of that gate—the sun is different and the air feels… it just feels different from inside. It was a whole different world. A whole different sun, a whole different feel. I feel the touch of the air on my skin now. And it's a joy. Every nuance of awareness like that is an absolute joy.

ROSE: When I went to San Francisco last night—it's just so much traffic and so much things going so fast that my eyes was trying to pick up everything at the same time and it actually made me dizzy. I got nauseated from it. I got dizzy 'cause I couldn't focus on what I was doing. I'm trying to look everywhere at the same time. My eyeballs were just going, "Whoop!"

CHARLES: You do have a different appreciation for life that I think people don't understand. I try to live each day like it's the last day that I'm livin'. I don't care about people's opinions or what they say, I'm going to enjoy life, you know. I'm not out here trying to break the law or get myself in trouble. That's not even a concern to me because that was never my standard.

ROSE: I still feel like I did the day that I went in.

STOLL: Exactly.

ROSE: I did not miss a beat. I'm just taking off from that day forward, ten years ago. It's weird.

FAMILY

ROSE: I'm a father of four. And I'm dealing with a sixteen-year-old going on thirty—wearing makeup like Britney Spears. She's out of control. And I can't tell her she can't dress like this, or wear makeup like this, because I was never there for her. All my kids have really suffered since I've been gone. Their mother left them five years ago. My mom's been raising them. If it wasn't for my mom, they'd be in a foster home and adopted out, probably. They're not secure. Like, when I took off to come up here, my daughter told me, "Daddy, when you coming home?" I told her, "Don't worry, I'm coming home Monday." "You promise?" Like I wasn't coming home. She thought maybe I was going back to jail and they just let me out for a minute to spend some time with them. They're really insecure all the time. It's real sad. It irks me. Because of the ignorance of other people of the truth.

CHARLES: I'm going to share this with you all. That's my daughter.

[*Charles shows a picture of his daughter, who committed suicide in 1996*]

CHARLES: That's my daughter.

ROSE: Very beautiful.

CHARLES: That's all I have of her right now.

MONROE: That's all you have of her?

ROSE: You lost her?

CHARLES: Mm-hmm.

ROSE: I'm really sorry to hear about that.

CHARLES: She didn't want to [live] because of my situation. They sent me to Texas in '95 and she couldn't visit me anymore. In '96,

SURVIVING JUSTICE

she decided she didn't want to be here anymore. I can't say how much it affected people's family because, whatever I may say, the effects is what is real. Talk is one thing, but the effects that… When they send someone to prison it affects [what] that person's family is like. No one don't even consider that, because it's too big.

ROSE: It's too big.

CHARLES: No one will ever understand. And my daughter was trying. She was in her last year of college at UMass. In spite of everything else, she was fighting the struggle with me. She was right there, she was strong. But when they took me from Massachusetts, in the middle of the night, in a plane, in shackles, and sent me 1,600 miles away to Dallas, Texas. That's, for whatever reason… That had consequences.

JUSTICE

MONROE: You make the law if you're in power. And you make it to suit yourself. But there is a tremendous pressure. Giving the police credit—which is hard for me to do, believe me. There is a tremendous pressure on police and prosecutors. I have seen at least one prosecutor in Virginia who was drummed out of his job, in essence, because he dropped charges against someone where the evidence was not compelling. And that's frightening, too—that the public almost forces someone who would want to do the right thing to bend the other way. So it takes courage on the part of police and prosecutors to do the right thing.

STOLL: What is really scary with Bakersfield was that regardless of how many times the attorney general come out and said, "Hey, you made a mistake here; you're questioning the children improperly"… All this came out in 1987. It was a scathing, blistering… I mean, they just scorched Kern County. They said, "You didn't do a thing right." But [Kern County] did not go back

438

and say, "Okay, Stoll, we screwed you. Let's bring it back and look at it again."

DAVID POPE: You know, somebody once said that, you know, [what] scares them about the United States [is] that we have the jury system. Because, you know, people that don't know anything can decide your fate. Maybe that's something significant with my case in particular, because voice spectrograph [evidence] is not sound, but they decided to use it. In the whole history of Texas I got to be the lucky guy, right? So this goes before a jury of your grandma and your baby sister, and all these innocent people that don't know anything. And you know, it was a big charade where the state put this examiner up there. That's really why I stayed in there for so long. Because mine became this case law that was going to set a precedent.

ROSE: I thought they were there to help. I really did. I really thought, "You know what? I'm innocent and there is no way I'm going to prison." And I didn't worry. All the way through trial I wasn't worried. I wasn't worried until the day they came back and said, "Guilty." Then I got worried real fast! [laughs]

I believe that juries are not a good thing. Because if you have a jury, if you can write a novel of fiction. If a district attorney can come in here and say anything he wants and get away with it, they can make you out to be anybody. I can turn you into a straight monster, and if I put it in front of people, they're gonna believe it. And that's what's happening. They're going in there making this person out to be a total monster, when they're not—they're just a human being like everybody else.

And you know what? I'm not going to react to idiotic stuff like that. You know? It's like... stupid. Because you're not going to get nowhere. Because they're always right. We're wrong. We're garbage to somebody who has the say-so in your life.

MONROE: What you're saying is a total change of the jury system and the adversarial kind of justice that we have. And you can't call it justice. It's a game. It's a competition. It's one that is staged. And it is literally called—I don't like to use that word, but—a crap game. And I heard this expression over and over again. I said, "What does that mean?" because I couldn't, having grown up with this whole ideology that things should be accountable, and right, and just. You wrote papers in civics about it. And it doesn't exist. It's a myth. An absolute myth, and you're right, until something basic changes, and the public demands it. Two words: accountability and reliability.

ROSE: Right now all the district attorneys and the lawyers are all pitchers and catchers. What it means is they have a record. It's no longer about prosecuting the guilty and helping the innocent. It's "I have a record to uphold as a pitcher, I'm going to be nine and zero in my next ten trials," and, "I'm going to prosecute the next nine, and I don't care who is guilty or who is innocent because it's my style. It's my personality. And it's my job on the line. And I'm going to be the next judge. Or I'm going to be whoever I want to be because this is how good I am." And it's all self-gain. It's all about self. There is nothing else involved except self. They don't care about the next person.

I do not trust the law, period.

CHARLES: You know the question I ask? "If I was a criminal, why would I wait until I was thirty-four years old?" All of a sudden, thirty-four years old, I'm this big monster rapist. Come on!

MONROE: Don't you think it's easier to convict somone who's innocent, at least in cases like that?

CHARLES: Listen, I could indict a ham sandwich. [Laughter] I *can*!

MONROE: If you could go back and get every record from day

one, you could show how all of this took place. I would have a better chance of getting records if I had grown up in Bulgaria under the KGB. As a citizen and as a taxpayer I should have the right. Especially now that the court has overturned it, vacated the convictions and accused the prosecution and the police of misconduct in this.

I can tell Pete's feelings are still very, very raw. And he has every reason to feel this way. And he's absolutely right. But change can come. Reform can come with a lot of media exposure and encouraging the police and the prosecution to see that it's in their best interest. I keep telling myself, "There must be a lot of really good police officers that are out there." There are people who are good people, who want things to work right. And they're doing a very dangerous job and a very necessary job. So you can't condemn all the police and you can't condemn all the prosecutors. It's making everyone see that this is something that works for everyone's good. And it can happen. And I think we mustn't give up on that. We mustn't.

DISOBEDIENCE

STOLL: Sometimes we didn't have our cell searched for almost a year. But I worked for the captain and that probably had a lot to do with it: "You don't want me to tell the captain you were up tearing my shit up and I can't get my work done." "Oh, never mind, Stoll. That's okay."

Like, one guy made a building officer angry and he ended up wadding up some toilet paper and throwing it at the officer. He was on the second tier, and he threw it down on their desk. They came in there and they took every piece of property that you owned—everything, every possible piece of property. First they took all of your state clothes and threw them in this giant pile, okay? Then they took all your socks and all your underwear, and all your T-shirts and threw them into a big pile. And they took everything you owned to the office. So now here you were, trying to pick your clothing out from some other inmate's clothing. And you go back and you realize you have no TV, you have no radio, your tape player is gone. All your tapes are gone. They took everything.

Then you had to go back up to the office. Now, there's 1,100 other guys trying to get up to the office to get their stuff, too. But they taught that building a lesson. You know, they were mad at this one guy for what he did. And because we didn't control that one guy, which is not our job, and I told them that a million times. I must have told them a million times, "That's not my job." They went in there and just literally tore our stuff up.

ROSE: What happened to the guy?

STOLL: Oh, they locked him up. He said, "Oh, man, they're really going to be pissed this time."

ROSE: Have they ever flooded your building out?

STOLL: We've done that. Everybody takes their sheets, shoves it down their toilet so now there's no drain. And you just start flushing.

ROSE: Oh, God. We were swimming in our cell.

STOLL: We just tell them, "We're flooding." You hear a guy down there flushing his toilet and hollering out the window. "You son of a bitches!" And everybody—if you get into it—you just figure, "What the hell?"

ROSE: Yeah, when you got forty cells in the building filing up with 500 gallons of water… You take everything off the floor, everything off the second shelf, and put everything up on the top bunk. And you tape your vents with plastic bags.

LOLA VOLLEN: So what's the fun in it?

ROSE: There's no fun. You want something done. Like, when we did it, it was the middle of summertime and the air conditioning went out. And it was a Friday. The people that fix it don't come until Monday. It's ninety-nine degrees in our cell with the sun baking on the back of our window, and they won't let us leave the door open or call the guy to come over and fix the air real fast.

STOLL: So you make yourself a swimming pool?

ROSE: You make a swimming pool. You cover the vents and you fill the whole cell up with about six feet of water and you go swimming. But where's the water gonna go when you're done swimming?

STOLL: I had enough water in my cell one day to actually get my body floating, yes. But boy, when you pulled that sheet out; when you pulled that sheet and those towels away from the door! Man, that shit'll suck you right through that crack, it would be going out so fast! Holy crap, you gotta look out!

ROSE: It doesn't damage anything because everything's cement and steel anyway.

STOLL: It's just state crap anyway, so what the heck?

PRISON VIOLENCE

STOLL: As inmates, we understood that—okay... this really sounds terrible—[murder] was a respectable crime. Maybe you had a good reason for it. A lot of people that did kill somebody—the guy probably had it coming.

ROSE: You've got a lot of people in prison. They think that murder is a crime respected, because they didn't molest a little kid, but instead, they just took some little kid's daddy or mommy, or somebody like that. They're kind of really twisted on that subject. I never did understand that.

STOLL: Murder and violence rules in prison. Nobody protects a child molester. Nobody protects a child raper. Nobody protects a child killer.

MONROE: But not in the women's [prisons]. It's very different. A difference in atmosphere. A difference in everything. I think first of all, people knew that [mine] was a high-profile case... I found nothing disturbing about the women themselves.

ROSE: I told this guy when he asked me what I was there for and I said, "But I'm innocent, that's why I'm telling you. "

STOLL: And he said, "Oh, yeah, sure, partner."

ROSE: You got a problem, just deal with it. If not, just see you later. And it's happened six or seven times: First thing that comes to [their] mouth: "Well, if you were in prison and you got convicted, you had to be guilty of something." I said, "You're worse than the district attorney!" I said, "Oh, you're a judge now!"

STOLL: Here were people who were run over by the system...

CHARLES: You know what [a guy] did to me after? After I told him everything? You know what he said? He called me a "tree jumper." It's really terrible.

ROSE: It's really disrespectful.

STOLL: You call another inmate a tree jumper, it means you're waiting in a tree to jump on a woman when she goes by.

MONROE: So did you have to fight?

STOLL: Everybody does. It's an unbelievably macho thing, where the guys are.

CHARLES: I was shooting pool, and when I was done with [fighting an inmate], the pool stick was this long. The officers—you know what they did? When they see us fighting?—they ran and locked the door. And leave that guy for me to kill him.

STOLL: Because they really don't care about you, and all they're doing is protecting their life. But you can't blame them. They're going home at night. You know, it's their job.

The [guards] that we liked in prison were the guys we called "eight and a gate." They did their eight hours and they went out the gate.

CHARLES: That's right!

STOLL: And they didn't bullshit with you. They didn't screw with you. They left you the hell alone. But then you had these macho nitwits that didn't pass the state police exam. So now they're in charge of somebody that's "confined." So you got all these idiots in charge of you. It's like a bunch of eighth-graders watching a bunch of sixth-graders! Christ!

CHARLES: You know what I did? You know what I used to do? I used to go by the desk and I say, "Listen, man, you know what?" I say, "Let me tell you something, right? I got to live here. You visit eight hours a day. I live here; this is my home. Take your money and run. Just get your money and run. This is my house." That's what I used to tell them.

STOLL: See, Bubba—because that's what you tell them. You tell them when they come in. You'd say, "Look, man, I live here, partner." You come in here for eight hours; you're going to tell me what the hell is going on? You don't find any weapons in there or any drugs—just leave my shit alone and keep moving. And they respected you because you had that attitude. But it took a couple years to figure out that's the attitude to have. Because if you're in the wrong place and you have that attitude, they'll beat your ass: "Oh, you're a smart guy, huh?" Uh-oh! Yeah.

Most of the reasons that cause violence in prison, there was probably a good reason behind it. I'm not justifying it, I'm just saying there was probably a good reason. Because you got to realize that here's a person that's gonna do twenty years in prison. But if he screws up, he could do thirty years in prison. So if he's going to step out there and screw up, then he probably had a pretty good reason. I'm not condoning violence, but a lot of times, violence for violence's sake is necessary. Because that's just what the hell you're dealing with. It's a violent society. It's not a bunch of good guys that their camp bus took a wrong turn. I mean, shit—these are some really violent, ugly people that have hurt people all their lives.

And that's the only stories they tell. That's why for me it was so hard, because I had never been in any trouble. I had never been arrested. Now I've [got] counts of child molestation against me. I mean, that's a pretty damn big jump! I had never been in any trouble. I have never done anything. I was just a carpenter minding my own business.

What I'm saying is you got to realize you're not talking a normal, ordinary lifestyle. You're talking prison. You can't equate it to what you know. Because you don't know.

A NOTE ABOUT METHODOLOGY

This book grew out of a class co-taught by Lola Vollen and Dave Eggers at the University of California Berkeley Graduate School of Journalism. The task of the class, which comprised fourteen students over two semesters, was to interview the exonerees represented in this book, edit their transcripts into clear narratives, and to surround these narratives with sidebars explaining the issues pertaining to wrongful conviction and exoneration.

Many of the exonerees were first interviewed by Sarah Stewart Taylor, a reporter with expertise in prison issues. Later, each exoneree was interviewed by a UC Berkeley graduate student. Half of these interviews took place in Berkeley, when six of the exonerees were flown to campus to participate in the weekend-long roundtable discussion [see page 433], and a series of individual interview sessions. The rest of the interviews took place in the home cities of the exonerees. The interviews ranged in length from four hours to twelve hours. Once the recordings of these conversations were transcribed, the students then edited each transcript down to a clear narrative. In most cases, this process involved paring a raw transcript—on average, the transcripts were about 45,000 words—down to a narrative of about 12,000 words. In no cases were any changes made to the content or meaning of the exonerees' words. Editing was done to make the narratives concise, and as linear as possible. The edited versions were then sent to the exonerees for approval. Changes were made when passages or details were incorrect or unclear, though the editors sought to maintain each exoneree's distinct voice. The editors of Voice of Witness are dedicated to presenting the stories of the interviewees as accurately as possible; the only way to safeguard this, we feel, is to involve the interviewees throughout the process. The changes requested by the exonerees or their lawyers were commonly limited to those involving grammar and factuality. In addition to receiving the approval of all of those whose stories are told in *Surviving Justice*, all of the narratives were fact-checked against news reports, court records, police records, and documents and notes kept by the lawyers involved.

For more information about methodology, sidebar endnotes, and to see transcripts of many of the interviews, visit:

www.voiceofwitness.com

APPENDICES

APPENDIX A

The following are excerpts from the third edition of Criminal Interrogation and Confessions, *written by Fred E. Inbau, John E. Reid, and Joseph P. Buckley. This seminal work has been used since the mid-1960s to train police officers and investigators to conduct effective interrogations. The manual, presented here in its 1986 edition, contains extensive instruction on the employment of psychological tactics and deception for interrogations of both suspects and victims.*

[FROM THE INTRODUCTION]

... There is a gross misconception, generated and perpetuated by fiction writers, movies, and TV, that if criminal investigators carefully examine a crime scene, they will almost always find a clue that will lead them to the offender; and that, furthermore, once the criminal is located, he will readily confess or otherwise reveal guilt, as by attempting to escape. This, however, is pure fiction. As a matter of fact, the art and science of criminal investigation have not developed to a point where the search for and the examination of physical evidence will always, or even in most cases, reveal a clue to the identity of the perpetrator or provide the necessary legal proof of guilt. In criminal investigations, even the most efficient type, there are many, many instances where physical clues are entirely absent, and the only approach to a possible solution of the crime is the interrogation of the criminal suspect himself, as well as of others who may possess significant information. Moreover, in most instances, these interrogations, particularly of the suspect, most be conducted under conditions of privacy and for a reasonable period of time. They also frequently require the use of psychological tactics and techniques that could well be classified as "unethical," if we are to evaluate them in terms of ordinary, everyday social behavior.

To protect ourselves from being misunderstood, we want to make it unmistakably clear that we are unalterably opposed to the so-called "third degree," even on suspects whose guilt seems absolutely certain and who remain steadfast in their denials. Moreover, we are opposed to the use of any interrogation tactic or technique that is apt to make an innocent person confess. We are opposed, therefore, to the use of force, threats of force, or promises of leniency—any one of which might well induce an innocent person to confess. We do approve, however, of such psychological tactics and techniques as trickery and deceit that are not only helpful but frequently indispensable in order to secure incriminating information form the guilty, or to obtain investigative leads from otherwise uncooperative witnesses or informants...

... In Dealing with Criminal Offenders, and Consequently Also with Criminal Suspects Who May Actually Be Innocent, the Interrogator Must of Necessity Employ Less Refined Methods Than Are Considered Appropriate for the Transaction of Ordinary, Everyday Affairs by and between Law-Abiding Citizens...

... From the criminal's point of view, any interrogation is unappealing and undesirable. To him it may be a "dirty trick" to encourage him to confess, for surely it is not being done for his benefit. Consequently, any interrogation might be labeled as deceitful or unethical, unless the suspect is first advised of its real purpose.

Of necessity, therefore, interrogators must deal with criminal suspects on a somewhat lower moral plane than that upon which ethical, law-abiding citizens are expected to conduct their everyday business affairs. That plane, in the interest of innocent suspects, need only be subject to the following restriction: Although both "fair" and "unfair" interrogation practices are permissible, nothing shall be done or said to the suspect that will be apt to make an innocent person confess.

There are other ways to guard against abuses by criminal interrogators short of taking the privilege away from them or by establishing unrealistic, unwarranted rules that render their task almost totally ineffective. Moreover, we could no more afford to do that than we could stand the effects of a law requiring automobile manufacturers to place governors on all cars so that, in order to make the highways safer, no one could go faster than 20 miles an hour.

[FROM CHAPTER ONE]

... Remember that when circumstantial evidence points toward a particular person, that person is usually the one who committed the offense. This may become difficult for some investigators and interrogators to appreciate when circumstantial evidence points to someone they consider highly unlikely to be the type of person who would commit such an offense, for example, a clergyman who is circumstantially implicated in a sexually-motivated murder. By reason of his exalted position, he may be interrogated only casually or perhaps not at all, and yet it is an established fact that some clergymen do commit such offenses.

[FROM CHAPTER FOUR]

...Recognize that in everyone there is some good, however slight it may be. The interrogator should seek to determine at the outset what desirable traits and qualities maybe possessed by the particular suspect. Thereafter, the interrogator can capitalize on those characteristics in the efforts toward a successful interrogation. The following example may seem to be an implausible one, but it actually happened during an ultimately successful interrogation of the perpetrator of a brutal crime. Reference was made to the kind treatment he had rendered his pet cat! The suspect was told that if he himself had been treated similarly by fellow humans, he would not have developed the attitude that led to his present difficulty. This proved to be very helpful in eliciting his confession.

[FROM CHAPTER FIVE]

Evaluation of Verbal and Nonverbal Responses

VERBAL RESPONSES

The period of time within which a verbal response is made to a probing question may be the first indication of truth or deception. An immediate response is a sign of truthfulness; a delay in answering indicates the possibility that the answer may be deceptive. This analysis is based upon the theory that a simple, direct, and unambiguous question does not require much deliberation before an answer is given. A delayed response, however, usually reflects an attempt to contrive a false answer. Another significant factor is whether or not the suspect answers the question directly. An answer such as "Who me?" or "I was home all day" or "I don't own a gun" are not responsive answers to the direct question concerning the crime itself. They are evasive answers and typically are deceptive. The same is true of a suspect's attempt to deviate from the subject matter altogether by injecting a comment that is unrelated to the objective of the question.

Also indicative of deception is suspect's repetition of the interrogator's question or a request that the interrogator repeat it or clarify it. For example, the suspect may say, in regard to an inquiry of his whereabouts on the day prior to the crime, "Do you mean yesterday, sir?," or in an arson case, he may respond to a comparable question by asking "Do you mean did I start the fire?" even though he had just been asked a question only as to his whereabouts at the time of the fire. What this signifies is that the suspect is stalling for time in order to formulate what he thinks will be the most defensible response.

A suspect who hesitates in answering a question by saying "Let me see now," prior to saying "no" is seeking to achieve two objectives: 1) to borrow time to deliberate on how to lie effectively or to remember previous statements, and 2) to camouflage true guilty reactions with the expression of a pretended serious thought.

The truthful suspect does not have to ponder over an answer. He really has only one answer, and it will be substantially the same, regardless of any repetition of the inquiry. Truthful suspects are not required to depend on a good memory, whereas liars are vulnerable and must be particularly careful to avoid making conflicting statements...

... Any suspect who is overly polite, even to the point of repeatedly calling the interrogator "sir" may be attempting to flatter the interrogator to gain his confidence. The suspect who, after being accused, says "No offense to you, sir, but I didn't do it," "I know you are just doing your job," or "I understand what you are saying" is evidencing his lying about the matter under investigation. A truthful suspect has no need to make such apologetic statements, or even to explain that he understands the interrogator's accusatory statements. To the contrary, the truthful suspect may very well react aggressively with a direct denial or by using strong language indicating anger over the implied accusation...

NONVERBAL RESPONSES

... Generally speaking, a suspect who does not make direct eye contact is probably being untruthful. However, some consideration should be given to the possibility of an eye disability, inferiority complex, or emotional instability, any of which may account for the avoidance of eye contact. Also, some cultural or religious customs consider it disrespectful for a person to look directly at an "authority figure." Background information on the suspect, of course, may alert the interrogator regarding these or similar nondeceptive causes of a lack of eye contact...

EMOTIONAL CONDITION

In addition to precautions regarding the behavior symptoms of suspects, where doubt arises as to the validity of a crime reported by the purported victim, it is imperative to consider that the traumatic experience of the crime itself may produce reactions of nervousness or instability, which might be misinterpreted as indications of falsity. For example, a normally nervous-type victim who has just been robbed at gunpoint may be honestly confused or disoriented by the experience, and consequently may seem to be untruthful about the report of the incident. Or, a wife whose husband has been shot to death in her presence may have been so shocked by what she observed that her version of the incident soon thereafter may seem untruthful, when in fact she truthfully reported what occurred.

Another example of how misleading behavior symptoms may surface is one in which a male friend of a female murder victim was interrogated about her death. He displayed a number of symptoms, according to his initial interrogators. It was reported that he could not look them "straight in the eye," that he sighed a lot, that he had a disheveled appearance, and that he seemed to be going through a great deal of mental anguish. An investigator reported that "He looked guilty as hell!" During a subsequent interrogation, conducted by a professionally competent interrogator, however, it was ascertained that the suspect was emotionally upset because of the young woman's death and that he had been crying uncontrollably over it. He simply had not verbally or demonstrably disclosed to the interrogators the extent of his grief. The investigators mistakenly confused his emotional behavior as indicative of guilt, and therefore, he became the prime suspect. Later developments in the case produced factual evidence that totally exonerated him from any part in the murder.

[FROM CHAPTER SIX]

Tactics and Techniques for the Interrogation of Suspects Whose Guilt Seems Definite or Reasonably Certain — The Nine Steps to Effectiveness

The authors again wish to make clear that the word "guilt" as used in this text only signifies the interrogator's opinion. In no way does it connote legal guilt based upon proof beyond a reasonable doubt. Accordingly, it is in that context this chapter presents the tactics and techniques for the interrogation of suspects whose guilt, in the *opinion* of the interrogator, seems definite or reasonably certain. Among them are *the nine steps* to effectiveness.

GENERAL CLASSIFICATION OF OFFENDERS

The selection of interrogation procedures depends to a considerable extent upon the personal characteristics of the suspect himself, the type of offense, the probable motivation for its commission, and the suspect's initial behavioral responses. On the basis of these considerations, criminal offenders are subject to a rather broad, yet flexible, classification into either *emotional offenders* or *nonemotional offenders*.

Emotional offender refers to an offender who ordinarily experiences a considerable feeling of remorse, mental anguish, or compunction as a result of his offense. This individual has a strong sense of moral guilt—in other words, a "troubled conscience." Emotional offenders can be identified behaviorally during an interrogation in that they tend to be emotionally moved by the interrogator's words and actions. As the interrogation progresses, the emotional offender may develop watery eyes and body posture will become less rigid and more open, without crossed arms and legs. The subject's eye contact with the interrogator will become less frequent, eventually culminating in a vacant stare at the floor. Because of the "troubled conscience" feeling, the most effective interrogation tactics and techniques to use on such a suspect are those based primarily upon a *sympathetic approach* — expressions of understanding and compassion with regard to the commission of the offense as well as the suspect's present difficulty.

Nonemotional offender refers to a person who ordinarily does not experience a troubled conscience. He may react emotionally, but usually to a lesser degree than that experienced by emotional offenders. During interrogation, the nonemotional offender may offer token, unchallenging denials of guilt that are stopped easily. The suspect is quite content to allow the interrogator to talk, but the words fall on seemingly deaf ears as the suspect maintains a defensive, closed posture, including crossed arms, erect head and a cold, hard stare...

The most effective tactic and techniques to use on the nonemotional offender are those based primarily upon a *factual analysis approach*. This approach means appealing to the suspect's common sense and reason rather than to his emotions; it is designed to convince him that his guilt already is established and, consequently, there is nothing else to do but to admit it.

As a general rule, the majority of all offenders, emotional and nonemotional, possess emotional traits to some degree. For this reason, the sympathetic and factual analysis approaches often should be intermingled. Greater emphasis will be placed, however, upon one or the other, depending on the type of offender.

As a result of many years' experience, primarily on the part of the staff of John E. Reid and associates under the guidance of the late John E. Reid, (one of the co-authors of the present text), the interrogation process has been formulated into nine structural components — *the nine steps* of criminal interrogation. These nine steps are presented in the context of the interrogation of suspects *whose guilt seems definite or reasonably certain*. It must be remembered that none of the steps is apt to make an innocent person confess and that all of the steps are legally as well as morally justifiable. For those persons who have qualms or reservations about utilizing some of the steps, this chapter subsequently presents various justification factors.

In utilizing *the nine steps* approach to an effective interrogation, the interrogator should keep in mind two points:

1. The numerical sequence does not signify that every interrogation will encompass all nine steps, or that those that are used must conform to a specific sequence.

2. As each step is used, the interrogator should be on the alert to evaluate whatever behavioral responses the suspect may be displaying; the responses themselves may be suggestive of the next appropriate step.

BRIEF ANALYSIS OF THE NINE STEPS

Step 1 involves a direct, positively presented confrontation of the suspect with a statement that he is considered to be the person who committed the offense. At this stage, the interrogator should pause to evaluate the suspect's response. Before proceeding to the next step, the interrogator should repeat the accusation. The tone and nature of this reception will depend upon whether the suspect seemed passive or voided a positive denial after first being accused. If passive, the second accusation should be expressed with the same or even greater degree of conviction. Care must be taken, however, to enunciate very clearly the second accusation so as to obviate the possibility of any misunderstanding. If the suspect's reaction to the second confrontation is as passive acts the one to the initial confrontation, that fact in itself is an indication of deception. On the other hand, if the suspect is quite direct and forceful in denying the first accusation, the second accusation may be reduced in tone and nature and the interrogator should proceed to *Step 2*, even though *Step 1* created a lessening confidence in his initial assumption of the suspect's guilt.

In **Step 2** the interrogator expresses a supposition about the reason for the crime's commission, whereby the suspect should be offered a possible moral excuse for having committed the offense. To accomplish this, the interrogator should attempt to affix moral blame of the offense upon some other person (e.g., an accomplice), the victim, or some other particular circumstance (e.g., an urgent need by the suspect of money in order for the suspect to support himself or family). If a suspect seems to listen attentively to the suggested "theme," or seems to be deliberating about it, even for a short period of time, that reaction is strongly suggestive of guilt. On the other hand, if the suspect expresses resentment over the mere submission of such a suggestion, this reaction may be indicative of innocence.

Up to this point, a guilty person, as well as an innocent one, will have denied guilt. The interrogator should then embark upon **Step 3**, which consists of suggested procedures for handling the initial denials of guilt. Basically, this step involves cutting off the suspect's repetition or elaboration of the denial and returning to the moral excuse theme that comprises *Step 2*. An innocent person will not allow such denials to be cut off; furthermore, he will attempt more or less to "take over" the situation rather that to submit passively to continued interrogation. On the other hand, a guilty person usually will cease to voice a denial, or else the denial will be weak, and he will submit the to the interrogator's return to a theme.

Step 4 involves the task of overcoming the suspect's comments about the moral excuse element presented in *Step 2*. These comments will consist of what may be viewed as "objections" from the suspect, presented in the form of explanations as to *why the suspect did not* or *could not* commit the crime. These responses are normally offered by the guilty suspect, particularly when they come after the denial phase of the interrogation.

They are significant in that they constitute evasions of a bold denial by the substitution of the less courageous statement as to *why* the suspect did not or could not commit the offense under investigation. Such an objection causes less internal anxiety than the utterance of an outright denial.

Step 5 consists of the procurement and retention of the suspect's full attention, without which the interrogation may amount to no more than an exercise in futility. During *Step 5*, the interrogator will clearly display a sincerity in what he says. Helpful in achieving this is an increase in the closeness of the previously described seating arrangement between interrogator and suspect. The same is true of the physical gestures the interrogator can employ, such as a pat on the shoulder or, in the case of a female, a gentle holding of the suspect's hand.

Step 6 involves the handling of the suspect's passive mood. This step should occur when the suspect becomes quiet, displays a tendency to listen, or tries to avoid looking directly at the interrogator. Physical signs of "giving up" may begin to appear. At this point, there should be a reinforcement of eye contact between the suspect and the interrogator. Tears that may appear in the suspect's eyes at this time usually are indicative of deception and also of a "giving up" attitude.

Step 7 is the utilization of an alternative question—a suggestion of a choice to be made by the suspect between an "acceptable" and an "unacceptable" crime. This choice will be in the form of a question, such as: "Was this the first time, or has it happened many times before?" Whichever alternative is chosen by the subject, the net effect of an expressed choice will be the functional equivalent of an incriminating admission.

Following the selection of an alternative, **Step 8** involves having the suspect orally relate the various details about the offense that will serve ultimately to establish legal guilt. These details can include where the fatal weapon was discarded or where the stolen money was hidden and the motive for the crime's commission.

Finally, **Step 9** relates to the confession itself. This step involves the recommended procedure for converting an oral confession into a written one and is presented later in this text.

APPENDIX B

The following is an edited excerpt from a police interrogation of the thirteen-year-old rape victim in Peter Rose's case. The interrogation took place in Lodi, California on December 20, 1994. The identities of the interrogation participants have been concealed.

DETECTIVE ONE: So we have two stories that were out there: what really happened and what you told us. That's fine. I can accept that. What do you want me to tell your grandfather?

VICTIM: I don't know.

D1: Well, I'm gonna have to go out there and I'm gonna have to talk to him. OK? I wanna know what you want me to tell 'em. I wanna make this easy for you too. I wanna go out there and I wanna say: [your granddaughter] and I've had a long talk and we've decided that maybe things didn't happened that way she originally say and the case is pretty much over. You think he's gonna be able to accept that? He's gonna wanna know why. Why is the case over?

DETECTIVE TWO: Why is [the] police abandoning a rape case of a thirteen-year-old girl on her way to school.

V: First stories that I told you... it did happen, but I wasn't telling all the truth. He did hit me. I'm not lying. And he did take me behind that house. He did get my pants down. 'Cause, he did tell me that he was gonna kill me if I didn't listen to him, so I listened to him cause I didn't want him to hurt me. And then... he... did what he did.

D1: What did he do?

V: Pulled down my pants from behind me and stuck his penis in my vagina. He did; I'm not lying. I'm not... I'm... telling the truth.

D1: ... I'm still listening.

V: 'Cause you looked at me and I thought...

D1: Uh huh.

V: Then he stood up and walked me back out to the alley, and then he walked me back out further to a fence—I don't know which one it was.

D1: Yeah, but the first story you're saying this fence. No! It was *this* fence. No! THIS fence. You know. I can appreciate the fact what you're telling me is: you don't know what fence it was.

V: I don't know what fence. I was scared. I wasn't paying attention.

D1: OK. I can believe that. What happened to the guy you pointed out?

V: (pause) I didn't know if it was him. I just pointed anybody out. I was paranoid.

D1: Uh huh. So we've been chasing a ghost for three weeks.

D1 or D2: What was he really wearing?

V: I don't know.

D1: Well, you saw him standing across the street. What did his face look like?

V: I don't know. I didn't see.

D1: You looked at 'em. He wasn't hiding. You looked at 'em. You saw him standing across the street. He walks across, comes in behind you. And he didn't follow you for three blocks. That's a long, long ways to be following a little girl and just to decide to grab her and drag her off someplace. That's a long ways.

V: He did, though. He did follow me. Where the bricks are, at the church—that church, that's were I saw 'em.

D1: OK. (long pause) Do you know who this guy was?

V: No. I'm not sure though. Because I don't wanna say if it is or not.

D1: Tell me who.

V: His name is Pete. He lives on Sutter Street, and my [aunt] Wendy talked to his girlfriend and his girlfriend said that he wasn't home... that morning... and he's been... acting [weird]... ever since.

D1: How do you know Pete?

V: He used to live next door.

D1: Have you ever seen Pete on the way to school before? (long pause) OK. Let's cut to the chase a little bit. Was it Pete?

V: I don't know. Seriously, I don't know.

D1: What [does] acting weird mean?

V: She said that she—he's been acting weird lately. She said it—I didn't.

D1: OK. But did you come back with the same question that I have: What do you mean?

V: Yeah. She said I don't know; he's been acting weird lately.

D1: Like he's on drugs.

V: Like...

D1: Like he's drunk.

V: He's been paranoid, she said—like he's been paranoid.

D1: Is this why you didn't run, that morning? Because you recognized that person as, as Pete?

V: Deep down I... don't know.

D1: Is it possible—is it possible...?

V: It could be Pete?

D1: Yeah. And that you don't want to identify him because you're afraid of what—if you were wrong.

V: I don't know. I... can't say it is or not. What if it's not?

D1: If it's not, it's not. If it's not, it's not. OK, but you're going to have to give us an explanation here, because this is our fifth or sixth story, and this isn't—truly, I don't know about [Detective Two], but this is not what I expected you to tell us. Is it possible that there could have been something agreed upon that got out of hand that morning as far as you and this guy? Maybe you talked to him, and—you know, he told you that you were real pretty...

D2: And then when this is all done, he says, "If you tell anybody..."

V: He just told me that if I told anybody that he would find out, and I was thinking how would he find out? Find out by my aunt?

D1: We're asking you, dear.

V: I don't know.

D1: OK, but why this story versus the one you told us originally?

V: What do you mean?

D1: You tell us. You just gave [Detective Two] this version. We'll call it Pete's ver-

460

sion. The "Pete Story." Why tell the Peter Story now?

V: This is the truth.

D1: Is there any part of the Pete Story that you should fill in some more blanks—because you know full well who it is.

V: I'm not saying it's Pete. I think it's him.

D1: We're falling back to square one, rapidly. We started to move ahead.

D2: You started making some progress. Now you're changing your story.

D1: You're not sticking to it. You told us the Pete Story, and now you're backing off of it.

V: I don't understand what you're saying.

D1: You start the Pete Story—you tell us that, "I see this guy." You bring Pete into it but you can't justify why. Justify it for us, meaning tell us why you think it's him. Or, why you're not sure it's him.

D2: But just don't throw us the name and let us hang there, because you did that, and I wasted three weeks. What happened that morning?

V: What I told you guys.

D2: Why do you think it's Pete?

V: Because, afterwards his girlfriend told me, "I think it was him."

D2: You saw this guy; you're talking back and forth with him; you've seen him and talked with him before.

V: I didn't see his face.

D2: Yes you did. And if somebody's sitting there saying, "I'll find out about this," well, good. I hope he does. Because if he didn't do it, he doesn't have anything to worry about. But if he did do it, then he's my problem, not yours. OK?

D1: Let me ask you this. If I'm not in this room, would you share another story with [Detective Two]? OK—you're a thirteen-year-old girl and we're grown men, and we don't generally interview thirteen-year-old girls by ourselves, especially after hours with the Division closed up. I understand why you don't want to talk to me, and I don't take that personally because I'm very good at making people look themselves in the mirror. We just want to make sure that we can actually say, "That's it. That makes sense."

D2: So far, we're still not quite there.

D1: It's a heck of lot better than it was.

D2: But we're still not there.

D1: And I think you can probably see that in our faces. And you can probably understand why we don't 100 percent buy on that, just yet.

D2: What we gotta work on is [that] we think it's Pete, but you saw this guy. You talked with this guy; he's got his hands on you; he's taking you someplace you don't want to go; you're looking at him; you're looking at his clothes; you're describing him; you're listening to his voice; you've heard and seen Pete before. What makes you think that this guy you saw that day was Pete?

V: I want to explain things to you guys, but you guys don't listen to me. You guys always cut in. You asked me why did I think it's Pete. I didn't know who it was. I don't know who it was. Afterward, Pete's girlfriend told us about Pete—it had me thinking that it was Pete.

D1: You saw this guy that hurt you standing on the corner by the church, by the bricks—was it Pete?

V: I don't know. I didn't see his face all the way. I was across the street, and he was on this side.

D1: If you saw the side of your grandfather's face... Is it your grandfather?

V: Yeah.

D1: You've seen Pete before.

D2: You know him. He makes you feel uncomfortable.

V: I don't know him personally.

D2: I don't know Bill Clinton, but he makes me feel uncomfortable, and I recognize him when I see him.

D1: We're the same two guys still sitting here that want to help you, but we can't put words in your mouth. But we recognize there's more to a story than what you want to willingly say. I think you're scared.

V: I'm telling you guys the truth now. I'm telling you guys the story, and you guys are still not believing me.

D1: I didn't say that. I said I believe it. So far, I'm not saying you're lying to me. I'm saying I need you to fill in a little bit more. I know you're scared, believe me I know you're scared, because this is as close to telling the whole truth as you have been in this whole thing, and I want to believe you, but I don't want to see us take any steps backwards because it's taken us two and a half hours to get to where we are right now. And I don't want to see us take any steps backwards. Fill in some of these gaps for me.

If it happened the way you're telling us you should be able to fill in everything, OK? You were there; I wasn't there. You have to tell me the whole story.

D2: You've got "A," "B," "D," "F." We want "C" and "E" now in the story. OK?

D1: Let me draw you a picture. A picture's worth a thousand words. We're gonna call this the Pete Story, OK? These boxes are going to represent just what happened as you've told us so far in the Pete Story. There's this part you haven't told us yet. So, tell us this part that you haven't told us yet. Tell us this part; so it all makes sense, and we can go "Yeah! OK!" Tell us the entire story, front to end, and how we got to Pete.

V: OK.

D1: The whole thing, one time through, no gaps.

V: OK. I seen him at the church, where the cable car turns.

D1: Who?

V: I don't know.

D1: You almost said Pete; I watched ya.

V: Uh-hmm. I don't know if it's Pete or not. I don't want to say it is or not. And you guys keep on asking me, "Is it Pete? Is it Pete?"

D1: You're the one who said Pete. Not us.

V: I think it's Pete.

D1: OK.

V: I saw whoever person it was by the cable box, so I kept on walking. Then whoever it was crossed the street to my side. And he was still following me, so I turned to [a] house and knocked and nobody answered. And then... I'm not sure, but I think he probably went through apartments and went back to the alley to the phone. I was just gonna keep on walking towards my bus stop, and then I turned, and I noticed he was right there, so I walked faster, and then we were at the corner of one of the alleys, and he came up to me, and he put his arm around me, and he hit me.

Then he took me by a car, and he goes, "No, this is not a good spot." And I asked him what he was gonna do to me, and he told me that he just wanted me to watch him do something. And then he took me behind the house.

I tried to get away. And then we were up the alley towards the house, and I was trying to look at him, and he asked me to pull my pants down and I tried to keep them up and then he got my pants down and he tell me to get down, and then I got down and he told me to get on my hands and knees. So I did that and then...

D1: ...Did whatever...

V: I was embarrassed...

D1: I know, but I've got to know everything that was going on so I can go out there and put a stop to this thing. OK? You have to be able to tell me everything that was going on, and I know you're embarrassed, and you're not going to tell me anything that I haven't heard. OK. He takes you behind that house and...? He had you do something else, didn't he?

V: No, I don't know how to tell you that.

D1: What's this part you're having trouble tell[ing] me?

V: Between my butt...

D1: And... then what happened?

V: [Inaudible]... [crying]... I was... he let me go... he jumped over a fence and left...

D1: What else? Something more was going on behind the house, wasn't it? You wouldn't be crying like this—I've heard that story before, and you didn't cry like this then. I've heard that story before. You need to fill in all the blocks. Come on, you're doing great. Something's got you really scared right now, doesn't it? What is it? Come on.

V: ... kept turning me over, and then he made me...

D1: Does the thought of that embarrass you more? Tell me why.

V: Because it's invasion.

D1: Was his penis hard or soft when he made you suck it.

V: Hard.

D1: It was hard. Did anything come out of his penis in your mouth?

V: No.

D1: OK. Was there a reason why you didn't tell Wendy that you knew it was Pete?

V: I was embarrassed to, and I was scared like she would go by and tell him something.

D1: Let me ask you this. What embarrasses you or makes you feel the most uncomfortable about telling us that it's Pete?

V: I don't know.

D1: Well, you know, we've gone through quite a bit here, almost three hours' worth. Why is Pete such an obstacle to tell us?

V: Why am I scared to tell it? Because he's scary, he scares me and when he said he was going to kill me, that's what scared me most.

D1: But the reason you didn't want to—-let me make sure I have it right—because you were scared, because you were embarrassed because you had to suck his penis.

V: Uh-huh.

D1: OK. So, when this Pete put his penis in your butt, how long was he in there?

V: Like a minute and then it pulled away.

D1: Were you still on your hands and knees—so did you move forward?

V: Uh-huh, and then he pulled me back.

D1: And then put his penis in your vagina?

V: Uh-huh.

D1: What does his penis look like?

V: It's... I really don't know how to explain...

D1: Is it huge?

V: It's kind of long?

D1: Show me on your hands how long do you think it is?

V: About like this.

D1: Okay, now you're showing me something that is about nine to ten inches.

V: I don't know, I didn't measure it.

D1: I understand. I understand that. But later on you might have to describe this. This guy has a wiener when he's hard only this big, you're telling me that it's this big: big discrepancy.

V: I don't know. I didn't really look, I closed my eyes I didn't want to look. I closed 'em. He put my head down and I closed my eyes real fast. And then he put in there, in my mouth. I tried to get away from him.

D1: OK, that's fine. I'm not saying that you're not saying the right thing. So did he put himself back in his pants? And you guys stopped?

V: Uh-huh.

D1: OK. Is there anybody, your best friend in the whole world, that you trust more than anything that you've told this story to?

V: No. I have a best friend, but I haven't told anybody nothing.

D1: Have you told anybody even close to what you've told us?

V: No, just the very first story I've told.

D2: Okay. Feel any better?

D1: Is there anything from this point on, that [Detective Two] or I still need some more puzzle pieces put in?

V: I don't know. I don't know what you guys want.

APPENDIX C

Excerpts from Massachusetts bill 104H8F, enacted December 30, 2004.
The bill provides compensation for the wrongfully convicted.

PART III. COURTS, JUDICIAL OFFICERS AND
PROCEEDINGS IN CIVIL CASES

TITLE IV. CERTAIN WRITS AND PROCEEDINGS IN SPECIAL CASES CHAP-
TER 258D. COMPENSATION FOR CERTAIN ERRONEOUS FELONY CON-
VICTIONS

ALM GL ch. 258D, ß 1 (2005)

ß 1. Eligibility for Compensation.

(A) A claim may be brought against the commonwealth for an erroneous felony conviction resulting in incarceration as provided in this chapter.

(B) The class of persons eligible to obtain relief under this chapter shall be limited to the
following:
(i) those that have been granted a full pardon pursuant to *section 152 of chapter 127*, if
the governor expressly states in writing his belief in the individual's innocence, or
(ii) those who have been granted judicial relief by a state court of competent jurisdiction, on grounds which tend to establish the innocence of the individual as set forth in
clause (vi) of subsection (C), and if (a) the judicial relief vacates or reverses the judgment
of a felony conviction, and the felony indictment or complaint used to charge the individual with such felony has been dismissed, or if a new trial was ordered, the individual
was not retried and the felony indictment or complaint was dismissed or a nolle prose-
qui was entered, or if a new trial was ordered the individual was found not guilty at the
new trial; and (b) at the time of the filing of an action under this chapter no criminal
proceeding is pending or can be brought against the individual by a district attorney or
the attorney general for any act associated with such felony conviction.

(C) In order for an individual to prevail and recover damages against the commonwealth
in a cause of action brought under this chapter, the individual must establish, by clear
and convincing evidence, that:

(i) he is a member of the class of persons defined in subsection (B);

(ii) he was convicted of an offense classified as a felony;

(iii) he did not plead guilty to the offense charged, or to any lesser included offense,
unless such guilty plea was withdrawn, vacated or nullified by operation of law on a basis
other than a claimed deficiency in the plea warnings required by *section 29D of chapter
278*;

(iv) he was sentenced to incarceration for not less than 1 year in state prison or a house of correction as a result of the conviction and has served all or any part of such sentence;

(v) he was incarcerated solely on the basis of the conviction for the offense that is the subject of the claim;

(vi) he did not commit the crimes or crime charged in the indictment or complaint or any other felony arising out of or reasonably connected to the facts supporting the indictment or complaint, or any lesser included felony; and

(vii) to the extent that he is guilty of conduct that would have justified a conviction of any lesser included misdemeanor arising out of or reasonably connected to facts supporting the indictment or complaint, that he has served the maximum sentence he would have received for such lesser included misdemeanor and not less than one additional year in a prison.

(D) The claimant shall attach to his claim certified copies of: the mittimus that shows the claimant's sentence to incarceration and; the warrants necessary to grant a pardon pursuant to *section 152 of chapter 127* or; criminal case docket entries or documents related thereto in the case of judicial relief.

(E) For the purposes of this chapter "conviction" or "convicted" shall include an adjudication as a youthful offender, if such adjudication resulted in the youthful offender's incarceration in a house of correction or state prison.

(F) The commonwealth and any individual filing an action for compensation under this chapter shall have the right to a jury trial on any action so filed. In the interest of doing substantial justice, with regard to weight and admissibility of evidence submitted by the claimant or the commonwealth, the court presiding at a jury-waived trial shall exercise its discretion by giving due consideration to any difficulties of proof caused by the passage of time, the death or unavailability or witnesses, or other factors not caused by the claimant, or those acting on the claimant's or the commonwealth's behalf. At a jury trial, the court shall consider these same factors as part of the exercise of its discretion when determining the admissibility and weight of evidence, and the court shall instruct the jury that it may consider the same factors when it weighs the evidence presented at trial. No evidence proffered by any party shall be excluded on grounds that it was seized or obtained in violation of the Fourth, Fifth or *Sixth amendments to the Constitution of the United States*, or in violation of Articles 12 or 14 of Part the First of the Constitution of Massachusetts.

ALM GL ch. 258D, ß 2 (2005)

ß 2. Concurrent Sentence and Time Credited.

A claimant shall not be entitled to compensation from the commonwealth for any incarceration or portion thereof, which was or will be credited toward a sentence for, or during which the claimant was also serving a concurrent sentence for the conviction of another crime. In those cases in which only a pardon from the governor is used to support a pending action against the commonwealth brought under this chapter, the subsequent exercise of the governor's authority to revoke such pardon pursuant to *section 152 of chapter 127* shall immediately negate the validity of any such pending action and the superior court shall immediately issue a summary judgment in favor of the commonwealth on such grounds.

ALM GL ch. 258D, ß 3 (2005)

ß 3. Jurisdiction.

A civil action brought against the commonwealth under this chapter shall be brought in the county where the claimant was convicted or in Suffolk county. The superior court shall have exclusive jurisdiction of all such actions. All civil actions brought pursuant to this chapter shall in all manner proceed by and be governed by the rules of civil procedure except as otherwise expressly provided in this chapter.

ALM GL ch. 258D, ß 4 (2005)

ß 4. Defense of Action; Offering and Acceptance of Award.

Service of process for a civil action brought pursuant to this chapter shall be made upon the attorney general for the commonwealth who shall defend the commonwealth against all such claims. The attorney general shall immediately notify the district attorney for the county that prosecuted the felony that forms the basis for the claim. Any district attorney so notified by the attorney general shall immediately notify any individual meeting the definition of "victim", as set forth in section 1 or chapter 258B, of the felony conviction that forms the basis of the claim. Any such victim shall be allowed, but may not be compelled, to testify or furnish other evidence. If such victim is unavailable to testify or decides not to testify, his prior recorded testimony, given under oath at a relevant proceeding, shall only be admissible after judicial review and determination that such testimony, or portion thereof, may be helpful to the factfinder. The attorney general shall consult with the appropriate district attorney relative to the merits of such action and, following consultation, shall have discretion to determine whether to proffer as evidence any documents, records, testimony or other information brought forward to the attorney general by such district attorney in defense of the commonwealth at a time deemed appropriate by the attorney general. The attorney general may arbitrate or settle any claim for damages filed under this chapter, but any award or settlement in excess of $ 80,000 shall be made only with the prior approval of the secretary of administration and finance. The acceptance by the claimant of any such award or settlement shall be in writing and shall, except when procured by fraud, be final and conclusive on the claimant, and shall constitute a complete release of any claim by the claimant against the commonwealth and a complete bar to any action by the claimant against the commonwealth by reason of the same subject matter.

ALM GL ch. 258D, ß 5 (2005)

ß 5. Damages.

(A) Upon a finding or verdict that the claimant has met the requirements of section 1 by the requisite standard of proof and is not barred from compensation by section 2, the court or the jury shall determine the damages that shall be payable to the claimant. In making such determination, the court or jury shall consider, but not be limited to, the consideration of: the income the claimant would have earned, but for his incarceration; the particular circumstances of the claimant's trial and other proceedings; the length and conditions under which the claimant was incarcerated and; any other factors deemed appropriate under the circumstances in order to fairly and reasonably compensate the claimant. The court, in its discretion, may admit expert testimony on these or any fac-

tors. The court may include, as part of its judgment against the commonwealth, an order requiring the commonwealth to provide the claimant with services that are reasonable and necessary to address any deficiencies in the individual's physical and emotional condition that are shown to be directly related to the individual's erroneous felony conviction and resulting incarceration through documentary or oral evidence presented to the court or jury by the claimant as part of the claim if the claimant provided in his original claim for compensation under this chapter:
(i) the nature of the services that he seeks; and
(ii) the agencies, departments or commissions of the commonwealth from which he seeks to receive such services. Any such agency, department or commission so named in the claim shall be entitled to reasonable notice of the court proceedings pertaining to the possible ordering of such services and shall be given an opportunity to be heard on whether such agency is the appropriate entity to provide such services if so ordered.

The court may also include in its judgment an order that entitles any claimant who wishes to apply for and receive educational services from any state or community college of the commonwealth including, but not limited to, the University of Massachusetts at Amherst and its satellite campuses, a 50 percent reduction of the tuition and fees applicable to such services at said institutions. Once the damages have been determined, the court shall enter a judgment against the commonwealth for the claimant in an amount certain, payable in either a lump sum or in annuity installment payments set by the court; provided, however, that any such annuity installment payments shall have fixed limits on their annual amount and on the time period which they shall be paid to the claimant. A judgment against the commonwealth may not include punitive or exemplary damages. The total liability of the commonwealth for any judgment entered under this chapter shall not exceed $ 500,000. Notwithstanding any general or special law to the contrary, the clerk of court shall not add to the judgment and the commonwealth shall not be liable for paying, any prejudgment or post judgment interest on damages. Subject to section 4, relative to award or settlements, the rights and remedies afforded to certain individuals by this chapter are not intended to limit in any way any rights or remedies that such individuals or other individuals may be entitled to exercise and pursue under chapter 258.

(B) In awarding damages under this section, the court or jury shall not offset the award by any expenses incurred by the commonwealth or any political subdivision of the commonwealth including, but not limited to, expenses incurred to secure the claimant's custody, or to feed, clothe or provide medical services for the claimant nor shall the court offset against the award the value of any reduction in tuition or fees for educational services or the value of services to be provided to the claimant that may be awarded to the claimant pursuant to this section.

(C) The commonwealth shall not be liable to levy of execution on any real or personal property to satisfy a judgment ordered pursuant to this chapter. Any judgments ordered by the court pursuant to this chapter shall be paid from funds appropriated by the general court for such purpose. Payments by the commonwealth under this chapter are made to remedy the claimant's injury of unjust incarceration. Only those portions of a judgment that are paid or retained as compensation for services in bringing a claim under this chapter by an attorney representing the claimant pursuant to a signed agreement with the claimant or otherwise shall be subject to taxation by the commonwealth.

(D) The court shall give due consideration to the possible bifurcation of court proceedings to separate the consideration of issues to be resolved by the court, as required by sections 1 and 2, from the determination of reasonable damages and other relief as required by this section.

ALM GL ch. 258D, ß 6 (2005)

ß 6. Frivolous and Bad Faith Claims and Defenses.

Any party to an action filed under this chapter is entitled to make a motion seeking costs, expenses and interest for wholly insubstantial, frivolous or bad faith claims or defenses advanced by the opposing party during proceedings under this chapter as set forth in section 6F of chapter 231 and is also entitled to the rights of appeal afforded parties in a civil action following a decision on such motions as set forth in *section 6G of said chapter 231.*

ALM GL ch. 258D, ß 7 (2005)

ß 7. Criminal Records.

(A) Upon the entry of a judgment in favor of a claimant under this chapter and following a separate hearing on the matter, the court shall enter an order either directing the expungement or sealing of those records of the claimant maintained by the criminal history systems board, the probation department, and the sex offender registry that directly pertain to the claimant's erroneous felony conviction case, including documents and other materials and any samples obtained from the claimant. The commonwealth, as well as any other law enforcement agency that may be directly affected by such expungement or sealing of such records including, but not limited to, the district attorney that prosecuted the felony case against the claimant, shall be given reasonable notice and an opportunity to be heard on the issue of whether such records, documents and materials shall be so expunged or sealed. In making its determination as to whether such records, documents and materials shall be so expunged or sealed, the court shall consider the interests of privacy and justice pertaining to the claimant's erroneous felony conviction as well as the probable effect of such expungement or sealing on relevant law enforcement entities and their ability to appropriately investigate and prosecute other persons for the felony which forms the basis of the claim or other crimes that may relate to the information contained in such records, documents and materials.

(B) Following a separate hearing conducted by the court, the court may also order the expungement or sealing of those records that directly pertain to the claimant's erroneous felony conviction case that are currently in the care, custody and control of other state, municipal or local departments, agencies, commissions or committees, including law enforcement entities. Any such agency, commission, committee or entity shall be given reasonable notice and an opportunity to be heard on the issue of whether such records, documents and materials shall be expunged or sealed pursuant to this section. In making its determination as to whether such records, documents and materials shall be expunged or sealed, the court shall consider those factors required for consideration by the court in paragraph (A).

(C) Any order to expunge or seal entered by the court shall provide that, in any employment application, the claimant may answer "no record" as to any charges expunged or sealed pursuant to this section in response to an inquiry regarding prior felony arrests, court appearances or criminal convictions.

(D) The charges and convictions expunged or sealed shall not operate to disqualify the claimant in any examination, appointment or application for public employment in the service of the commonwealth or any other political sub-division thereof, nor shall such charges and convictions be used against the claimant in any way in any court proceedings or hearings before any court, board or commission to which the claimant is a party to the proceedings.

ALM GL ch. 258D, ß 8 (2005)

ß 8. Statute of Limitations.

A claim for compensation brought under this chapter shall be commenced within 2 years after either the grant of a pardon or the grant of judicial relief and satisfaction of other conditions described in subsection (B) of section 1. Any action by the commonwealth challenging or appealing the grant of such judicial relief shall toll the 2 year period. Every action brought pursuant to this chapter that is not commenced within the time required by this section is forever barred from consideration by the courts of the commonwealth.

ALM GL ch. 258D, ß 9 (2005)

ß 9. Commonwealth to Provide Required Documents.

(A) A court granting judicial relief consistent with the criteria set forth in subclause (a) of clause (ii) of subsection (B) of section 1 shall provide a copy of this chapter to an individual seeking such relief at the time the criteria of said sub-clause (a) of said clause (ii) of said subsection (B) of said section 1 are satisfied. Such individual shall be required to acknowledge receipt of a copy of this chapter in writing on a form established by the chief justice for administration and management of the trial court. This acknowledgement shall be entered on the docket by the court and shall be admissible in any proceeding filed by a claimant under this chapter.

(B) The parole board, upon the issuance of a full pardon under *section 152 of chapter 127*, shall provide a copy of this chapter to an individual granted clemency at the time warrants necessary to grant the pardon are issued. Such individual shall be required to acknowledge receipt of a copy of this chapter in writing on a form established by the parole board, which shall be retained on file by the parole board as part of its official records and shall be admissible in any proceeding filed by a claimant under this chapter.

(C) If a claimant granted judicial relief or a full pardon shows he did not properly receive a copy of the information required by this section, he shall receive a 1 year extension on the 2 year time limit provided in section 8.

APPENDIX D

State Compensation Laws and Statutes as of September 2004

State	Passed	Maximum Award
AL	2001	Minimum $50,000 per year of incarceration; possibility for more
CA	2000	$100 per day of incarceration
DC	1981	No maximum, no punitive damages
IL	1945	<5 years = $15,000, <14 years = $30,000 max, >14 = $35,000†
IA	1997	$50 per day and lost wages up to $25,000/year, attorney's fees
ME	1993	$300,000, no punitive damages
MD	1963	Actual damages (amount of money from lack of employment, etc.)
MO	2003	Educational aid to persons exonerated by DNA testing
NH	1977	$20,000
NJ	1997	$20,000/year or twice claimant's income in year prior to conviction
NY	1984	No limit
NC	1947	$10,000 per year; maximum of $150,000
OH	1986	$25,000 per year, lost wages, costs, attorney's fees
OK	2004	$175,000; no punitive damages
TN	1984	$1 million
TX	2001	$25,000 per year, maximum of $500,000
VA	2004	90 percent of income (max. twenty years); $10,000 tuition
WV	1987	"Fair and reasonable damages"
WI	1913	$5,000 per year, maximum of $25,000

†Plus cost of living adjustment

Time Limit for Filing	Requirements for Eligibility
Two years after exoneration	Conviction vacated/reversed and charges dismissed
Six months after release	Pardon for innocence
No limit	Pardon, conviction reversed
N/A	Pardon for innocence
Two years	Conviction vacated or reversed, charges dismissed
Two years from pardon	Pardon for innocence
N/A	Pardon on grounds that conviction was in error
N/A	N/A
Three years	"Found innocent"
Two years from release/pardon	None
Two years	Pardon or conviction reversed, charges dismissed
Five years	Pardon for innocence
Two years	Conviction vacated or reversed; charges dismissed
No time limit	Conviction vacated and charges dismissed; pardon
One year	"Exoneration" or pardon for innocence
Two years	Pardon or granted relief on basis of innocence
N/A	Conviction vacated
Two years	Pardon, reversal; charges dismissed or acquittal
N/A	Proof of innocence

Source: "When Justice Fails" University of Chicago Roundtable. Adele Bernhard (2004)

APPENDIX E

The following is a compilation of recommended reforms and reviews for reducing the risk of wrongful convictions in the U.S. criminal justice system. This list was assembled from recommendations by The North Carolina Center on Actual Innocence; the Innocence Project; the National Association of Criminal Defense Lawyers; The National Institute of Justice; The Illinois Governor's Commission on Capital Punishment; The American Bar Association; and articles by Barry Scheck, Jim Dwyer, and Peter Neufeld.

EYEWITNESS IDENTIFICATIONS

Eyewitness testimony cannot be faultless, but a number of simple safeguards have been shown to make it more reliable. Sequential lineups, in which witnesses view photos or individuals one at a time, produce fewer misidentifications than simultaneous lineups. "Blinded" lineup administrators, who do not know which members of the lineup are suspects, are less likely to influence or cue the witness. Research has indicated that witnesses should not be presented with only one photo or individual; in 2003, the North Carolina Actual Innocence Commission recommended that there be at least seven non-suspects per suspect included in every photo lineup, and at least five for live lineups. In Illinois, the Governor's Commission on Capital Punishment recommended that juries be informed of the shortcomings of eyewitness identifications, including their racial complications, in order to ensure that such evidence is not accepted unquestioningly. New Jersey has implemented lineup reforms; Illinois has begun to do so through pilot programs, and North Carolina now uses sequential, blinded identification.

FORENSIC LABORATORIES AND DNA TESTING

Labs often lack training, accreditation, and funding, and the expense and expertise required for DNA tests make them difficult for defendants and inmates to obtain. Forensic error can be reduced through standards and oversight—protocols for lab workers and procedures for the collection, preservation, and processing of evidence, set by an outside agency that maintains an evaluatory role. Such an organization was created in Texas in May of 2005, when the state Legislature established the Texas Forensic Science Commission. The widely recognized value of DNA tests has led to calls for expansion of their availability. Lab capacity, both for storage and analysis, is presently insufficient—a 2003 study by the National Institute of Justice estimated that "350,000 rape and homicide cases await DNA testing." This is essentially a question of resources: more personnel and more money must be obtained to make improvements possible. Existing assets can also be extended. The NIJ study observed that "A significant amount of staff time is devoted to tracking and managing evidence samples" rather than conducting tests, tasks which can be automated to a much greater degree. And grants that are now available only to state-run labs can be opened to local jurisdictions as well. The Justice for All Act, passed in 2004, authorized $25 million in grants for post-conviction DNA testing over five years, but more is needed. Thirty-eight states now allow for post-conviction testing, but not all of those programs are broad enough to qualify for Justice for All Act grants.

PROSECUTORIAL AND POLICE MISCONDUCT

Oversight and transparency are seen as the bases for reform of investigator misconduct. Videotaped interrogations can prevent improper coercive practices, or at least reveal their role in any confession. Pretrial evidence discovery can be made more accessible and comprehensive: defense attorneys could be allowed to request more information and confirm that all relevant material has been disclosed, including the details of any deals between prosecutors and jailhouse informants. And sanctions and training can be put in place for both police officers and prosecutors to discourage both the withholding of evidence for the sake of making a better case and the excessive reliance on witnesses who might be compromised by incentives or otherwise unreliable. To some degree, simply emphasizing the risk of wrongful convictions in training sessions can encourage awareness and avoidance of them on the part of investigators.

EFFECTIVE COUNSEL

As with forensics shortfalls, many of the prevalent flaws in defense can be mitigated through improvements in personnel and funding, which currently vary widely between jurisdictions but are uniformly lacking. Public defenders are overworked and underpaid, and reversing those two trends is an essential step. The Justice for All Act established $75 million in Capital Representation Grants over five years, which can be used to "establish, implement, or improve an effective system for providing competent legal representation to indigents charged with capital offenses"; under the Act, equal funds must be provided to prosecutors. And in June of 2005, the Montana Public Defender Act established a statewide public defender office to replace that state's inadequate county-based system and lessen the gap between resources afforded to prosecutors and those given to public defenders; similar reforms have been proposed in Michigan, Louisiana (where public defense is funded primarily by traffic tickets), Virginia, and North Dakota. With more time and more resources, defense lawyers would be able to better prepare for trial, obtaining their own experts and conducting necessary investigations. They would be less pressured to enter inappropriate but expedient pleas. Ineffective assistance of counsel claims on the appellate level can also be encouraged and considered more thoroughly, and defense lawyers can be held to a higher standard by the bar.

DEATH PENALTY MORATORIUMS

Since the reinstatement of the death penalty, 120 people have been exonerated while on death row, and the flaws that led to those wrongful convictions have yet to be effectively corrected. A moratorium would temporarily suspend executions while a legislative review is conducted to determine reforms that could reduce the risk of executing the innocent. The only state with a moratorium in place now is Illinois; it was instituted by former Governor George Ryan in 2000 and has been allowed to continue under the current governor, Rod Blagojevich. Maryland declared a moratorium in 2002, but it was lifted by Governor Rob Erlich when he took office in January 2003. According to the American Bar Association, which supports a moratorium, twenty-one states and the U.S. Congress had introduced moratorium legislation as of March 2003.

INNOCENCE COMMISSIONS

Innocence commissions are meant to investigate the causes of wrongful convictions when they are identified and recommend preventive measures. The Innocence Project identifies as the key features of such commmissions "subpoena power, access to first-rate investigative resources, and political independence," as well as the inclusion of members of all levels of the justice system—"prosecutors, judges, police officers, defense attorneys, and forensic scientists." Innocence commissions in every jurisdiction would mean that any exoneration would be followed by an inquiry and lead to policy recommendations. North Carolina, Connecticut, and Virginia have established commissions; in North Carolina, as a result, eyewitness identification procedure reforms were adopted and an Innocence Inquiry Commission to review the innocence claims of convicted felons was approved by the House in August 2005.

GLOSSARY

Accessory. A person who intentionally assists another in committing a crime. An accessory is not necessarily present during the crime, but may be involved in planning, driving a getaway car, or concealing **evidence**.

Acquittal. A judgment of a court, based either on the verdict of a **jury** òr a judicial officer, that the **defendant** is not guilty of the offense(s) of which he or she was charged.

Aggravated. (as in aggravated **assault**, aggravated **rape**, aggravated **robbery**) A term denoting crimes committed with violence; the presence of a deadly weapon; reckless disregard for another's safety; or intent to cause harm, bodily injury, or to commit another crime.

Appeal. A request to a higher court seeking a reversal of the decision of a trial court. After the **lower court** judgment, the losing party (called the *appellant*) must file a notice of appeal, request transcripts or other records from the trial court, file briefs with the appeals court citing legal reasons for overturning the ruling, and show how those reasons relate to the facts in the case. No new **evidence** is admitted on appeal because it is strictly a legal argument. The other party (called the *respondent* or *appellee*) files a *responsive brief* countering these arguments. The appellant then rebuts that response with a *reply brief*. The appeals court may sustain the original ruling, reverse it, send it back to the trial court, or reverse in part and affirm in part. For state cases there are supreme courts (called courts of appeal in New York and Maryland) which are the highest appeals courts, and most states have lower appeals courts as well. For federal cases there are courts of appeal in thirteen different **circuits**, and above them is the U.S. Supreme Court, which selectively hears only a few appeals at the highest level. See **habeas corpus**

Appellate court. A court with jurisdiction to review decisions of **lower courts**.

Arraignment. The hearing in which a person charged with a crime first appears before a judge or magistrate and is advised of the **charges** against him or her and the penalties for the charges. The judge determines if the **defendant** has an attorney or needs one appointed to him or her by the court, accepts the defendant's **plea** or request for a delay, sets **bail**, and schedules future court appearances.

Assault. The threat or use of force on another, whether successful or not. **Assault with a deadly weapon:** To threaten or harm with the use of a dangerous weapon. **Sexual assault:** Any form of sexual contact, including **rape**, that is forced upon a person without consent or one who is unable to give consent.

Autopsy. Medical or forensic examination of a dead body to determine the cause of death.

Bail. Money or property exchanged for the release of an arrested person who has been charged with a crime. Judges may refuse to allow bail in more serious cases, such as **murder** or treason, or where the **defendant** might be a danger to the community.

Blood type. (also **blood group**) One of the classes (designated A, B, AB, or O) into which most of the body's cells, including those in blood, can be separated on the basis of the presence or absence of specific proteins on the cells' surfaces.

Book. To make a record of a person's arrest, with details of the person's identity (including a photograph and fingerprint), particulars about the alleged offense, and the name of the arresting officer.

Capital. (as in offense, **conviction**, or punishment) Punishable by death.

Charge. A formal allegation that a person has committed a specific offense.

Circuit. A district established within the state or federal judicial system. The U.S. Court of Appeals, for example, is divided into thirteen circuits spread across the country.

Civil lawsuit. A legal action taken in a court of law by one person or entity against another. Civil lawsuits pertain to private rights and privileges, and do not include criminal matters. A **habeas corpus** action, however, is also classified as a civil action, although it challenges the validity of a criminal **conviction**. See **habeas corpus**

Clemency. Mercy or leniency, especially the power of the president or a governor to **pardon** a criminal or commute a criminal **sentence**.

Composite sketch. An artist's rendering, usually of a suspect's face, based on **witness** descriptions.

Conflict of interest. A situation in which a lawyer representing two clients simultaneously represents opposing aims. The lawyer may be disqualified from representing both clients if the dual representation adversely affects either client, or if the clients, after being fully advised of the conflict and their rights, do not consent to the dual representation.

Conjugal visits. Visits allowed for the spouses of prisoners, which may include access to a private room intended for sexual relations.

Convict. (1) A person who has been found guilty of a crime and is serving a **sentence** of imprisonment; a prison inmate. (2) To find a person guilty of a criminal offense following a criminal **trial**, a guilty plea, or a plea of *nolo contendere* ("no contest").

Conviction. The act or process of judicially finding someone guilty of a crime; the judgment (as by a jury verdict) that a person is guilty of a crime.

Corporal search. A search of the body usually conducted on inmates moving between facilities or preparing to enter the visitation area of a **prison** or **jail**.

Corrections. The agencies or facilities concerned with the custody, confinement, supervision, or treatment of alleged or convicted criminal offenders.

Corroborate. To confirm or give support to a piece of information or **evidence** that supports a claim made at **trial** by lawyers or **witnesses**.

Counsel. One or more lawyers representing a client.

Cross-examination. The questioning of a **witness** to discredit or undercut previous **testimony**. Unlike direct examination, questions during cross-examination are limited to the subjects covered in the direct examination of that witness. However, the attorney may ask **leading questions**.

Death penalty. A death sentence imposed as punishment for serious crimes, such as **murder**. As of September 2005, the death penalty remained legal in thirty-eight states, the federal government, and the U.S. military.

Death row. The area in a prison where those sentenced to death are confined.

Default judgment. A decision made in favor of the plaintiff when the **defendant** fails to appear in court, respond to a plaintiff's claim, or comply with a court order.

Defendant. The person or entity charged with a crime in a criminal **prosecution**.

Defense. The **evidence** and methods adopted by a **defendant**; the party representing this person.

Deposition. Testimony given under oath, generally before a trial.

Direct examination. The questioning of a **witness** by the party that has called that witness to give **testimony**.

Disbarment. The act of expelling a lawyer from the practice of law, due to misconduct or an ethical violation.

Discovery. The pretrial disclosure of pertinent facts or documents by one or both parties to a legal action or proceeding.

Dismissal. A decision by a judicial officer to terminate a case without a determination of guilt or innocence.

District attorney. (also **DA**) A public official elected in a county or district to represent the state in criminal cases. The district attorney's duties include investigating alleged crimes in collaboration with law enforcement, and filing criminal **charges**.

DNA. Deoxyribonucleic acid, a chromosomal double chain (the famous "double helix") found in the nucleus of each living cell, the content of which determines each individual's hereditary characteristics. DNA's relevance to the law lies in the theory that each person's DNA is different. Thus, cells from any part of the body can be used to identify and distinguish an individual from all other people, and help identify the source of any biological evidence associated with a crime.

DNA profiling. The process of examining DNA to determine its origin. DNA profiling is used to indicate parentage or to identify individuals as possible sources of biological evidence (bones, teeth, hair, saliva, etc.).

DQ alpha. A specific area on the **DNA** strand used to characterize DNA.

Using the seven variations (*alleles*) of DNA on this area of the DNA strand, individuals can be categorized into twenty-eight different DQ alpha types. Determination of an individual's DQ alpha type involves a **polymerase chain reaction**-based test.

Evidence. Any type of proof legally presented at **trial** and allowed by the judge, which is intended to convince the **jury** of facts pertinent to the case. It can include oral **testimony** of **witnesses** or experts on technical matters, documents, public records, objects, photographs and **depositions**. **Circumstantial evidence:** Evidence intended to establish a fact by showing surrounding circumstances which logically lead to a conclusion of fact. **Corroborating evidence:** Evidence that supports a proposition that is already supported by some evidence. **Exculpatory evidence:** Evidence that may establish a criminal **defendant's** innocence. The **prosecution** has an obligation to disclose exculpatory evidence in its possession when the evidence may be material to the outcome of the case.

Exhumation. The retrieval of a buried human corpse, usually for purposes of forensic investigation.

Extradition. To hand over a person accused or **convicted** of a crime to the state or country where the crime was committed.

False Confession. An admission of guilt by a **suspect** who did not commit the crime. False confessions are often obtained through deception, threats, or force.

Felony. A serious crime punishable by imprisonment for more than one year, or by death. Examples are **murder, rape**, and **burglary**.

Forensic evidence. The results of scientific inquiries conducted in order to corroborate legal claims.

Grand jury. A group of people chosen from voter rolls to sit for at least a month—sometimes a year—on a panel to decide whether the prosecution's **evidence** against the accused justifies formally charging him or her (see **indictment**).

Grievance. An injury, injustice or wrong that gives ground for a complaint; the complaint itself.

Habeas corpus. (Latin for "you have the body") A formal challenge of the legality of an individual's imprisonment or detention. In addition to being used to test the legality of an arrest or commitment, the writ may also be used to obtain review of the **extradition** process; the right to, or amount of **bail**; or the jurisdiction of a court that has imposed a criminal sentence. The writ of habeas corpus can be employed procedurally in federal district courts to challenge the constitutionality of a state court conviction.

Indeterminate sentence. (1) A **sentence** of an unspecified duration, such as one for a term of ten to twenty years. (2) A maximum prison term that a parole board can reduce after the inmate has served the minimum time required by law.

Indictment. The formal written accusation of a crime made by a **grand jury** and presented to a court for **prosecution** against the charged person.

Informant. (also **snitch**) One who incriminates others who may or may not be involved in a crime, especially in exchange for financial rewards.

Interrogation. The questioning of a **suspect** or **witness** by law enforcement officials.

Jail. A place of confinement for individuals found guilty of minor crimes or awaiting **trial** or **sentencing**, usually under the jurisdiction of local governments. See **prison**

Jailhouse lawyer. A **jail** or **prison** inmate who gives legal advice and assistance to other inmates.

Judgment. A court's final decision of the rights and obligations of the parties in a civil case, criminal **prosecution**, or appeal in a lower court.

Jury. A group of twelve citizens chosen from county voter rolls who hear the **evidence** presented at **trial** and determine whether the accused is guilty or not guilty.

Juvenile. A person who has not reached the legal age (usually eighteen) at which one is treated as an adult by the criminal justice system.

Leading question. A question which suggests an answer, usually answerable by "yes" or "no." These are forbidden during the direct examination of witnesses to ensure that they are not coached by a lawyer, but are allowed during **cross-examination**.

Lineup. A method used by law enforcement to have a victim or **witness** identify a **suspect** from a row of people. During the procedure, an officer asks the victim or witness if any of the individuals in the lineup committed the crime.

Lockdown. The act of confining prisoners to their cells to regain control over a **prison**, usually in the event of a protest or riot.

Lower court. The court with original jurisdiction over the **prosecution** of persons accused of misdemeanors or certain felony offenses.

Magistrate. A judicial officer with the power to arraign those accused of crimes, set **bail**, hear **discovery** disputes and try cases involving minor crimes.

Mens rea. (Latin for "guilty mind") Criminal intent or recklessness. To prove that a **defendant** is guilty of murder, the **prosecution** must show that the defendant had such intent while committing the crime.

Miranda rights. In *Miranda v. Arizona (1966)* the United States Supreme Court ruled that a **suspect** in police custody must be informed of certain constitutional rights before interrogation including the right to remain silent, to have an attorney present during questioning, to have an attorney appointed if the suspect cannot afford one and to be told that anything the suspect says can be used against him or her in court.

Mistrial. A trial that ends prematurely because of some irregularity that prejudices a party's right to a fair **trial**, or a deadlock by a jury without reaching a verdict after lengthy deliberation (a *hung jury*).

Modus operandi. (also **MO**) A particular way or method of doing something, especially as it relates to well-established methods of committing a crime.

Motion. Written or oral application requesting that a court make a ruling. **Post-trial motion:** A requested application after a judgment is entered, such as a motion for a new trial.

Mug book. A collection of photographs of previously arrested persons that may be shown to victims and **witnesses** in cases in which a **suspect** has not yet been determined.

Murder. The intentional killing of another human being. **Capital murder:** Murder punishable by death. **First-degree murder:** Murder that is willful, deliberate, premeditated, or that is committed during the course of another serious felony. Depending on the state, a murder may qualify for first-degree murder if the person murdered was of a special class such as a police officer, or under "special circumstances" such as multiple murder or the use of poison. **Second-degree murder:** Murder that is not committed under any of the circumstances of first-degree murder.

Preliminary hearing. A test of the charge against the accused. The **prosecution** must present **evidence** and **witnesses** that indicate that an offense has been committed, and that there is probable cause to believe that the person accused is responsible. The accused may cross-examine witnesses and may present evidence if he or she wishes.

No contest. (also *nolo contendere*) A **plea** given by a **defendant** who does not wish to argue charges against him or her. No contest pleas are often given in plea bargain situations to avoid problems in later civil suits where an admission of guilt can lead to negative consequences.

Overturn. To invalidate or rescind a previous decision, as when courts reverse wrongful convictions.

Paralegal. (also **legal assistant** or **legal analyst**) A person who assists a lawyer in duties related to the practice of law but is not a licensed attorney.

Pardon. To use the executive power of a governor or president to forgive a person **convicted** of a crime, thus removing any remaining penalties or punishments and preventing any new **prosecution** of the person for the crime for which the pardon was given. A pardon strikes the **conviction** from the convicted person's legal record. A pardon may be given to a rehabilitated person, or can terminate a **sentence** and free a prisoner when the president or governor is convinced that the trial was unfair or there is doubt about guilt.

Parole. The release of a prisoner before his or her full sentence has been served. Release is granted for good behavior on the condition that the parolee must regularly report to a supervising parole officer for a specified period.

Parole board. A governmental body that decides whether prisoners may be released from **prison** before completing their **sentences**.

Penal. Of, or relating to, penalty or punishment, especially for a crime.

Perjury. (also **false swearing** or **false oath**) The act or instance of a person deliberately making false or misleading statements while under oath.

Petition. A formal written request made to a court.

Plea. An accused person's formal response of "guilty," "not guilty" or "**no contest**" to a criminal **charge**.

Polygraph. (also **lie detector**) A device used to measure the legitimacy of statements. This is done by recording and measuring involuntary physiological changes in the body during questioning. Results are not allowed as **evidence** in most states.

Polymerase chain reaction. (also **PCR**) A technique developed to amplify certain sections of a **DNA** strand so that they can be tested by DNA fingerprinting technology.

Postconviction relief. Legal action taken by the **defendant** and/or an attorney acting on the defendant's behalf, after **conviction** and **sentencing** in a criminal trial, specifically appeals and **habeas corpus** petitions. The defendant may challenge conduct of the **trial**, competency of **counsel**, admission of **evidence**, juror or **prosecutorial misconduct**, or seek to introduce new evidence (such as **DNA**) in an attempt to have a conviction **overturned**.

Post-traumatic stress disorder. A psychiatric disorder that can occur following the experience or observation of life-threatening events. PTSD exhibits itself through nightmares and flashbacks, difficulty sleeping, and feelings of estrangement. These symptoms can be severe enough and last long enough to significantly impair the person's daily life.

Prejudicial comments. Any inappropriate or biased comments made in front of the jury by **witnesses**, lawyers or judges that might affect the **jury**'s impartial **judgment** of the case.

Prison. A secure facility, usually under state or federal control, designed for the confinement of persons serving sentences for serious crimes. **Low-security prison:** A facility designed for non-violent offenders, typically with dormitory-style housing and without barbed wire or guard towers. **Medium-security prison:** Prisons with strengthened perimeters (often double fences with electronic detection systems), mostly cell-type housing, a wide variety of work and treatment programs, a higher staff-to-inmate ratio than low security prisons, and greater internal controls. **Maximum-security prison:** Prisons with highly-secured perimeters (featuring walls or reinforced fences), multiple- and single-occupant cell housing, a high staff-to-inmate ratio, and close control of inmate movement. Inmates involved in gangs, drugs, riots, or other problems in other prison facilities may be sent to a maximum-security prison where contact between prisoners is closely monitored and extremely limited. Access to law libraries, work, treatment programs, and exercise facilities is also limited, if allowed at all.

Private investigator. In criminal cases, an individual retained by **counsel** to conduct an independent exploration of the **charges** and **evidence** against the accused. The investigator will review law enforcement reports of the crime, interview prospective **witnesses**, examine evidence, and attempt to find evidence which will help the attorney's case.

Probable cause. Reason to suspect that a person has committed or is committing a crime. Under the Fourth Amendment, probable cause must be shown before an arrest or **search warrant** may be issued.

Probation. A court-imposed **sentence** that allows a convicted individual to remain in the community instead of being incarcerated. During probation the individual must abide by conditions, such as drug testing, a curfew, or staying within a particular county or state, and is subject to the supervision of a probation officer.

Pro bono. (also ***pro bono publico***; Latin for "the public good") Legal services that are performed as a public service, free of charge.

Pro se. (also ***in propria persona***; Latin for "for oneself") The decision and act of representing oneself in a court proceeding without the assistance of a lawyer.

Prosecution. (1) The party instituting or conducting legal proceedings against someone in a criminal **trial** or lawsuit. (2) A criminal proceeding in which the **evidence** against an accused person is presented to a **jury** or judge.

Prosecutorial misconduct. The **prosecution's** improper or illegal act (or failure to act), especially involving an attempt to persuade the **jury** to wrongly convict a **defendant** or impose an unjustified punishment.

Protective custody. A restrictive form of confinement akin to **solitary confinement** imposed on inmates for their own security or well-being. Protective custody is frequently employed for inmates convicted of sexual crimes against children, or whose position or physical characteristics leaves them especially vulnerable to harm from the general **prison** or **jail** population.

Racketeering. A federal crime involving the organizing of, and conspiring to commit criminal activity.

Rape. The act of forcing sexual intercourse without consent upon another person, or upon a person incapable of giving consent.

Rape kit. A collection of forensic **evidence** taken from a **rape** victim's clothing, hair, material under fingernails, and bodily orifices (rectum, mouth, and vagina).

Rebuttal. In-court time given to contradict the evidence or arguments of an adverse party (the **prosecution** or **defense**).

Recidivism. The repetition of criminal or delinquent behavior, especially when it results in recurring incarcerations.

Rehabilitation. The combined and coordinated use of medical, social, educational, and vocational measures used to assist individuals reentering society after **incarceration**.

Remand. To send a case back to a **lower court** for reconsideration.

Robbery. The act or attempt to take property in the possession of another person with the use or threat of force. **Armed robbery:** Robbery committed by displaying a weapon with the intent to subdue the victim.

Runner. A person, usually an inmate, who illegally distributes packages, drugs, and/or money for prisoners.

Sally port. A secured area through which officers and other individuals pass into certain areas of a **prison**.

Segregation. (also called **administrative segregation**, or **ad seg**) Placement of an inmate in a secured, separate unit for the safety of the institution for reasons that may include alleged gang affiliation, investigation of a disciplinary offense, or repeated misconduct.

Sentencing. The phase of a criminal trial, following the **verdict** or **judgment**, in which the court assigns punishment to a **defendant** who has been found guilty.

Sentence. The **judgment** pronounced by the court pertaining to the punishment to be inflicted upon the defendant; the punishment itself.

Snitch. See **informant**

Solitary confinement. (also the hole) The complete isolation of a prisoner from other inmates.

Spectrograph. A machine that analyzes a human voice by separating and mapping it into elements of frequency, time lapse, and intensity (represented by a series of horizontal and vertical bar lines) to produce a **voiceprint**.

Statement. An account of a person's knowledge of a crime taken by law enforcement officials as part of their investigation of the offense.

Statute of limitations. A time limit for prosecuting a crime, based on the date when the offense occurred. The purpose of such a statute is to require diligent **prosecution** of known claims, and to make sure that claims will be resolved while **evidence** is still available and **witnesses'** recollections are still fresh.

Sua sponte. (Latin for "of one's own will") Generally used in reference to a court making a decision on its own initiative without a motion by one of the parties.

Suspect. A person believed to have committed a crime or offense.

Testimony. Evidence that a **witness** under oath gives during a hearing or **trial**.

Trial. A formal examination of **evidence** and determination of legal claims that is overseen by a judge.

Unlawful flight. The act of evading arrest or **prosecution**.

Vacate. An action taken by a court to legally annul a **conviction**.

Verdict. A judge or **jury's** decision of the **defendant's** guilt or innocence.

Voiceprint. A pattern of curved lines and whorls that are made by a **spectrograph** machine that measures human vocal sounds for the purpose of identifying an individual speaker.

Warrant. A judicial **writ** authorizing officers to make searches, seizures, or arrests. **Search warrant:** A judge's written order authorizing a law enforcement official to investigate a specified place and seize evidence related to a crime. **Death warrant:** A warrant authorizing a warden or other **prison** official to carry out a death **sentence**; it typically sets the time and place for a prisoner's execution.

Wiretapping. The use of an electronic device to listen in on private telephone conversations. Such activity is illegal unless conducted pursuant to court order, based upon a showing of probable cause by law enforcement.

Witness. A person who testifies under oath at a **trial** or hearing. **Alibi witness:** A witness who testifies that the accused was in another place at the time that the crime occurred.

Writ. A court's written order commanding the addressee to do, or refrain from doing, a specified act.

Sources:
The Merriam-Webster Dictionary, New rev. edition. (Springfield, MA: Merriam-Webster, 2004.)
Black's Law Dictionary, 7th Edition. Garner, Bryan A, ed. (St. Paul, Minn.: West Group, 1999.)
Dressler, Joshua, *Cases and Materials on Criminal Law,* 3rd Edition. (St. Paul, Minn.: West Group, 2003.)
The New Oxford American Dictionary, 2nd edition. McKean, Erin, ed. (United Kingdom: Oxford University Press, 2005.)
Lockyer, Bill. *Crime and Delinquency in California.* (Sacramento, California: California Dept. of Justice, 1998.)

To see citations for the sidebars in this book, visit:

www.voiceofwitness.com

PHOTO CREDITS

World Photos / Gary Kazanjian
7. Stoll with lawyers: AP/Wide World Photos

CHAPTER VII: BEVERLY MONROE

1. Monroe headshot: courtesy Beverly Monroe
2. Monroe with children: courtesy Beverly Monroe
3. Joseph Burrows: courtesy Center on Wrongful Convictions at Northwestern University
4. "Monroe's hope for freedom..." headline: courtesy Beverly Monroe
5. Monroe celebrates her release: courtesy Beverly Monroe
6. Monroe with her daughter Katie: courtesy Beverly Monroe

CHAPTER VIII: MICHAEL EVANS AND PAUL TERRY

1. Evans headshot: AP/Wide World Photos
2. Terry headshot: courtesy Pamela Hawkins
3. Jim McCloskey headshot: AP/Wide World
4. Evans talks to reporters: AP/Wide World
5. Gregory Bright and Earl Truvia: courtesy Lola Vollen
6. Ernest Duff headshot: © Courtney Jones
7. Pamela Hawkins and Paul Terry (May 2005): courtesy Pamela Hawkins
8. Pamela, Beverly, and Paul Terry (1964): courtesy Pamela Hawkins
9. Terry after his trial: courtesy Pamela Hawkins
10. Terry in undated photo: courtesy Pamela Hawkins
11. Terry and Hawkins (February 1993): courtesy Pamela Hawkins

CHAPTER IX: DAVID POPE

1. Pope headshot: courtesy David Pope
2. Pope at seventeen: courtesy David Pope
3. Voice spectrograph readouts: courtesy David Pope
4. Technician in Houston crime lab: AP/Wideworld Photos / Pat Sullivan
5. Marvin Anderson: AP/Wide World Photos
6. "Man freed by new evidence" headline: courtesy David Pope
7. Pope a year after release: courtesy David Pope

CHAPTER X: JOSEPH AMRINE

1. Amrine headshot: From Salon.com
2. Calvin Burdine: AP/Wide World Photos
3. Amrine in April 1995: Missouri Department of Corrections
4. Missouri State Penitentiary: *Columbia Daily Tribune* / Jenna Isaacson
5. Prison rape panel: AP/Wide World Photos
6. Officers at Florida State Prison: AP/Wide World Photos
7. Amrine at a press conference: AP/Wide World Photos
8. Amrine with his niece: AP/WideWorld Photos

CHAPTER XI: PETER ROSE

1. Rose headshot: *Sacramento Bee* / Brian Baer
2. Rose and his children: courtesy Susan Rutberg
3. Randy Greer and daughter: Photo © Ken Light
4. Rose hugs son: *Sacramento Bee* / Brian Baer
5. Dr. Edward Blake in laboratory: © Courtney Jones

CHAPTER XII: KEVIN GREEN

1. Kevin Green headshot: From *The Innocents* / Taryn Simon
2. Private First Class Kevin Green: courtesy Kevin Green
3. Richard Dexter: courtesy Judy Lybarger
4. Green at San Quentin Prison: courtesy Kevin Green
5. Kevin and Kelly Green: courtesy Kevin Green

CHAPTER XIII: ROUNDTABLE DISCUSSION

1. David Pope headshot: courtesy David Pope
2. Beverly Monroe headshot: courtesy Beverly Monroe
3. Peter Rose headshot: courtesy Susan Rutberg
4. John Stoll headshot: AP/Wide World Photos
5. Ulysses Rodriguez Charles headshot: from *The Boston Herald*

INTERVIEW AND SIDEBAR CREDITS

CHAPTER I: CHRISTOPHER OCHOA

Interviews conducted by Arwen Curry
Sidebars by Ella McPherson (polygraph tests);
Candace Chen and Arwen Curry (dating);
Courtney Jones and Ella McPherson (apologies)

CHAPTER II: JUAN MELENDEZ

Interviews conducted by Leonie Sherman
Sidebars by Alex Carp (prosecutorial misconduct), Aileen Kerun (prison conditions); Colin
Dabkowski (prison healthcare); Dominic Luxford
(suicide)

CHAPTER III: GARY GAUGER

Interviews conducted by Michael Chandler and
Sarah Stewart Taylor
Sidebars by Colin Dabkowski and Neil Berman
(interrogation tactics); Lola Vollen and Nicole
Hill (psychological toll of wrongful conviction)

CHAPTER IV: JAMES NEWSOME

Interviews conducted by Sarah Stewart Taylor
and Sarah Wiener-Boone
Sidebars by Arwen Curry (misidentification);
Simon Henderson and Eliabeth Zitrin (biased
juries, jailhouse lawyers); Ella McPherson (prison
education)

CHAPTER V: CALVIN WILLIS

Interviews conducted by Sarah Stewart Taylor
and Jonathan Jones
Sidebars by Rick Opaterny (DNA costs); Emily
Taguchi Klingensmith (compensation)

CHAPTER VI: JOHN STOLL

Interviews conducted by Anna Sussman
Sidebars by Candace Chen (McMartin trials);
Abner Morales and Colin Dabkowski (solitary

confinement); Alex Carp (lack of official review)

CHAPTER VII: BEVERLY MONROE

Interviews conducted by Krista Mahr and Colin
Dabkowski
Sidebars by Alex Carp (Miranda rights); Michael
McCarrin (snitches)

CHAPTER VIII: MICHAEL EVANS AND PAUL TERRY

Interviews conducted by Sarah Stewart Taylor,
Jori Lewis, and Colin Dabkowski
Sidebars by Nicole Hill, Colin Dabkowski, and
Rick Opaterny (innocence projects, life after
exoneration)

CHAPTER IX: DAVID POPE

Interviews conducted by Rebecca Goldman
Sidebars by Dominic Luxford and Stephanie
Spiro (flawed experts); Lola Vollen and Colin
Dabkowski (religion in prison)

CHAPTER X: JOSEPH AMRINE

Interviews conducted by Traci Curry and Sarah
Stewart Taylor
Sidebars by Colin Dabkowski (ineffective coun-
sel); Abel Haro (prison rape, prison violence);
Courtney Jones (executions)

CHAPTER XI: PETER ROSE

Interviews conducted by Sarah Wiener-Boone
Sidebars by Dominic Luxford

CHAPTER XII: KEVIN GREEN

Interviews conducted by Sarah Stewart Taylor
and Krista Mahr
Sidebars: Colin Dabkowski (spousal murders);
Candace Chen (marriage); Momo Chang (parole)

ABOUT THE EDITORS

Lola Vollen is a physician specializing in the aftermath of large-scale human rights abuses. She has worked with survivors of systemic injustices in Somalia, South Africa, Israel, Croatia, and Kosovo. Working with Physicians for Human Rights, she developed Bosnia's mass grave exhumation and identification program. She is the founder of the Life After Exoneration Program, which helps exonerated prisoners in the United States with their transitions after release. She is a visiting scholar at the University of California, Berkeley's Institute of International Studies, co-editor of the Voice of Witness series, and a practicing clinician.

Dave Eggers is the editor of *McSweeney's* and the author of three books, including *How We Are Hungry* and *A Heartbreaking Work of Staggering Genius*; a finalist for the Pulitzer Prize and the winner of the Addison Metcalf Award from the American Academy of Arts and Sciences. As a journalist, his work has appeared in the *The New Yorker*, *The New York Times*, *Esquire*, the *UK Guardian*, and other publications. His first book of oral histories, *Teachers Have It Easy: The Big Sacrifices and Small Salaries of America's Teachers*—co-edited and -written with Daniel Moulthrop and Nínive Calegari, appeared in July of 2005. During 2004-2005 he taught at the UC Berkeley Graduate School of Journalism and with Lola Vollen, he is a founding editor of the Voice of Witness series.

The VOICE OF WITNESS SERIES

The Voice of Witness series allows those most affected by contemporary social injustice to speak for themselves. Using oral history as its foundation, Voice of Witness seeks to illustrate human rights crises through the voices of its victims, and in some cases, its participants. These books are designed for readers of all levels—from high school and college students to policymakers—interested in a reality-based understanding of ongoing injustices in the United States and around the world.

Coming in 2006:

AFTER THE FLOOD:
The Victims of Hurricane Katrina Speak

With far too little help from those who owed it to them, the poor bore the brunt of the Gulf Coast disaster. Evacuations left many behind, and the few facilities that did exist for refugees quickly became miserable, dangerous places. Read the startling, day-by-day stories of the unlucky ones who lost their homes only to find that they had nowhere else to go.

Coming in 2007:

SLAVERY IN SUDAN

After decades of civil war, Sudan's central government began to use a new weapon against the Sudanese People's Liberation Army. Arab militias were armed and encouraged to abduct women, girls, and young boys from the black African region of southern Sudan, where the rebels were based. Thousands were forced into servitude in the Arab north. The conflict has slackened, and many abductees have made their way back home. In this book, some of them will recount their terrible ordeal.

VOICE OF WITNESS
WWW.VOICEOFWITNESS.COM